D1563712

Medical Miracles

Medical Miracles

*Doctors, Saints, and Healing
in the Modern World*

JACALYN DUFFIN

OXFORD
UNIVERSITY PRESS
2009

OXFORD
UNIVERSITY PRESS

Oxford University Press, Inc., publishes works that further
Oxford University's objective of excellence
in research, scholarship, and education.

Oxford   New York
Auckland   Cape Town   Dar es Salaam   Hong Kong   Karachi
Kuala Lumpur   Madrid   Melbourne   Mexico City   Nairobi
New Delhi   Shanghai   Taipei   Toronto

With offices in
Argentina   Austria   Brazil   Chile   Czech Republic   France   Greece
Guatemala   Hungary   Italy   Japan   Poland   Portugal   Singapore
South Korea   Switzerland   Thailand   Turkey   Ukraine   Vietnam

Copyright © 2009 by Oxford University Press, Inc.

Published by Oxford University Press, Inc.
198 Madison Avenue, New York, New York 10016

www.oup.com

Oxford is a registered trademark of Oxford University Press

Library of Congress Cataloging-in-Publication Data
Duffin, Jacalyn.
Medical miracles: doctors, saints, and healing in the modern world / by Jacalyn Duffin.
    p. cm.
Includes bibliographical references (p.   ).
ISBN 978-0-19-533650-4
1. Spiritual healing—Christianity—History. 2. Christian saints—History.
3. Miracles—History. 4. Canonization. 5. Medicine—Religious aspects—Catholic
Church—History. 6. Catholic Church—Doctrines—History. I. Title.
BT732.5.D84 2008
231.7'3—dc22   2008026678

9 8 7 6 5 4 3 2 1
Printed in the United States of America
on acid-free paper

For my brothers in blood

Dale Dotten,
Peter Galbraith,
Wycliffe Lofters, and
the memory of Bernard Longpré

Acknowledgments

The staff of the Vatican Secret Archives and the Vatican Library were unfailingly helpful during my exploration of their magnificent collections. Many colleagues, friends, and family members contributed to this book with enthusiastic interest, scholarly wisdom, and encouragement. Special thanks are owing to Susan L. Abrams, Bernard Cousin, Jeanne Drouin, Ross Duffin, Mary Fissell, Giulia Flesch, Francesco Guardiani, Bert Hansen, Anita Johnston, Len Husband, Father Roger Laberge, the late Sister Kathryn Lafleur, Joshua Lipton-Duffin, Harry Marks, Jennifer MacLeod, Sheila McCullagh, Father Paolo Molinari, Lois Myers, Anne Overell, Ana Cecilia Rodriguez de Romo, Todd Savitt, Giulio Silano, Terence Storm, Cherrilyn Yalin, Father William H. Woestmann, Jessica Wolfe, Robert David Wolfe, Adrian Wilson, Terry Jones and his online Patron Saints Index, several anonymous readers for the press, and the intrepid, good-natured staff of Bracken Library at Queen's University, especially Darlene Lake, Jane Reeves, and Susan Cochram, who brought the libraries of the world to Kingston.

Cynthia Read, my editor at Oxford University Press, was a wise and patient guide for this medic wandering on the turf of religious history. Her expert colleagues Jeffrey House, Meechal Hoffman, Daniel Gonzales, Stephanie Attia, and Mary Anne Shahidi also helped cheerfully and promptly. This project was supported by a Hannah grant from Associated Medical Services of Toronto and a sabbatical leave from Queen's University; I am deeply grateful for both. An earlier version of some material in chapters 3 and 4 previously appeared in *Bulletin of the History of Medicine* 81, no. 4 (2007): 699–729, © 2007 by The Johns Hopkins University Press.

Contents

Figures

Tables

Abbreviations

ASV	Archivio Segreto Vaticano
BAV	Biblioteca Apostolica Vaticana
Beat.	Beatification or beatificationis
Can.	Canonization or canonizationis
CCS	Congregazione delle cause dei santi [Congregation for the Causes of the Saints]
Miraculé(e)	Person who has experienced a miracle
RP	Riti Processi [trials of the SRC]
SCCS	Sacra Congregatio pro causis sanctorum [Sacred Congregation for the Causes of the Saints]
SRC	Sacra Rituum Congregatio, also Congregatio Sacrorum Rituum [Sacred Congregation of Rites]

Medical Miracles

Introduction

How This Book Came to Be

More than twenty years ago, in my capacity as a hematologist, I was invited to read a set of bone marrow samples "blind," without being told the reason why or any clinical details. The fourteen specimens were taken from one woman over an eighteen-month period. Using the microscope to examine slides of blood and bone marrow, I found that it had been a case of severe acute leukemia with a remission, a relapse, and another remission. I assumed that the patient must be dead and the review was for a lawsuit. Only much later did I learn, to my great surprise, that the patient was (and still is) alive. She had accepted aggressive chemotherapy in a university hospital, but she attributed her cure to the intercession of a Montreal woman, Marie-Marguerite d'Youville, who had been dead for two hundred years. This case became the capstone in the "cause" for Youville's canonization as the first Canadian-born saint. Again, I was surprised.

A few years later, in December 1990, I was invited, with my Jewish husband, to attend the canonization ceremony at St. Peter's Basilica. It was a moving experience, which we shared with the treating physician, Dr. Jeanne Drouin of Ottawa. There the postulants, led by their Canadian shepherd, Father Constantin Bouchaud, presented me with a gift that they deemed appropriate for a doctor who was also a historian: the *Positio,* or bound testimony on the miracle.[1]

CONGREGATIO DE CAUSIS SANCTORUM

P. N. 562

MARIANOPOLITANA

CANONIZATIONIS

BEATAE

Mariae Margaritae Dufrost De Lajemmerais

(viduae D'YOUVILLE)

FUNDATRICIS

SORORUM A CARITATE

(† 1771)

POSITIO
SUPER MIRACULO

ROMA
Tipografia GUERRA s.r.l.
Piazza di Porta Maggiore, 2
1989

FIGURE INT.I. Title page of the *Positio super miraculo* concerning the leukemia miracle cited in the cause of Saint Marie Marguerite d'Youville, 1989.

Suddenly, I realized that a record of my small part as a doctor in this remarkable tale would reside forever in the Vatican Secret Archives (*Archivio Segreto Vaticano*, ASV). In the same instant, the historian in me recognized that one such file must exist for every saint canonized in modern times. Until then, the Vatican Archives and Library loomed in my mind as remote, auspicious places of no relevance to my work. Now I began to crave them as the repository of hundreds of miracles just waiting to be explored. Would I be allowed to use those files? And if granted permission, could I understand them? Linguistically limited and oriented to nineteenth- and twentieth-century medicine, I had doubts about both possibilities.

In this book, I will describe the results of four increasingly long research trips to the Vatican from 2001 to 2007. At the outset, I was in search of answers to the following questions: What were the miracles worked through the intercession of new saints in modern times? How many were healings of physical illness? Who were the supplicants? What diseases were cured, and did they change through time? How many miracles, like "mine," entailed cutting-edge science and the testimony of skeptical, even atheist, physicians like me? What was the experience of other doctors whose medical work led them to a liturgical encounter? And how did the miracles transpire? In this book, the flood of answers to these questions about medicine and religion is shaped around four goals outlined below.

Definitions and Goals

For the canonization process of the Roman Catholic Church, happy outcomes do not automatically qualify as miracles. Even when good evidence establishes that the patient appealed to God or a saint at a crucial moment, recovery is not considered miraculous if any chance remains that it might have occurred naturally or through human intervention. Instead, such outcomes are acts of grace or special favors. A miracle is something stronger.[2]

Over the centuries, many philosophers have contemplated the definition and the existence of miracles. In philosophical and theological traditions, a miracle is an event of wonder, which lacks any other reasonable explanation; it can also serve as a "sign" of divine action.[3] Some insist that to merit the label, miracles must represent a rupture of natural laws. Others argue that such a rupture is unnecessary for an event to qualify as miraculous; rather it must remain unexplained by science. The latter group of scholars suggests that miracles tell us about history of science, culture, and society. Still others contend that miracles can never exist, and that all religious belief is unnecessary, even dangerous superstition.[4]

I do not pretend to have understood all the nuances of this erudite debate. My interest was sparked by that unusual case of leukemia so long ago. Leukemia is a relatively new disease; its first descriptions date from the mid-nineteenth century. Before it became a disease, would recovery from the symptoms of fever, bleeding, and weakness have seemed miraculous? And in our own era, how can we designate a miracle in a person who has accepted chemotherapy? In short, the historical curiosity was sparked by a medical encounter, and it was naïve of the scholarly debates over definitions and faith. The gift copy of the *Positio* containing the medical evidence suggested a historian's way to find answers. I was particularly interested in learning about what had once been considered miraculous in the past, and how that might have changed through time into the present. That was the first goal of this book.

For some time, I tried to avoid those debates about definitions of miracle. As the work proceeded, however, it crept toward defining "miracle" after all—but it was a *pragmatic* definition "from below." The Vatican records tell of events that large numbers of people once considered miraculous. As a result, they *were* miracles, and, for that matter, they still are. A representative sample allows us to discover what miracles are and have been in the Roman Catholic tradition. That definition became the second goal.

This ensemble of records is also a privileged source of social, religious, cultural, and medical history. It holds enormous possibilities for many applications in different fields. A third goal of this book is to draw attention to the rich potential of these files for other scholars whose interests and expertise extend beyond the confines of medical history.

Finally, my fourth goal is to engage medical practitioners in a discussion about the meaning and function of medicine and religion. I have been struck by the looming presence of medical science in these religious records, and how the converse is not true: medicine seems to ignore religion, and has done so for a long time. Indeed, many of my clinical colleagues are suspicious or uncomfortable with this research. Medline, the repository of up-to-date medical literature, barely addresses religious healing. Most references to *miracle* in that vast database resemble those in newspapers; the word is used hyperbolically to indicate precisely the opposite of the religious meaning: new drugs or procedures that are clearly the products of human ingenuity. Spirituality as a source of healing is rarely addressed in this literature. Sometimes, medical authors debunk miracles or argue for abolishing those beliefs to eliminate false hope.[5] Aside from the few recent but controversial trials on the effects of prayer and distant healing, the religious role in sickness is relegated to consolation and comfort in the face of therapeutic failure and death.

Doctors may believe that they have cured their patients, when patients actually credit God via the saints. If a multiplicity of approaches to healing is accepted by our patients, then we physicians should at least try to understand how that works. One of the outcomes of this work, for me, was finding unanticipated parallels in the "doing" of medicine and the "doing" of religion—parallels that suggest similarities in the dynamic relationship between knowledge and experience. Therefore, my fourth goal of engaging medical practitioners is to raise their awareness of medicine as a semiotic endeavor, not unlike religion, and to foster greater tolerance for the multifaceted experience of illness and recovery. For that reason, I dedicate this book to my hematology mentors who taught me the joyful elegance of observing and interpreting signs in our patients and their blood.

Sources for This Research

To determine a miracle in the Roman Catholic tradition, a detailed inquiry, called a "process" or a "trial," is necessary to establish that the event happened and lacks a scientific explanation. These inquiries leave records of testimony, and for the most part those files constitute my sources.

The files on miracles are carefully constructed to serve the canonical tradition. Indeed, they are generated and shaped by that tradition. Each *positio*, or deposition, is the record of an inquiry. It contains one or more stories, told and retold through documents and the words of many witnesses: clerical, medical, and laypeople. If possible, witnesses include the "miraculé" who received the divine intervention, as well as family, friends, neighbors, notables, priests, nuns, monks, and doctors. The investigation usually takes place in the hometown or cathedral city nearest to the site of the miracle. Records in the Vatican Archives are sealed for the six most recent papacies—currently, from 1939 forward. Since the eighteenth century, however, some records have been printed, bound like books, and deposited in the Vatican Library. These sources, together with the summaries (or compendia) that are printed at the time of each canonization, make it possible to study some of the late-twentieth-century miracles for which the archives are still closed. I attempted to examine at least one record, preferably that of the final miracle, for every cause completed since 1588. More on the research and records can be found in appendix A.

In examining these sources, I have identified more than 1,400 miracles pertaining to 229 different canonizations and 145 beatifications from 1588 to 1999. The study begins with a saint canonized in 1588, because in that year the current rules of canonization were first laid down as part of Counter Reformation changes. A special Congregation was created to preside over the process. These 1,400 miracles, referred to throughout as "the [or "my"] collection," contain at least one miracle (if any were identified) for each canonization since 1588, and for many beatifications too.

A conservative estimate suggests that my collection represents a survey of a third to a half of all miracles deposited in the ASV for use in the canonizations since 1588. It is amplified by information supplied by other sources.

The canonization process for a saint, called the *cause,* can take many years. The saints whose causes I have examined were born over the course of a thousand years, from 928 to 1922; the miracles ascribed to them were worked from an undated medieval past through 1272 to 1995. The first and most surprising discovery is that almost all the miracles—approximately 95 percent—are healings from physical illness, and for most, doctors provide testimony.

Vatican Records as a Source of History

The miracle files for canonization resemble those generated by the Inquisition. The Inquisition records have been brilliantly explored by scholars, such as Emmanuel le Roy Ladurie, Carlo Ginzburg, and Michael Goodich.[6] They reveal the everyday lives and religious feelings of people who were not in a position to leave their own traces. The canonization records have similar potential. Here we find the abstract thoughts of working-class people on the nature of transcendence; the shaky, handwritten crosses of illiterate mothers certifying their "voices" as recorded by celibate male clerics; the admissions of wealth or poverty and the confessions of devotional practices by religious, medical, and laypeople, be they humble or elite.

I am far from being the first historian to look into the history of miracle cures. The existing literature provided a stimulating and challenging guide, and several exciting new works have appeared since I began this project. Special attention has already been given to the miracles of ancient and medieval saints extracted from the "pre-Congregation" hagiographies (prior to 1588).[7] Some studies connect the stories to intriguing theories of narrative.[8] Several scholars using statistical methods have pointed to ancient and medieval miracles as a valuable source for the social history of popular religion and culture.[9]

In terms of medical history, Joseph Ziegler studied physicians in the Vatican records from the thirteenth to the fifteenth centuries.[10] Katharine Park used corporeal miracles to explore Renaissance attitudes to dissection.[11] Caroline Bynum probed miracle tales to uncover aspects of female spirituality and gendered attitudes to the body and to food.[12] David Gentilcore used the depositions to amplify his study of healing and healers in early modern Italy.[13]

Gentilcore concentrated on the canonization records since 1588. In general, however, these later documents have attracted somewhat less attention than their medieval equivalents. Nevertheless, their potential has been recognized in a handful of excellent studies. Some focus on specific times and places, such as Naples,[14] Venice,[15] or the Loire Valley and Brittany.[16] Angelo Turchini dissected the process that resulted in the 1610 "construction" of Saint Carlo

Borromeo.[17] Simon Ditchfield used his engaging analysis of a cleric's role in the post-Congregation canonization process of early seventeenth-century Milan to argue that modern history began in the religious approach to evidence and investigation.[18] Pierre Delooz conducted a sweeping *Annales*-style investigation of the political and sociological ramifications of canonization from the fifteenth to the twentieth century.[19] In a famous article, Peter Burke applied these same principles to the saints canonized in the first century after the changes.[20] These studies concentrated on the saints and the canonization process rather than on the miracles.

In addition, a few devout historians of religion have published inspirational and accessible summaries of the recent miracles, based on privileged access to the ASV and the Archive of the Congregation for the Causes of the Saints.[21] Historians of the Vatican have also consulted these records to illustrate Church procedures and their change.[22] Similarly, scholars who study religious hospitals or shrines, especially Lourdes, have highlighted the blend of medical and spiritual functions.[23]

To the best of my knowledge, no one has yet attempted to survey all the canonization miracles of the last four centuries—perhaps with good reason. From a practical perspective, this collection defines what some miracles have been and probably still are. It also sheds light on the interconnected workings of religion and medicine in the context of illness and healing that sparked my original questions.

Rather than a chronological summary of the miracles over four centuries, I have structured this book around themes emerging from medical history: the Hippocratic triad of patient, illness, and doctor. Chronology appears within each chapter. In chapter 2, the patients and their saints are described. Chapter 3 explores the problems that were solved miraculously, usually, but not always, diseases, and how they changed through time. Chapter 4 focuses on the special experience of physicians whose evidence was increasingly in demand from the earliest times into the present. Chapter 5 reviews how these many players interact in the gestures and devices of appeal and in the drama of the cure itself. The conclusion connects the findings to my original questions about religion and medicine, showing parallels in function and emphasizing timelessness in responses to illness in clerics, physicians and the sick people whom they serve.

In chapter 1, we begin with a history of the process that created these sources highlighting the contributions of a few key figures from both medicine and the Church.

I

Making Saints

Miracles, Medicine, and
Evidence since 1588

Miracles are not holdovers of magical superstition from an early age.
They are modern. Wonder resides in many aspects of life, but the set
of miracles studied for this book is a product of a specific tradition
within the Roman Catholic Church: the process of saint making, or
canonization. In its current form, this procedure began around 1588
and has continued to evolve under the influence of popes and physicians, some of whom are described in this chapter. Because miracles
answer to the needs of this process, they are also shaped by it.

The History of Canonization in Brief

The veneration of worthy predecessors is universal and timeless.
Hinduism, Buddhism, Judaism, and Islam recognize multiple holy
people and attribute wondrous events to them.[1] The ancient Greeks
and Romans also celebrated a cult of heroes. In the Roman Catholic
tradition, a dead person becomes a recognized saint through canonization, the history of which is well documented.[2] Scholars have
pointed to parallels between Christian sainthood and the older forms
of honoring the dead, sometimes implying that the saints had deliberately or inadvertently become the homologues of ancient heroes
and minor gods.[3] The celebrated departed have long provided inspir-
ing examples of lives well lived and practical help for afflicted mortals
still on earth. For millions of people in the world, they still do.

Until 1588, sanctity in the Roman Catholic tradition was a matter of consensus and local veneration. Apostles, martyrs, hermits, and healers were remembered for great religious devotion and remarkable feats of endurance, charity, or healing—acts considered miraculous during their lifetimes and beyond. These stories imbued their biographies until "lives of the saints" grew into the almost predictable, laudatory, and hortatory form, known as hagiography.[4]

Around the year 1100 the Church in Rome began to take an increasingly judicial interest in establishing the grounds for confidence in the lives and deeds of saints. Saints had been recognized locally through the proclamation of bishops, but decisions about saints were increasingly subjected to papal approval. Around the year 1300, formal arguments were constructed to challenge claims for sanctity.[5] One of the most interesting and accessible of these collections is the 1318–19 testimony of hundreds of witnesses who were interrogated on the miracles of Chiara of Montefalco.[6]

By the sixteenth century, the saints and their spectacular deeds were among the many targets of Martin Luther, John Calvin, and other reformers. They contended that some saints had never lived, and they decried the sensationalism attached to miracles.[7] Better it would be, in their view, to accept suffering and death as challenges to faith rather than to seek personal exemptions from the cruel realities of existence. In response to these and other Reformation criticisms, the Catholic Church launched a series of conferences held at intervals from 1545 to 1563, and known as the Council of Trent (figure 1.1). The Tridentine (adjective from the Latin word for Trent) reforms acknowledged the problems identified by critics and tried to introduce order, credibility, and confidence into the labyrinth of ancient customs in all areas of Church operations.

As a result of this Counter-Reformation, several new committees, or "congregations," were created by Pope Sixtus V. First among them was the Sacra Congregatio Romanae, created in 1542 and reorganized in 1587 to establish new rules for the practices of the old and darkly famous Inquisition in examining evidence for charges of heresy. Another was the Sacra Rituum Congregatio, or Holy Congregation of Rites (SRC), established in 1587 and charged with gathering and challenging evidence concerning the lives and deeds of potential saints.[8] Hence, in discussing saint making, we speak of pre- and post-Congregation eras. It is the latter that concerns us in this book.

The SRC presided over all aspects of saint making for the next four centuries. From 1588 on, a pamphlet-sized *Vita* or *Compendium* was printed in the year of every canonization to summarize the life, virtues, and miracles of each new saint; the practice continues today. A few decades later, the tasks

FIGURE I.I. Council of Trent, fresco by Pasquale Cati da Iesi, circa 1588, in the church of Santa Maria in Trastevere, Rome.

of the SRC were further defined by Pope Urban VIII (1568–1644). He formally separated beatification and canonization into two distinct processes, and he extended Vatican control over both. He insisted on stringent rules of evidence for the biography and miracles of potential saints. But he also formalized an "equivalent" process that allowed for consideration of long-dead individuals, as exemptions or *casi excepti,* for whom documents were lacking. A special office was created to concentrate on legalistic arguments against the canonization and seeking natural explanations for asserted miracles.[9] The leader of this office was called the *promotor fidei* (promoter of the faith), colloquially known as the "devil's advocate." The new rules were immediately put to use. In his twenty-one-year reign, from 1623 to 1644, Urban VIII beatified thirty-seven servants of God, and canonized five saints, all but one through the exempted process.

A century later in the 1730s, the procedures were documented, revised, and codified by Prospero Lambertini (1675–1758), who had served as promoter of the faith and would later become Pope Benedict XIV.[10] Additional summaries of the regulations were printed, as were lists of professors, physicians, and surgeons who were entitled to comment in the processes.[11] Lambertini's many contributions will be examined more fully below.

With some modifications, these 250-year-old rules still govern the process now. In 1917, a wait time of 50 years after the death of a potential saint prior to consideration for canonization was reduced to 5 years. In 1969, Pope Paul VI divided the SRC into two, creating a congregation for Divine Worship and another devoted solely to canonization, called the Sacra Congregatio pro Causis Sanctorum, or Congregation for the Causes of Saints (CCS—the word "Sacra" was removed in 1984). The CCS maintains its own archive in a modern building at the end of the Via della Conciliazione, left of the entrance to St. Peter's Square.

Paul VI further emphasized the papal role in beatification. Although decisions about beatification were taken in Rome, the ceremonies had been left to local bishops and cardinals. When he traveled, Paul VI chose to preside over beatification ceremonies; consequently, all postulants tended to seek the Pope as officiant. As a result, beatifications were increasingly held in Rome.

In 1983, John Paul II expanded the possibilities for new saints from many countries and diverse walks of life. In single ceremonies, he canonized large groups from many non-European countries, although he was not the first pope to do so. He reinterpreted the role of the promoter of the faith by reducing the staff of canon lawyers and the power in the position. Cases are now assessed largely on the evidence of the exemplary life; much relies on the scholarship of biographical text. Miracles are still necessary, but some people close to the procedures speculate about a future when they may be dispensed with. Benedict XVI appears set to continue the trends. As Joseph Cardinal Ratzinger and like his papal namesake of the eighteenth century, he, too, had served as promoter of the faith before becoming pope. In that capacity, he published several tracts of spiritual guidance that are directly related to the process of saint-making.[12] Already, Benedict XVI has bent the twentieth-century, five-years-after-death rule in consideration of John Paul II who will likely join several other papal saints recognized in modern times.[13] Benedict XVI may further decentralize the process of beatification by returning the ceremony to cardinals and bishops.[14]

The Importance of Credible Evidence

On the surface, the canonization process seems to have little in common with the Inquisition, itself subjected to Counter-Reformation revision and centralization by Sixtus V. In the Inquisition, people were interrogated to explore their beliefs and practices and to root out heresy; the consequences could include excommunication, imprisonment, fines, and other punishments. Torture was sometimes used to extract confessions. The wealthy were able to purchase pardons or dispensations, or they could hire proxies to serve penalties. Less fortunate people became the imprisoned or executed victims of the Inquisition. The *New Catholic Encyclopedia* points out that capital punishment was imposed by civil, not clerical, authorities. The functions of the Inquisition continue in the Congregation for the Doctrine of the Faith (often called the Holy Office). This office made controversial headlines in July 2007 by proclaiming the Roman Catholic Church as the one true church and the pope its infallible leader.

In contrast to the Inquisition, the canonization process focused on happier subjects. Failure to convince the authorities of a miracle or of sanctity had no more dire consequences than disappointment and delay. These differences notwithstanding, the processes of Inquisition and canonization bear a number of similarities. Being products of the Tridentine reforms, they both centered on a forensic, even skeptical, approach to assertion, argument, and interpretation. They were predicated on doubt and demonstration. Claims of either heresy or sanctity had to be anchored in solid evidence deriving from credible witnesses. In both procedures, the scrupulous methods of the interrogators were intended to leave no stone unturned, no question unasked. With these rigorous methods, Church officials would respond to the criticisms of reformers by proving that they opposed superstition, ignorance, and intolerance and that they took counsel from distinguished professors and wise physicians.[15]

Liturgical advice on how to conduct the inquiries included up-to-date science and knowledge of the full range of human frailties that might hide the truth. Simon Ditchfield argues convincingly that the forensic nature of these Counter-Reformation activities laid the foundation for the methods of modern history.[16] The canonization process included two types of legalistic scrutiny: the first, into the supposedly exemplary life of the saint; the second, into the claims that the would-be saint had worked miracles.

Miracles in the Canonization Process

In the canonization process, the Church does not create a saint—it merely acknowledges sanctity. During the ceremony, the pope proclaims a saint with the single word: *dicernimus*—"we recognize it." If the deceased is truly a saint, she resides in heaven with God. Only God can work miracles, but the saint can intercede on behalf of those who appeal to her. A happy outcome is called an "act of grace"; however, if it is thought to exceed the boundaries of nature and craft, it may be subjected to further scrutiny and designated a "miracle," thereby becoming evidence—a "sign"—of the saint's holiness in proximity to God.

Several steps mark the road to canonization; each can take many years. First, a scholarly biography of the would-be saint must be prepared with meticulous documentation to establish that she or he actually existed, possessed "heroic virtues," and led an exemplary life. If this biography is accepted, the servant of God will be recognized as "venerable." Then comes beatification, for which at least one miracle is required; then, the servant of God is known as "blessed." For the final step of canonization at least one additional miracle is required.

Since the late sixteenth century and to this day, no person who died a natural death can become a saint without working miracles; and no event can be recognized as miraculous without deep deliberation that usually includes the participation of physicians. A few special exceptions are made. Martyr saints have long been exempt from the requirement to have worked miracles, although miracles are often attributed to them.[17] Other exemptions occur through the "equivalent" process of Urban VIII that allows casi excepti to bypass the requirements of biographical documentation and miracles. This latter process is somewhat similar to that which prevailed prior to 1588, but it is necessary to produce evidence that the saint actually existed, led a good life, and is venerated; the decisions are taken in Rome. Usually casi excepti enjoy no shortage of attributed miracles, but witnesses are long dead, leaving little opportunity for their investigation. For sixteen post-Congregation canonizations, no miracles have been identified in the Vatican Secret Archives (ASV) or the Vatican Library; six pertain to martyrs. A few other would-be saints have been exempted from the need for miracles at the stage of beatification.

Within the SRC (now the CCS), the office of the promoter of the faith, or "devil's advocate," challenges the evidence. Formally created in the seventeenth century, the roots of this office go back even earlier to the Avignon papacy, two centuries before the Council of Trent. The office tests the robustness of the evidence for sainthood by raising doubts at every step: finding imperfections in the exemplary life, contesting claims of the postulants, identifying errors in medical judgment, and unmasking deception or wishful thinking on the part of the postulants or the person who experienced the miracle (called the *miraculé[e]*, or recipient). Essentially, this office is tasked with finding scientific explanations for asserted miracles.

By the late seventeenth century, doubts about miracles were printed in meticulously crossed-referenced books, *Positiones super Dubio,* some of which reside in the Vatican Library. For example, a 1677 *Dubio* in the cause of Domingo of Jesus and Maria contains an extraordinary four-page table of thirty-seven witnesses, literally a "spreadsheet" with five columns referring to the manuscript testimony and dates of each deposition; Domingo has yet to be beatified.[18] Later printed *Dubios* extended to multiple tables involving hundreds of witnesses. The rules codified in the 1730s by Prospero Lambertini, before he became Pope Benedict XIV, were based on his own extensive service as devil's advocate from 1708 to 1727 or 1728.

Medicine in the Canonization Process

Miracles of healing have been prominent since biblical times, and they appear frequently in medieval hagiographies. For example, Vauchez found that cures of illness constituted 80 to 90 percent of the collections of medieval miracles that he gathered.[19]

In 1588, the Church reformers expected that medical miracles would continue in the process of the future, and they anticipated a need for medical evidence. Many of the new saints, such as Carlo Borromeo of Milan, had been known for curing illness and helping victims of epidemics during their earthly lives. Pope Sixtus V took a special interest in medicine and the provision of care. In 1586, he invited the Fatebenefratelli to establish their hospital on the ancient healing site of the Isola Tiberina; their founder, John of God, would be canonized a century later.[20] The words for "healing" and "miracle" were often used interchangeably in the reports of canonizations. But as much as the clerics might condone medicine, they do not usually practice it. Conversely, most doctors are not known for religious devotion or theological scholarship; the few canonized physicians are exceptions that almost prove the rule.[21] The mechanisms used in these reorganized investigations had to allow medicine and religion—two elaborate canons of wisdom with opposite premises—to communicate with one another.

In the early years after the creation of the SRC, the miracles cited in the canonization processes seem to have differed little from those of their medieval precursors. The first saint canonized immediately after the creation of the congregation in 1588 was Spaniard Diego d'Alcalá (also Didacus). Dozens of posthumous miracles were summarized in two printed sources that followed the completion of his process; each had been the object of investigation.[22] For example, in a single miracle concerning the recovery of a young woman from paralysis, no fewer than eighty witnesses were said to have been questioned.[23] Thirteen of Diego's miracles were described in detail, and at least three became famous for having involved royalty: cures of King Henry IV of Castile, of his daughter, and of the seventeen-year-old Prince Carlos, son of Philip II of Spain.[24] Details on the last will be given in chapter 5. Like his medieval predecessors, Diego was even credited with having saved a "valuable mule," the only cure of an animal found in my entire collection.[25] A biographer claimed that an additional 130 miracles had been the subjects of "sworn testimony" duly given "judicious consideration," although they were not described; consequently, he invited his "dear reader" to think how many more of Diego's miracles must remain unproven simply for want of witnesses or investigation.[26]

This over-the-top response to the Counter-Reformation demand for evidence set the bar for the earliest canonizations. In the ASV, I have located manuscript records corresponding to only three of the eleven canonizations prior to 1623 and the reign of Urban VIII. Consequently, the best sources for miracles prior to his reign are the official summaries, the *Compendia* or *Vitae*, published at the moment of canonization. These printed summaries contain vignettes of miracles worked before and after the death of the saint, like those of Diego, though never so numerous. (See table 1.1.) Healings predominate.

Taken collectively, the miracles of the first post-Congregation canonizations form a solid bridge to a medieval past. *Vitae* for Diego and Francis Xavier mention Arabs and Jews, suggesting a plurality of culture that soon faded in later collections.[27] The *Vita* on Isidore concentrates on twelve miracles, but it also describes, sometimes in detail, a cluster of thirty-nine other miracles that had not been approved by the SRC. They had not been rejected; rather, the cluster remained uninvestigated because the authorities were satisfied with the weight of evidence in the first twelve. Clusters of miracles were holdovers from medieval hagiographies; usually they were grouped by type of diagnosis with no names or dates and little evidence of inquiry. They were a feature of the causes for Diego, Ramon of Penyafort, Bruno, and four other saints canonized in the seventeenth century.[28] But reports on clusters of miracles virtually disappear after 1700.

The cause for Carlo Borromeo is especially interesting. Known as an "apostle" of the Council of Trent, Borromeo had helped implement the changes to

TABLE 1.1. Miracles and Sources for Twelve Canonizations and One Beatification, 1588–1623

	Born	Can.	Source[a]	Miracles	Healings (percent)
Diego d'Alcalá	1400	1588	V, C	86	81 (91)
Hyacinth Odrowacz	1185	1594	V	3	2 (67)
Ramon of Penyafort	1185	1600	ASV, V	19	18 (95)
Pope Gregory VII	1020	1606	V	4	1 (25)
Francesca Romana	1384	1608	V	11	10 (91)
Luis Bertran	1526	1608[b]	C	10	9 (90)
Carlo Borromeo	1538	1610	ASV, C	17	15 (88)
Filippo Neri	1515	1622	V	6	6 (100)
Francis Xavier	1506	1622	V	16	11 (69)
Ignatius Loyola	1491	1622	V	10	10 (100)
Isidro Labrador	1080	1622	V	13	11 (85)
Teresa of Avila	1515	1622	ASV, V	5	4 (80)
Bruno	1035	1623	V	cluster	all (100)

[a]V = Vita; C = Compendium.
[b]Beatification (canonized 1671).

church procedures. During his life, he had been devoted to care of the sick and was often depicted tending to those stricken by plague.[29] He died just before the SRC was established and became one of the first saints canonized under the new order that he had helped to create. In addition to its other justifications, Borromeo's canonization was recognition for his contribution to the process itself. Turchini has analyzed the manuscript and printed testimony on over a hundred miracles considered in the Milan investigation.[30] In the ASV file on his cause, fifteen of the seventeen miracles were healings from illness that had occurred between 1593 and 1604. The file also includes an exceptional report on the costs of the process.[31] Spurred on by eagerness, the cause moved so quickly that it broke the new rule of a fifty-year wait: Borromeo had been dead a mere twenty-six years.

These early canonizations reveal that the Counter-Reformation changes demanded an approach that would allow investigators to gather, understand, and challenge those medical and scientific witnesses. At first, postulators aimed for overwhelming numbers of miracles and witnesses, but soon the clerics strove to recognize quality of evidence as well as quantity. The shift in emphasis was endorsed by the ecclesiastical historian, Cesare Baronio, who wrote in 1609 that the quantity of sources counted less than their reliability: "we should not judge the truth of history from the number of historians, but rather how much faith we might place in any of the arguments of a single author."[32]

The effect can be felt in the miracle files analyzed in this study. The first canonizations after 1587 featured many miracles with just a few witnesses for each. But a trend was established: fewer miracles, each with many witnesses. During the reign of Urban VIII, the average number of miracles assessed in each investigation dropped considerably, whether expressed in terms of the year of testimony or of canonization (figure 1.2). Investigators also left traces of their rising interest in the quality of evidence for miracles. For one thing, transcripts of testimony, during and following the reign of Urban VIII were preserved, and the office of the promotor fidei began to print detailed doubts, as described above. Furthermore, the organization of these documents reflects meticulous attention to detail of witnesses and corroborations.

Andrea Corsini, bishop of Fiesole, was the only saint canonized by Urban VIII through the full process. The record of inquiry into his miracles was conducted in 1606 before Urban's election as pope; it contains a detailed summary of more than sixty-four miracles, each with meticulous cross-referencing to the testimony of numerous witnesses; some witnesses were examined on several different miracles.[33] The votes of the cardinals with accompanying statements in favor of Corsini's cause were also published in 1629, together with the usual *Compendium*.[34]

This scrupulous attention to evidence and its preservation was joined by another trend toward more open accountability. In subsequent causes through the reigns of several other popes, the objections of the devil's advocate were occasionally published as a *Dubio* or as *Animadversiones*. These analytical

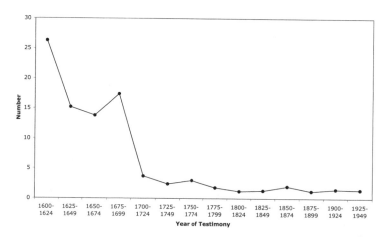

FIGURE 1.2. Average number of miracles in the archival records of each process by year of testimony (N = 149 files in ASV containing a total of 563 miracles).

documents applied pressure to the claims of postulants; they adhered to exacting standards of logic and science.[35] Nevertheless, a few seventeenth-century investigations, like Corsini's, continued to cite a host of miracles and many witnesses resulting in lengthy documents that resembled their medieval precursors.[36] In subsequent centuries, collections of the numerous miracles that flowed in the years immediately following the death of a would-be saint were handled differently; they would be gathered in files concerning reputation and labeled *fama* (fame), to distinguish them from the full inquiries into miracles.

The Role of Paolo Zacchia

Several writers contributed to the accommodations between religion and medicine. Among the most influential was the Roman physician and lawyer Paolo Zacchia (1584–1659). Born in Rome as the Tridentine reforms were being implemented, Zacchia was educated at the Jesuit Collegio Romano and rose to prominence during the reign of Urban VIII. Eventually he became the chief doctor (*archiatro*) of the papal states, a position somewhat like that of United States surgeon general. He served as the personal physician to two popes, Innocent X (1644–1655) and Alexander VII (1655–1667). Innocent X presided over five beatifications, and Alexander VII canonized five saints, three through the equivalent process. Zacchia's writings indicate that he offered advice on interpretation of the miracles investigated by his pontifical patients. His works were long cited within the canonization records, and he probably sat as an expert on several trials.[37] He died four years into the reign of Alexander VII, leaving his papers to nephews, and he was buried in the newly renovated Santa Maria in Vallicella (Chiesa Nuova) in central Rome.[38]

Talented in poetry, music, and translation, Zacchia wrote a number of medical essays and three books. His short treatise *Il vitto quaresimale* (1637) was a disquisition on Lenten diet and lifestyle intended to maintain health while observing the forty-day fast. His second work, *De mali hipochondriaci* (1639), was a treatise on the nature, causes, characteristics, and treatment of "hypochondria," a physical disease and not a mental disorder as its name might imply to contemporary readers. The vast array of symptoms ranged from vomiting and weight loss to headache, dizziness, and swollen hemorrhoids. Among the recommended treatments was *brodo de gallo* (chicken soup). Both these books were written in Italian.

Zacchia's third book, *Quaestiones medico-legales* (figure 1.3), was his masterpiece. Published in installments of nine volumes (or *libri*) over three decades from 1621, the *Quaestiones* (also *Quaestionum*) was a monumental survey, in

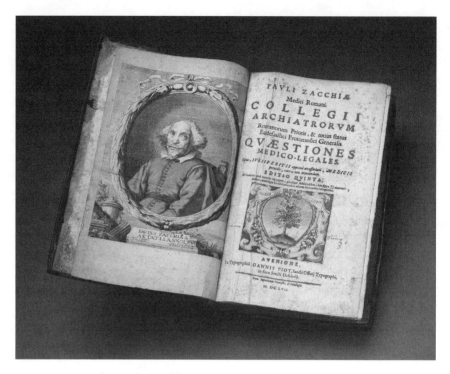

FIGURE 1.3. Paolo Zacchia and his *Quaestiones medico-legales,* 1657, frontispiece and title page. Courtesy National Library of Medicine, Bethesda.

Latin, of all medical topics from the perspective of legal and religious concerns. The first complete editions followed his death. It was reprinted many times in several different countries during the seventeenth and eighteenth centuries. Posthumous editions open with *Encomia,* or praise, from distinguished physicians. They also include variations on a list of the approximately one thousand authors cited by Zacchia (alas, without indexing, although an extensive index is devoted to subject matter). A testimony to his eclectic erudition, the list names ancient writers, such as Hippocrates, Aristotle, Galen, Dioscorides, and Celsus; early moderns, such as Jodocus Lommius, Andreas Vesalius, Daniel Sennert, Georg Wedel, and Girolamo Cardano; and literary, historical, and legal writers, including Herodotus, Homer, Ovid, Plautus, Pliny, Plutarch, and Virgil.

Zacchia frequently referred to German Protestant Daniel Sennert (1572–1637) and to Girolamo Cardano (1501–1576), the Padua-educated physician who had claimed friendship with the great anatomist Andreas Vesalius. Cardano was a prolific author; his vast oeuvre included a frank autobiography, in which he told how the tragedy of the wrongful execution of his son had devastated his life. Cardano sometimes found himself in trouble with the law and at odds with the Church, but he professed deep religious faith. He believed in miraculous portents, especially those derived from dreams, causing some historians to describe him as an early "interpreter" of dreams. Even as a child, Cardano was acquainted with saintly intervention: during a dreadful illness, caused either by plague or an over indulgence of green grapes, his parents prayed to his namesake, Saint Jerome, with happy results. Cardano had another brush with saintliness in his friendship with the much younger, scholarly bishop of Milan, Carlo Borromeo.[39]

Through Zacchia, the medical views of Cardano, hardy in medicine and passionate in religion, were brought to the canonization process. Sometimes Zacchia disagreed with him, yet he always referred to his work with respect. In his section on miracles, he referred to Cardano's views of the power of sleep and prophecy, and he cited the evidence used in several causes, as will be explained below.

But Zacchia contributed much more to the dialogue between medicine and religion. Historians of law and legal medicine have long recognized him as a founding "father": the Italian journal of forensic medicine, established in 1921, honors his memory in its name, *Zacchia: Archivio di medicina legale, sociale, e criminologia*. Recent scholarship delves into the origins of modern medicolegal dilemmas by reevaluating portions of the *Quaestiones*. Stemming from this renewed interest, we have excellent, but selective, translations with interpretation of Zacchia on the fetal soul,[40] mental illness,[41] poisoning,[42] corporeal evidence,[43] medical malpractice,[44] women's health,[45] sex within marriage,[46] and jurisprudence.[47] Much remains to be studied.[48] At the time of writing, the *Quaestiones* still awaits complete translation into a modern language.

Zacchia approached each topic with the same lawyerly emphasis on evidence and skepticism that characterized the science and the religion of his time. The recent studies reveal a startling modernity in his views. For example, he recognized that sexual relations in marriage were important for women as well as for men, even when one person of the couple was impotent or infertile.[49] In keeping with Church doctrine, he did not condone marriage in the absence of sex—an intriguing stance from our perspective, because some of the few married couples who have been canonized chose to live as brother and sister. With respect to abortion, he considered late abortion to be more dangerous and sinful than early abortion, and he adopted a position against Thomas Aquinas about the moment in which the soul was instilled in the fetus.[50]

The nine books of Zacchia's *Quaestiones* cover an eclectic array of medical topics, seemingly in no particular order. They were eventually assembled in two tomes, ending with sixty sample consultations, called *consilia*. The posthumous editions contain a third tome, edited in part by the author's lawyer-nephew,

Lanfranco, and consisting of the consilia (expanded to a total of 85) and 100 decisions from the Roman Rota. Zacchia used these cases to illustrate the application of points made in his book. He argued for the authority of medicine over law and for the greater weight of physician evidence over that provided by other professionals, such as midwives or caregivers. He also championed an expanded role for medicine in society.[51]

Miracles enjoy a large section in Zacchia's *Quaestiones* (Liber 4, titulus 1, first printed in 1628). After defining "miracles," he presented the range of their manifestations with biblical precedents, including prophecies, ecstasy and rapture, prolonged youth, miraculous death, and resurrection. He described the natural decomposition of corpses and instructed observers in the use of modern anatomy and chemistry to investigate claims of "incorruptibility," or absence of decay. The eighth of the eleven "questions" on miracles examined healings from various illnesses, citing medical authors who could provide reliable touchstones for an assessment of recovery from physical illness. These possibilities were dealt with in groupings that betray a strange (to us) nosological classification under labels that described either the sufferers or their diagnoses: lunatics, paralytics, demoniacs, withered (*aridi*); the blind, mute, or deaf; fever, dysentery, bleeding, and prolonged labor; leprosy and dropsy; sterility and miraculous conception; snakebites, wounds, ulcers, and birth defects.[52]

According to Zacchia, for a healing to be miraculous, several elements were necessary: the prognosis had to be incurable—either because of the diagnosis itself or because of the extent of the illness; and the recovery should be complete and instantaneous. Nothing should suggest that the cure might have been accomplished through nature or medical treatment.

Why Zacchia came to write of these matters is not known. One might reasonably speculate that as a prominent Roman physician with ties to the Vatican, he had been invited to comment on the miraculous claims being assessed by the SRC. Indeed, in this chapter and the consilia, he analyzed miracles under consideration for three candidates for sainthood: Lorenzo Giustiniani, canonized in 1690; Felice of Cantalice, canonized in 1712; and Pope Gregory X, beatified in 1713.[53] In these discussions, he referred to precedents from the causes of at least eight other saints, some of whom were canonized in his lifetime: Diego d'Alcalá, Hyacinth, Ramon of Penyafort, Carlo Borromeo, Andrea Corsini, Teresa of Avila, Maria Maddalena de'Pazzi, and Francisco Borgias. The recent death of future saint Roberto Bellarmino was also mentioned.[54] Sheltering incomplete causes, Zacchia named neither the potential saint nor the postulants when a decision went against the miracle; this reticence avoided prejudicing the reception of future evidence.[55]

Zacchia's approach catered to the needs of skeptical clerics, who were ill-informed about medicine and struggling to implement the new tradition of juridical argument. Medical experts working for the Vatican continued to cite Zacchia in their commentaries well into the twentieth century.[56] His influence on the canonization process, both personal and intellectual, cannot be over-estimated, even if it may still be difficult to grasp.

Prospero Lambertini and the Doctors

The most prominent name in canonization history is that of Prospero Lambertini, who in 1740 became Pope Benedict XIV (figure 1.4). Born and raised in Bologna, where he spent much of his life, he was a canon lawyer by training, schooled in rhetoric, logic, and history. His election to pope came at the end of a tedious, six-month conclave. Endowed with Enlightenment curiosity and a lively sense of humor, Lambertini was familiar with many of the illuminati of the medical school in his home town and he took a great interest in scientific investigations. He claimed friendship with the older Roman physician Giovanni Maria Lancisi (1654–1720), who from 1688 had served as personal doctor to three popes.

Lambertini is described as having a mercurial temper, softened by a fondness for children, and a shyness, if not outright discomfort, in his dealings with women. Nevertheless, he was the academic patron of two brilliant women destined to become the first female professors of Europe: experimental physicist Laura Bassi and mathematician Maria Gaetana Agnesi.[57] An erudite who adored books, Lambertini held an appointment as custodian of the Vatican Library from 1712 until 1726. He also served as secretary to the Congregation of the Council from 1718 to 1727. The latter position placed him at the heart of the affairs of the Curia (papal court), and carried weighty responsibilities akin to those of Cabinet Secretary in Britain, or Chief of Staff to the President of the United States, or Clerk of the Privy Council in Canada. Overlapping with these tasks and for two decades, from at least 1708, was his previously mentioned service within the SRC as promotor fidei, the devil's advocate.

Benedict XIV was known for his energy, intellectual prowess, and conciliatory skills. He had a diplomatic talent for peacemaking, which he applied to relations with the Eastern Orthodox Church, and with Austria, France, and Spain. Criticized for being "great in the study; small in the field," he was concerned with frugality and rejected the self-aggrandizing posturing that had characterized some earlier papacies, despite the urgings of his entourage.[58] He has been

FIGURE I.4. Pope Benedict XIV (Prospero Lambertini) surrounded by books, by Giuseppe Maria Crespi, circa 1740. Pinacoteca, Vatican Museums, Vatican State. Photo courtesy Scala/Art Resource ART 192997.

variously accused of sympathy for the Jansenists and hostility for the Jesuits, and vice versa.[59] These views are heavily colored (and obscured) by the opinions and allegiances of those who have written about him. Nevertheless, it is safe to say that Benedict XIV supported the centralization of Church endeavors, not because the duty had been bestowed by God, but because a measure of quality control would produce reliable results.[60]

Benedict XIV was assailed by the intelligentsia and leaders of Europe seeking favors. Thus, he ran into trouble with the Church in France for corresponding with François Arouet, known as Voltaire. Hoping for entry into the French Académie, Voltaire approached the pontiff through at least three different channels, seeking a papal endorsement of his play "Mahomet." From his tongue-in-cheek reply, Benedict XIV seems to have seen through the manipulation even as he granted approval; later he was irritated by the stir that his response had caused in France.[61] His wit was legendary, and his jokes have been collected. Our concern is with only one of his many roles: the presence of medicine in the canonization process.

By the time Prospero Lambertini stepped into the office of the promoter of the faith, the procedures of evidence, investigation, counterargument, and analysis were well established. Nevertheless, during his time, the average number of miracles investigated in each inquiry dropped still further and continued to decline into his papacy; large collections of many miracles in a single file became a thing of the past (figure 1.2).

Numerous investigations were conducted into miracles while Lambertini served as devil's advocate, but few seem to have passed muster by resulting in canonizations. The promotor fidei was expected to test the evidence and raise objections, but it is doubtful that Lambertini personally interrogated witnesses because most of the miracles had taken place in an earlier century. While he held the office, four regular canonizations took place, all in 1712. Six more canonizations took place during his papacy. During his lifetime, many trials investigated other miracles that would be applied to canonizations by future popes.

One canonization certainly drew Lambertini's attention: that of Caterina of Bologna. It was celebrated in 1712 with a costly festival in his native city. Lambertini would have reviewed the Dubio that had been prepared by a predecessor and published in 1681. It challenged the evidence on no less than 170 miracles, eight of which were dealt with in some detail. The first two concerned incorruptibility and the fragrant odor emanating from the saint's body, which is still visible for all to behold in a chapel adjacent to Bologna's Corpus Domini Church. Six other miracles were cures from illnesses that had transpired long before Lambertini was born: a dislocated foot; a gunshot wound; a grave illness with convulsions and headache; a dislocated hand; a breast cancer; and a fever with lethargy and delirium. Physicians, identified by name, gave evidence in all six cases; sometimes their comments were amplified by the testimony of pharmacists and barber-surgeons. The miraculé in the fifth miracle was himself an "illustrious" doctor of Bologna, Albertus Carradorius; he recovered from a grave illness in 1655 at age fifty-nine and lived at least another decade to provide testimony on his own cure and on another of a breast tumor in a twenty-one-year-old nun.[62]

The 1712 canonization of "politically inept but personally holy" Pope Pius V may have introduced some awkwardness for Lambertini.[63] Pius V had excommunicated Queen Elizabeth I of England, thereby placing Catholics in that country in a quandary: religious devotion could mean political treason. Indeed, Lambertini's experience wrestling with this evidence may have inspired his later chapter on the virtues anticipated in any would-be saint who had once been pope.[64] He admitted that canonization of a pontiff could be a delicate matter, but he thought that recognition of unique contributions was good for the well-being of the Church. Four miracles were described in the *Compendium* summarizing the process for Pope Pius V: one was the prediction of success in battle; another, the increase of flour for making bread in a monastery; two others were healings, the most recent of which was the recovery of a doctor's wife from postpartum fever in 1678.[65] In 1713, a year after the canonization of Pius V, an eight-page, private publication described another healing that had taken place in May of the same year: a sixty-two-year-old woman recovered from a two-year history of nervous disease causing paralysis; she had invoked the saintly pontiff while holding one of his shoes.[66] The story was published in Rome, perhaps as an offering of thanks.

Felice of Cantalice was another of the saints canonized in 1712. His corpse was also incorrupt, but the *Compendium* published at the time of the ceremony referred to other miracles that had taken place in his "temple," featuring six in particular, none of which had been among those studied by Zacchia. All six were undated, physical healings, and the miraculé was named in each: eye infection (in a three-year-old boy); arthritis; club foot; multiple grave illnesses; knee pain; and acute fever (in a four-year-old boy).[67] A similar array of eight medical healings were described in the 1712 canonization of Andrea Avellino based on testimony recorded in 1681 and challenged in a *Dubio* published in 1695.[68]

Lambertini's scrupulous attention to detail and his fascination with science and medicine are apparent in the printed *Dubios* in the causes of Giovanna Maria della Croce, Pierre Fourier, and Jan Dukla.[69] A major preoccupation in the cause of Pierre Fourier was the revival of two little boys, Giambattista and Nicolo, aged six and four, who had been run over by a cart in 1670; the promotor fidei cited both Zacchia and Lancisi.[70] In analyzing other miracles, vast tables were assembled, containing names, occupations, and ages of a hundred or more witnesses for each miracle, usually with one or more physicians. Twice, someone—perhaps Lambertini or a secretary—annotated the printed record by hand with the votes of the cardinals on the asserted miracles.[71]

The manuscript records also emphasize the importance of detailed testimony: after every numbered article in a 1749 file appear the words "according to well informed testimony."[72] The files of Lambertini's era are carefully arranged, easy to follow, with cross-references, numerous witnesses, and fault-less attention given to asking every question of every witness, and recording the answers. The effect often meant that each witness had to be asked the same questions twice or even thrice.[73]

After Lambertini left the office of promotor fidei, he spent three years as bishop of Ancona from 1727 and was raised to cardinal in 1728. In 1731, he replaced the archbishop of Bologna who had left for the conclave in Rome where he would be elected Pope Clement XII; in nine years, Lambertini would succeed him once again. Meanwhile, the future pope engaged with the scientific and cultural products of his hometown. He attended the lectures and demonstra-tions of local intellectuals and heard physicist Laura Bassi defend her disserta-tion. In response to the request of anatomists, Lambertini granted permission to dissect cadavers, and he defended the importance of public instruction in anatomy, both verbally and in print. This published notice cited distinguished medical writers Marcello Malgpighi, Daniel Le Clerc, and Thomas Sydenham, and closed with the observation that no less spiritual a man than the dying François de Sales had willed his body to *la Notomia* for the benefit of the Catho-lic faith and church.[74]

During this Bologna period, Lambertini completed his master work, *De servorum Dei beatificatione et beatorum canonizatione* (1734–38), noted above. This book is a detailed summary and codification of the procedures for can-onization; it refers to a voluminous number of case examples. His experience as devil's advocate motivated and informed the process. He wrote to a clerical friend describing his labor:

> I did not find it hard to devote myself to this theme. I undertook the
> work all the more gladly because the procedure followed in can-
> onizations was then practically unknown to anyone but the people
> actually engaged in it . . . I was not tired out by the investigations I
> had to make, but just as one hardly notices the discomforts of a long
> journey when one is traveling in company, so I forgot my fatigue in
> the joy of having fellow workers to help me [in] my task. I should
> have been frightened at my isolation lest I should go astray, if I had
> really been alone. When my mind dictates my heart guides my pen,
> because I am so happy to be useful to religion.[75]

These words notwithstanding, Lambertini worked mostly alone. The "compan-ions" were the many authors whose books he consulted and loved.

Multiple editions and summaries of *De servorum Dei* were published; however, just as for the work of Paolo Zacchia, only small portions have been translated into modern languages. The section on "heroic virtues" was translated into English in three volumes in the 1850s.[76] An analytical summary, with most examples removed, was printed in French in 1865.[77] Biographer Renée Haynes summarized the work in English.[78] Unlike Zacchia, however, Lambertini himself has been the object of many scholarly studies and biographies from the moment of his death forward. Among the remarkable resources on his life is a biography by his friend Louis-Antoine Caraccioli; the correspondence with Pierre Guerin Cardinal de Tencin, who was archbishop of Lyons and a minister under Louis XV; and a never-delivered radio address by Pope Pius XII.[79]

Lambertini's influence on the canonization process and his fascination with medicine and science are especially evident in his approach to miracles. He insisted on consideration of all sources of doubt; therefore, familiarity with advances in medicine and science was essential. In a lengthy passage of *De servorum Dei*, he explored varieties of miracles. For example, attention was given to miracles that contest the actions of evil, such as conversions from heresy and redemption from sin. Also Lambertini referred to astronomical miracles, and to "negative miracles," which entail the prevention or avoidance of disasters. Most of the discussion, however, concentrated on miracles of physical healing and the need to distinguish cures owing to the power of nature, suggestion, or medicine from the truly miraculous. In other words, Lambertini placed even greater emphasis on medicine in the assessment of miracles than had Urban VIII.

The many medical authors cited by Lambertini include the ancients, such as Hippocrates, Galen, and Celsus, as well as more recent physicians, such as Zacchia, Lancisi, Fabricius of Acquapendente, Hildanus, Vallesius, Daniel Sennert, Thomas Willis, and Thomas Sydenham (a fellow sufferer from gout). Newly recognized diseases and novel methods of assessing them were included. For example, around 1706, Lancisi had been charged by his patient, Pope Clement VII, to investigate the apparent increase in sudden death; subsequently, he described the condition of ruptured aneurysm. This new disease was discussed by Lambertini with Lancisi named as discoverer.[80]

Lambertini stressed heroic virtue as the trigger for canonization: miracles need not be investigated until the candidate for sainthood has already met the requirement for an exemplary life. Indeed, it seems that heroic virtue had already become the most important step in the procedure. If the miracle might later be shown to have arisen through natural causes, the canonization would nonetheless have been justified, as it was for martyrs. This sanguine attitude to temporal relativity is an important aspect of the Church's approach to miracles that does not always sit well with medical and scientific observers today.

Lambertini's proclivity for demonstrating proof—beyond the shadow of a doubt—fostered a taste for miracles of a certain kind. For example, suspicious of flagellants, he wrote that mortification of the flesh is to be expected from saintly people, citing (perhaps strangely) Ovid to endorse mortification. But he sided with Hippocrates to advocate moderation: for example, he thought it appropriate that the young Jesuit Luigi Gonzaga had been denied flagellation, which he had repeatedly requested, during his final illness.[81] Suspicious of credulity, Lambertini followed chemical experiments intended to elucidate the process involved in the liquefaction of the blood of the Neapolitan patron St. Januarius (Gennaro).[82] He pointed out that cures from seizure disorders must be carefully studied because the condition could have natural remissions. In this context, he asked for reports on the famous convulsionaries of St. Médard in Paris. He separated the symptoms of hysteria from the wandering womb and declared that cures of this disease should not be considered miraculous.[83] Ever concerned about charges that the Church had been too lenient on superstition and magical thinking, he distanced the canonization process from its pagan roots, and he criticized the popular customs of reciting prayers three times and offering up novenas.[84]

Like Zacchia, whom he cited often, Lambertini insisted on careful presentation of evidence and argument, demonstration and doubt. Haynes recounts a charming tale about his lawyer's aptitude for this work. As a young apprentice, prior to 1700, Lambertini had attended an investigation into the fasting of an elderly nun. Convinced of her sincerity, the judges were about to close their inquiry when Lambertini begged to ask a question: "Mother do you open your bowels every day?" The startled nun replied, "Yes, of course." Lambertini then argued that preservation of this regular function should be impossible in a person with an empty gut; her claim was exposed as a fabrication.[85]

That story may itself have been a fabrication about our lover of truth, but another tale of equal probity is more reliably attributed to Lambertini himself. A Protestant Englishman visiting Rome was shown a collection of evidence gathered for consideration by the Curia. Impressed with the "authentic" evidence, the "heretic" observed that the miracles would be hard to refute. The prelate then said, "Of all these miracles, which seem to you to be so firmly established, not one has been approved by the Sacred Congregation of Rites, since the proofs were rejected as insufficient."[86]

One cannot help but wonder if Lambertini's departure from the position of devil's advocate had something to do with the little flood of regular canonizations that took place during the six-year reign of Benedict XIII, from 1724 to 1730. Was his reticence overruled? In 1726, no less than eight saints were canonized through the usual process. The causes for three of these saints cite long lists of undated medical miracles, some of which might have been investigated by Lambertini. In the sixty-one miracles that I have examined from these

1726 canonizations, only four were not medical: two pertained to the incorrupt corpse of the saint; one was preservation during an earthquake; and another was a case of demonic possession. The fifty-nine other miracles in these causes were healings of ailments, in which more than half—thirty-two—described the role of doctors often with their testimony.

Even as pope, Lambertini may have kept the brakes on the canonization process. In his eighteen-year reign, he beatified twenty-eight, but canonized only seven, two through an equivalent process. One of his beatifications in 1747 concerned Girolamo Miani (Jerome Emiliani), founder of the Somaschi order of clerical teachers who had first instilled Lambertini's love of learning. His own Bolognese ancestor, the child Imelda Lambertini (b. 1322), was a candidate for beatification: she had died at age nine in a state of ecstasy as she beheld the Eucharistic host that had been denied her because of her youth. During Lambertini's lifetime, Imelda's cause made no progress at all; her beatification did not take place until 1826 by an "equivalent" process. His hesitation may have had more to do with his practice of avoiding charges of nepotism, something he did rather well, much to the chagrin of his nephews.[87]

I have examined 210 miracles pertaining to canonizations and beatifications held during the time of Lambertini's influence, from roughly 1702 to his death in 1758. Another 46 miracles in my collection were investigated during the same period and applied to causes that were completed after his death. For at least 125 of these miracles, testimony had been gathered between 1595 and 1700, well before Lambertini enjoyed any influence on the process. Of the total of 256 miracles, 22 were not medical: 10 pertained to the corpse of the saint; 12 others involved visions, salvation from fire or storms, and the expulsion of demons. In the reports of at least 116 of these miracles (45 percent), medical evidence was given by doctors; this effect was more pronounced in the 46 miracles investigated in Lambertini's time and used in later causes (34 of 46, or 79 percent). The proportion increases if the analysis is limited to miracle files for which I have been able to examine the complete testimony rather than a summary (22 of 25, or 88 percent).

Thus, among the miracles that were investigated during Lambertini's period of influence (whether or not they had occurred during his lifetime), more than 90 percent were healings and more than half included doctor testimony. By the time of his death, nearly 90 percent of the investigations heard from physicians.

To the end of his days, Lambertini remained fascinated by medicine and devoted to his native Bologna; often he found ways to combine the two loves. In 1742, he founded a school of surgery in that city, endowing it with surgical instruments given by the King of France. In 1745, also in Bologna, he established the Accademia Benedettina for learned discussion, naming the woman mathematician, Agnese, a founding member. In 1746, he commissioned another set of anatomical models of wax and terra-cotta for Bolognese instruction in obstetrics. In Rome, he befriended the Fatebenefratelli and visited their hospital on the Isola Tiberina.[88] He also expanded the ancient hospital Santo Spirito in Sasso with a costly new wing and contemplated the unorthodox plan of reserving a bed there for himself. The loud protestations of his entourage forced him to abandon the idea and hire a new doctor, Marc Antonio Laurenti.[89]

But the papal doctors could do little to help their eighty-three-year-old patient. As his reign drew to a close, he suffered so much from gout that he was unable to walk or stand during Mass. He died quickly of pneumonia in May 1758 and was buried in St. Peter's Basilica. If a cause has been launched for the canonization of Prospero Lambertini, I have found no trace. Without being a saint, he can surely be regarded as an honorary "doctor" of the Church, in the medical, if not the theological, sense of the term.

Into the Nineteenth Century

This project began as a search for the final miracles in every cause for canonization. The full array of the chronological distribution of miracles appears in figures A.1 and A.2, and tables A.1 and A.2. A curious gap emerged: relatively few miracles had occurred in the early nineteenth century. Was this pattern a product of clerics or of popular culture?

One explanation lay in the fact that canonizations were infrequent in this period of both religious and medical skepticism. In the seven decades from 1768 to 1838 inclusive, only five saints were canonized, all in 1807 by Pope Pius VII. Furthermore, the relatively rare canonizations during that time relied on miracles that had been worked much earlier. European political history provides another explanation for the relative absence of miracles. During the late eighteenth century, many religious orders had been closed, especially in Austria, Hungary, France, and Bohemia. Soon Napoleon Bonaparte's influence in Spain and Italy had similar results. The suppression of religious orders and colleges continued well into the mid-nineteenth century in many parts of Italy during unification.[90] The relative absence of nuns and priests meant that few were available to guide the public to potential saints; fewer still would be able to bring asserted miracles to the authorities. People may have experienced happy outcomes following invocation of holy figures, but the mechanisms for gathering and investigating miracles were lacking. In the same period, miracles, though fewer, were geographically more diverse and included inquiries that had been conducted in places as far away as Turkey, Canada, and the United States.

By the second half of the nineteenth century, miracles once again flowed to the attention of the Vatican authorities. At this time, the files display traces of routinization: two miracles were carefully investigated for each step of beatification or canonization. Blank forms were printed to ensure that all the required information would be provided and organized for "asserted miracles."[91] Some files show signs of having been read and reread, especially in marginal annotations made, perhaps, by the office of the promotor fidei or by postulants wishing to respond to his criticisms.[92] By the early twentieth century, investigations from Italy, Spain, and France once again predominated, although the new geographic diversity persisted.

With the 1983 reforms of John Paul II, a canonization required only one miracle after beatification. This reduction in the requirement for miracles might have hastened the process, but it simultaneously increased the level of scrutiny. The ASV index reveals that several archival volumes may now be devoted to the investigation of a single miracle; however, little more can be said because the files from this era are sealed.

The Consulta Medica

Medicine continues to pervade the process of saint making. In 1949, formalizing routines that had been in place for two centuries, the SRC annexed a college of physicians, the *Consulta Medica*, or Medical Council, which provides a steady supply of experts to study the scientific evidence in proposed miracles. The council may have been new, but it simply created a standing committee out of preexisting practices, giving it statutes and regulations.[93] The body persisted after 1969, when the CCS was created.

The Consulta Medica continues; service is prestigious and restricted to distinguished physicians who are practicing Catholics. Mostly, they are male academics from the vicinity of Rome who are paid honoraria for their contributions.[94] Giuseppe Giunchi, the Roman physician who served as the head of the Consulta Medica for more than two decades, wrote a frank memoir of his experience for the celebration of the four hundredth anniversary of the SRC in 1988. He described several difficulties that attend this work, not the least of which is the challenge posed by statistics. The weight of expectations embedded in medical statistics is to be respected; however, he said, when the evidence of an event is solid, the use of statistics to oppose it is a form of denying the truth in particular circumstances. For those serving on the medical council, belief is important. "Without faith," he wrote, "there can be no miracles."[95] Soon after, Kenneth Woodward interviewed internist Franco de Rosa and transplant surgeon Raffaello Cortesini, who have also served on the Consulta; the latter was cited in the media on a miracle for the cause of Mother Teresa, and he plans a book on his experiences. These doctors point out that no two cases are alike, that detailed documentation is essential, and that errors stem from mistaken diagnoses and lack of information. But some healings simply cannot be explained through science.[96]

From 1588 forward the business of saint making was ever more intimately associated with illness and earthly medicine. The unattended healings that had been prominent in the pre-Congregation hagiographies gave way to increasing emphasis on witnessed physical healings with medical testimony. The works of Paolo Zacchia and Prospero Lambertini reveal the preoccupation with medicine. As pope, the latter consciously revised and explained the procedures because, he said, those who carried out the will of the Church were themselves human.[97] He did not deny the possibility that miracles might be seen in cures from diseases that had yet to be recognized; nor did he deny the possibility of genuinely miraculous cures of diseases thought to be psychosomatic. But he wrote, "If a miracle of healing is to be recognized and proclaimed, it must involve such a 'physical disease as can only' (normally) 'be cured by scientific medicine.'"[98]

This seemingly paradoxical restriction emerged from that Counter-Reformation demand for credible evidence, and all tests of evidence emerged from the best knowledge of fallible human beings. Thus the elaborate workings of law and medicine were brought into the service of religion. This observation underscores two points: first, that most miracles were expected to be healings from illness; and second, that the only way to challenge or endorse claims of transcendent experience was through mastery of scientific wisdom.

2

The Supplicants
and Their Saints

In 1844, in the small town of Roccasecca, unmarried, illiterate, and impoverished Maria made a marginal living by cooking, cleaning, and weaving. At age thirty-two, she was alarmed to feel a lump the size of a small nut in her left breast. Every day it grew bigger, harder, and more painful. Overcoming her modesty, she showed it to the regional doctor whom she had known since childhood; he immediately referred her to a surgeon and two other physicians. All agreed that it was a cancer, by now the size of an egg, and that it should be cut out. Anesthesia was utterly unknown, and the prospect of an operation further terrified Maria. With the lump steadily increasing in tenderness and size, she went to her priest, who told her of the cause of Paolo della Croce, although Roccasecca was the birthplace of Thomas Aquinas. For twenty days and nights, Maria prayed to the uncanonized Paolo, witnessed by the woman who shared her bed. The night of October 20–21 she passed in agony, but by morning, the lump had vanished. She hastened to show the surgeon and a young friend. Two years later, Maria and her companions were summoned, together with the doctors, to tell their experience at an inquiry. Maria listened attentively to her own words read by the scribe, and then she solemnly confirmed their truth by signing her name with a cross.

Source: Paulus a Cruce Danei, ASV RP 2356 (1846), n.p.

In a much-cited paper, the late Roy Porter urged medical historians to look for the patient in the medical past; he drew on rich examples from early modern diarists to emphasize the point. His essay represented the medical side of a trend that has come to be called medical history "from below."[1] Indeed, doctors and other elites have had the advantage over patients in shaping our view of the past; they left more numerous and more obvious records.

Famous exceptions describe what it was like to be sick in various times and places. One of the earliest stories to have attracted attention is that of the second-century neurotic Aelius Aristides, who traveled the ancient world for fifteen years or more, seeking a cure for we know not what. His account belabors his desperation, the inadequacies of his physicians, and the wild smorgasbord of therapies, both medical and religious, that he attempted in his quest for relief. It is frequently used by historians.[2]

For medical history "from below," the canonization files are a privileged source. They encompass first-person testimony about suffering and attempts to find healing. In this chapter, I will describe the people whose experiences became the focus of the miracle inquiries and the extent to which they changed through time. As we have seen, hagiographies from an earlier period often featured miracles, perhaps as a way of shoring up credibility of the saint. But the purposes of those earlier accounts differed from the ones in this study. They usually concerned the celebration of the powers of established saints; they were not subjected to the legalistic process of canonization. As a result, some caution must be exercised in drawing comparisons between the populations of miraculés before and after 1588.

The majority of miracles recorded in the canonization files from the last four centuries are the stories of ordinary people rather than elites; some, like Maria, were poor and illiterate. Witnesses were asked to describe their income, financial status, living arrangements, and devotional practices, as well as the events considered miraculous. Granted, the transcriptions of in-person testimony are filtered through the minds and hands of the clerical investigators and scribes; however, these depositions come as close as imaginably possible to recording "voices" from the past of those who usually are "voiceless." They hold enormous potential for social and demographic history. As scholars of the medieval and early modern period have already shown, the possibilities extend to mentalities and microhistory of well-circumscribed areas.[3] Several brilliant new studies have exploited this potential in analyzing miracles at a single shrine or several shrines in a region.[4] Some have focused on the miracles after 1588.[5] In short, historians whose interests lie beyond religion or medicine have much to learn from these documents about community, authority, wealth, class, and power. But my central focus is medical, and I leave it to others to extend the observations into those realms.

In addition to the "patients" or miraculés, this chapter will also describe the saints and blesseds who were invoked to work the miracles. Originally, I had planned to set aside consideration of the identity of saints in favor of their deeds. It seemed that the saints had already been "done": several excellent studies have analyzed canonization from sociological perspectives in various periods and places; the most sweeping of these is the meticulous work of Pierre Delooz.[6] Gradually, however, I realized that the "selection" of both the saints and the people who appealed to them was far from random. Some bond must have existed between the recipient of the miracle and the future saint. Furthermore, the records of miracles are classified according to saints: they cannot be requested without knowing their names.

Saint and Subject

Several factors enter into the selection of saints canonized since 1588. The social, cultural, national, and political functions of canonization are well known. Canonization of a locally venerated figure pleases citizens of that nation and strengthens their ties to the Church. At least three kings of Spain were directly involved in promoting the causes of Diego of Alcalá and Isidro Labrador.[7] The process for Diego, described in chapters 1 and 5, featured the cure of a prince, which was said to have been instrumental in mending sixty years of hostility between Rome and Spain.[8] These nationalistic functions persist; the cause of a saint can be "fast-tracked" if her origins correspond to the traveling agenda of a pope. For example, John Paul II presided over a number of canonizations on his journeys. Similarly, on May 11, 2007, during his visit to Sao Paolo, Pope Benedict XVI canonized the first Brazilian-born saint, Frei Anthony of St. Anne Galvão. The cause of Blessed Mary MacKillop of Australia is frequently touted in nationalistic terms in books, articles, and websites, as is the search for a miracle, which was launched after her beatification in 1995.[9]

On another level, saints inspire and select each other, leading to national, social, occupational, and intellectual groupings. For example, Angela Merici was canonized in 1807 for founding the order of teaching nuns in memory of the pre-Congregation Saint Ursula. Inspired to nursing from a vision of St. Vincent de Paul, Catherine Labouré was drawn to care for the sick; in 1830, her vision of the "Immaculate Conception" soon became the subject of her Miraculous Medal. In 1858, barely four years after her medal had been approved by Pope Pius IX, the same words, together with a vision strikingly similar to the image on the medal, came to the uneducated girl, Bernadette Soubirous of Lourdes.

The son of a Spanish farmer, Pedro Claver became an American missionary through the influence of his countryman, Alfonso Rodriguez. The Spanish educator Enrique de Ossó y Cervelló founded institutions in memory and admiration of Teresa of Avila. Thirteen of the many Jesuit saints canonized within the period under study were born between 1501 and 1599; many knew each other in relationships of service, education, or spiritual advice. The canonizations of individual members in these groups may have been separated by centuries, but the spatial locus of their following and intercessions was often narrowly confined. In many cases, their mortal remains lie only a few steps apart: the Jesuit church of St. Ignatius in Rome holds the tombs of Luigi Gonzaga, Roberto Bellarmino, and Jan Berchmans; the nearby Chiesa del Gesù holds the tomb of Ignatius Loyola and a monument to Francis Xavier. This vast interconnected array of extant saints participates in extending the geographical fame of future saints and in shaping the logic that guides suffering people in the search for help.

Some long-established saints are viewed as patrons of certain diseases because of their own illnesses or the way that they died: St. Lucy for eye disease; St. Agnes for breast cancer; and St. Roch and St. Sebastian for plague. The same is true for post-Congregation saints. Indeed, an exemplary life often includes care of sick people during epidemics, founding of hospitals, and forbearance during painful ailments. Many of the first saints canonized after 1588 had served in outbreaks of plague, including Diego, Isidro, and Carlo Borromeo. As a result, people with similar problems may choose to appeal to a certain candidate for sainthood because of that attribute. A few such examples can be found in this survey. Teresa of Avila, herself paralyzed for three years, was said to have healed a priest from a contracture of his arms and chest and a four-year-old child from congenital deformities.[10] A Jesuit priest with kidney stones appealed to the Jesuit novice Luigi Gonzaga, who suffered from kidney disease before he died of plague at age twenty-three.[11] John of God, known to have endured a spell of insanity, interceded for a woman with fever who had lost her senses for ten days.[12] Gemma Galgani, who had tuberculosis, was invoked to heal a girl with a type of tuberculosis on her skin.[13] Ezeqiel Moreno y Díaz, who had died of malignancy, was invoked by a woman with cancer in 1986.[14] A similar connection was noted in the first miracle said to have been attributed to the intercession of Pope John Paul II and reported in spring 2007: the cure of Parkinson's disease in a French nun.[15] These diagnostic correlations are exceptions; nationality was a stronger link.

The saints derive from at least thirty-eight different nations on five continents (table 2.1). Of the twenty-eight canonizations in the first century following the Tridentine revisions, twelve were Spanish, eight Italian, and five French.[16] These wealthy, Roman Catholic nations have produced the most saints,

TABLE 2.1.   Nationalities of 400 Saints and Blesseds in This Collection, 1588–1999

Australia	England	Japan	Poland
Austria	France	Lebanon	Portugal
Belgium	Germany	Lithuania	Scotland
Canada	Herzegovina	Madagascar	Spain
Chile	Holland	Majorca (Spain)	*Sudan*
Corsica (France)	Hungary	Mexico	Switzerland
Croatia	India	Monaco	Ukraine
Czech, Moravia	Ireland	Paraguay	USA
Denmark	Italy	Peru	Venezuela
Ecuador			

Note: Countries in *italics* have no corresponding miraculés in the study.

but a few canonizations in the seventeenth century recognized the sanctity of persons from farther away. Polish saint Hyacinth (Jacek Odrowacz) of Cracow was canonized by the equivalent process in 1594. Peruvian Rosa of Lima was canonized in 1671 to become the first American-born saint. After her death and prior to her canonization, she was said to have worked eight undated miracles, all healings from physical illness, including the recovery of a native prince (nobilis Indiae) from a leg ailment of three years duration.[17]

A potential saint can be invoked only by those familiar with her deeds and reputation. As a result, forthcoming saints tend to work their miracles at home. The miraculés in this collection are even more diverse than their saints and represent forty-eight nationalities on five continents (table 2.2). Their tales are written in a multitude of languages, usually with a Latin or Italian translation.

For the majority of these stories, a narrow geographic correspondence prevails between the origins of the miraculé and those of the saint (table 2.3).

TABLE 2.2.   Nationalities of 1,400 Miraculés in This Collection, 1588–1999

Argentina	Ecuador	Japan	Poland
Australia	*Egypt*	*Kenya*	Portugal
Austria	England	Lebanon	Scotland
Belgium	France	Lithuania	*Slovenia*
Brazil	*Guatemala*	Madagascar	*South Africa*
Canada	Germany	Majorca (Spain)	Spain
Chile	Herzegovina	Malta	Switzerland
Colombia	Holland	*Mauritius*	*Turkey*
Corsica (France)	Hungary	Mexico	Ukraine
Croatia	India	Monaco	*Uruguay*
Czech, Moravia	Ireland	Paraguay	USA
Denmark	Italy	Peru	Venezuela

Note: Countries in *italics* have no corresponding saints or blesseds in the study.

TABLE 2.3. Nationalities of Saints and Blesseds and Sites of Miracles

Saints' Origin	Percent Miracles in Same Country	Percent Miracles in Other Countries	Percent Unknown Location	Total Miracles
Spain	61	4 S. America 3 India	27	323
Italy	74	1 S. America 2 other Europe	22	672
France	68	7 USA or Canada 5 Africa or S. America 10 other Europe	9	209
Poland	54		30	43
Germany[a]	48	25 other Europe	13	23
Netherlands	58	32 Switzerland	11	19
Portugal	17	33 India	39	18
Belgium	60			15
Switzerland	60	20 Austria 20 S. America		6
Czech	75			4
UK/Ireland	75	25 Italy		4
Lebanon	100			3
USA	50		50	8
Canada	100			6
Mexico	67	33 C. America		3
S. America	46	4 Spain	50	26
Africa	67	33 Italy		3
India	100			3
Ukraine	100			8
Australia	100			1

[a]Germany includes Prussia and Austria.

Because the earliest and greatest number of saints were Spanish, Italian, and French, people of these nations have predominated as recipients of miracles in the last four centuries. This adherence goes well beyond nationality to the strictly local, such as the province, county, birthplace, or burial site of the saint.

Jesuit missionaries who lost their lives in evangelical travels were invoked by people in Asia and both American continents on the instruction of teachers and clerics (table 2.4). These connections reflect the history of colonization. For example, at least ten miracles cited in the cause of Francis Xavier and six in that of João of Brito were worked in India.[18] Similarly, in 1889, the French founder of the Christian Brothers, Jean-Baptiste de la Salle, was invoked to heal a Canadian monk of the same order from a paralytic ailment.[19] In the early twentieth century, Italian-born Antonio Maria Pucci helped to cure a Chilean

TABLE 2.4. Sites of Ninety-Five Miracles of Jesuit Saints

Country	Percent
Unknown	35
Italy	11
Spain	16
Other Europe	13
North America	7
South America	1
India	17

man of a fractured pelvis.[20] German Maria Theresia Gerhardinger was beatified on the basis of the 1973 healing of a Brazilian nun from lymphoma.[21] In 1981, a family in Venezuela appealed to Spaniard Maria Rosa Molas y Vallvé to reattach the amputated finger tip of a five-year-old boy bitten by a piranha.[22]

Selection of Miraculés

Appealing to a not-yet saint is risky business indeed. Why would anyone expend what could be a last breath on a figure whose holiness has yet to be confirmed? Would it not be more reliable to appeal directly to God, or to an established saint? Some religious sources imply that "saints-in-waiting" are more receptive to appeals, for two reasons: they are eager to be canonized for the "good news" inspiration that will flow from publication of their exemplary lives; and they are less "busy" than the regular saints or the Deity himself. Nevertheless, the gestures of appeal to nonsaints must be viewed as courageous: the supplicant trusts in the future success of the cause. She casts a vote of confidence in the holiness of the saint and in the validity of the process. And she does so at the singular moment between life and death that will come to each and every one of us, usually only once.

Sometimes, the sick person had never heard of the saint and is urged by the cajoling or the occasional deception of others; in those cases, the trust is placed in human caregivers who are committed to promoting a cause. In 1749, a nun explained how she came to appeal to Jan Berchmans: a lady had visited her niece in the same convent, bringing word of Berchmans; another nun had his image.[23] The promotional efforts of Austrian Father Weninger, discussed below, brought Pedro Claver to many mid-nineteenth-century Americans who had never heard of him. In 1925, a man who had been hiking in the mountains near Barcelona collapsed with raging peritonitis and was conveyed to a monastery by his friends; the Jesuits instructed him in the life of Roberto Bellarmino to whom he made his appeal.[24]

Several witnesses claimed that they had already appealed to recognized saints before turning to the lesser known candidate. In 1602, an elderly nun, Angelica Landriana, testifying in the cause of Carlo Borromeo, said that she had previously invoked the recently canonized saints Hyacinth and Ramón of Penyafort without success; an image illustrating her 1602 appeal and thanks-giving was included in a vita of 1610 (figure 2.1).[25] In 1627, a mother had prayed to the medical saints Cosmas and Damian to help her infant son, before turn-ing to François de Sales.[26] A man tried many other saints before appealing to Maria of the Five Wounds to heal his swollen testis.[27] Revealing strong Jesuit

FIGURE 2.1. The elderly nun Angelica Landriana appeals to Carlo Borromeo and gives thanks for her cure from hydropsy. This miracle was cited in the canonization process. Bonino, *Nonnulla praeclara gesta*, 1610.

allegiances, a nun prayed to "St. Ignatius, St. Luigi Gonzaga, and all the Jesuit saints," before turning to Jan Berchmans who had yet to be canonized.[28]

A lovely story describes the recovery of a thirty-six-year-old watchmaker from a painful leg injury in 1904. A Protestant, the man had never heard of Madeline-Sophie Barat, nor was he familiar with the custom of seeking intercession. The 1906 testimony on his miracle explains how the nuns guided the man to her tomb, revealing neither the destination nor the reason. He converted following his cure. Perhaps the conversion added weight to the miracle; Barat was beatified in 1908.[29]

Occasionally the bond between sufferer and saint is no more complex than that of a shared name. Recall that the parents of future physician Jerome Cardano had appealed to St. Jerome on his behalf to heal a childhood illness.[30] By the naming process of baptism, the family deliberately (or inadvertently) places a child under the protection of certain saints and would-be saints. The name offers direction in a crisis. Sometimes the sufferer attended a school, or joined the order founded by the saint, or it was nuns or priests in her sphere who had done so.

Thus in 1604, an infant Carlo was cured of blindness from birth after an appeal to Carlo Borromeo and his case was included in the cause and in vitae published at the canonization (figure 2.2).[31] In 1753 a little Polish boy whose given name was "Jan Kanty" was the first of eleven people said to have been healed by the intercession of Jan Kanty.[32] Two Jeannes, both cured in 1743, appeared among the miraculées of the French queen, Jeanne de Valois.[33] In 1863, Belgian Sister Maria Alphonsa attributed her recovery to her namesake Alfonso Rodriguez.[34] In 1915, a child named "Marie-Madeleine" was healed by Marie-Madeleine Postel.[35] Two of three healed by Ursuline-founder, Angela Merici, bore the name "Angela"; the third was an Ursuline nun.[36] Some of the connections were more tangential: in 1921, Dutch Jesuit Peter Kanis was invoked to cure a nun who had taken the name Sister Ignatia, presumably to honor the Jesuit founder.[37] These examples are merely a few chosen from numerous instances in the collection.

Clusters of Miraculés and Miracles

As explained in chapter 1, the inquiries conducted prior to 1700 would sometimes focus on large numbers of miracles, presented in clusters. Around a shrine huge crowds of supplicants would assemble to make, what one biographer called, a "theater of the sorely afflicted, a Probatica pool of incurables."[38] Gathering evidence would entail interrogation of hundreds of people who had

Carolus Naua infans cœcus natus ꝑ nerita S.Caroli lumen oculorū recipit

L'anno 1604 d'Otobre Lucina moglie di Filippo Naua in Milano partorisce un Figliuolo al quale fu posto nome Carlo e questo nacq

nce cieco senza la sostanza de gli occhi, in uece della quale haueua gran copia di materia uerde, e puzzolente S.Carlo apparisce a Clara Fighola di 5 anni Benedice il Figliuolo e li restituisce gl'occhi

FIGURE 2.2. The newborn infant Carlo Nava recovers from blindness after his mother Lucina appealed to Carlo Borromeo. This miracle was cited in the canonization process. Bonino, *Nonnulla praeclara gesta*, 1610.

witnessed multiple events; the report would describe an extremely local and highly active "social network" promoting the cause of the saint.[39] For the majority of these clusters, the transcripts and details of the actual testimony are now lacking and we know of their existence from their groupings, usually by diagnosis, in the publications at the time of the canonization (table 2.5).

Thirty files of testimony prior to 1700 have been studied in this collection. Three exceptional manuscripts in this group reveal the Counter-Reformation

TABLE 2.5. Clusters of Miraculés by Half Century of Canonization

From year	1588	1600	1650	1700	1750	1800	1850	1900	1950
to year	1600	1649	1699	1749	1799	1849	1899	1949	1999
No. of clusters	4	4	17	2	0	0	1[a]	1[b]	0

[a]1892 analysis of testimony on St. Falco, delivered in 1532, and of a set of 25 votive offerings presented between 1579 and 1719.
[b]A 1638 printed summary of 41 miracles attributed to Alessandro Sauli and probably applied to his beatification in 1741; he was canonized in 1904.

approach to investigating large clusters of miracles during the transition in preference from many miracles to few. They also describe social networks of tightly knit communities, united by a mission and by ties of work and blood. It is not known if they typify earlier investigations whose records may have been lost, or if their format is new and owing to the heightened attention to evidence following 1588.

The first is the 1606 record of testimony on more than sixty miracles attributed to Andrea Corsini, who had been bishop of Fiesole near Florence. Dozens of Fiesole people—men, women, and children—came forward to recount their experiences and explain their relationships to each other. Only five miraculés in this group were in religious orders: two monks and three nuns. The vast majority of miraculés and other witnesses worked in industries related to the wool trade, especially carding and weaving; many lived in poverty. Two were successful artists: Lorenzo Cresci and Bernardo Pucetti. Cresci was working on a painting in the church above Corsini's tomb when he was cured of tertian fever (malaria).[40] Another witness was a thirty-seven-year-old Florentine, Michelangelo Buonarotti, who claimed to be well off, "in need of nothing"; however, he did not explain what connection, if any, he may have had to the more famous artist of the previous century.[41] With the attention on corroboration, the file seems to stand midway between a *fama*, reporting on a reputation, and a judicial investigation into miracles.

The second such file was generated sixty years later, when dozens of people came forward in two separate inquiries to describe miracles attributed to Maria Maddelena de' Pazzi. Most miracles took place near her tomb in Florence. But the geographic range was broader than in the Corsini file: witnesses reported on at least a dozen miracles worked at a distance in either Naples or Sorrento.[42] The gathering defines a distinct segment of Florentine society in 1663–64, whereas the events recollected happened at intervals over the preceding fifty years. Thirty miracles in this collection of sixty-two involved nuns or monks associated with Pazzi's convent community. Identifying herself as a daughter of Caterina de Medici, Mother Maria Pacifica, the fifty-one-year-old prioress of the convent testified on four different miracles.[43] But the witnesses also included laypeople involved in a wide array of occupations—schoolboys, housewives, and traveling merchants. The 1669 canonization took place in Rome as the new rules stipulated; however, Maria Maddalena's origins and her influential network are evident in the church chosen for the ceremony: San Giovanni dei Fiorentini.

The third and last of these large investigations in my collection took place in France in 1682 and concerned more than seventy miracles attributed to Pierre Fourier de Notre Dame, founder of congregations in eastern France. Most of the dozens of witnesses were French. The file contained a tiny sub-cluster of two double miracles: the two brothers resuscitated from having been run over by a carriage in 1670 (mentioned in chapter 1), and another pair of brothers both healed of hernia in 1673.[44] Again religious miraculés were in the minority: ten nuns and one monk. However, witnesses came from several different communities centered on Lorraine, including Besançon, Toul, Gray, and "Multiponten" (possibly Pont à Mousson), and extending to Paris and Nantes. In terms of geography, the corresponding "network" is even less circumscribed than those for Corsini and Pazzi earlier in the century. The widespread effects and fame of this would-be saint may also reflect a change in methods of invocation, as will be discussed in chapter 5.

The overwhelming mass of evidence in Fourier's file seems to have posed a challenge for the young Prospero Lambertini, as mentioned in chapter 1. In his work for the promotor fidei, he helped to analyze and organize the 1682 record in preparation for publishing doubts and criticisms on several occasions between 1702 and 1726. The cautions seem to have been effective: Fourier was beatified in 1730—only after Lambertini had left the office of promotor fidei and before he became pope; he was not canonized until 1897, following another French miracle investigated in 1885.[45]

Family and Local Connections

The end of the seventeenth century saw the waning of quantity in the approach to evidence of the miraculous. But the interconnectedness of witnesses to each other did not vanish. As the number of miracles under investigation declined, fewer witnesses were called in total, but many more witnesses were examined for each miracle. Even the inquiries that addressed only one or two miracles contain overlapping surnames and relationships through birth and marriage.[46]

Examination of all the miracle files in the cause of French shepherdess Germaine Cousin illustrates the range of such a collection. Four separate files contain information on seven miracles: six were healings that had taken place at her tomb in Pibrac near Toulouse; one was the increase of flour in an orphanage near Bourges. The six miraculés included a seven-year-old girl, a twelve-year-old son of a farmer, a young woman merchant and a nun, both aged twenty-two, a dressmaker of twenty-four, and a thirty-five-year-old woman. Details of these appeals will be presented in chapter 5. They took place over three decades between 1828 and 1858, but the testimony was gathered in a narrower, thirteen-year range between 1846 and 1859. Some witnesses reappear in each of the different investigations: two doctors in particular. However, a doctor who had testified in 1846 subsequently died prior to the cure of another former patient, and he could not be summoned for the 1856 investigation.[47]

In small towns, people who appealed to a would-be saint might be related to the religious and medical professionals who testified in their cases. In 1908, a doctor described the care of his elderly aunt.[48] Sometimes, more than one miracle would occur in an extended family; the two events would be investigated simultaneously.[49] This practice greatly simplified the work of the investigators, but it thoroughly complicates the historian's task of untangling the record.

On a few occasions, witnesses were related by blood to the prospective saint. From 1656, a relative of Caterina de'Ricci who lived near Gubbio collected an annotated list of more than fifty miracles, in a conscious effort to contribute to her cause. Although his raccolto was not the product of an inquiry, it is kept in the ASV together with the testimony on two miracles from a century later.[50] In 1773, during an investigation of miracles ascribed to the venerable Salvatore Pagnani, several witnesses and a miraculée declared that they were his nieces or great-nieces. These blood relationships may have done nothing to advance his cause which is still awaiting beatification.[51] In 1853, a nun who was one of the miraculées for Sardinian saint Ignazio of Laconi was said to have been his sister.[52] Similarly, a forty-eight-year-old Corsican nun rejoiced to learn that Theophilus of Corte had been her great-uncle; she related this connection to the fervor of her 1905 appeal and its success.[53] In 1907, witnesses describing the miracle of thirty-three-year-old Rosalie, a farmer in southern France, claimed blood ties to the martyr Pierre Chanel. Rosalie found relief from her long-standing tuberculosis in 1904 by praying to Chanel and making a pilgrimage to Lourdes in the same year. She insisted that her recovery was owing to Chanel, not to the Virgin, nor to the as-yet-uncanonized Bernadette Soubirous; yet her case was one of the rare healings published in the *Journal de la Grotte*. Three years later the distinguished Dr. Gustave Boissarie claimed that her cure was one of the "most important" of those he had witnessed.[54]

Finally, bonds between supplicant and would-be saint were forged by similar occupations and trajectories of faith. Thirteen of twenty-six cures in priests
had followed appeals to would-be saints who had been priests, bishops, or pope.
Along the same lines, the intercession of an English Catholic convert, Cuthbert
Mayne, was sought in 1884 by forty-one-year-old Joseph, himself an English
convert who suffered from exquisitely painful leg ulcers.[55]

Socioeconomic Considerations: Elites, Paupers, and Illiterates as Witnesses

In the earliest hagiographies, a special place is accorded elite miraculés, as if
their involvement were more impressive or more credible. The custom persisted in the first century following the Tridentine changes. Miracles involving nobility, such as kings, princes, counts, countesses, and bishops, figure
more prominently in the records of the sixteenth and seventeenth centuries
(table 2.6). Nobles also often appear as witnesses in these early modern records,
even when they did not experience or witness miracles. For example, thirty-one
personages, most elderly counts, bailiffs, lawyers, canons, and other officials,
testified in the 1632 process concerning Jeanne de Valois. They spoke of her
fame, the hordes of supplicants, and the many votive offerings left at her tomb,
but they could offer few specific details about the miracles under investigation.[56] Doctors and their family members also formed a special type of elite
miraculé; they appeared regularly across all centuries, as will be discussed in
chapter 4. With the exception of physicians, the number of elite witnesses is
negligible after 1800.

In this context of socioeconomic status, widows deserve special mention for
their steady presence. In the early investigations, they appear more often than
single or married women, perhaps owing to their higher status as autonomous

TABLE 2.6. Social Status of Miraculés by Half Century of Testimony

From year to year	1588 1599	1600 1649	1650 1699	1700 1749	1750 1799	1800 1849	1850 1899	1900 1949	1950 1999	Total
Nobility	9	9	16	1	0	0	1	2	0	38
Widows	0	5	5	3	2	2	1	3	4	25
Doctor families	1	7	4	3	1	0	2	2	3	23
Impoverished	0	17	3	2	2	2	2	7	2	37
Illiterate	0	0	1	3	4	2	3	0	0	13

people of independent means. For example, only five women were among the thirty-one witnesses in the aforementioned 1632 process on Jeanne de Valois; all were widows.[57] In contrast, later investigators tended to emphasize the poverty and vulnerability of widows.

Impoverished and illiterate miraculés appear at a steady rate, until the twentieth century. Even in wealthy households, the testimony of poor and illiterate servants about their masters was included. Often enough, a servant had been the only person to have attended an employer in illness. In one investigation involving a medical family, testimony came from numerous physicians, but also from four servants, at least two of whom were illiterate.[58] On at least one occasion, the idea of appealing to the would-be saint seems to have come from a servant or tenant, "a woman living in my house."[59]

An interesting feature of trying to identify witnesses in the seventeenth- and eighteenth-century miracles is their relative ignorance of (or indifference to) their own ages and lapse of time. Ages were expressed approximately—*in circa, mas o menos*—whereas regular declarations of the actual date of birth did not become frequent until the nineteenth century. One woman testifying in 1790 did not even pretend to give her age, stating bluntly, "I do not know how old I am."[60] The most recent example of collective innumeracy appeared in an 1870 file pertaining to the cure of an impoverished Sicilian fruit seller's sore arm; all witnesses, except the doctors, were illiterate, and most did not know their ages.[61] Instead, the people confidently and reliably situated events in juxtaposition to the seasons or religious festivals, but they disagreed over the length of time that had passed between an event and the testimony, sometimes by as much as ten years.[62]

The decline of both nobles and the poor in the records of the twentieth century might be connected to the rise of democracy and the welfare state in Europe—fewer princes and paupers were around. But it also has something to do with changing attitudes to evidence. In the early years, privileged status implied reliability and authority; it also signified education that conveyed a facility with the process itself, and it meant financial resources to pursue the cause. In the later years, poverty of witnesses might not have increased their credibility, but it tended to enhance the romantic wonder of the miracle.

Gender of Miraculés

Gender seems to have been another factor in selection of patients, especially in the nineteenth and twentieth centuries when women saints and miraculées both increased in numbers.[63] Two-thirds of canonizations between 1588 and

TABLE 2.7. Saints, Blesseds, and Miraculés by Gender

Miraculés	Saints or Blesseds	
	Female (N = 414) (percent)	Male (N = 986) (percent)
Female (N = 779)	32.7	67.3
Male (N = 621)	25.6	74.4

1999 were of men or groups of men (171 male versus 83 female). A new influx of women saints began in the nineteenth century. Overall in this collection, female saints and blesseds were responsible for thirty percent of all miracles: 25 percent among those canonized or beatified before 1700 and 37 percent for those after 1900. During the four centuries studied, both men and women appealed to holy people of the opposite sex. Men displayed no hesitation in turning to women saints: 28 percent of the successful favors granted to men were attributed to women, and 25 percent of those to women (table 2.7).

At first, miracles in men were slightly more frequent than in women. After the late eighteenth century, nearly twice as many female miraculées appear than male (tables 2.8a, 2.8b, and figure 2.3). The relatively greater number of miracles worked in women more recently needs explaining. It could reflect a

TABLE 2.8a. Gender of Miraculés by Half Century of Canonization in This Study (absolute numbers)

From year to year	1588 1599	1600 1649	1650 1699	1700 1749	1750 1799	1800 1849	1850 1899	1900 1949	1950 1999
Female	29	81	90	101	27	30	81	121	198
Male	63	84	110	101	16	13	57	65	109
Unknown[a]		7	1					1	2

[a]Excludes unknown supplicants for nonmedical miracles.

TABLE 2.8b. Gender of Miraculés by Half Century of Canonization (percentage of miracles)

From year to year	1588 1599	1600 1649	1650 1699	1700 1749	1750 1799	1800 1849	1850 1899	1900 1949	1950 1999
Female	32.6	44.8	44.8	48.1	71.1	69.8	57	63.7	62.9
Male	70.7	46.4	54.7	48.1	42.1	30.2	40	34.2	34.6

Note: Totals may not equal 100 percent because both men and women appear in clusters and because unknowns are excluded.

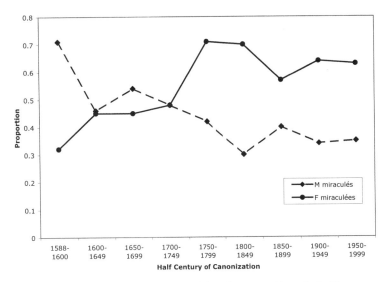

FIGURE 2.3. Proportion of male and female miraculé(e)s by half century of canonization ($N = 1,361$).

greater willingness on the part of church officials to listen to their evidence. But female witnesses testified frequently in every century, even in cases involving male miraculés. It may also be explained by theories of women's more active involvement in religious practices, especially in the last two centuries.[64] Similarly, it may reflect a relatively greater comfort in speaking publicly of health and religious matters. In other words, miracles may have been experienced no less often by men, but they were less willing to discuss them.

Another possible explanation for the predominance of female miraculées could relate to the observations of Caroline Bynum and other feminist scholars about religious practices. They suggest that women are simply more corporeal than men, owing to their conspicuous and cyclical biology: menstruation, gestation, parturition, lactation, and the preparation of food. These functions serve as constant reminders of their physicality and the intimate connection of their bodies to propagation, life, and death.[65] Support for these ideas comes from the jarring stories of placid nuns cutting the bodies of their newly dead sisters to retrieve hair, digits, hearts, and other organs. This scholarship often refers to Colette de Corbie's vision of the dismembered baby Jesus served on a plate, and to Chiara of Montefalco, whose fresh corpse was sliced open by her sisters and found to contain the shape of a crucifix inside her heart.[66]

The story of a similarly hardy removal was told by an elderly nun in the *fama* of Marie-Euphrasie Pelletier. During Pelletier's life as superior of her order, a nun died in the "odor of sanctity." Marie-Euphrasie determined that the cadaveric heart should be removed, but rigor mortis had firmly fixed the arms of the deceased over her chest. Pelletier commanded the corpse to open its arms; the body obeyed instantly—in death as in life—and the heart was retrieved.[67]

The vast majority of the 762 healing miracles in women are similar to those of men; however, at least 70 miracles scattered across the four centuries (or ten percent) entail the complications of birthing. These will be further discussed in chapter 3. During the first half of this same period, we know that men rarely attended labors and deliveries. Therefore, we must notice, even if we cannot fathom, the motives and wishes of these sometimes illiterate women who chose to recount intimate moments of their sexuality and reproduction to celibate male clerics.

Men appealed to the candidates for sainthood in only slightly fewer numbers than women (608 vs. 748). Just as female patients suffered ailments unique to their biology, men developed health problems that reflected their physiology and active lives. For example, they suffered more hernias than women and more accidents, including car crashes, shipwrecks, and falling off horses and buildings. The specifics will be further developed in chapter 3.

Perhaps because of their greater wealth and autonomy, it was the male patients who seemed most often to have been medical travelers, reminding us of the medical quest of the second-century neurotic Aelius Aristides. For example, a forty-two-year-old Italian businessman had been a health pilgrim for at least five years until 1749 when he was cured of a "cancerous tumor." His wanderings seem to have been motivated by his work as much as his poor health. Nevertheless, he saw doctors in every place that he visited. The consultants were Italian, German, and Spanish, working in Vienna, Bologna, Venice, Padua, and Palermo. All recommended surgery, but he found healing through the intercession of Serafino of Monte Granario.[68]

Miraculés in Religious Orders

A religious occupation—such as nun, abbess, monk, priest, or bishop—was frequently found among those who had experienced miracles, but it did not describe the majority (table 2.9). Again, women were more numerous: there were at least 195 nuns (5 of whom were superiors) and 72 monks, priests, or bishops. Although saints who had been clerics during life predominate, miraculés who were clerics were in the minority for every period examined. This finding might be surprising if one imagines that the truthfulness of clerical witnesses would be considered unassailable and should lead to favoring their experiences.

TABLE 2.9.   Religious Miraculés by Gender and Half Century of Canonization

From year to year	1588 1599	1600 1649	1650 1699	1700 1749	1750 1799	1800 1849	1850 1899	1900 1949	1950 1999	Total
Female cleric	1	10	21	23	5	5	20	35	65	187
Male cleric	0	11	25	26	2	4	16	14	14	112
All miracles	89	181	201	210	38	43	142	190	315	1409

Again it is tempting to seek an explanation for the relative absence of clerical miraculés in the social history of religious practices. Could it be that religious witnesses were automatically judged as biased for the cause, and therefore, excluded in favor of laypeople? Or did ingrained humility and reticence dictate silence on matters of personal illness and cure? Further tending to diminish the presence of clerical miraculés, those in religious orders may have assimilated the church's relative discomfort with the sensationalism of miracles; consequently, they might hesitate to offer received graces for scrutiny to avoid charges of bragging or gullibility. Sometimes fellow clerics who had been bystanders were more adamant about the power of the intercessions than were the miraculés themselves. An explanation for this discrepancy resides in the extreme illness of the person who was cured—an observation that applies to all miraculés, not only the religious. The nearly fatal symptoms hampered recollection, and religious subjects might have been less susceptible to the hints and urgings of others about what had transpired while they lay ill.

In looking over the ensemble of healings in religious persons and comparing them with others, few differences can be found in terms of average age, nature of the illness, presence of physicians, gestures of appeal, or numbers of witnesses. Male and female religious appealed to saints of both sexes in approximately equal proportions to the ensemble, but male clerics in this study never appealed to saints who had not been in holy orders during their lives (table 2.10). Testimony on these events in clerical people might be amplified by that of laypeople serving as domestic servants, cooks, or laborers in a religious community, and the attending physicians. All miracles personally experienced by clerics were healings from physical illness, although they sometimes provided bystander testimony on nonmedical miracles, involving food or the corpse of a saint whose body lay in the local church.

Clerics who were members of a saint's order were aware of the exemplary life, and often they resided near the tomb. Three examples illustrate this point. The 1657 recovery of a nun from a grave injury to her hand was among more than a hundred miracles gathered for consideration in the cause of her founder,

TABLE 2.10. Saints and Miraculés by Gender and Clerical or Lay Occupations

Miraculés	Appeals to Female Saints (percent)		Appeals to Male Saints (percent)	
	Clerics ($N = 362$)	Lay ($N = 52$)	Clerics ($N = 952$)	Lay ($N = 34$)
Female cleric ($N = 191$)	47	2	50	1
Female lay ($N = 588$)	22	5	70	3
All females ($N = 779$)	28	5	65	2
Male cleric ($N = 72$)	32	0	68	0
Male lay ($N = 549$)	22	3	72	3
All males ($N = 621$)	23	3	72	2
Total ($N = 1,400$)	26	4	68	2

Caterina of Bologna.[69] In 1830, a Spanish monk appealed to the founder of his order, Miguel de los Santos (Argemir), and was cured of consumption.[70] In 1912, a Canadian nun of Sherbrooke, Quebec, was healed of pulmonary tuberculosis following a novena to the founder of her order, Marie-Leonie Paradis, who had died only one week earlier.[71]

Unlike the miraculés in medieval hagiographies, illustrious clerics were only rarely found in this collection. An *archiprete* of Gavi, healed in 1822, was among the recipients of miracles bestowed by Giovanni Battista Rossi.[72] A century later, a bishop who had been serving in Africa suffered from amebic dysentery of such severity that it defied the ministrations of the Institut Pasteur; he was cured in 1925 after witnessing the translation of the relics of Bernadette Soubirous of Lourdes.[73] A mother superior led prayers for food in the nonmedical miracle attributed to Germaine Cousin; evidence came from other nuns, the carpenter, and an abject *tourrière*, assigned to a bakery, who responded to the usual question: "I am poor."[74]

Most clerical miraculés were ordinary members of their convents or novices, but their dramatic recoveries drew testimony from the whole community. Thus in 1779, the rapid cure, attributed to Angela Merici, of an Ursuline nun who had been paralyzed and mute brought testimony two years later from the prioress and the domestic servant, both of whom had seen the event.[75] Similarly, in 1859, a mother superior, several local women, and attending doctors testified to a cure from paralysis of a twenty-two-year-old nun in the previous year.[76] A transcendent experience in a low-ranking member of the convent hierarchy might eventually translate into special attention or a future promotion.

For example, in 1885, a French abbess described the miraculous cure of a knee injury that she had sustained as a novice nearly twenty years earlier.[77] Another such example is the story of an American novice, Mary, described below.

Many religious witnesses are present in the healings of laypeople too. Those who might otherwise be unaware of a cause were directed to candidates for sainthood by their spiritual advisors. It is rare to find any file in which a priest or a nun does not testify either to the extraordinary events or to the character of the main witness. Sometimes it is the priest who directed the invocation or administered the last rites.

Occasionally the influence of a cleric could be crucial to a cause. For example, in the seventeenth century, a priest advised nuns to pray to Juan de la Cruz for an ailing sister.[78] Similarly in 1860, a nun urged her dying religious sister to pray to André Fournet after the last rites had been administered.[79] And in 1910 another nun suggested that a young laywoman make a pilgrimage to Lourdes in honor of Jean-Baptiste Vianney to seek a cure for her tuberculosis.[80]

Similarly, and defying the usual geographic restrictions, Father Francis Xavier Weninger, a Jesuit priest who had been born in Austria in 1805, was particularly influential in the United States.[81] He served the cause for a Spaniard, Pedro Claver, who had died of natural causes in Colombia. Weninger brought word of the would-be saint to at least four American cities by giving "relics," including images and medals, to sick people: a sixteen-year-old girl with a paralyzed arm in Philadelphia in 1858;[82] an eighty-two-year-old woman with a painful cancer on her face in Milwaukee in 1861;[83] and a child with visual problems and a forty-three-year-old man with broken ribs and posttraumatic pleuropneumonia, both in St. Louis in 1863.[84] Weninger also claimed to have used the relics in New York City for an Irish woman with sore fingers.[85] Some witnesses admitted that they had never heard of Claver until Father Weninger came into their lives. His reputation in this cause is well known. The testimony on the cures, much of it in German, was applied to the canonization, which took place in 1888.

In the cause for the Canadian Marie-Marguerite d'Youville, the miraculée stipulated that suggestions for her 1978 appeal came from friends and family, especially an aunt who was a nursing nun in the Sisters of Charity order founded by the saint. She indicated that other saints and blesseds had been tried without success.[86]

The stories about clerical patients offer captivating glimpses of private moments in monastic life: replication of familial roles of care, admonishment, and encouragement; the cyclical life of prayer; the communal joy in a happy outcome. In 1909, a forty-eight-year-old nun of St. Louis, Missouri, who had been vomiting blood, felt herself so well following an appeal to Marie-Euphrasie

Pelletier that she went looking for something to eat; the incredulous sisters ordered her back to bed.[87]

In a bizarre accident in 1815, a monk was descending the staircase of his monastery when he stumbled, collided against the stone wall, and was pierced in the chest by his own crucifix. The wound developed weeping fistulae that refused to close until he appealed to Alfonso Maria of Liguori. First among the many witnesses of his healing was the seventy-year-old house physician who described his frustrated efforts to cure the monk with quinine, cupping, barley water, and setons.[88]

Memories could persist for many years in convent communities. For example, the dreadfully lame Sister Alexandra of Le Puy, France, had dragged around her paralyzed leg with a cord; her story was told in 1921 by a succession of elderly nuns who had been novices at the time of the cure fifty-three years earlier.[89] In 1986, nearly thirty years after her cure, Chilean Sister Ophelia described how she had resigned herself to death, until the mother superior ordered her to pray for recovery from bronchiectasis. She accepted religious and medical interventions, thinking "perhaps God has more work for me." When she made a sudden and complete recovery, she was astonished.[90]

This last case above sheds light on why religious people might pray for a cure within a philosophical framework that demands acceptance of God's will. The question often arose in my mind. But as many of these stories have revealed, seeking medical help is not incompatible with religious faith; some would contend that *not* to do so is a sin.[91]

Children

The healings of children form a poignant set of miracles. More than three hundred cures of children appeared in this collection. Child patients were of both sexes and ranged between 20 and 25 percent of the totals in each period of canonizations, except for the early nineteenth century (table 2.11). A gender discrepancy is more obvious in young people than it was in adults: healings in boys predominated until the twentieth century; and overall, miracles in boys appear more often than in girls (195 vs. 123).

The numerous appeals for children discredits contentions that parents of earlier centuries were more resigned than are we to the loss of offspring of either sex. Building on the observations of Ariès, Stone contended that deep emotional attachments were imprudent in early modern times, owing to the high mortality rate and belief in immortality of the soul; he argued that family relationships were marked more by economic interests than affection. This

TABLE 2.11. Children in the Miracles by Half Century of Canonization (includes infants)

From year to year	1588 1600	1600 1649	1650 1699	1700 1749	1750 1799	1800 1849	1850 1899	1900 1949	1950 1999	Total
Girl	6	8	16	22	4	0	13	23	30	122
Boy	12	28	30	38	5	3	18	26	34	194
Unknown	0	1	1	0	0	0	1	0	0	3
Total	18	37	47	60	9	3	32	49	64	319
All miracles	89	181	201	210	38	43	142	190	315	1,409
Percent miracles in children	20	20	23	29	24	7	23	26	20	26.6

view has been challenged by many scholars, including Finucane and Hanawalt, who pointed to the value of sources on miracles. [92]

For the twentieth century the percentage of child miraculés in my collection is higher than other studies have previously reported.[93] No evidence could be found that female saints were more frequently invoked to heal children (tables 2.12a and b). Nevertheless, some saints of both sexes seem to "specialize" in children, either because they had died young themselves or because they had spent their lives in mothering, teaching, or caring for orphans. Youthful saints may be invoked slightly more frequently for the young. In the fourteen miracles ascribed to eight saints who had died before age twenty-one, the miraculés had an average age of eighteen.

Children were the beneficiaries in four of the fifteen miracles ascribed to the Jesuit novice Luigi Gonzaga: three boys and one girl.[94] Among the miracles described for the 1954 canonization of Domenico Savio, a singer who died at age 15, was the 1927 recovery of a seven-year-old boy from typhus. So desperate was the lad's condition that his doctor had already completed the death certificate for the "little cadaver" (cadaverino). Testimony given in 1931 came from the boy's mother and the doctor.[95]

Saints who had been teachers were sometimes invoked for ailing children. Two of the four miracles in cause of Maria Domenica Mazzarello, founder of a girls' school, were healings of little girls. The first occurred in 1916 when four-year-old Ercolina, who shared one of the saint's many names, recovered from rickets and the sequelae of polio; her file contained before and after photographs.[96] The other, which took place in 1945, was the cure of seven-year-old Giancarla from a coma owing to kidney failure; she, too, had the "aspect of a cadaver" and had been given the last rites.[97] On New Year's Eve 1919, a hospital nurse urged invocation of the Italian teacher Lucia Filippini to heal a twelve-year-old girl of

TABLE 2.12a. Children Miraculés and Appeals to Saints by Gender (includes infants)

	Percent Female Saints	Percent Male Saints
Girl (N = 122)	35	65
Boy (N = 193)	22	78
Unknown (N = 6)	33	67
Total (N = 323)	27	73

Note: Overall miracles ascribed to female saints represent 30% of the total; those ascribed to male saints represent 70%.

TABLE 2.12b. Infant Miraculés and Appeals to Saints by Gender

	Percent Female Saints	Percent Male Saints
Infant girl (N = 13)	46	64
Infant boy (N = 23)	13	87
Unknown infant (N = 3)	33	67
Total (N = 39)	25.6	74.4

Note: Overall miracles ascribed to female saints represent 30% of the total; those ascribed to male saints represent 70%.

iatrogenic (postoperative) hypoparathyroidism. This child was all the more precious to her family because her brother had already died of diabetes, a disease then still lacking effective treatment.[98]

These examples might suggest a tendency for teachers or mothers to "specialize" in children, but the same saints also interceded for adults. For example, Mazzarello's cause also recognized cures in two grown women.[99] Similarly, a thirteenth-century Moravian mother, Zdislava of Lemberk, was credited with the 1989 cure of a forty-nine-year-old male physician from coma owing to cardiac arrest.[100]

At least thirty-seven of the miracles in children pertained to infants (table 2.13). Most were cited in canonizations or beatifications of the twentieth century; twenty occurred after 1900. Several baby boys are mentioned in earlier centuries, but only one infant girl appears in the records before the twentieth century: a newborn in the 1588 cause of Diego d'Alcalá.[101]

In other words, the illnesses of neonates and babies, especially females, scarcely appear in these records until it was common practice to invite physicians for their delivery and care. As will be shown in chapter 4, this observation probably has more to do with the Church's preference for "objective" testimony,

TABLE 2.13. Infant Miraculés by Half Century of Canonization

From year to year	1588 1599	1600 1649	1650 1699	1700 1749	1750 1799	1800 1849	1850 1899	1900 1949	1950 1999	Total
Female infant	1	0	0	0	0	0	0	1	8	10
Male infant	1	5	1	3	0	0	2	3	7	22
Unknown infant	0	2	1	0	0	0	0	0	2	5

such as that provided by the miraculés themselves and especially by doctors. It should not be construed as any lack of affection for tiny children in a more distant past. Even the terse Latin summaries of the child stories vividly proclaim the despair of frantic parents. As will be shown in chapter 5, they prayed beside their sick children, or carried them to shrines, with sobs and lamentation. When recovery was granted, they rejoiced. If, however, doctors were not involved, the report of a good outcome rarely came to the attention of the Vatican.

Sometimes the cure followed months of parental persistence over a child's chronic disabilities. In 1785, a printer who lived in Rome's Piazza Barberini ran all over the city seeking help for his four-year-old son whose painful, arthritic knee had repeatedly opened to ooze a sinister pus. The illness persisted for more than a year, keeping the child in bed or wrapped in his mother's arms. Finally the printer met a doctor at the Trevi Fountain who suggested that the family appeal to a saint. Not knowing which saint to choose, the father stopped passersby with his request. He viewed it as great good fortune that a Capuchin told him of the cause for Lorenzo of Brindisi. The parents immediately brought their son to the Capuchin chapel in Rome. Telling the story a decade later, the father declared that the lad was now perfectly healthy, attending school, and fully capable of walking from the Piazza Barberini to the Vatican; in winter he took the "vehiculo."[102] Parental persistence is apparent in other stories of disabled children as will be shown in chapter 5.

In 1915, a fifteen-year-old French girl had grown progressively blind in her left eye from age six. Interrogated about the onset of her illness in childhood, she described how the problem began with a sore throat; soon blood streamed from her eye and an increasingly thick veil descended over her vision. She matched stages in the deterioration to different ages in her life. With her mother, she began a novena at the tomb of the Blessed Marie-Madeleine Postel. Her sudden cure came during Mass at the elevation of the host. Mother and daughter were admonished for their noisy outburst of wonder. Her cleared vision was not perfect, but the "before and after" measurements showed progression from 10 percent to 70 percent of normal sight.[103]

A similar case formed part of the cause for beatification of Conrad of Parzham. At her precipitous birth in 1917, tiny Elisa had been dropped on her head. She spoke not a word until age two, and at three, she still did not walk. Her impoverished, seventy-year-old father was convinced that the deformity of her legs, in the shape of an X, was owing to the birth injury and the privations of war, further aggravated by his inability to afford medical attention. When he learned of another child's cure, he resolved to pray to the would-be saint; his three-year-old daughter began to walk instantly.[104] One of the two additional miracles for Conrad's canonization four years later concerned the 1928 cure of teenaged girl from pulmonary tuberculosis.[105]

Testimony on child healings usually came from parents or grandparents. But occasionally children were invited to describe distant memories. Echoing down the decades between us and them, their words convey foggy recollections from a barely verbal existence. Certainly, in the years between recovery and evidence, these dramatic tales would have been embellished and crystallized through repetition within families.

For example, in the case of the printer's son described above, the boy himself was the final witness. At age 15, he could scarcely remember his knee ailment of ten years earlier.[106] Eleven-year-old Francesco, the son of an Italian surgeon, was also a witness to his own healing of typhoid five years earlier in 1816. When asked for his occupation, he said, "I go to school and I go to Mass." As will be shown in chapter 4, the father was convinced that the recovery had been miraculous, but the boy himself was uncertain. "I don't remember anything," he said repeatedly. But he did recall pain and vomiting and being given various drinks. More clearly he remembered the moment of recovery: "I called mama to help me get out of bed."[107] In 1948, an inquiry heard from ten-year-old Giancarla, whose recovery three years earlier from uremic coma was described above.[108]

Sometimes the ailments of children reflected their liveliness and serve to remind us that they have always been prone to accidents (figure 2.4). Finucane's study of medieval canonizations found at least a quarter of the miracles pertaining to children involved accidents hauntingly similar to those of today.[109] In my own collection, around 1745, a little girl of about four years old dislocated her spine in an "imprudent game" that entailed being tossed in the air. For three long years, she was miserably paralyzed, with limb atrophy and complete numbness, even to "boiling water," until her parents appealed successfully to José de Calasanz.[110]

Similarly, in 1870, vivacious, twelve-year-old "Marietta" was playing "gymnastic games" with a rope and ladder at her home in Palermo when she fell from a height onto a broken chair that penetrated five centimeters into her

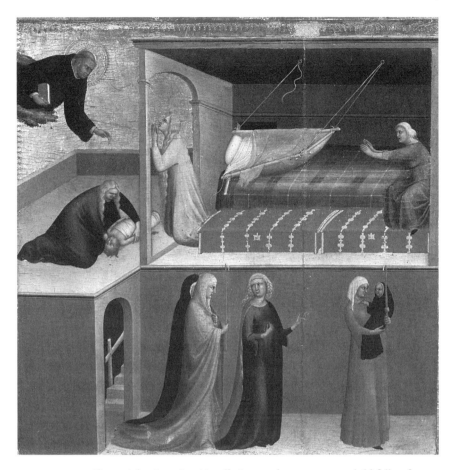

FIGURE 2.4. Above right, Agostino Novello intercedes to rescue a child fallen from its cradle; below, the family gives thanks. Agostino died in 1309 and was beatified in 1759. Altarpiece by Simone Martini, 1324, Pinacoteca Nazionale, Siena. By permission of the Ministero per i Beni e le Attività Culturali. Photo courtesy Soprintendenza PSAE di Siena & Grosseto.

back between the fifth and sixth ribs. She began coughing bright red blood. The horrified family summoned their physician, conveniently residing in the same building and aptly named, Conforto. He immediately applied leeches. But they also placed an image of Andrea of Burgio directly on the wound. She was cured within a day, as the whole family and the doctor testified nine years later. Conforto readily pronounced the recovery a miracle, although he had never heard of the venerable monk. A sister described her vivid memories, although she had been only five years old. And now a healthy, marriageable, young woman, Marietta spoke herself.[111]

FIGURE 2.5. Rita of Cascia intercedes to save a child from drowning in a well. She was canonized in 1900. Painted ex-voto, seventeenth century, Monastery of Santa Rita, Cascia. Carpentieri, *Per grazia ricevuta*, 1992.

Another accident from childhood play resulted in the briefest though not the least disturbing of illnesses in the collection. In 1921, young Juan was fooling around with a bottle of "oxygenated" water when it exploded, sending shards of glass into the right eye of his twenty-one-year-old sister, Maria del Pilar. The wound pierced the choroid and ciliary body of her eye and leaked vitreous humor. Following an appeal to Joaquina de Vedruna de Mas, Maria's eye was normal again in less than twenty-four hours. Testimony was gathered seven years later from Maria, her brother, their parents, and several physicians. This miracle became one of two considered for the 1940 beatification of Joaquina.[112] Suggesting that the saintly mother of nine may have been a minor "specialist" in pediatrics, both miracles considered for her 1959 canonization were cures of infant girls: one from pneumonia with tension pneumothorax in 1949; the other from diphtheria in 1950.[113]

Sometimes grown-up children were required to explain remote events made all the more distant by the original illness. In 1923, a Torino teenager, Octorini, had been racing his new bicycle "too quickly" down a hill when he crashed, hit his head, lost consciousness, and developed traumatic meningitis.

Medical efforts to save him were to no avail, but he recovered following an appeal to Maria Bertilla Boscardin. In the long process that led to her canonization in 1960, he was summoned to testify at least twice: first in 1929 and again in 1938, when he had become a thirty-year-old laborer as yet unmarried. One can only speculate on what effect this continued preoccupation with his adolescent folly had on his psyche and his faith.[114]

Often the child miraculés could provide little information; however, their healthy, youthful presence probably spoke much more loudly than words. And, whether or not their stories were shaped by elders, the testimony of child witnesses is a remarkable source worthy of more attention by historians.

Elderly

Miracles were not confined to the young. Healings of the elderly can be found for canonizations in every century from the sixteenth to the mid-twentieth century. Again, the stories illuminate the social situation of people rarely able to leave records. Sometimes the aged miraculés were abject paupers marked by vulnerability. The story of Lucia, a midwife, described below, represents one of these.

In contrast, elderly widows of wealthy merchants could be left to manage large households. For example, testimony on the 1759 cure of a seventy-year-old widow from the seemingly minor problem of an ear polyp offers a fascinating glimpse into the domestic setting: her four grown children, one a forty-year-old priest, still lived with their mother. She seemed to wield extraordinary power over them and her physician with whom she negotiated vigorously about treatment. A thirty-six-year-old servant also testified. Almost effortlessly, the widow solicited a cure from José de Calasanz by standing at her window, facing a convent, invoking his name, and crossing herself three times. The testimony was obtained in 1761, the year of canonization; but this healing was not described in the *Compendium*.[115]

Wealth may have been a selection factor in the miracles of the elderly because they can afford servants and doctors who linger as witnesses after they die. Without witnesses, there will be no investigation. Only one of the thirty-seven miraculés over the age of seventy (thirteen men and twenty-four women) described herself as poor and dependent on friends.[116] In his 1761 recovery from left arm paralysis, a seventy-two-year-old *speziale* from Ascoli was attended by at least seven physicians and a servant, all of whom gave evidence.[117] Similarly the 1848 cure of a Neapolitan widow, Fortunata, at age seventy-six, was described by herself, a daughter, a son, two attending doctors, and the servant who helped her pray to Maria Francesca of the Five Wounds of Christ.[118]

Absent Patients: The Missing and the Dead

Some miracle files describe healings in people who seem not to have testified, although nothing indicates that they had died. Possibly they had moved away and were deposed at another time and place in records filed elsewhere. Perhaps their testimony was deemed unnecessary.

For example, a poverty-stricken tailor, Carlo, was cured of paralysis in 1741. The testimony gathered four years later contains the evidence of three priests and a physician, but nothing from Carlo.[119] Was his report kept elsewhere? Had he died? Or, is it possible that evidence from an illiterate miraculé was deemed unnecessary?

In favor of the latter possibility is the fact that "absent patients" seem to be more numerous in a distant past. Perhaps the investigators of long ago had greater confidence in skeptical experts or pious clerics than in the potentially credulous laypeople whom they served. For example, sometime before 1740 in the cause of Peter Kanis, an entire family experienced food poisoning and three of four people died; however, a doctor was the only witness to the illness and recovery of the survivor, although several others testified to the fame of her cure.[120]

Another missing patient was the Corsican, Flora, who had been healed at age nine of tuberculosis with abdominal ascites. Testifying in 1919, some twenty years later, witnesses claimed that she was now a healthy, married woman living in Marseilles.[121] Occasionally, the absence of the miraculée was never explained.[122]

Sometimes, however, no testimony could be gathered from a miraculé because he or she was already dead. When I first encountered this situation, I was surprised: how could a *healing* be designated in a person who was dead? By the end of my research, I realized that it was a fairly regular occurrence. A miracle cure is no guarantee of immortality. Restoration of health is merely death postponed. The process of investigation is long; furthermore, the amassing of local information about a cluster of miracles may take place before the canonization process is officially launched; the process triggers a retrospective investigation.

At least sixty miracles from a total of more than fourteen hundred concerned people who had died before the investigation was complete. This practice is by no means passé. No less than thirty-two of the deceased miraculés were recent, having been involved in causes ending between 1984 and 1995.[123] The frequency of this situation suggests that when miraculés go missing, they may be presumed dead.

When the miraculé is known to have died, the witnesses have an additional problem: they are constrained to prove that she or he succumbed to a disease entirely different from the one that was cured. Abundantly clear in the twentieth-century cases, it is also evident in earlier files. For example, in December 1678, seventeen-year-old Isabella, wife of a doctor, lay dying of fever following a stillbirth. On Christmas day, her mother, brother, and husband appealed to Pope Pius V. Isabella recovered and eventually became the mother of five boys and a girl, but by 1704, when her miracle was investigated, she had been dead seven years and her husband was remarried. He and the other medical witnesses made it clear that her death at age thirty-six was from another kind of fever that had lasted three days.[124]

Far from conveying immortality, a miracle cure is tied to recovery from a specific illness. This variation makes the files of dead miraculés doubly laden with medical evidence: the first illness must be deemed incurable by human intervention, whereas the second, which was indeed fatal, must differ from the first.

In several cases of dead witnesses, an older person had been cured, only to die before the process began. For example, in 1789, a sixty-eight-year-old priest was suddenly cured of an incarcerated hernia, the result of an accident; his physicians insisted that he would die without surgery. He refused the operation and appealed to Giovanni Giuseppe (Calosinto). Eleven years later, in 1800, he died of "hydropsy" of the chest; testimony into both his illnesses—the hernia and the hydropsy—was gathered in 1802; medical evidence supported both diagnoses and emphasized their differences. It formed what must have been a convincing miracle, as it was described in four archival files and the *Compendium* of 1839.[125]

Another case in the same cause was remarkably similar. In 1791 an Italian priest was cured at age seventy-one of an acute stomach ailment so severe that he had been given the last rites. Four years later, he, too, succumbed to water on the chest (hydropsy).[126]

Similarly, in 1933, seventy-two-year-old Josephine was cured of a seven-year illness with a weak heart (cardiomyopathy). She had used the Miraculous Medal to invoke its designer, Catherine Labouré. Testimony came from Josephine's daughter, her sister, and a pharmacist nephew, together with the attending physicians. They described how she celebrated her sudden cure with champagne. After three more years of good health, she caught influenza while visiting her daughter, and died. The process took place a year later in 1937.[127]

The two cases described above were investigated only a year after the death of the miraculé. They suggest that the permanent departure of the key witness may have stimulated the postulants to gather records of special memories in anticipation of a time when all witnesses might be gone. This observation is further supported by the story of Lucia, a poor midwife (*levatrice*) of northern Italy, who maintained that she had recovered in 1902 at age seventy-four from an incarcerated hernia through the intercession of Giuseppe Cafasso. Sixteen years later, on January 3, 1918, she died at age eighty-nine. Soon after, a formal inquiry questioned her friend Luigia, another midwife, and collected certificates prepared several years earlier. The postulants were presented with a letter that Lucia had written back in 1906 apologizing for not having done her duty to speak sooner, a failing that left "a thorn in her heart." Her death drew official attention to her transcendent experience.[128]

Another investigation apparently triggered by the death of the miraculé invites a different theory. Perhaps the cured person had posed an obstacle to the recognition of a miracle. Salvatore, a Sicilian, was cured in 1937 at age fifty-one of Pott's disease of the spine; he lived to age eighty-five. His much younger wife and her brother were the key witnesses in testimony, delivered sixteen years after his death and fifty years after his cure. As evidence for Salvatore's good health, the family produced poignant 1953 photographs of him with his six-year-old daughter. But no letters or statements came from Salvatore himself. The cure was attributed to Sicilian Giuseppe Benedetto Dusmet, beatified in 1988.[129] By suggesting that Salvatore may have opposed scrutiny of his cure, I do not mean to imply that he refused to believe it was miraculous. But I wonder if the *publicizing* of these private events, including the evidence for his decrepitude and his good health, may have gone against his desires or his taste. His death left the family members free to do as they thought best.

The interval between a cure and its investigation could sometimes be so long that it suggests a retrospective search for miracles in order to shore up a process that was finally beginning to move ahead for other reasons, be they political, social, or biographical. An example of this possibility can be found in testimony given in 1920 about events of a half-century earlier, when a thirty-year-old Majorcan nun attributed her cure from pulmonary tuberculosis to the intercession of Caterina Thomas of Palma. She lived for another thirty-six years and died in 1906 of "chronic meningitis," which itself is now considered a possible manifestation of tuberculosis. The investigation into this miracle was conducted fourteen years after her death, fifty years after her cure. As in the case of Sister Alexandra, told above, convent memories could persist for a long time. The Majorcan witnesses were a handful of elderly nuns and the miraculée's eighty-five-year-old, poverty-stricken sister whose information about the 1870 illness came from recollected conversations with nurses. The only physicians still available were those who had presided over the nun's final illness.[130]

Many, but by no means all, of the dead witnesses were elderly. Examples of cures in young people who soon died further underscore the tight connection between a miracle and a specific illness. Parents of baby girl Pierina, born in 1894 with a dislocated hip, described the lengthy saga of specialist consultations, leg braces, and immobilization that had left the child miserable as well as lame. Her mother and sisters appealed to Giuseppe Cafasso, instructing little Pierina to utter the words, "Blessed Cafasso pray for me." Five years later, the family was devastated when this special child died at age seven from pulmonary edema (heart failure). Testimony of the miraculous healing of her hip was given in 1918, seventeen years after her death; it, too, may have been triggered by the aforementioned death of the midwife Lucia earlier that year.[131]

One of the most remarkable files that I encountered was that of a New Orleans novice, Mary, healed of pulmonary tuberculosis at age twenty, and dead of "congestive fever" at age twenty-one. Distinct from other such cases is an autobiography and several letters that Mary had composed in February 1867, sometime between her cure and her death. In articulate prose, she emerges as a witty, intelligent, young woman who joked with her physician and was resigned to her fate. The sister nuns had offered many prayers, and Mary doubted that there was "any saint left in heaven that they had not implored." Then she turned to Jan Berchmans. She laid his image over her mouth, and he came to her in a vision, placing a finger on her tongue. Quickly her health returned, but it held for only a few months. Having been healed once by divine grace, she refused medical therapy for the second illness until her superior ordered her to consent as an act of obedience. But the doctor's efforts were futile, and she succumbed to a fever that had "nothing to do with the original complaint." The personal testimony was amplified twenty years later with the fond memories of her convent sisters.[132]

Mary's story could be included in the Congregation files only because the investigators were convinced that the disease that killed her in 1867 differed from the disease that resolved in 1866. For these inquiries, a credible diagnosis was just as important as a credible witness. In fact, the disease itself serves a kind of witness, and that is the subject of the next chapter.

3

The Miracles

Diseases, Corpses, and Other Wonders

I first encountered the canonization process as a hematologist back in 1986, when I was asked to read a set of bone marrow slides. Only after I had completed the work to describe a case of aggressive leukemia was I told the amazing news that the patient was not only still alive, but her remission was being considered as a miracle. How could that be? Her diagnosis was relatively new and her chemotherapy treatment had been "state-of-the-art."

Until 150 years ago, leukemia did not exist as a diagnostic possibility. Symptoms that we now associate with the disease would have been labeled something else, possibly hemorrhage, fever, or weakness. If a patient suffered a little, prayed, and recovered, no one would have been startled because no one would have predicted a dire outcome. A miraculous cure of leukemia was possible only after the concept of leukemia, together with its dangerous prognosis, had become available. From the 1970s, remissions were possible with chemotherapy, but rarely would doctors construe them as cures.

In the months and years that followed, I was even more surprised by the up-to-date scientific detail demanded by the investigators in examining the case. The historian in me wondered if this reliance on medical science was recent or old.

As a result of this experience, it was curiosity about what might have constituted other miracles in the Vatican Archives that drove my initial research. At the outset, I had no idea what proportion of the miracles would prove to be healings from illness. If cures had been frequent, my main questions were, what diseases were involved, and how might they have changed through time? Within the first few days at the Vatican, I learned that healings were indeed the most frequent form of miracle in the canonization processes of the past four centuries, and that they are increasing. The diagnoses, however, keep changing.

Frequency of Healings as Miracles

Miracles of healing have always figured in Christian writings beginning with the life of Jesus as told in the Gospels. Some scholars write of Christianity as a religion of healing across two millennia.[1] Medieval miracles also include healings with cures ascribed to well-established holy figures, such as the Virgin Mary or St. Peter. Large studies based on thousands of medieval miracles confirm that healings predominate.[2] But cures were not always in the majority. For example, in twelfth-century manuscripts describing more than a hundred miracles worked by Notre Dame de Rocamadour, fifty (or about 40 percent) were cures of various illnesses; the majority encompassed other things, such as preservation from fire or drowning, the restoration of property, punishments for bad behavior, and cures of animals.[3] An analysis of early fourteenth-century miracles attributed to the Virgin featured only two healings out of a selection of thirteen; the rest concerned apparitions, money, language, and faith.[4] Similarly, in the cause for Giovanni da Capistrano, launched shortly after his death in 1456, early documents show that he was credited with numerous healings; however, equal, if not greater, significance was accorded other feats, such as liberation from captivity, expulsion of demons, and conversions.[5]

Commenting on the importance of cures in the miracle process, Vauchez detected a slight decline in healing miracles from 90 percent to 80 percent of the saintly repertoire between the fourteenth and fifteenth centuries.[6] A similar study of miracles in seventeenth- and eighteenth-century Naples found that cures represented 68 to 79 percent of the total.[7]

My study shows that physical healing was the single most important form of miracle at the time of the Tridentine reforms, and that it continued to rise into the present. The vast majority of the more than 1,400 miracles in my collection entailed recovery from physical or mental illness. They rose from a "low" of 87 percent of all miracles in the seventeenth century to 96 percent in the twentieth (table 3.1). The trend becomes even more obvious when the miracles are sorted by year of testimony.

FIGURE 3.1. Family appealing to Santa Rita to intercede for the recovery of a woman bedridden with illness. Painted ex-voto, 1931, Monastery of Santa Rita, Cascia. Carpentieri, *Per grazia ricevuta*, 1992.

This focus on medical miracles was fostered and shaped by the demands of the process and by the intellectual contributions of men like Zacchia and Lambertini.

Cures of Specific Diseases

The Role of Diagnosis

Many aspects of these stories are fairly constant through time, including the people, their doctors, and their gestures of appeal. Also the forms of illness and recovery altered little. But the names for the diseases that were healed—the

TABLE 3.1 Healing Miracles by Century of Canonization

	16th C.	17th C.	18th C.	19th C.	20th C.
Healings	82	334	237	173	486
All miracles	89	382	248	185	506
Percent of total	92	87	96	94	96

diagnoses—changed a great deal. In fact, the diseases are the most mutable aspect of these records.

On one hand, the diseases change to include new diagnostic possibilities for previously unrecognized conditions. For example, I found two cases of multiple sclerosis from the mid-twentieth century,[8] one of myasthenia gravis from the mid-1970s,[9] and six cases of either leukemia or lymphoma (from 1961 forward).[10] But other diseases that we tend to think of as old, even ancient, such as pneumonia and tuberculosis, were rarely named as such in the seventeenth-century records. They, too, rose in later investigations with shifts in diagnostic preoccupations. In a distant past, people suffering from what we might *now* label as these problems were likely said to have "fever" or "wasting."

On the other hand, certain diseases vanished from the files, sometimes because they occur less frequently now, and sometimes because they had actually disappeared for epidemiological, medical, or conceptual reasons. The vanished ailments include smallpox, which was eradicated in the late 1970s; epidemiologically it no longer exists. Diseases also declined in these records after they became treatable with new medicines: diabetes and general fevers both waned in the collection after the advent of insulin and antibiotics. If a disease disappears for conceptual reasons, it is because the same symptoms shift from being formulated as one diagnosis to another. For example, prior to the early nineteenth century, the widespread condition that we call "tuberculosis" was many different diseases, with different names, depending on the symptoms and specific location in the body.

Some diseases persist through time, having been the object of healings in all four centuries examined. Cancer, fractures, arthritis, blindness, and what I will call "neurological" illnesses were steadily prevalent in all time periods. But the investigators insisted on ever more stringent proof of diagnosis with, for example, tissue pathology in cancer, X-rays in orthopedics, bacterial culture in fevers, and imaging scans or nerve-conduction studies in neurology. Demands for those proofs created some of the most interesting challenges for the doctor witnesses, as will be shown in the next chapter.

In consequence of these historical considerations, changes occurred in the diagnoses considered "amenable" to miracle cure. The changes correspond to alterations in prevalence, shifts in disease classification (called *nosology*), and the waxing or waning of general confidence in the likelihood of cure either by nature or by human skill. In other words, certain diagnoses "arise" as worthy of divine cure, depending on time and place.

Because the diagnosis was often printed in the *Compendium* summaries, abundant information on this aspect of the process is available, even when archival documents are lacking. In general, using all 1,306 medical miracles for which

I have a "diagnosis," cures before 1800 were of visible conditions detectable by anyone—patients, lay caregivers, and medics alike: skin disease, fevers, blindness, convulsions, paralysis, and lameness. Similar problems had been the basis of miracle cures in medieval times.[11] In the early modern period, the diagnoses in my collection reflect the symptom-laden classification systems of the nosologists who dominated medical wisdom at that time. They are accompanied by thick description of symptoms, but they also contain newly appreciated diagnostic labels. In the nineteenth century, the diagnoses amenable to miracle cure concentrated on specific internal organs and newly conceived fevers, such as tuberculosis, diphtheria, gastritis, and typhoid. These broad changes reflect the new preoccupations of medical scientists and perceived advances in both diagnostics and in therapeutics, as will be explained in the specific examples below.

Some patients suffered from more than one condition. In the ensuing analysis, their diagnoses are sorted independently. As a result, information from a single miracle may appear in two or more places below.

Tuberculosis

Tuberculosis is probably the most frequently appearing disease in these records. Caution must be exercised in identifying it retrospectively. The word was not coined until the 1830s when some seventeen different, symptom-based diseases were collapsed into a single entity.[12] Daily fevers, bloody cough, shortness of breath, wasting, consumption, and phthisis are among the conditions that represent "apparent tuberculosis" gathered in table 3.2. These figures probably underestimate the prevalence of the disease in the miracle files because most are lung ailments, whereas the frequent involvement of bone, kidney, and brain by tuberculosis was not appreciated until the nineteenth century.

Conditions that represent tuberculosis increase steadily in the miracle files into the twentieth century. The most striking rise, early in the nineteenth century, relates to its naming and unification. At that time, many experts insisted on its terminal character almost as a sine qua non.[13] In other words, tuberculosis had the gloomy prognosis that we now associate with cancer. Although its cure was thought to be impossible, its diagnosis became more precise and accessible owing to new technologies, such as the stethoscope. These two factors—the unification and the new technologies—help to explain the relatively recent rise of this old disease. Later, however, the advent of surgical and medical treatments for tuberculosis, coupled with the realization that it could sometimes heal spontaneously, coincided with a disappearance of the diagnosis from the miracle files in the latter half of the twentieth century. Of the datable cures of tuberculosis, only a few occur after 1950: one had been contracted in France in

TABLE 3.2   Some Diseases Cured by Century of Canonization

	16th C.	17th C.	18th C.	19th C.	20th C.
Apparent TB	0	8	8	16	79
Fever[a]	9	43	33	11	25
Malaria	1	5	3	2	0
Scurvy	0	0	1	4	1
Resurrection	6	10	4	1	0
Heart disease	1	2	4	3	22
Unconscious[b]	1	2	1	0	13
Lung	0	2	1	2	13
Kidney/urine	1	6	5	6	21
Liver	0	0	0	1	14
Gut	1	11	9	16	78
Cancer[c]	0	7	11	19	41
Orthopedic[d]	9	39	27	39	59
Mental illness	1	7	1	1	3
All miracles	89	382	248	185	506

[a]Excludes tuberculosis, malaria, and postpartum fever.
[b]Includes coma.
[c]See also table 3.4.
[d]See also table 3.5.

1950 and cured in 1955[14] (table 3.3). Two other cases suggestive of tuberculosis were cured in 1959 and 1960 respectively; however, in both those cases, tuberculosis was incidental to something else that was the main problem and it had been contracted much earlier in 1937 and 1942, respectively.[15] Many people have died from tuberculosis in the past fifty years. Conceptually speaking, however, control of that disease now seems to fall within the grasp of human art. It no longer "arises" as a problem yielding only to a divine solution. Hence, tuberculosis rose and fell in the miracle trials.

Smallpox, Malaria, Fevers, and Epidemic Disease

The same might be said of fevers—and not only those that are now susceptible to antibiotics. They rise and fall throughout the record, depending on incidence

TABLE 3.3   Tuberculosis Miracles by Decade of Cure, 1890s to 1970s

	1890	1900	1910	1920	1930	1940	1950	1960	1970s
No. of cures	9	5	3	20	11	12	5	1	0

and on medical knowledge. Smallpox provides a good example. It appeared ten times for canonizations from the sixteenth century to the twentieth; however, all but one of the illnesses had occurred before Lady Mary Wortley Montagu's promotion of variolization in the early eighteenth century, and long before 1796 when Edward Jenner described vaccination. The single exception and most recent healing of smallpox was of a fifteen-year-old girl: in 1897, she developed a fever originally thought to be measles until the characteristic rash announced the diagnosis and threatened her eyesight. Her doctors were horrified to discover that they had been dealing with smallpox, because she had been properly vaccinated.[16]

Another striking example of fading disease is provided by the periodic fevers, or what is now called malaria. Characterized by dramatic rise in temperature at regular intervals with teeth-chattering chills followed by drenching sweats, the condition was called "tertian" or "quartan" fever depending on the number of days between attacks. Endemic in Italy until the mid-twentieth century, the general populace was well acquainted with the diagnosis and its danger.[17]

Eleven examples of the miraculous cure of periodic fever were found in these files. Clusters of "a few tertians" and "a few quartans" were also mentioned in the sixteenth-century process of Diego d'Alcalá. Five were for canonizations in the seventeenth century, three in the early eighteenth century, and two for the 1897 canonization of Pierre Fourier, whose miracles were investigated in 1682. In fact, the most recent testimony on a malaria cure was gathered in 1704 on the 1678 illness of seventeen-year-old Isabella, wife of a doctor, described in the previous chapter and below.

The abrupt disappearance of this common and debilitating disease from the canonization record corresponds well to the advent of specific treatment. True, malaria was controlled by water management plans in later centuries, but it was the discovery of effective medication that best explains its disappearance from these records. Cinchona, or Jesuit bark, was brought to Europe from Peru by missionaries in the mid-seventeenth century. It contains the substance quinine, which would be isolated from the organic material in the early nineteenth century. Supplies are said to have been scarce during the seventeenth century. Much later, in 1834, a doctor described his difficulty in obtaining the medicine when he originally thought (mistakenly) that his patient had malaria.[18] From this study it is clear that by the turn of the eighteenth century, the very existence of an effective remedy had penetrated the minds of doctors, patients, and clerics. Indeed, in the most recent of the malaria cures, Isabella's doctor-husband claimed to have given her cinchona without success.[19] The convoluted interweaving of historical events with the miraculous is especially intriguing with this disease: the Jesuits who noticed the bark and brought it to Europe were companions of those sainted for their dangerous missions. After 1705 and having a specific remedy, malaria persisted in Europe, but it no longer "arose" as a condition amenable to a miraculous cure.

Other fevers of various types appear regularly in the files and constitute a significant proportion of the miracles (table 3.2). In the early period, in at least sixteen cases, the word *fever* was used alone, with no specific adjectives to describe it. Most of these diagnoses were from the seventeenth century; two appeared in testimony from 1719 and 1726. Before and after that period, fever usually took another descriptor, with adjectives such as *acute* (5), *ardent* (3), *continuous* (9), *hectic* (5), *malignant* (13), *pernicious* (3), *pestilential* (6), and *putrid* (1). These adjectives reflect the up-to-date nosological priorities of the era in which the diagnoses were made. Beyond description, they connected the patient's illness to well-circumscribed symptom patterns that were diagnostic entities in the prevailing medical canon.

To illustrate this point, six cases refer to the miraculous cure of "pestilential fever," a name for what we might call "plague," although contemporary physicians purported to distinguish between them.[20] Plague itself was named in three other miracles: in one the arrival of the corpse of Francis Xavier coincided with an alteration in wind direction, which stopped the spread of plague; and two cures date from 1656 and 1738. In 1656, Naples and Rome experienced a devastating epidemic that claimed tens of thousands of lives.[21] The miracle cure of 1656 came from a little town, near Naples, where fifty-six people had already died: an unhappy mother was among the throng at the shrine of Caterina de'Ricci, holding the "dead" body of her seven-year-old daughter; the child was revived.[22]

As soon as new names were attached to patterns of febrile illnesses, they rapidly appear in the canonization files. Typhoid fever provides a good example. It was given a vivid clinical description in the mid-seventeenth century, but it was indistinguishable from typhus until 1837. Following this distinction typhoid became the target of public health reformers and was much discussed by laypeople.[23] In this collection, typhoid fever appears in eight cures: five Italian, two French, and one Argentinean. They occurred between 1816 and 1933 in seven different causes ending from 1867 to 1994. Thus, typhoid "arose" as an object of miracle cure during the nineteenth and early twentieth centuries. Appendicitis provides a similar example and will be discussed below.

Perhaps strangely, I found no miraculous cures of cholera, although it was responsible for several devastating pandemics beginning in 1832. The idea that would-be saints were never invoked for this dire condition is untenable. More likely, the rapid progression of cholera from onset to death or cure, in just a matter of hours, left little opportunity for intervention, be it medical or spiritual. Equally, if not more significant, would be the absence of opportunities for gathering evidence of medical failure or of divine healing. In addition to the short duration, chaos during epidemics of cholera, smallpox, or plague surely diminished the all-important documentation of individual illnesses and appeals during the period in which canonizations were relatively rare. Furthermore, their virulence may have carried off eyewitnesses. The absence is striking and invites more investigation.

Fever declined in the twentieth century; its later appearances were usually as a complicating symptom rather than as a diagnosis. Its decline is related both to the changing priorities for anatomical, rather than symptom-based, diagnoses and later to the advent of antibiotics. From a scientific perspective, fever no longer constituted an adequate diagnosis, whereas its cure could be attributed to human intervention. As a result, fever no longer "arose."

Venereal Disease

Somewhat surprisingly, venereal disease made eight appearances in these files: all but one involved females, four of whom were nuns; one was a child. The seven healings took place from 1682 to 1955. For the only male, it was simply mentioned as part of his past medical history. Gentilcore describes another cure of a man from 1747.[24] The records that I have found resort to euphemism to avoid naming the disease. Nevertheless, they establish its identity and absolve the women sufferers of moral wrongdoing by emphasizing its hereditary nature: "contracted in the womb," from the "incontinence" and "indiscretion" of fathers.

Since its recognition in the early sixteenth century, syphilis was known to take many forms. The symptoms that afflicted these women included arthritis, paralysis, convulsions, sore mouth, and skin ulcers. Some appear to have always understood their diagnosis. A nun whose parents had both died within a year of her birth told how she had been raised by her "nonna" and had always been "subject to a certain wicked disease."[25] For a syphilitic orphan, entering a convent as a novice would have provided a safe destiny. Perhaps, religious houses and their attending physicians were alerted to children with hereditary syphilis on a regular basis. By the twentieth century, novices were routinely examined for any illness.[26]

From at least one nun, doctors withheld the diagnosis of syphilis, calling it "an infection." The deception surely created a few awkward moments: at first, during her treatment with salvarsan, the arsenic derivative introduced specifically for syphilis in 1910; and then again later during their testimony in 1928.[27] The most recent cure of what might have been syphilis occurred in 1955, well after the advent of penicillin: an Egyptian housewife had been diagnosed at least twenty years previously and treated to no avail with many drugs, including salvarsan; by the time penicillin became available, her disease was considered inveterate and incurable.[28]

Only one person in this collection was miraculously cured of gonorrhea: a married woman from Madagascar whose arthritic knee improved in 1933. Medical experts emphasized that the recovery was all the more remarkable because it had taken place prior to the advent of penicillin.[29] The only man in this group admitted to having had gonorrhea in his past, but his miracle was the cure in 1848 of another ailment, said to have been unrelated, although we might disagree: a hard swollen testis diagnosed as cancer.[30]

Two of the five saints invoked to heal the women with venereal disease were men. The relative absence of male patients is intriguing. Given the widespread prevalence of the conditions and their vicious symptoms, there can be little doubt that men prayed for release from such misery. Perhaps some could even attribute cures to intercession. If they existed, these cases were not brought to the attention of the church, possibly because of the presumed moral culpability of the male sufferer.

Scurvy

Scurvy posed a serious problem for medical practitioners during the eighteenth century. The concept of vitamins was unknown, even as navy surgeon James Lind conducted experiments. He proved that the dreaded ailment was a nutritional deficiency that could be cured and prevented by citrus fruits and juices. The research culminated in his treatise of 1753, but it was little known until the end of the century. In my collection of miracles, only six people were miraculously cured of scurvy, or "scorbutic" conditions. Most suffered from bleeding and sores of the mouth, gums, or skin—symptoms that could readily be confused with secondary syphilis. Indeed, a nun, described above, was diagnosed with both diseases and her diet was an object of therapy.[31]

Five of the six people with scurvy were cured in the eighteenth century: three certainly prior to Lind's treatise; three probably after, the most recent in 1808, although the miracle was applied to a later canonization (table 3.2). Physiology was specifically addressed in the analysis of at least two scurvy cures, with use of the concepts of "animal economy" and "*la machina*" and numerous citations from contemporary literature.[32] Although these numbers are small, they suggest that the narrow chronological window for the presence of scurvy in these records is tied to medical history: it "arose" when it was a pressing problem for investigation and diagnosis; it faded with general awareness of the newly found specific therapy.

Resurrection

Resurrection from death appeared twenty-one times in the early files and then disappears (table 3.2; figure 3.2). Six such reports formed part of the cause of Diego d'Alcalá.[33] Miracles of resurrection were cited in four canonizations in the eighteenth century and one from the nineteenth, all based on testimony gathered no later than the seventeenth century. Adult men were raised from dead in two clusters cited in the process for Diego d'Alcalá. All others involved children, three of whom were newborns: four girls and fourteen boys (one miracle entailed two brothers).

When details are available, these stories emphasize the great distress of the parents and stand as further evidence in the debate over of how early modern people loved their children and were not resigned to their loss, as mentioned in chapter 2. In one case, the boy was the son of a widow and all the more precious for being her only child.[34] In the two most recent cases from 1678 and 1682, physicians had certified the deaths. The latter case was the revival of two brothers crushed by a cart from the cause of Pierre Fourier, much studied during the time of Lambertini.[35]

One reason for the disappearance of resurrection from the miracle repertoire may have been increasingly stringent methods for detecting death. Zacchia claimed that death could not be determined with certainty until the cadaver began to decay.[36] This hypothesis implies that the children raised in the seventeenth century had not been *really* dead by later standards. However, it is all too easy to cast such facile aspersions upon our predecessors. We are challenged by the example of a resurrection corroborated by a convinced physician.

A thirty-five-year old doctor was attending a festival on August 5, 1678, when he happened on a group of sobbing women gathered around a distraught mother who held the lifeless body of her three-year-old son. She begged the doctor to do something. He later testified that the child was "without pulse, without warmth, without sensation or movement, nor any sign of vital operations." A "large contusion" covered his forehead, said the physician, and he perceived an apparent dislocation of the neck. "I judged him to be dead." The next day he went to the church expecting a funeral and instead found a multitude, in the midst of which stood the same little boy whom he had pronounced dead, solemnly holding a candle before the image of Andrea Avellino; all the women were rejoicing.[37]

As this example suggests, even if the children were not *really* dead, they surely were moribund with what now might be labeled as unconsciousness

FIGURE 3.2. Margherita of Cortona restoring the life of an injured boy. She was canonized in 1728. Watercolor by Adriano Zabarelli based on a fresco by the Lorenzetti brothers no longer extant. Manuscript 429, figure vi, circa 1639, Biblioteca del Comune e dell'Accademia Etrusca, Cortona.

or coma. But both these concepts belong to a more recent period: the word *coma* appears in fifteen miracles, all but one occurring after 1895. Another explanation for the disappearance of resurrection from the canonization records may be increased skepticism in the Church, possibly spilling over from Protestantism, that there could be any resurrections other than those of the New Testament.[38] If lay witnesses thought that a "raising" had occurred, they might have been discouraged from bringing it forward.

Yet the absence of resurrection may be more apparent than real. The phenomenon may still appear in different ways, and invites reconsideration of what may have been meant by resuscitation in the earlier centuries. For example, the recent advent of coma suggests that some "deaths" of the past might have been labeled deep unconsciousness in our time. Similarly, heart disease had been rare in the earlier miracles. In this collection, as will be shown below, heart disease rose in miracle cures of the twentieth century. Four of these cases included cardiac arrest; one was the result of an accidental electrocution. When heart miracles are compared to resurrection from death, the one type of cure seems to have replaced the other.

Anatomical or Organic Diseases

By the early nineteenth century, medicine was increasingly enamored of diagnoses that were equated with changes in specific organs of the body. This new way of identifying disease began to eclipse the disease categories that were anchored in symptoms. Beginning in the eighteenth century, the trend flourished with the rise of new modalities in the physical examination, such as percussion (1761), auscultation (1819), biopsies (after 1850), and eventually X-rays (1895) and other imaging techniques. These methods made it possible to detect alterations in the organs of the body before the patient had died.

This shift is evident in the miracles (table 3.2). For example, as noted above, heart disease—so frequent in our own time—is strikingly rare in the earliest records. Three such miracles occur in testimony prior 1617. Two miraculés were cured of "pain in the heart"; and another of "palpitations"; however, the first condition may have been a metaphorical expression for melancholy.[39] The next case of heart disease, called "cardialgia," came from 1731; the promotor fidei engaged in a discussion of whether or not it could be a real and possibly fatal disease, citing ancient and modern literature.[40] The remaining nineteen cases came after 1758. The anatomical pathology of the heart was a subject of great interest during the eighteenth century, when authors challenged the ancient notion ascribed to Hippocrates that the heart itself could not be sick.[41]

As a result, these miracles show once again that the clerics were considering up-to-date medicine.

The newness of heart disease is evident in testimony delivered in 1822 on a cure of a serving woman living "decently" in the care of her employer, an eighty-two-year-old Roman widow. Without using a stethoscope, which had only just been invented, the doctors decided that she had been suffering from pericarditis and a ventricular aneurysm. To back up their unusual claims, they cited prestigious authorities, such as Benivieni, Morgagni, Sauvages, and Cowper. They even mentioned the hotly debated new theory of "ossified" (hardened) coronary arteries.[42]

The transitional moment between older styles of the eighteenth century and modern methods is apparent in the case of a nun examined in 1825 for the cure of swelling, or dropsy. Her doctors had prescribed the relatively new drug of digitalis (foxglove leaf) as a diuretic, and they had examined her swollen belly by palpation looking for enlarged organs and by percussion (tapping) looking for "undulation." In analyzing their findings, they indulged in a physiological discussion of balance, suggesting that suppression of her menses might have caused her to cough blood. They cited an eclectic mix of scientific authors, typical of the period, including Hippocrates of the fifth century B.C., Giorgio Baglivi of the seventeenth century, and the early-nineteenth-century English chemist William Hyde Wollaston.[43]

Diseases of the chest exemplify the anatomical trend in diagnosis and treatment. Pleurisy is characterized by sharp pain on deep inspiration and was known since antiquity.[44] Seven people were cured of it in various causes, but the most recent of these cases was an illness from 1780.[45] In other words, though still well recognized, pleurisy became a symptom rather than a disease in its own right amenable to miracle cure. Similarly, pneumonia is a very old disease, also well known to the ancients.[46] However, the appearance of pneumonia as a diagnosis in these records seems to have awaited the advent of the anatomical methods of examination and the stethoscope. Twelve such cases were found. One relied on testimony given in 1682, in the much studied process of Pierre Fourier.[47] The rest pertain to cures that took place in 1817 or after. Having made a late appearance, it disappeared early. Only one pneumonia case can be said to have been cured miraculously following the advent of antibiotics: it was a secondary diagnosis in the setting of a more severe cardiac problem that was also cured.[48] Therefore, pneumonia waxed and waned according to its detectability and its treatability.

Seven miracles involving other lung conditions—bronchiectasis, emphysema, aspiration, cyst, and abscess—appear in the records. All postdate the stethoscope. These observations do not imply that lung disease was infrequent in earlier times. On the contrary, they add further evidence to the observations made above about the ways in which both practicing physicians and clerics ordered medical knowledge. For example, the many cases called "fever" in the earlier centuries may have corresponded to illnesses labeled pneumonia had they presented in a later period. Doctors might have considered the diagnosis, but such deliberations were neither transmitted nor credited. Until the eighteenth century, anatomical localization was unimportant for diagnosis.

The kidney is mentioned in miracles as early as 1600. Until the twentieth century, however, all instances were of urinary retention, stones, or both. Conversely, renal stones occur only once after 1674, as an incidental finding in a more severe biochemical diathesis.[49] Indeed, urinary stones are thought to have been more prevalent in a distant past, owing to the greater frequency of prolonged, untreated infections. But their disappearance may also reflect an increased comfort with, or availability of, surgical treatments for stone, the history of which extends into antiquity. Bright's disease of the kidney was detected in a woman suffering from postpartum fever in 1864.[50] Nephrotic syndrome appeared in a Czech monk cured of many illnesses in 1955.[51] Two cases of renal failure were cured in 1933 and 1982.[52] One other renal problem—floating kidney—was a new disease when it was mentioned in 1913; yet a moving kidney now is of little pathological significance.[53]

Liver disease appeared in fourteen cases; seven were hepatitis. Like pneumonia, hepatitis was known since antiquity. But again like pneumonia, the organic location of a febrile illness, be it in liver or lung, was rare in these records prior to the nineteenth century.[54] One of this group was cured in the 1740s, another in 1839; the remainder occurred in the twentieth century. Three other liver conditions were the result of metastases from cancers originating elsewhere. Another three were cirrhosis, complicated by portal hypertension; they occurred in a German woman, cured in 1957, and in two Italian men: one, called Liborio, cured in 1957, and the other, a policeman, cured in 1961. Neither the German woman nor the policeman drank alcohol, but Liborio had been a heavy drinker all his life. A tissue diagnosis with liver biopsy was available only for the woman. For Liborio, experts were vexed by the absence of a tissue biospy and refused to pronounce upon an "anatomical" cure. Nevertheless, they were impressed by the clinical evidence: Liborio's massive ascites (abdominal fluid) had been drained four times, removing more than eleven liters from his belly. His condition resolved to such an extent that he returned to his grueling work, demanding an expenditure of 6,000 calories a day; he lived ten more years, only to die of a seizure disorder.[55]

Liver disease was also cured in 1928 in a Sardinian woman with an echino-coccal cyst (a parasite from dogs), and in 1987 in an American child suffering from an accidental overdose of acetaminophen.[56]

Gastrointestinal diseases were always abundant and represented nearly 9 percent of all miracles. The early cases were symptomatic, described as vom-iting, diarrhea, or abdominal pain. In the seventeenth century, ten miracles involved the cure of hernia; three of apparent rectal prolapse (intestinorum descensu); and eight of dysentery, of which six were hemorrhagic (bloody flux). Hernia then disappears from the files. Its eighteenth-century departure seems to predate the advent of effective surgical treatments; however, it implies that some human management, perhaps in the form of trusses and manual reduc-tion, had become available. Hernia reappears in the twentieth century when four people were cured not from hernia per se, but from its near fatal complica-tion—strangulation, necrosis, and gangrene—emergencies deemed beyond the power of medicine or surgery to control.

Anatomical diagnosis of the gastrointestinal tract did not appear until the nineteenth century, as it did for other body systems. Historians have shown that the stomach and intestines were a special focus of medical preoccupa-tion in the eighteenth and nineteenth centuries. Doctors doing autopsies to investigate deaths from various fevers noticed a bright red color to the inner lining of the gut and concluded that it was the "seat" of inflammation.[57] In these files, gastritis makes its first appearance in the 1833 testimony on the cure of an eighteen-year-old Majorcan girl three years earlier.[58] At that time, it was a fashionably new diagnosis.

Peritonitis is another abdominal condition that did not receive its first description until the early nineteenth century.[59] It appears twenty times in these records, all but one (from 1891) occurred in the twentieth century. Nine were identified as tuberculous peritonitis; one was in the setting of postpartum fever; the remainder were the result of various abdominal problems, including rup-tured or twisted bowel, appendicitis, and pancreatitis.

Appendicitis is related to peritonitis and was also well described by the early nineteenth century. It is said to have captured the public imagination in 1901, when surgeon Frederick Treves operated on the new King Edward VII, delaying the coronation and saving his life.[60] The five instances of appendicitis found in these miracles show that it is a disease of the twentieth century; they date from 1930 to 1953. Gall bladder disease with biliary obstruction appeared thrice, from 1920 to 1937. Intrasusception, a dire intestinal problem, occurred once: the 1946 cure of an infant girl.[61] Most of these anatomically defined con-ditions of the stomach and intestine now fall into the category of surgical dis-eases, to be discussed below.

TABLE 3.4. Miraculous Cancer Cures by Century of Canonization

	16th C.	17th C.	18th C.	19th C.	20th C.
Breast	0	1	5	5	6
Skin	0	4	3	8	1
Stomach	0	0	0	2	3
Intestinal	0	0	0	1	11
Bone	0	0	0	0	3
Uterus/testis	0	0	0	2	4
Melanoma	0	0	0	0	2
Lung	0	0	0	0	1
Lymphoma/ leukemia	0	0	0	0	6
All cancers	0	7	11	19	41
All miracles	89	382	248	185	506

Cancer

Miracle cures of cancer and tumors are present in all eras and comprise a significant proportion of the whole. The words used to describe them change through time: *scirrho, malignant ulcer, tumor, carcinoma,* and *cancer.* When these diagnostic labels are combined, it is clear that cancer steadily increases through time. Several reasons can explain why. First, cancer is usually a disease of the elderly; an increase in life expectancy can be correlated with an absolute increase in the incidence of the disease. Second, until the advent of antibiotics in the twentieth century, infectious conditions, such as tuberculosis, posed equally desperate outcomes. Third, prior to the new modalities of physical examination, some cancers would have been attributed to tuberculosis and its predecessors because of the similarity of symptoms: pallor, wasting, and bleeding. Finally, the rising trend to anatomical diagnosis, provided by surgical biopsies, meant that the detection of internal changes was more frequent from the second half of the nineteenth century. Until then, cancer was readily detected on the skin, limbs, or breasts, but not in the internal organs (table 3.4).

Orthopedic and Neurological Disease

Problems of bones and joints were frequent at all times and constituted at least 10 percent or more of the miracles in every century studied. They took the form of lameness or other disability brought on by injury, illness, or birth defects (table 3.5). Those of the early period were numerous but cannot be "diagnosed"

TABLE 3.5. Orthopedic Miracles by Century of Canonization

	16th C.	17th C.	18th C.	19th C.	20th C.
Club foot	0	4	0	2	3
Arthritis	0	2	4	7	12
Fracture	2	9	6	9	11
Dislocation	0	1	3	5	4
Lame	5	13	5	7	6
Tubercular	0	0	0	3	19
Deformities	2	9	1	6	3
Total	9	39	27	39	59
All miracles	89	382	248	185	506
Percent of total					
Miracles	10	10	11	21	12

retrospectively into the categories familiar to us. Vauchez dealt with the problem by referring to them all as "contracti" of "various sorts," and he demonstrated that they constituted the vast majority of miracle cures in the later Middle Ages.[62] In their decline, he cited the rising presence of doctors with more precise diagnostic practices and shifts in the gestures of appeal.

The apparent spike in orthopedic problems for nineteenth-century canonizations is owing entirely to fourteen such cures in the 1682 testimony used for the canonization of Pierre Fourier two hundred years later. In other words, they stem from an earlier time. Fractures and dislocations will be discussed below with surgical diseases.

Cures of the unspecified "contracted," "withered," and "deformed" limbs of unknown cause that were common in medieval times appeared in twenty-one people, most during the seventeenth century; one in 1744. More specific forms of bony or joint disease appeared in tight chronological spaces. Gout or "podagra" was seen in five miracles; all based on testimony gathered between 1604 and 1682. The subsequent silence invites speculation on the role of Thomas Sydenham's magisterial description of 1683. It also suggests that he wrote at a time when gout was a major preoccupation. Pott's disease of the spine, a specific tubercular condition of the vertebrae, described in 1779, appeared in ten cures dating from 1908 to 1941.

In some situations, it was difficult to classify the ailments into either neurological or orthopedic designations because both seemed relevant. Applying these categories facilitates our comprehension, but it is anachronistic. For example, the use of the word *paralysis* in the seventeenth century could refer to a person rigid with severe arthritis, or to someone struck down with apoplexy, or to what we might call stroke. All too frequently the information available was insufficient to make a distinction; in any case, such a distinction was not important at that time. Indeed, on some occasions, such as head injuries, both designations might still apply.

So-Called Neurological Conditions

Making the blind to see, the deaf to hear, and the lame to walk was the stock in trade of biblical miracles. The Vatican records show that people with these problems had recourse to their saints on a regular basis; sometimes their appeals were met with a cure. The description of a cluster of miracles in the *Compendium* for Jean-François Regis shows the influence of the Gospels: in his cause, paralytics were made to move, the blind to see, the sick to heal, the dying to revive, the lame to walk, and inveterate sinners to repent.[63]

When early modern people complained of a problem with vision or hearing, it could result from cataract, infection, or earwax, things now considered likely to recover naturally or with surgery and drugs. For these people, however, the end result was the same as the intractable, neurological causes of our time: blindness or deafness, bringing isolation and poverty as a result. Consequently, we must designate neurological conditions as "apparent" (table 3.6).

Paralysis and epilepsy declined proportionately but did not disappear. The two most recent instances of paralysis in these records are cures from 1972 and 1977. In both cases, investigators established the diagnosis through standard neurological procedures.[64] The three most recent examples of epilepsy cures were in children in 1945, 1962, and 1983. In all three cases, the seizures were complications of underlying illness such as fever or brain pathology.

TABLE 3.6. Apparent Neurological Problems by Century of Canonization

	16th C.	17th C.	18th C.	19th C.	20th C.
Skull fracture/head injury	1	9	1	2	6
Eye disease	6	28	12	8	23
Ear disease	2	6	6	1	7
Epilepsy	4	6	7	5	5
Apoplexy	0	1	3	2	1
Paralysis	4	17	17	8	21
Meningitis				0	21
Myelitis/polio				1	4
Encephalopathy/coma					17
All miracles	89	382	248	185	506

The problem in accepting these "neurological" cures as miraculous is the well-known possibility of spontaneous remission in many conditions, including epilepsy, multiple sclerosis, and myasthenia gravis. If a cure follows an invocation, skeptics will call it "coincidence" owing to a natural remission; they will also expect a relapse. Repeated follow-up examinations are usually provided in answer to this concern.

The relative decline of neurological conditions in my collection may be related to two phenomena: the rise of the neurological examination and the (re)definition of hysteria through the concept of conversion reaction. Both constitute arguments for skeptics against wonder in the miracle cures.

The first argument relies on confidence in the modern neurological examination. Today we think of blindness, deafness, seizures, and paralysis as conditions of the nervous system. But it is important to understand that the neurological examination, as it is known today, did not arise until a fairly narrow period beginning in the late nineteenth century; it was well established by the early twentieth century.[65] In earlier times, however, these end points constituted full-fledged diagnoses in and of themselves, and the physiological origins were not important.

The second argument trades on ideas about hysteria. In the same late-nineteenth-century period, hysteria was transformed from the antiquated idea of uterine suffocation to the modern concept of conversion reaction in the work of figures like Jean-Martin Charcot and Sigmund Freud. These two changes—the neurological examination and the definition of hysteria—roughly correspond to years during which hysteria was raised as an objection by some Vatican experts. More on this subject appears below in the discussion of mental illness and in chapter 4.

Diseases of Women

Miracles involving pregnancy, labor, delivery, and recovery appear at a steady rate until the twentieth century, when they decline slightly (table 3.7). In the seventeenth century, a large proportion of miracles dealt with aspects of a difficult delivery including prolonged or painful labor, and unusual presentations, such as breech or transverse lie (when the baby is sideways inside the mother). Their decline, beginning in the nineteenth century, reflects a wider use of forceps beyond a narrow elite. Further decline in the twentieth century relates to the rising prevalence of Cesarean birth. Although labor miracles appear in a few recent canonizations, only one actually occurred after 1771: the 1951 recov-

TABLE 3.7. Obstetrical Miracles by Century of Canonization

	16th C.	17th C.	18th C.	19th C.	20th C.
Sterility	1	1	0	0	0
Labor	1	9	7	3	2
Bleeding	0	0	2	3	6
Fever	0	2	6	2	3
Dead baby	1	5	2	0	2
Other	1	6	3	1	5
Total	2	17	16	8	14
All miracles	89	382	248	185	506
Percent of total miracles	2.2	4.5	6.5	4.3	2.8

ery of both mother and premature baby from obstructed labor and a transverse lie; the doctors had been planning destruction of the child.[66]

Postpartum hemorrhage and fever, both serious complications of childbirth, were also present. Cures of bleeding persist into the twentieth century, when specific anatomical and physiological causes were identified, such as placenta previa, abruptio placenta, disseminated intravascular coagulation (DIC), and shock. Postpartum fever, however, declined. One of three twentieth-century canonizations involving fever after delivery was based on testimony gathered in 1638: the woman had been in much greater danger from a concomitant hemorrhage. In the other cases, the infection had spread to peritonitis.[67] The decline in postpartum fever reflects the advent of sterile procedures in the latter third of the nineteenth century and of antibiotics in the twentieth. In other words, control and cure of postpartum fever, like that of other infectious illnesses, had come within the reach of medical care. Whether or not prayers had been offered, recovery could be ascribed to human remedies. Even when mothers and caregivers were inclined to give credit to the saint, the church was not.

In ten cases, the miracle consisted of saving the life of the mother although her child had died, a dangerous situation that may have provided the original impetus for male practice.[68] Of these, to us, unhappy cases, six were from the sixteenth and seventeenth centuries, two from the eighteenth century, and the most recent from 1952. Something about these stories was not compelling. For example, Zacchia described another case approved by the Rota in 1628 involving a woman, Alessandra, who had appealed to Pope Gregory X in 1625; however, doubts swirled around her miracle and the pontiff was not beatified until almost a century later in 1713.[69] Similarly, testimony was given in 1773 on a mother's survival despite a prolonged labor and her fetus dying in transverse lie; but the alleged intercessor, Salvatore Pagnani, has yet to be beatified.[70] The two most recent cases in which this situation applied were for a canonization in 1904 and a beatification in 1989; however, the miracle in the first had occurred in 1613; and in the second, the 1952 stillbirth was incidental to the recovery from postpartum peritonitis and hemorrhage.[71] In other words, survival of a stillbirth may once have seemed wondrous, but it lost that attribute with the advent of forceps and Cesarean delivery.[72]

Altered products of conception were of interest to clerics and physicians alike. They occur when the egg and sperm unite, but rather than making a child, they become a distorted growth. Recognized since antiquity, these relatively rare abnormalities include hydatidiform mole, which is a tangled cystic mass of blood vessels, and choriocarcinoma, which is an aggressive malignancy. Some have argued that these unusual events placed the mother in a spiritually awkward situation, as if they signified grievous sin, such as carnal relations with the devil. But the canonization records do not support that hypothesis; at least two women with these problems became miraculées. The first was a seventeen-year-old nun, who suffered a three-month illness involving stomach upset and vaginal hemorrhage in 1699; two physicians testified that after her appeal, she suddenly passed a mole the size of an orange with a rush of blood that soaked her bed. The sexual origin of the mole was not discussed in her case, although it had been recognized in the literature.[73] The case of choriocarcinoma occurred in 1937 in a married woman from Taranto.[74]

Evidence of attendants at deliveries rose steadily across the four centuries. This finding reflects the well documented trend to medicalization of birth; however, it could also be a product of the canonization process itself, which increasingly relied on independent witnesses. Deliveries without witnesses could not generate convincing evidence. Doctors testified in at least forty-four of the seventy obstetrical cases from as early as the seventeenth century at the dawn of physician-attended birth.[75] The pressure for witnesses may also explain why only four instances of answered prayers for sterility appear in this collection, all from testimony prior to 1683.[76] More on birth attendants and midwives will be discussed in chapter 4.

Ten miracles involved gynecological problems unrelated to pregnancy and labor. In keeping with anatomical diagnoses of other body parts, all but one were from 1818 or later. Six cases concerned cancer, and there was one each of prolapsed uterus, menstrual difficulty, uterine fibroids, and burns following ovarian radiation. In the latter two cases, the miracle entailed recovery, not only from the underlying problem, but also from the side effects of medical treatment. In other words, they were cures of iatrogenic diseases, which will be discussed below.

TABLE 3.8. Cures of Chronic and Acute Ailments by Century of Canonization

	16th C.	17th C.	18th C.	19th C.	20th C.
Chronic	5	25	24	36	127
Acute	2	54	80	27	212
All miracles	89	382	248	185	506

Duration of Illness: Chronic versus Acute

For approximately half of the miracles (666), there is enough information to determine the length of illness (table 3.8). No consistent pattern emerged. In the sixteenth and nineteenth centuries, chronic ailments of longer than a year's duration predominated. Sometimes, it appears that the chronicity of an ailment added value to the claim of a miracle because the problem had repeatedly defied nature and human remedies; furthermore, witnesses would abound.

Similarly, the average duration of illness over all four centuries is 2.8 years with little variation by century of canonization (table 3.9). Only in the sixteenth century did the average duration of illness exceed the overall average. More than two thirds of illnesses from that period persisted longer than a year. But canonizations in every century entailed some miraculous cures in ailments of two and three decades' duration.

Surgical Problems: Accidents, Wounds, and Operations

In the early centuries of this study, surgical practice was concerned with the dressing of wounds and setting of bones. Doctors occasionally drained abscesses or effusions and performed emergency amputations, but operations inside the head, thorax, or abdomen did not appear until the advent of anesthesia and antisepsis in the mid-nineteenth century.

Surgical problems, therefore, include the treatment of injuries. These problems constitute about 10 percent of miracles in every century, and a quarter to one third involved children. In the nineteenth and twentieth centuries, women

TABLE 3.9. Duration of Illness by Century of Illness (years)

	16th C.	17th C.	18th C.	19th C.	20th C.
Average	4.8	1.6	2.1	2.5	2.8
Maximum	30	34	21	30	36

TABLE 3.10 Accidents, Injuries,[a] Falls, and Drowning by Century of Illness

	16th C.	17th C.	18th C.	19th C.	20th C.
Men	2	15	12	9	12
Boys	2	11	4	2	10
Women	0	6	4	12	16
Girls	0	1	8	2	8
Total	4	33	28	24	46
Percent of total miracles	5	9	11	13	9
All miracles	89	382	248	185	506

[a]Includes fractures and dislocations.

suffered trauma more frequently than men (table 3.10). Accidental falls were relatively more frequent in the seventeenth century. Wounds caused by knives or guns were mercifully rare; possibly, such injuries were usually fatal, or victims of violence, so often violent themselves, were deemed unsuitable miraculés (table 3.11).

Fractures and dislocations were common in every era (table 3.5). Forty-eight instances appear across the four centuries; two fractures also involved dislocation. Accidents with ladders, horses, carriages, and automobiles were cited as the cause. To confirm the diagnoses, doctors testified in at least thirty-two cases; records have been preserved in eighteen. Special emphasis was often placed on the rapidity of cure, because fractures usually knit naturally through time. Others cases focused on the failure of bones to unite despite the use of orthopedic devices.

For example, in 1606, a surgeon told how he was summoned to attend a little boy whom he found at the bottom of a well, with "all his bones broken"; the child recovered in a single day, only to die a week later of something else.[77]

TABLE 3.11 Causes of Injury[a] by Century of Canonization

	16th C.	17th C.	18th C.	19th C.	20th C.
Wounds	1	9	9	9	11
Burns		1	2	0	4
Gunshots		0	2	2	1
Stabbing		0	2	1	0
Falls		12	5	2	3
Drowning with injury		2	3	2	2

[a]Excludes fractures and dislocations; see table 3.5 above.

In 1817, a woman fell from a ladder while carrying a sack of grain; two doctors found her with internal injuries and a dislocated hip, which they described with the anatomical precision of their era as the "removal of the head of the femur from the acetabulum."[78] In 1856, two doctors testified on the radical recovery of a thirty-year-old woman with a severely dislocated hip that had resulted in a leg-length discrepancy of six inches. She was unable to walk and had twice gone to Sette for sea baths, but to no avail.[79]

In the twentieth century, the healing of broken bones was often incidental to that of more severe injuries. For example, the most recent case was the result of a 1989 car accident in an eight-year-old Lithuanian boy: he suffered fracture of the base of the skull with grave intracranial lesions, including a subdural hematoma that required surgical evacuation, later complicated by cardiac arrest and coma.[80]

Avoiding the agony and deformities of recommended surgery was a form of miracle that began in the late eighteenth century when doctors began to offer operative treatments, usually amputations. A timely cure made the surgery unnecessary. This type of miracle increased into the twentieth century partly because surgical options had also increased (table 3.12).

The existence of surgery as definitive treatment might imply that miracles could not be discerned in patients so managed. But surgery had long been part of the saintly repertoire, as portrayed in the famous "transplantation" miracle of the doctor saints Cosmas and Damian.[81] A miracle garners credibility when the patient's condition has defied the best treatment of the era. Once surgery became the standard of care, it must have been applied for the investigators to accept both the diagnosis and the desperate prognosis. In the twentieth century,

TABLE 3.12. Avoidance of Surgery and Operations Performed by Century of Canonization

	17th C.	18th C.	19th C.	20th C.
Avoidance of surgery	0	7	8	20
All operations	0	5	9	67
Incision/draining	0	0	1	5
Amputation	0	0	0	1
Biopsy	0	0	0	9
Laparotomy	0	0	0	4
Appendix	0	0	0	8
Cancer	0	0	4	9
Heart	0	0	0	5

Note: See also fractures and dislocations in table 3.5 above.

many miracles were recognized in people who had previously been treated with surgical operations, ranging from simple biopsy to exploratory laparotomy to coronary artery bypass.

Typifying the miracles that entailed avoiding surgery is the case of the twenty-two-year-old German woman who, in March 1929, was helping her parents in the woods when she was struck by a falling tree that injured her right arm. The wound stubbornly refused to heal; over the course of seventeen months, she developed osteoarthritis, diagnosed as *metastatic synovitis*, and finally, gangrene. Her doctors sadly recommended amputation on the premise that it was necessary to "sacrifice a member to save the life." She agreed, but the night before her operation, she prayed to Conrad of Parzham; the following morning, she was cured, to the amazement of all.[82]

Sometimes, the opposite situation occurred, and miracles followed surgery. A Spanish engineer had undergone an operation and transfusions for gastric bleeding in 1982, but his illness progressed to hepatic encephalopathy and coma.[83] Reminiscent of Ambroise Paré's famous phrase "I bandage them, but God heals them," this postoperative healing was construed as having been worked by God through the intercession of the saint and the surgeon's hand. Because miracle stories are most convincing when the patient's deteriorating condition defies best practice, to be in a position to qualify, best practice must have been given and failed. Doctors and their up-to-date medicine are essential to the clerics. More on this subject will be discussed in the following chapter.

Mental Illness

Miraculous cures from mental illness were always rare and decline in frequency through time. Thirteen such cases, which include diagnostic words such as "insania," "disturbed," "deranged," or "lost mind," have been identified in ten women and three men. They figure as evidence in canonizations into the twentieth century; however, all but two were based on testimony delivered prior to 1700 (table 3.2).

Four cures in this group occurred in clerics—three Carmelite nuns and a monk—whose stories were among the many miracles in the cause of the Florentine saint Maria Maddalena de' Pazzi. At age twenty-nine, Sister Daria developed a "mental affliction," with furor, babbling, writhing, and biting, that lasted two or more years; her condition defied the ministrations of four doctors who finally "abandoned" her. The cure followed a vigil and invocation on the saint's feast day, May 25, 1626. A few years later, Daria was noted for her patience and stability and was appointed teacher of novices. Testifying thirty-seven years after her cure, the witnesses included her biological sister and other nuns.[84] The story of Sister Colomba was similar. Her wild agitation, biting, and kicking failed to respond to the doctor's prescription of bleeding, baths, and medicines; she recovered after an invocation on the same feast day in 1634.[85] Without specifying a date, the mother prioress recollected the cure of another mental affliction of three years' duration in a priest.[86] Finally, Sister Lucretia told of her own recovery from a mental disturbance in 1645, after promising to pray nightly at the tomb for a year.[87]

The word *pazza* (crazy) was used by the witnesses to describe these ailments, characterized by irrational speech and violent behavior. Given the paucity of such cases in other causes, it is tempting to speculate that the saint was preferentially invoked because of her name. That the four disturbed clerics in her cause had been attended by one or more physicians demonstrates that madness was at least partially medicalized in the seventeenth century.

Sister Lucretia's case was remarkable for its firsthand testimony about an episode of insanity. Only one other case, that of the widow Elisabetta, provides similar insight, but it is not included here because her problem was labeled "demonic possession" and will be discussed below.

A single cure of mental illness took place after the early eighteenth century: the 1890 cure of a Torino woman from a disorder diagnosed as "mental alienation." She, too, had been treated by a physician who provided testimony.[88] This case was one of seventeen miracles cited in the cause of Giovanni Bosco; the other sixteen were cures of physical ailments.

In the mental illness group, I have included two women who were miraculously cured of "uterine suffocation," or hysteria. In the first, a noble woman of Florence attributed her 1607 recovery to the intercession of the Jesuit novice Luigi Gonzaga. Her story constituted the fourteenth miracle in a collection of fifteen.[89] In the second, sometime in the same century, an Italian nun recovered from a fifteen-year illness, diagnosed as a hysterical condition and characterized by "atrocious convulsions"; she attributed her cure to the intercession of Giuliana Falconieri.[90] Further details are lacking, but both cures of hysterical suffocation became recognized miracles, as they were described in the *Compendia* summaries.

In contrast, from at least the nineteenth century forward, imposing a diagnosis of hysteria was sufficient to disqualify the cure as a contender for a miracle. Lambertini, and Zacchia before him, had both been concerned with hysteria and imagination as a cause of sickness.[91] In my collection, the earliest case, in which hysteria was mentioned to discount the significance of a patient's cure, occurred in the official doubts raised in the cause of Pierre Fourier in 1726, during the time of Lambertini. Sister Ursula was said to have recovered from tertian fever that had rendered her moribund; the office of the promotor fidei cited Lancisi to argue that hysteria could result in equally sudden recoveries.[92]

By the nineteenth century, doctors testifying in inquiries were expected to clarify whether or not the patient had been hysterical. Expert consultants were well aware of the possibility, but not every treating physician had considered it. To illustrate this point, consider the case of the eighteen-year-old girl from Majorca, mentioned above, who was cured of gastritis in July 1830. She suffered long-standing stomach spasms that two of several doctors had labeled "hysterical." At least one doctor and all other witnesses, including a surgeon, pronounced her recovery "miraculous."[93] But this case was not compelling, and yet another miracle, a cancer cure, was collected before completion of this process.[94] In 1902, a diagnostic contest between paralysis and hysteria was waged between two doctors testifying in the cause of Emilie de Rodat; further details will be given in chapter 4.[95] Similarly, in 1938, the diagnosis of a woman with severe abdominal pain was a matter of debate between two treating physicians, one of whom called her a "grand hysteric"; however, this impasse did not delay the cause of João de Brito, possibly because he was a martyr.[96] In another investigation concerning a cure of goiter in 1973, a psychiatrist and a surgeon debated whether or not the miraculée was hysterical.[97]

In at least thirty-one other healings, occurring from 1866 to 1966, over a wide range of diagnoses, from paralysis to tuberculosis to cancer, the possibility of hysteria was raised and rejected as a significant negative. These discussions, all on women, seem to peak in the 1930s and then decline (table 3.13).

Prior to 1850, hysterical loss of function was not well characterized and could not easily be distinguished from other causes. After the mid-twentieth century, however, the neurological examination, described above, was established and pervasive. Treating doctors would never have left themselves open to such criticism by failing to perform the requisite tests. As a result, the rise and dissemination of the neurological examination may also account for the late-twentieth-century decline in discussions about the possibility of hysteria; the question was raised and dismissed at source.

TABLE 3.13 Cases in Which Hysteria Was Considered by Quarter Century of Testimony

From year to year	1800 1824	1825 1849	1850 1874	1875 1899	1900 1924	1925 1949	1950 1974	1975 1999
No. of cases	0	3	2	3	8	9	0	2

Belying the professed readiness of physicians and clerics to accept hysteria as a real and disabling disease, by 1850 or earlier, a cure of that condition was thought to be far less impressive than a cure of organic illness. This observation is not to condemn those doctors or priests for failing to accept or sympathize with their patients' suffering. Rather, it further defines the scientific parameters necessary for "diagnosis" of a miracle. In the seventeenth century, hysteria could be cured by miracle. By the nineteenth century, a cure for hysteria (fabricated or not) had fallen within the realm of human intervention; it did not "arise."

Psychiatric illness made an exceptional and ignominious appearance in the miracle files as the *cause* of a physical ailment. In 1844, a thirty-two-year-old woman recovered from a series of complaints that included vomiting blood and the new diagnosis of pericarditis. Her illness began twelve years earlier when she had been working as a nurse in a hospital for "les aliénés" near Orléans, France. She was attacked by a patient, "*une folle*" (a madwoman), and saved from certain death only by the quick actions of another "*folle* . . . who temporarily enjoyed her reason." Testimony was provided in 1846 by one of the two treating physicians and no less than four experts, including two famous French professors, J. C. Lallemand and J. C. A. Récamier. This tale of an irrational and unjust assault was woven into the texture of her illness as described by virtually all twenty-two witnesses whether or not they knew any other details about the case.[98]

Iatrogenic Disease

The increasing medicalization of the modern world is evident in the cures from iatrogenic diseases, which rose steadily in the files (table 3.14). The earliest case stems from the eighteenth century, and a nurse was the key witness; it will be described in chapter 4.[99] The two gynecological cases, mentioned above, serve as examples. The woman with uterine fibroids was a forty-seven-year-old housewife from Madagascar who had been treated with a hysterectomy in 1975; soon after, she developed a life-threatening infection of the abdominal wall that progressed to gangrene and hypovolemic shock. She recovered after invoking the African monk Scubilion Rousseau.[100] The woman whose ovaries had been irradiated was a forty-four-year-old Polish widow who had received

TABLE 3.14 Cures of Iatrogenic Disease by Century of Canonization

	1700s	1800s	1900–1949	1950–1999
Iatrogenic disease	1	2	5	20

this treatment for osteomalacia in 1921. But she suffered severe burns that formed ulcers oozing pus; the cure followed her invocation of the Polish martyr Andrzej Bobola, in 1922.[101]

The cures of iatrogenic disease increase dramatically for causes in the second half of the twentieth century. Because a large proportion of mortality figures are now said to be owing to doctor-caused disease, this observation is in keeping with the range of illnesses in modern society. Recovery from the iatrogenic illness of perforated bowel following a 1980 endoscopy is the object of a miracle investigated in Spain.[102] In my collection, at least thirteen of the twenty such cures after 1950 were of life-threatening problems that followed what should have been life-saving surgery. This grim array of deadly conditions ranged from wound infections, abscesses, fistulae, and adhesions, to septic shock, hypovolemia, cardiac arrest, and encephalopathy. Other doctor-caused problems were owing to toxicity from treatments: burning of a neonate's eyes with concentrated silver nitrate; several other radiation burns; and the accidental swallowing of an irritant (cantharides, or Spanish fly) intended only for the skin.

Doctors do not like to blame each other. As awkward as these interrogations must have been for those responsible for harm, the complete records on iatrogenic cures include evidence from treating physicians. Sometimes as many as twelve doctors were named, and up to six testified. In cases of iatrogenic illness, medical experts were also especially numerous.

The Nonmedical Miracles

Although they are few in number and decline through time, the nonmedical miracles of the last four centuries are an interesting subgroup. Using a strict rule for identifying "medical" miracles as recovery from illness, 105 miracles of the total of 1,409 (or 7.4 percent) could not be called "medical." One exceptional "healing" is included in this collection because it entailed the recovery of a "valuable mule."[103] Less numerous than in the medieval hagiographies, these nonmedical miracles cover the same array of wonders, including preservation of the corpse, expulsion of demons, religious conversion, punishment, and liberation from prison (table 3.15).

Corpse

Fully a third of this intriguing group of nonmedical miracles concern the incorruptibility (preservation) or sweet odor of the corpse of the saint. In the

TABLE 3.15 Nonmedical Miracles by Century
of Canonization

	16th C.	17th C.	18th C.	19th C.	20th C.
Corpse	1	12	7	3	5
Flood/well	0	4	1	2	0
Fire	0	1	2	1	0
Earthquake	0	0	1	0	0
Multiplication	0	6	3	1	1
Vision	2	2	1	1	2
Demons	3	7	1	1	1
Accident	0	5	0	0	1
Other	0	6	0	1	3
Total	7	48	19	12	20
All miracles	89	382	248	185	506

fourteenth century, these corporeal miracles, sometimes involving dissection to retrieve organs, seem to have been recognized in the bodies of female saints, although women are in a minority in the pantheon of saints.[104] No such predominance appears in my collection; male saints outnumber female in these corporeal wonders (table 3.16). Twenty-nine miracles of the corpse involving twenty-two saints were found. In these settings, anatomical testimony was often provided by physicians who cited scientific authorities, such as Carlo Taglini, Ambroise Paré, Daniel Sennert, Théophile Bonet, Giambattista Morgagni, Antoine-Laurent de Jussieu, Henri Milne Edwards, and Paolo Zacchia.[105] As explained in chapter 1, Pope Benedict XIV was especially interested in anatomical evidence. Miracles for at least nine of the canonizations during his lifetime entailed incorruptibility and fragrance of the saint's corpse.[106] For example, four hundred years after her death, the corpse of Chiara of Montefalco was credited with new miracles; observers testifying in 1726 noticed the eyes opened and moved, while the feet swelled, seemingly in sympathy with suffering of sisters in her convent during an outbreak of influenza.[107]

TABLE 3.16 Miracles Involving the Saint's Corpse by Sex
and Century of Canonization

	16th C.	17th C.	18th C.	19th C.	20th C.
Female	0	2	3	2	1
Male	1	10	4	1	4
Total	1	12	7	3	5

So frequent an occurrence was the finding of incorruptibility that exhumation of the body of the would-be saint was part of the canonization process. This "fleshy" and interventionist attribute of Counter-Reformation Catholicism contrasted with the spiritual and transcendent piety of Protestants.[108] Regular visitors to Catholic churches expect to find the bodies of saints and would-be saints displayed and venerated as holy relics. The practice has captured the attention of nonreligious people and websites on the topic abound.[109] Beyond the miraculous preservation of the corpse itself might be many healings attributed to touching or seeing it. Several specific examples will be described in chapter 5.

But these cadaveric miracles, frequent though they were, seem to have provided only weak evidence for sanctity in modern times. In almost every cause that included a miracle pertaining to the saint's corpse, other miracles of healing were also included. Eventually, the finding of miraculous preservation was deemed to be indistinguishable from mummification induced by environmental circumstances of humidity and temperature. Because the finding could apply to the remains of people who had not lived exemplary lives, it constituted insufficient evidence for saintliness.

Similar observations apply to the mystical phenomenon of the stigmata, the wounds that resemble those of Christ's passion. Records of this occurrence have persisted since at least the time of St. Francis of Assisi, and nearly fifty modern saints or blesseds received the stigmata during life, including Padre Pio, canonized in 1999. The church holds no official position on the matter.

It seems that in the modern canonization process, stigmata have been incidental to the final decision. In my survey, I found only one process with testimony on stigmata: a 1909 investigation in the cause of Gemma Galgani.[110] However, the same inquiry also contained evidence on the cure of a woman from arthritis of the knee, whereas the *Compendium* printed in 1940 ignored both and cited two different miracles of physical healing in a father and his daughter.[111]

Until recently, the apparent absence of stigmata in official miracles may be procedural; testimony concerning this phenomenon must be acquired soon after the saint's death from people who had known her in life. It becomes part of the biography or the *fama* and appears too soon for the traditional rhythm of canonization.

Expulsion of Demons

Seen as a task for holy people from biblical times forward, the expulsion of evil spirits cannot, strictly speaking, be regarded as a form of medical miracle. It figures among Christ's miracles as described in the gospels and is often mentioned in the lives of saints recognized prior to 1588. Its presence in the canonization records after 1588 is limited to the sixteenth and early seventeenth centuries (figures 3.3 and 3.4).

Thirteen instances of the miraculous recovery from demonic possession appear in records pertaining to ten canonizations from 1588 to 1904; but none was more recent than 1638. Two were clusters: a group of eleven women in the cause of Zita, and another group of four for Chiara of Montefalco. Of the others, seven involved women miraculées, one of whom was a nun; four were lay men. None represented the only or final miracle in any cause. Indeed, literally dozens of other miracles of physical healing were also included in these same causes. In other words, expelling demons may have constituted an important preoccupation in the seventeenth century, but it was not a strong argument for canonization. It faded from the evidence just as rapidly as mental illness.

One case is remarkable for its firsthand testimony. A wealthy widow, Elisabetta, testified in 1606, together with her brother and a servant that her illness had resolved without doctors after an appeal to Andrea Corsini on New Year's Eve 1597. She also gave evidence on two physical healings from 1605: her own recovery from fever and that of her twelve-year-old daughter from earache. On both occasions, physicians and surgeons were consulted.[112]

I did not designate the recoveries from demonic possession as "medical" miracles. Nevertheless, certain aspects of the stories suggest that behavioral and emotional phenomena, conceived of as "possession" in the seventeenth century, were already being subsumed into a medical framework as mental illness. In other words, the early modern use of terminology involving demonic possession shows that it may have been thought of as disease. Our reasons for thinking otherwise may be based on a far too literal interpretation of the language. Support for this notion can be found in a closer inspection of the cases.

In at least two expulsions, medication was prescribed to no avail, as if seeking a doctor's advice was an appropriate response to demonic possession.[113] In another involving a young girl, the main symptom was her "black character."[114] In two others, the words "evil spirits" seem to be used interchangeably with terms that imply unhappiness or anger, similar to our own use of the expression, "low spirits."[115] Some overlap occurs in the language used in cases of possession and of madness. The widow Elisabetta said that she had been afflicted with "unworldly spirits"; she also described a servant relieved of "bad spirits."[116] In the case of Sister Daria, cited above, her problem was variously identified as "molested mind," "dementia," and "madness," for which at least four doctors had been consulted.[117]

At least two early modern physicians, Girolamo Cardano and Paolo Zacchia, dealt with demons within a medical context. The former claimed his

FIGURE 3.3. A man possessed of a demon and his friends appeal successfully to Santa Fina at her tomb. Shutters of a reliquary attributed to Lorenzo di Nicolo di Martino, 1402. Museo Civico, San Gimignano, Italy.

FIGURE 3.4. Anastasia Magi is liberated from evil spirits following an
appeal through an image of Carlo Borromeo. This miracle was cited
in the canonization process. Bonino, *Nonnulla praeclara gesta*, 1610.

father was possessed of a demon like a familiar,[118] whereas the latter discussed
demonic possession medically alongside lunacy, paralysis, blindness, and deafness in his chapter on miraculous cures of illness.[119]

These observations about medical involvement hold true for what authors
have written about demonic possession in medieval times. Using similar sources
but from a much earlier period, Michael Goodich indicated that signs of medieval demonic possession included many physical symptoms—such as fever,

disorientation, eating disorders, compulsions, insomnia, convulsions, trembling, rigid muscles, speechlessness, foaming saliva, memory loss, screaming fits, grinding teeth, uncontrolled weeping, and the uttering of obscenities, blasphemies, and insults—only some of which might later be designated as insanity.[120] Similarly, for a case of demonic possession considered in the 1601 process on Carlo Borromeo, the only witness was a doctor (figure 3.4).[121]

Other scholars point to the similarity of symptoms for possession, hysteria, and epilepsy. Indeed, by the eighteenth century, believing oneself to be possessed could be construed as evidence for mental illness.[122] The medicalization of religious events extended into the late nineteenth century as physicians continued to wrestle with what constituted "normal" or "abnormal" religious behaviors in a process that Giordana Charuty has labeled "the psychiatrization of beliefs."[123] In the nineteenth century, medical attention reevaluated a famous sixteenth-century case of possession as illness.[124] More recently, retrospective analysis of possessions has likened them to the modern diagnosis of dissociative personality disorder.[125] Finally, in 1985, a psychiatrist turned the issue upside down when he advocated reverting to the concept of possession as a helpful metaphor in the recognition and management of depression.[126]

Little more can be said about possession because the cases are rare and because madness itself also disappears from the files. This observation of early modern medicalization may help to explain the frequency of demonic possession in a more distant past. It may also provide a new, less Whiggish approach to narratives of demonic possession in earlier times.

Other Nonmedical Miracles

Punitive miracles are those that cause a person to suffer because of heresy, sin, or maligning the saint.[127] In my collection, they are intriguing but scarce: only five instances appeared. In the cause of Diego d'Alcalá, an unbeliever was visited with severe leg pain that did not relent until he truly accepted the saint's holiness.[128] The 1610 *Vita* of Hildebrand (Pope Gregory VII) told of a man struck mute for speaking evil.[129] Similarly, the 1729 *Vita* of Bohemian lawyer and controversial martyr Jan Nepomuk described retributive justice meted out until heretics would convert and sinners repent.[130]

Two examples of punition were variations upon healings. A despairing mother refused to pray to Isidro Labrador for her little girl because he was not yet canonized; the child deteriorated; when her mother relented, a cure followed.[131] A Spanish man recovered from headache and fever in 1702, but the same symptoms returned when he failed to keep a vow made in his invocation of Juan de la Cruz.[132] No miracles involving punishment appeared after the canonization of Jan Nepomuk in 1729.

Liberation miracles entail escape from prison. They are predicated on the notion that the confinement is cruel, unjust, and immoral, a product of irrational tyranny. They characterize medieval stories, but are little apparent in this collection. Liberation appeared only once in the 1690 *Vita* of Juan de San Facondo de Sahagún, within a cluster of five that also included salvation from fire and flood.[133] After 1588, popular wisdom may have deferred more to authority: perhaps, people came to think that prisoners belonged in jail; their liberation was not miraculous, but frightening.

The remainder of the "nonmedical" miracles in my collection entail events that Lambertini called "negative miracles": preservation of life without injury from starvation, accidents, or natural disasters, such as fire, floods, earthquakes, and falls (figure 3.5). In this study, accidents causing injury, including drowning and fractures, involved illness and caregivers and were considered "medical."

Escaping accidents without injury seems to have been common only in the seventeenth century. The descriptions are lively: two involved runaway mules; another, the narrow miss of ships immersed in fog.[134] In August 1702, two young men—Pietro and Paolino—emerged unscathed from a flash flood of the river Orba where they had been fishing. Frantically trying to stay afloat amidst crashing logs and debris, they appealed to Pope Pius V; one of their fathers did exactly the same as he watched in horror from the shore. Grasping at a branch, the youths were saved when it stuck in the mud. This miracle seems not to have been decisive as it was not described in the *Compendium*. Nevertheless, it may have triggered the investigation into two earlier events of 1678 and 1683, respectively, because inquiries on all three were conducted in 1704.[135] More on emergency invocations will be discussed in chapter 5.

Increase in food supplies, or "multiplication," especially of flour, bread, and oil, characterized eleven miracles, most occurring in collective households, such as orphanages and monasteries. For example, in 1718, a vinegar cruet was replenished in the kitchen of an orphanage, where a sick woman could eat nothing but dressed salad; the 1762 testimony entailed a succession of elderly residents who recollected the event of almost half a century earlier.[136]

Twice, water surfaced during dry spells.[137] Once in 1609 sufficient food appeared to feed a crowd of paupers assembled to celebrate the saint.[138] A miracle of multiplication can go on to contribute to later miracles of healing. For example, water from miraculous springs and wells associated with saints could be applied to later cures. In the cause of Isidro Labrador, five of thirteen

FIGURE 3.5. Agostino Novello interceding to save a falling child. Agostino died in 1309 and was beatified in 1759. Altarpiece by Simone Martini, 1324, Pinacoteca Nazionale, Siena. By permission of the M-inistero per i Beni e le Attività Culturali. Photo courtesy Soprintendenza PSAE di Siena & Grosseto.

miracles were healings following immersion or ingestion of water from "his fount."[139]

Another example of the multiplication of miracles from a miracle of multiplication is found in the cause of Maria Maddalena de'Pazzi. In 1626, the nuns were preparing to celebrate the glory of Paradise with a special display of light when they ran out of oil. Sister Eugenia appealed to the saint and the problem was solved.[140] Perhaps the supply ran low again, because the events were repeated in 1654 when Sister Reparata also offered an invocation for oil.[141] This *olio multi-plicato* was piously conserved and used at least six times, between 1645 and 1663, to anoint other supplicants who were subsequently healed of their illnesses.[142]

Visions as miracles appeared in the dossiers of eight causes; none were final miracles. Two were for martyrs, and the apparitions occurred at the sites of martyrdom.[143] The records of testimony on these two miracles are not available, but they probably predated the changes of 1588. Both causes contained additional files with numerous healings, as did all other causes with vision miracles. A vision in the twentieth-century cause of Maria Goretti was particularly moving. Sometimes called a martyr to virginity, she died of stab wounds at the age of twelve resisting the sexual attack of nineteen-year-old Alessandro Serenelli. While incarcerated, he had a vision of Maria and converted. His story was used toward the beatification in 1947; since that time, however, his family disputed the charge of attempted rape. Another miracle file for Goretti dated 1948 is still under seal. The *Compendium* printed at the time of her canonization refers only to an unspecified intercession and recalls the practice of dispensing with miracles for martyrs.[144]

Over time, the nonmedical miracles in my collection appear to wane, especially when expressed as a percentage of the whole. Nevertheless, their numbers are probably too small to insist on a trend with confidence. Among nonmedical miracles, only four could be dated to events of the twentieth century. One was the Goretti vision and another the stigmata of Gemma Galgani, both described above. In the third, Marcel, a nineteen-year-old Swiss student, was mountain climbing in 1940 when the weather turned violent. He prayed to his compatriot Marguerite Bays. The rope linking him to three other climbers snapped and his companions fell to their deaths, but Marcel was saved.[145] The fourth was a miracle of multiplication: in 1960, twenty-two Spanish witnesses testified that in 1949, Juan Macias had interceded to increase the supply of rice in a shelter that he had founded.[146]

Given that the rate of canonization increased after 1940, the absolute decline in nonmedical miracles represents an even greater relative decline that places ever more emphasis on healings. Moreover, doctors were summoned to give evidence in these nonmedical miracles too, and not only on the corpses. Sometimes they were asked to comment on the potential consequences of negative miracles had they not occurred. The rare archival files with no physician evidence at all were mostly from the seventeenth and eighteenth centuries.[147] Only one such file came from after 1800: it concerned the 1845 provision of food in a convent shelter for young women; the nuns had been reduced to calculating the quantity of loaves that could be made from remaining supplies when suddenly the bins were filled with flour. Testimony came two years later from the nuns, a carpenter, and a baker.[148] But the same cause included investigations on six other miracles, all healings with physician testimony.

TABLE 3.17a Late-Twentieth-Century Miracles by Organ System
(total 134)

Organ System	Number	Examples
Cardiac	9	Arrest, ventricular fibrillation, myocarditis, coronary artery
Vascular	4	Ruptured aorta, ischemic ulcers, phlebitis, varices
Respiratory	13	Insufficiency, emphysema, asthma, bronchiectasis, bronchiolitis
Neurological	28	Encephalopathy, subarachnoid hemorrhage, spinal stenosis, myasthenia gravis, multiple sclerosis, meningoencephalitis
Gastrointestinal	28	Peritonitis, bleeding ulcer, pancreatitis, ulcerative colitis, volvulus
Liver	9	Cirrhosis, fulminant hepatitis, abscess
Genitourinary	6	Nephrotic syndrome, renal insufficiency
Gynecological	10	Toxemia, abruptio, postpartum hemorrhage, infection
Eye	4	Uveitis, uveal prolapse, corneal wound
Ear	1	Otitis media
Endocrine	2	Thyroid adenoma
Bone and Joint	8	Polyarthritis, congenital dislocation of hip, club foot
Blood, lymphatics	6	leukemia, lymphoma
Other	6	Skin, wounds, infections, tumours

Note: Some illnesses involved more than one organ system.

TABLE 3.17b Late-Twentieth-Century Miracles by Pathological Process
(total 134)

Disease Type	Number	Examples
Atherosclerosis	15	Coronary artery disease, stroke
Immunological	6	Lupus erythematosus, polymyositis
Cancer	25	Breast, stomach, bowel, leukemia, lymphoma, melanoma, sarcoma
Hemorrhage	5	Postpartum bleeding
Trauma	18	Drowning, subdural hematoma, fractures, aspiration of foreign body, run over by tractor, wounds
Chronic disease	7	Cirrhosis, club foot
Infection	19	Septicemia, subphrenic abscess, gangrene
Tuberculosis	6	All contracted before 1951
Iatrogenic disease	15	Transfusion reaction, radiation dermatitis
Postoperative	11	Infection, adhesions, shock, fistulae

Note: Some illnesses involved more than one type of disease.

The miracles from 1950 to 1999 concentrate almost exclusively on a wide array of serious diseases involving all organ systems and many pathological processes (tables 3.17a and b).

By placing increasing emphasis on medicine and physical healing in canonization, the Church does not deny the possibility of transcendent experiences in other forms. Rather, the miracles used in the canonization records signify something much more than an account of wondrous events; they must also serve the rigorous standards of the process itself. Consequently, the rising presence of medicine in these files is a product of the procedural demand for reliable evidence from credible witnesses and knowledgeable experts. It seems that medical miracles have what it takes to make a saint. With the tremendous emphasis on healing, the increased medicalization of the modern world, and the importance of medical testimony even in the nonmedical miracles, physicians emerge as key players in these investigations. They are the topic of the following chapter.

4

The Doctors

Medical Knowledge in the
Canonization Process

In March 1816, in the ancient port of Gaeta, eight-year-old Francesco, son of a surgeon, lay unconscious in the final stages of fever. Sickly for most of his short life, he was known for a strange pulsation in his chest that had been diagnosed as a chronic aneurysm. With this attack of fever, his fragile condition deteriorated drastically, and after nearly four weeks, the attending doctors abandoned hope. But Francesco's desperate parents prayed and urged their drowsy boy to swallow water in which they immersed a fragment of the cloak that had once belonged to Paolo della Croce. To their amazement, both the fever and the chronic problem rapidly resolved. Testifying three years later, Francesco's surgeon-father insisted that the recovery had been miraculous, and he drew on his professional experience to explain why. To his dismay, the medical confreres doubted this judgment; the boy could have recovered naturally, they said. On deeper questioning, the most vociferous opponent grudgingly admitted that he had been absent at the time of the cure. His opposition was based not on observation of the illness but rather on his understanding of how the world must work. Whose evidence would count most?

From: Paulus a Cruce Danei, ASV RP 2355 (1819), 53v (Dr. Sotis, absent), 61–64 (miraculé), 66–76v (Dr. Placitelli), 79v–90 (father).

To my surprise, both as a doctor and a historian, I quickly learned that the Vatican does not and never did recognize healing miracles in people who eschew orthodox medicine to rely solely on faith. The canonization officials strive to consider the latest in science; they do not want to be manipulated by the wiles of sensationalists or the aspirations of the gullible. Doctors provide an antidote to these problems with their medical knowledge, their ostensible objectivity, and even their skepticism. Within a process, they participate in a multiplicity of ways: mostly as attendants of the sick, but also as experts, neighborly witnesses, or patients themselves. The quality of the evidence depends on their medical skill in diagnosis, therapy, and prognosis. In many cases, medicine is under investigation along with the miraculé; judgment of the doctors' skill may affect the outcome. In this chapter, we will explore the experiences of doctors who were invited to testify in the inquiries on miracles.

The practice of consulting doctors on miracles had been established long before 1588, as is attested by the work of scholars on medieval canonizations.[1] Doctor testimony had also been solicited on healings from earlier centuries that were applied to post-Congregation canonizations.[2] In my collection, virtually all testimony on cures referred to treating physicians by name, even if they did not testify in person. Of all the medical miracles for which complete files were examined, the majority contain physician testimony (figure 4.1). The predominance of doctors increases through time and becomes more evident when expressed by century of testimony. Even the brief summaries of healing miracles frequently referred to physician participation (table 4.1). Doctors crowd these records.

For the earliest canonizations between 1588 and 1610, printed records and *Compendia* describe medical witnesses in more than thirty miracles; however, transcripts for most of those investigations are not in the ASV.[3] For example, three distinguished doctors examined the corpse of Diego d'Alcalá;[4] and at least thirteen healings cited in his cause had been attended by physicians.[5] A sizable minority of seventeenth-century healings in my collection did not mention physicians, but each of the same causes included other miracles with medical testimony.

Actual physician testimony is also found in the seventeenth-century post-Congregation causes for which archival transcripts remain, including Carlo Borromeo, Andrea Corsini, Pasqual Baylón, Pedro Alcántara, Maria Maddalena de'Pazzi, François de Sales, and Tomás de Villanueva. Sometimes many physicians gave evidence on a single case. In 1663, no fewer than six doctors were mentioned, three of whom testified, on one miracle among the many in the cause of Maria Maddalena de'Pazzi.[6] For another case in the same cause, the inquiry heard from all four of the doctors involved.[7] Similarly, for a healing in the cause of Caterina of Bologna, four of eleven witnesses summoned in 1674 were physicians.[8] The maximum number of doctors mentioned in a single miracle was nineteen; their names appeared in 1926 testimony for the cause of Joaquina de Vedruna, beatified in 1940.[9]

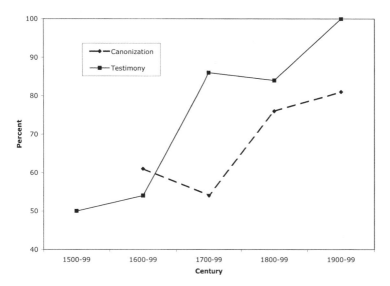

FIGURE 4.I. Doctor testimony in complete records, shown as percent of miracles in each century of canonization and of testimony ($N = 512$ healing miracles).

Reflecting the medicalization of the western world, the average number of doctors making an appearance in each record increases from approximately 0.3 for canonizations of the sixteenth century to 2.7 in the twentieth (table 4.2). These numbers increase when the calculation is limited to those files for which we have complete testimony (table 4.3) and range over the centuries from an average of approximately one doctor mentioned to four. The trend is apparent whether it is expressed by century of canonization (as shown in the tables) or by century of cure or testimony.

Similarly, the proportion of doctors who actually testify also rises steadily through the centuries from approximately 20 percent of those named to greater

TABLE 4.I. Doctors Mentioned in Brief Records of Miracle Healings with or without Testimony by Century of Canonization ($N = 801$ incomplete records, brief summaries, *Compendia, Positiones*, etc.)

	16th C.	17th C.	18th C.	19th C.	20th C.
No doctor	69	103	69	28	182
Doctor	14	70	43	21	202
Total	83	173	112	49	384
Percent with doctors mentioned	16.9	40.5	38.4	42.9	52.6

TABLE 4.2. Average Number of Doctors Mentioned and Testifying in Each Healing Miracle by Century of Canonization (N = 1,312 miracles)

	16th C.	17th C.	18th C.	19th C.	20th C.
Mentioned	0.3	0.9	1.03	1.8	2.66
Testifying	0	0.17	0.4	0.98	1.99
Percent of doctors mentioned who testify	0	18.9	38.8	54.9	74.7

than 70 percent. Turchini's work supports this estimate: in a 1601 investigation in Milan, 17 of 65 cases (or 26 percent) contained physician testimony; however, of the 14 actually selected for further investigation at least 8 (or 57 percent) had contained medical evidence.[10] In other words, even in the early seventeenth century, testimony from doctors may have helped a miracle move forward. The same cases described in my own sources reveal that doctors had been involved with 92 percent of the healings attributed to Carlo, whether they gave evidence or not.[11]

In this collection, an average of one doctor was named in each record of the seventeenth century, but only a small proportion can be said to have given evidence in person. Their opinions and actions were described by other witnesses, including the miraculé, or nuns, monks, and priests. Perhaps greater credence was given to witnesses in holy orders; alternatively, doctors might have been uninvited or unwilling to testify. For canonizations after 1700, however, at least a third and usually more of the physicians mentioned in a record provided testimony in person.

One of the striking features of the earliest miracles is a formulaic reference to physicians who had "despaired of," or "abandoned," their patients. For an observer today, these terms might suggest callous behavior; however, giving up on treatment seems to have been part of proper medical decorum since antiquity.[12] Referring to the great physician of the second century A.D., one

TABLE 4.3. Average Number of Doctors Mentioned and Testifying in Each Healing Miracle with Detailed Records, ASV, and *Positiones* (N = 922)

	16th C.	17th C.	18th C.	19th C.	20th C.
Mentioned	N/A	1.01	1.33	4.17	3.53
Testifying	N/A	0.19	0.49	1.31	2.4
Percent of doctors mentioned who testify		18.4	36.8	31.4	68

N/A = not applicable; no archival files on miracles for sixteenth-century canonizations.

witness said that the doctors had "left the patient to the discretion of nature, following the advice of Galen."[13] Such restraint reduced financial hardship for the patient's family and eliminated accusations of false hope against the doctors. In addition, Christian tradition required the physician to indicate when to summon the priest. At least forty-two such cases of medical despair have been found; all but three are based on testimony from 1682 or earlier. Only one from the twentieth century entails direct testimony from the "despairing" doctor himself, the word being his own. The rest are described by others. Sometimes they occur in ill-defined clusters: "many immediate and perfect cures in those of whom physicians and surgeons had despaired."[14] The formula of medical "abandonment" and "despair" stood as a sign of serious disease, adding to the wonder of the recovery. It occurs so frequently that it must be received as code for "incurability," if not impending death. In other words, as Vauchez observed for the medieval period, doctors appear in these early records simply to demonstrate that the patient was seriously ill and medicine had been useless (figure 4.2).[15]

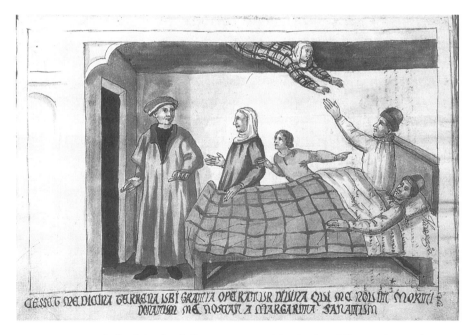

FIGURE 4. 2. A physician (on left) turns away as Margherita of Cortona intercedes to cure a sick man, shown in two positions. She was canonized in 1728. Watercolor by Adriano Zabarelli based on a fresco by the Lorenzetti brothers no longer extant. Manuscript 429, figure viii, circa 1639, Biblioteca del Comune e dell'Accademia Etrusca, Cortona.

TABLE 4.4. Surgeons and Physicians Distinguished in Miracle Records

	16th C.	17th C.	18th C.	19th C.	20th C.
One or more surgeons	0	27	35	43	57
One or more physicians	14	168	110	117	285

But during the seventeenth century, attending doctors did more than despair and sometimes provided in-person descriptions of care that they had delivered. In my collection, physicians testified on at least forty-five miracles in sixteen different causes of the seventeenth century, beginning with the earliest inquiries for which testimony could be found in the ASV: Carlo Borromeo and Andrea Corsini, in 1604 and 1606, respectively.[16] Surgeons also were present in every century and testified in many cases, either as the solo treating doctor, or together with physicians (table 4.4). At that time, surgery and medicine were separate but related professions, the former given to the work of the hand and taught by apprenticeship; the latter of higher status and related to academic learning through books. In these records, physicians outnumber surgeons in every century, although demographically speaking their relative proportions would be reversed.

Other health providers testified, including dentists, physiotherapists, pharmacists, and midwives. A variety of words are used to describe them: *cerusico* (6 cases), barber (4), phlebotomist (2), apothecary (2), pharmacist (8), midwife (17), or *speziale* (3). In other cases, people in these same occupations sometimes testified as bystanders rather than caregivers. Except for nurses and midwives discussed below, little information can be gleaned about the plurality of healers known to have worked in early modern Europe and into the nineteenth century.[17] With its concern for scientific authority, the canonization process seems to have favored medical orthodoxy over all other forms.

After 1800, only one complete miracle file contains no medical testimony at all: it was an analysis of votive offerings that had been left at the tomb of St. Falco during the sixteenth century.[18]

The Centrality of Medical Testimony: Arrival of Experts

Gradually, the physician's testimony took on as much or even greater significance than that of the "miraculé." If the doctor refused, the process could not proceed. In many cases, beginning with testimony from 1697, the medical

TABLE 4.5. Average Number of Treating Physicians versus Expert Physicians in Each Healing Miracle from All Sources by Century of Canonization (N = 1,312)

	16th C.	17th C.	18th C.	19th C.	20th C.
Treating doctor (T)	0.27	0.83	1.1	1.3	1.4
Expert doctor (E)	0	0.01	0.05	0.7	0.7
Ratio E:T	0	1:83	1:22	1:2	1:2

practitioner was the first witness questioned.[19] In five extreme examples, a doctor appears to have been the only witness questioned; in those cases, possibly but improbably, the records of other witnesses may be missing.[20]

In second half of the seventeenth century, the evidence of treating physicians was amplified and corroborated by independent medical observers: at first in writing, then in person. These "experts" (*periti*) came from near the hometown and were engaged, much as I had been, to examine the records and attest to the current good health of the miraculé. In my collection, experts appear as early as 1606; frequently they had examined the miraculé on the day of the inquiry.[21] One of the first independent experts may have been Paolo Zacchia, who commented on several miracles for the causes of Lorenzo Giustiniani, Felice of Cantalice, and Pope Gregory X.[22]

Eventually the percentage of expert doctors in the files increased until it matched that of the attending physicians (tables 4.5 and 4.6). Some late twentieth-century files contain evidence from many more experts than attending doctors. Not surprisingly, the experts often disagreed with treating doctors and with each other, as will be shown below.

From the 1920s, at least twenty years before the creation of the Consulta Medica, names of expert Roman doctors recur in printed *Positiones*. They seem to have been selected on the basis of their specialties according to the characteristics of the miracle, and they usually studied the cases from their homes in or near Rome. Sometimes they traveled to participate in the investigations in person.[23] Until the late twentieth century, the experts were male.

TABLE 4.6. Average Number Treating Physicians versus Expert Physicians in Each Healing Miracle that Mentions Doctors by Century of Canonization from Complete ASV or Printed *Positiones* (N = 679)

	16th C.	17th C.	18th C.	19th C.	20th C.
Treating doctor (T)	1.57	1.69	2.34	2.1	1.4
Expert doctor (E)	0	0.01	0.11	1	1.2
Ratio E:T	0	1:169	1:21	1:2	1:1.7

Women Caregivers

Although the doctors were mostly male, the testimony of women caregivers appeared in these records from their inception. Female family members who traditionally attended the sick always gave evidence in every century. But at least seventeen midwives and more than fifteen unrelated nurses were mentioned in cases from as far back as the early seventeenth century. Midwives testified in person at least fifteen times from as early as 1606 to as late as 1971. The numbers parallel what is known from other historical information about physician-attended birth (table 4.7).[24] Around 1604, two midwives revived two different stillborn babies through invocation of Andrea Corsini. The events were described as resurrections rather than resuscitations. One midwife had baptized the infant in case it should die before the priest could attend; a surgeon also commented on the case.[25]

As early as the seventeenth century, midwives worked alone or with the doctors. Their opinions could be crucial to the testimony. Two midwives, Barbara Salvanna and Elisabeth Vilar, explained the danger of a transverse presentation in a 1618 delivery. This case lay in the archives for two centuries until it was reopened for further consideration in 1824. The later readers added medical commentary from well-respected, contemporary authors, such as Daniel Sennert and Friedrich Hoffman. Although the final observers were situated in the early nineteenth century, they accepted the obligation to reckon with the opinions of the midwives within the standards of their own time.[26] By the twentieth century, a midwife was never the sole caregiver witness.

The earliest case in which an unrelated hospital nurse gave testimony occurred in 1750. It was also the earliest iatrogenic miracle in the collection. Fleurie, a twenty-six-year-old pauper, was cured of a festering wound that had eroded through the muscles and tendons of her arm. Her nurse was adamant

TABLE 4.7. Attendants Cited in Obstetrical Miracles by Century of Canonization

	16th C.	17th C.	18th C.	19th C.	20th C.
No attendants	2	8	9	1	2[a]
Physician only		4	5	4	10
Midwife only		3	0	2	0
Both		2	2	1	2
Attended		9	7	7	12
Total	2	17	16	8	14
Percent attendants		53	44	88	86

[a]The invocations in these two cases were made in 1613 and 1853.

that its cause was a sloppy phlebotomy done by a careless physician. Adding to this grievous error, the doctor's bedside manner was appalling: he spoke in Latin, which Fleurie could not understand.[27] Another nurse played a prominent role in the 1921 testimony concerning the recovery of a twelve-year-old girl from iatrogenic tetanus.[28]

Women doctors begin to appear in the files in the early twentieth century: Dr. Matilde Voigt, born in 1886 with an M.D. degree from Heidelberg, testified as an expert on the 1920 healing of a three-year-old girl from rickets and mental retardation.[29] Notwithstanding the Church's long commitment to male authority, the gender of the caregivers did not seem to influence this process. It was their experience as witnesses and their expertise in science that was needed.

Doctors, Their Income, and Its Sources

Because all witnesses must give an account of their means, it is possible to find some doctors ready to admit that they were "well off,"[30] lived "decently,"[31] relied on "diverse incomes,"[32] or enjoyed "abundance and every comfort."[33] Others claimed more modest situations, being "neither rich nor poor" and maintaining families from the "proceeds of the profession."[34] But no doctors lived in want. Patients, however, as explained in chapter 2, sometimes claimed to be poor, especially in the early centuries. An appeal to religion during illness might provide a way of avoiding medical expenses; however, at least twenty-nine of thirty-eight people who were poor had consulted physicians, sometimes as many as six for a single illness.

Occasionally people refused to see a doctor out of allegiance to religion; they would declare that the cure came without medical help—*senza remedio dell'arte*.[35] But rarely did anyone claim to have been avoiding the cost of a doctor. I found only one such case: the 1606 testimony of a father concerning his infant son.[36] Two others admitted that they could not afford lavish journeys to spas recommended by doctors whom they had consulted.[37] It is impossible to imagine that many others did not do likewise; however, cases lacking medical evidence and corroboration seem not to have met the standard of credibility demanded by the Congregation procedures. By 1800, if a patient was cured without seeing a doctor, the story might be wonderful, but it stood little chance of investigation by the authorities.

Judging by their testimony, physicians attended rich and poor alike. One specific group of poor people regularly turned to medicine: clerics. A nun replied to the usual question: "I have taken a vow of poverty; consequently, I am poor."[38] Yet neither poverty nor religion deterred nuns or priests from consulting physicians. Using the entire collection including summaries, at least

155 of 254 clerics (61 percent) saw at least one doctor during illness, compared with at least 544 of 1065 (51 percent) of all others. The discrepancy increases when these calculations are limited to only those miracles for which we have full testimony: 87 of 109 clerics (80 percent) versus 257 of 403 others (64 percent). The higher percentage of physicians appearing in the record is owing to experts consulted after the cure. Convents and monasteries were steady consumers of medicine.

Doctors and Their Own Families as Miraculés

Sometimes, in addition to their roles as attendants or as experts, physicians appeared in a nonprofessional capacity as witnesses to healings in neighbors, family members, or themselves. Miracles worked in ailing doctors are special. The earliest in my collection was a surgeon who attributed his recovery from a lethal head wound to Francesca Romana.[39] Another surgeon credited Francis Xavier with the 1597 cure of his headache and eye disease; the 1622 record states that he had first consulted colleagues and tried to treat himself.[40] An "illustrious" physician, mentioned in chapter 1, attributed his 1655 cure to Caterina of Bologna; he lived at least nineteen more years to testify on another miracle in the same cause.[41] Similarly, for a different cause, a doctor was cured in 1699; a few years later, he testified on his own healing and yet another in his brother.[42]

The most recent examples of doctors as miraculés date from the 1980s. They include the 1981 cure of a sixty-two-year-old Brazilian of a sacral ulcer following coronary bypass surgery and ascribed to Gaspare Bertoni.[43] In 1984, a sixty-three-year-old physician-veterinarian recovered from lung disease following his invocation of the Spanish priest Enrique de Ossó y Cervelló.[44] And in 1989, a forty-nine-year-old Czech doctor survived cardiac arrest and deep coma following his physician-wife's appeal to the thirteenth-century Moravian mother Zdislava de Lemberk.[45]

Members of doctors' families were also present from the earliest times. Little Margaret, daughter of a physician, was a miraculée in the cause for Ramón de Penyafort, canonized in 1600.[46] Another example occurred in the 1816 story of Francesco, son of the Gaeta surgeon, told in the opening to this chapter. Perhaps owing to the medical disagreement, his case was not decisive; the final miracle in that cause was the healing of a breast tumor that opens chapter 2.

A medical family was particularly prominent in two Spanish miracles of 1928 and 1929, both attributed to the intercession of Vincenza Maria Lopez y Vicuña. Being offspring of sisters who had both married physicians, the two subjects were cousins, one a doctor. In 1928, the six-year-old cousin, Agnes, was cured of meningitis; testimony came from her medical father and a medical brother. The following year, her older cousin, the newly graduated doctor, Joseph, recovered from pulmonary tuberculosis. Initially, however, his own physician-father suspected that Joseph had contracted syphilis while he was away at medical school. The negative Wassermann test proclaimed the young man's virtue even as it eliminated the diagnosis of venereal disease.[47] The investigation of both cures was conducted concurrently in 1940, and Vicuña was beatified in 1950.

Doctor-Patient Relationships

Some physicians did not cultivate open communication with their patients. Normally hidden, the differences between thinking and saying would be exposed in an inquiry. In 1928, a French doctor admitted that he had lied about the diagnosis of a little girl to avoid frightening her parents; he told them that she had "scrofula" rather than rickets. The lie posed a problem in the claim of a miracle. It also emerged that the doctor believed that the girl's father was suffering from severe tuberculosis of the bone. Nevertheless, the man kept blaming his disability on a motor accident, and the doctor did not dissuade him. Adding to the woes of this poor family, the man's truck had been destroyed in a fire. The doctor's dissimulation stemmed from an honest effort not to make things worse, but it meant that the family members and the physician were speaking of different things.[48]

In 1929, an Italian doctor decided that the opposite course—truthfulness—was the best policy in preparation for sad losses. He warned the family that their baby boy would soon die of pneumonia; he promised to return for signing the death certificate. During the long illness, he had visited nearly every day, but one day he did not return. The family seemed to resent his absence, although the baby recovered during that night. As the father told it, the house was crowded with visitors, watching and waiting, and the mother was falling over with fatigue, but he urged her to join him in prayer to Pompilio Pirrotti. The next morning, the doctor was surprised to see the father in his shop and went in to express his condolences, thinking that the child must have died. "Don't you know anything, doctor?" exclaimed the annoyed father. He curtly explained that while the doctor stayed away, the baby had revived and sucked hungrily at the breast as he had not done for four whole days. In their testimony, the mother and an uncle rendered the doctors' work as "abandonment."[49] It is not known if this "well-off" doctor presented a bill.

Dismal doctor-patient relationships were exposed in the inquiry on the cure of Adele, an Italian-born nun living in a French convent. She suffered from recurrent ear infection that had spread to the bone, causing mastoiditis and meningitis. She was operated a first time in 1939, but when the condition recurred in 1941 and a second surgery was proposed, she hesitated. She preferred to go home to her village and "accept God's fate." The enraged doctor insisted that she come to his office, where he accused her of committing the sin of suicide should she ignore his recommendations. Even the nurse described his actions as "terrible." Adele signed herself out of hospital, and her community established a novena to Jeanne de Lestonnac, following which she soon recovered. But the story did not end there. Adele bravely returned to see the "terrible" surgeon and some of his colleagues, forcing them to acknowledge her recovery. No fewer than eleven doctors are mentioned in her file, five of whom testified. Adele was still alive and working at age seventy-two, thirty-nine years after her cure.[50]

Science in Medical Testimony

Conceptual Shifts

Up-to-date science is apparent in the doctors' words and actions, and in the ideas and technology on which they relied. Three areas reveal change through time of conceptual priorities: crisis, mensuration, and heredity. They are most obvious in the history-taking practices of physicians.

The concept of crisis as a method of natural healing goes back to Greek antiquity. A crisis entailed worsening symptoms: a peak in fever or increase in vomiting, diarrhea, and other evacuations, such as bleeding or draining of pus. Early modern physicians anticipated it as part of the physiological process in curing acute illness. One of the hallmarks of an unusual healing, for doctors who were familiar with the theory, occurred when a patient recovered in the *absence* of a crisis. Zacchia claimed that if a crisis took place, the healing could not be miraculous.[51]

In testimony from 1681 to 1939, at least eleven miracles entailed observations by physicians about the absence of a crisis: four in the sixteenth century, three in the eighteenth, three in the nineteenth, and one in 1939. The abrupt rise and slow fall of commentary on absent crises corresponds to the period in which physicians were beginning to question and reject the utility of the antique idea.

Heredity also has roots in ancient notions of disease and is indicated in language reflecting the constitutional makeup of a patient in terms of humors and susceptibilities. The word *temperament,* for example, occurs at least seventeen times in medical testimony from 1757 to as late as 1935.

By the late nineteenth century, and for a host of fascinating reasons, medical interest in heredity was reinvigorated with new degeneracy theories and the rise of genetics. It translated into special attention being devoted to familial antecedents: the health of parents, siblings, and other relatives. Deep questioning about the family history might provide possible explanations for the ailment. This practice is clearly visible in eleven instances of medical testimony from 1866 to 1935. The most recent case was that of a nun with meningitis; doctors emphasized her long-standing poor health and the strong family history of tuberculosis, and death certificates of her young sibs were included.[52]

Eventually a patient's own past became an important factor in present health. Like a form of personalized heredity, it was as if people were somehow descended from their own health experiences. Detailed medical questioning on the personal as well as the familial antecedents of the miraculés becomes increasingly evident after 1925.

Another conceptual and methodological change was the rise of measurement, or mensuration. As shown in chapter 2, people tended not to count their years or recall dates until the nineteenth century. Similarly doctors tended to provide qualitative, rather than quantitative, observations about their patients' health. For example, the pulse might be weak, rapid, or full, but actual counting of the beats per minute was rare until the late nineteenth century.

One of the earliest examples of mensuration came not from physicians, but from the 1847 testimony on a miracle of multiplication: careful calculations were given for the quantity of flour needed to make the requisite number of loaves.[53] In medical testimony, measurement of limb length and the angles of joints began in the second half of the nineteenth century. Records of the weight gain or loss appeared closer to 1900. Turning knowledge into numbers is also reflected in the gradual shift from use of the word *natural,* to express health, to *normal.* In my collection of miracles, the word *normal* appears by 1834 in an investigation from Italy that also heard the word *natural* from another witness.[54]

Technology in Diagnosis

Up-to-date science is also reflected in new technologies. They appear in the Vatican records soon after their invention because the treating doctors had used them or because experts criticized their lack. For example, testifying in 1819, the doctors involved with young Francesco of Gaeta, described above, had been using the modalities of percussion and tactile fremitus to explore the lad's chest problem. Similarly, the stethoscope, first publicized in that same year of 1819, appeared in these records in the diagnosis of an illness that began in 1832 and was cured in 1837: the doctor described a precordial lift and the sounds he heard by direct application of the ear.[55] Following this miracle, diagnosis of most heart or lung problems entailed auscultation as a matter of course. Indeed, in 1846, Joseph C. A. Récamier was invited to comment as an expert on findings in a young woman with pericarditis; he was a famous associate of the even more famous René Laennec, inventor of the stethoscope. In the same case, another doctor went into great detail about the heart sounds, producing a short primer on the relatively new topic, only to dismiss heart disease in this young woman. He offered an iatrogenic explanation for why it had been considered: the "redness of her cheeks" spoke of the "emotion" caused by the investigation. He ended by asking, "how can one expect a young girl to be subjected to so many consultations without blushing and without a few palpitations of the heart?"[56]

A thermometer may have been used in an Italian woman cured of postpartum fever in 1881;[57] temperatures were also recorded for people cured in 1892 and 1897.[58] Similarly, as tuberculosis waxed in importance throughout the nineteenth century, failure to demonstrate Koch's bacillus to confirm the diagnosis was a matter of concern by 1885, only three years after Robert Koch had discovered it.[59] Photographs appeared in files from 1899.[60] X-rays together with fluoroscopy appeared less than five years after Roentgen's famous demonstration of 1895;[61] an actual X-ray image taken in 1905 was included in a file from the following year.[62] Blood pressure measurements soon followed by 1917.[63] The aforementioned Wassermann test, elaborated from 1901 to 1906 to identify syphilis, appeared in its capacity as a "scientific fact" synonymous with venereal disease by 1928.[64] Similarly, the Widal test, developed in 1896 to facilitate diagnosis of typhoid fever, appeared in testimony from 1928.[65] EEG, invented in 1925, may have taken longer: it was used in two illnesses from 1965, although the delay is likely more apparent than real because complete files for this period are sealed (table 4.8).[66]

TABLE 4.8. A Few Diagnostic Procedures in the Miracle Files

	Introduced	No. of Yrs. to Cure	No. of Yrs. to Can.
Stethoscope	1819	11	48
Thermometer	1868	13	20
Koch's bacillus	1882	3	65
X-ray	1895	5	25
Fluoroscopy	1896	4	38
Blood pressure	1905	8	35
Wasserman test	1906	23	59

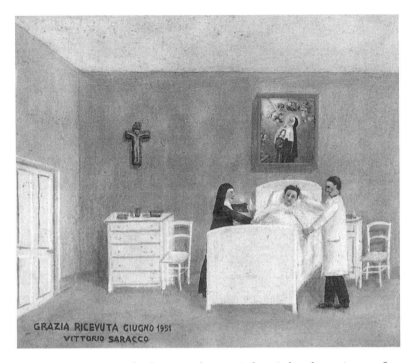

GRAZIA RICEVUTA GIUGNO 1951
VITTORIO SARACCO

FIGURE 4.3. A nun and a doctor tend a man in hospital under an image of
Santa Rita to whom he attributed his cure. Painted ex-voto, 1951, Monastery of
Santa Rita, Cascia. Carpentieri, *Per grazia ricevuta,* 1992.

In thinking of hospitals as technology, and in keeping with what we know
of their rise, it is perhaps significant that 90 percent of the miracles in which
hospitals are mentioned were worked during the twentieth century (figure 4.3).
Portions of hospital charts, such as nurses' notes, temperature graphs, and labo-
ratory reports, appear from 1906 forward.[67] This latter observation owes much
to the advent of technology for making copies.

Technology in Therapeutics

Evidence of "cutting-edge" science was not confined to diagnostics, but also
extended to therapeutics. Miraculously cured patients were treated with the
best modalities available, be it drugs or surgery.

Bleeding, in several different forms including phlebotomy, cupping, and
leeches, appeared frequently in testimony given from the early seventeenth
century to the early twentieth. Similarly, vesicants and blisters were used
until 1868, as were setons, which entail inserting a thread into the skin to

encourage draining. Magnetism was attempted in the mid-1840s for the nun with pericarditis examined by Récamier.[68] Electrical treatments, including the short-lived belts and batteries, appeared from 1900;[69] they continue in the use of cardioversion following arrest of the heart.[70] One patient had been managed with open heart massage in 1983.[71] Radiotherapy had been given to at least three miraculés from 1950 forward (figure 4.4).[72]

As for drugs, they, too, followed up-to-date standards of practice. Their arrival in these records replicates the history of medical therapeutics. Jesuit bark, or cinchona, appeared by the late seventeenth century, as discussed in chapter 3. Mercury was given to a *speziale* with a paralyzed arm in 1761.[73] Digitalis was prescribed for a young girl in 1825.[74] Insulin therapy was regular treatment for a woman with a gangrenous foot who had been diabetic since 1928.[75] Cortisone and ACTH hormones were used in a woman with hepatic coma in 1953.[76] Miracles were also discerned in people who had received new antimicrobial drugs: a nun given salvarsan in 1927;[77] a woman who took streptomycin in 1946;[78] a boy treated with sulfa in 1945;[79] and a baby girl and a nun, both of whom had taken penicillin in 1951.[80] Cytotoxic chemotherapy was administered in cases of malignancy from at least 1973 when a Brazilian nun was treated with "MOPP" chemotherapy for lymphoma; however, she attributed her cure to the intercession of Maria Theresia Gerhardinger.[81]

FIGURE 4.4. A man receives radiation therapy while he appeals to the Virgin. Anonymous painted ex-voto, 1955. Madonna del Monte, Cesena, Italy. Photo courtesy Scala/Art Resource, NY, ART339797.

In short, the length of time for a new technique to appear in these records had more to do with the time needed to generate the type of illness requiring that intervention than it did with any aversion to the use of novel treatments on the part of the religious patients and authorities. Table 4.9 gives a few more examples.

Doctors flaunted their scientific prowess by referring to future possibilities; some of these hypothetical interventions never did become practicable. An example from just prior to the advent of antibiotics illustrates this preoccupation with the future. In 1934, physicians reflected on their care of a little boy eight years earlier; he had been dying of disseminated tuberculosis complicated by a streptococcal infection. They regretted that the child's condition and the narrow time frame made it impossible to attempt preparation of a special vaccine to save his life.[82] Such a treatment never became standard practice for that disease.

As explained in the last chapter, avoiding recommended surgery was a continuing source of miracles: eighteen of the thirty-five such examples occurred prior to 1900. Conversely, only twelve of eighty-one cures associated with surgical treatment had occurred prior to 1846, the year of an important public demonstration of ether anesthesia. (See chapter 3, table 3.12.)

In contrast, sixty twentieth-century miracles were discerned in patients who had actually undergone a wide array of operations, including appendectomy, tonsillectomy, cholecystectomy, thyroidectomy, splenectomy, nephrectomy, hysterectomy, prostatectomy, lung resection, enterostomy, mastoidectomy, pyloroplasty, bone grafting, removal of adhesions, coronary bypass, and exploratory laparotomy. In chapter 3, the example of a Spanish engineer typified the scenario of a postoperative miracle. The most recent example displays the enormous

TABLE 4.9. A Few Therapeutic Procedures Mentioned in the Miracle Files

	Introduced	No. of Yrs. to Cure	No. of Yrs. to Can.
Cinchona	ca. 1650	ca. 28	62
Vaccination	ca. 1790	ca. 24	77
Chloroform	1847	19	41
Salvarsan	1910	17	24
Pneumothorax	1912	36	63
Radium	1921	17	29
Radiotherapy HV	1930	20	56
Sulfa	1937	8	47
Penicillin	1944	7	41
Coronary bypass	1968	13	21

complexity of these cases. An American Jesuit who suffered from glaucoma and polymyositis had undergone multiple operations in the 1980s, including coronary bypass, prostatectomy, and repair of a herniated disc; however, the miracle, attributed to the intercession of the French Jesuit Claude de la Colombière, was his cure, in 1990 at age seventy-six, of acute-on-chronic respiratory insufficiency with radiographic reversal of pulmonary fibrosis.[83]

These claims about the up-to-date medical knowledge are based on what I have merely happened to notice. Earlier uses of innovative technology and therapeutics may reside elsewhere in files that I have not examined. In a sense, then, these records can serve as a touchstone to the point of general acceptance of new technologies and treatments as standards of investigation and care.[84]

Physician Reactions: Honor, Defensiveness, and Disagreement

In their testimony, doctors displayed a wide range of reactions to the events. Some seemed honored to have been involved in the process; they waxed eloquent about themselves and the case. Sometimes, their own faith as devout Catholics meant that they had been moved by the brush with transcendence, and they were eager to testify. A doctor who gave evidence on three of seven miracles investigated in 1711 said that he had been consulted for yet another cause fourteen years earlier.[85] Two centuries later, in 1939, a physician explained that he appeared willingly and out of "no human sentiment, neither of love, nor fear, nor hope, nor lucre, nor any other human concern, but only for the greater glory of God and the glorification of the Blessed."[86] Typifying responses of the devout and reminiscent of Ambroise Paré, a physician replied to a nun's expression of gratitude in 1860 by saying, "It's not I who has cured you, but the Good Lord."[87]

Even less observant doctors entered into the process with solemn dignity. The physician of a small community might be the town's only secular professional, and his participation as an authority was his duty, if not his due. A summons to testify could be a declaration of his importance.[88]

Such expectations of local authority seem to be reflected in the doctors' role in endorsing cures. Not only were they obliged to testify on the diagnoses and treatments at an investigation, they were often summoned immediately after a healing by patients and their families to "witness" recoveries, long before the healing became the object of an investigation. Thus, in 1705 a physician worked through his own disbelief at a nun's sudden, unexpected cure from paralysis by having her walk up and down the choir of her church.[89] Similarly, two doctors and a surgeon who had labored long and hard for four months in

1775 to treat a twenty-year-old woman with fever and swollen abdomen were roused in the middle of the night to do nothing other than verify her complete recovery.[90] They might have wondered why it could not wait till morning; I wonder if they sent a bill.

Other doctors seem to have been deliberately or inadvertently left out of the loop. They expressed surprise at the summons to an inquiry because they did not realize that their patients had recovered or because they did not know that their patients credited divine powers instead of their own. For example, for five years ending in 1924, a doctor looked after an Italian nun with a tumor in her lower belly; he and others had recommended surgery, which she always refused. When he was called to treat her for an acute infection in her chest, he asked about her abdomen and discovered that the tumor had been cured miraculously some time earlier without his being told.[91]

Sometimes physicians appeared to be defensive about their actions and opinions. Testifying in 1908, a Corsican doctor justified his failure to order a bacteriological examination on the pleural effusion of a forty-nine-year-old nun three years earlier. He was forced to the abject admission that his diagnosis of tuberculosis had been merely "clinical." With the benefit of hindsight, the three expert colleagues refused to accept that the nun's ailment, though "grave," had been tuberculosis and, therefore, beyond a natural cure.[92] This disputed healing was not decisive for the cause; more evidence was needed. Consequently, a 1919 inquiry examined a cure of twenty years earlier in a nine-year-old Corsican girl. She had been thought to suffer from tubercular ascites; once again, the bacteriological examination had been neglected by the attending doctor who had considered, but rejected, a paracentesis. The "miraculée," said to be married and living in Marseilles, appears not to have testified.[93]

Similarly, in 1938, two Italian doctors of Liguria defended their failure to perform a lumbar puncture because, they argued, it would have been exquisitely painful and "purely academic" in a man who was obviously dying of meningitis. Given the patient's florid, clinical appearance, including positive Kernig and Bruzinski signs, the absence of a bacteriological proof was deemed more forgivable in this case than it had been in the previous. His recovery, unlike hers, became the final miracle in the canonization process of Maria Giuseppa Rossello in 1949.[94]

As these cases of tuberculosis demonstrate, the aggravated illness of a patient was often the reason that doctors offered for not having performed the best techniques of diagnosis and treatment. In other words, they were left claiming that the patient had been "too sick" to receive the newest procedures. Such omissions always opened the door to criticism, and experts rushed through. Some of these awkward moments seem ironic to us now because the neglect of certain investigations and treatments might be construed as harmless, even beneficial. Others, like the following examples, are baffling.

In 1758, a woman with the new diagnosis of heart polyp was judged too sick to be bled, although that was the recommended treatment.[95] In 1927, the treating physicians of a nun with tuberculous paralysis knew that they had erred badly in omitting the rituals of percussion and auscultation when examining her chest, and in failing to perform the Babinski maneuver on her feet, especially when she had displayed hyperreflexia and clonus. (Apologies to the general reader: those seemingly obscure words will signify flagrant errors to anyone who is medically qualified!)[96] Surgeons were left squirming in 1954 when they reported on opening a woman's belly in an exploratory laparotomy, only to close it again when they found widespread carcinoma originating in bowel and invading the ureters; in their haste, they had failed to take a biopsy to confirm the obvious diagnosis. The exercise struck them as "unnecessary"; never once did they imagine that she would recover.[97]

The defensiveness of treating physicians was especially apparent when a long time had elapsed between the illness and the inquiry. It was also evident when practitioners hailed from the countryside and the experts were urban academics. Did interpersonal rivalry feed suspicion about diagnostic and therapeutic skill? And did financial ramifications stem from having one's clinical acumen exposed and exploded in public view?

In 1834, a professorial witness retrospectively criticized his more humble colleague's use of bleeding some nineteen years earlier in the care of a fifty-year-old woman with fever. Perversely, the supposed medical error made the cure all the more remarkable in his expert (but anachronistic) eyes: not only had the woman recovered from her illness, she had also managed to survive her doctor's backward treatment.[98]

Urban-rural rivalry seems to have played a role in disagreements over an 1892 case from Switzerland. Doctors were severely divided over the diagnosis and cure of Justine, a twenty-five-year-old dressmaker. Her own physician was convinced that she had been suffering from tuberculosis for eight years, on the basis of listening to her with a stethoscope only twice. That this doctor was also a farmer probably made it all the more difficult to stand up to the horde of sophisticated experts from Paris, Geneva, and Lausanne. They alluded to the most recent science and hinted that the problem was actually hysteria. One of the critics spoke with confidence that resonates sadly today: "I believed that Justine was hysterical, not as a result of my careful examination of her chest, but from the general appearance (*coup d'oeil général*) and because in women, nervousness combined with anemia is almost always connected to some disease of the sexual organs." Justine herself complained of the arrogance of these consultants, one of whom bluntly told her, "*Poitrinaire* [weak in the chest] you were; *poitrinaire* you remain." Another evinced the opinion (now considered incorrect, as noted on page 75) that "all consumptives have no remedy but the grave." A younger consultant criticized the treating doctor's failure to order a culture for the tuberculosis germ; but in 1885 when she was cured, he himself had not begun practice nor was the test itself widely available, having been invented only three years previously. Notwithstanding the suspicion that Justine might be hysterical, all the medical witnesses acknowledged the physical asymmetry of her chest; strangely, however, they could not agree on which lung had collapsed, nor could they explain how hysteria had accomplished that feat. This raging dispute might have been resolved—or perhaps aggravated—had it taken place only three years later with the added benefit of X-rays.[99]

When experts decided that the treating physician had made a mistake, the entire miracle could collapse. Thus in 1892, a general practitioner of Louvain was challenged by professors over his diagnosis of paralysis owing to transverse myelitis (inflammation of the spinal cord) in a forty-one-year-old nun, herself a nurse and teacher. The four experts essentially ganged up on the G.P. by deciding that the good sister had been hysterical: her cure, like her disease, depended on the all-too-human power of suggestion. Ten years later, one of the experts in this case refused to budge from his original position; he offered the somewhat illogical reason that cures from transverse myelitis cannot occur by miracle, "because they are rare." Yet as the treating doctor argued with evident exasperation, none of the experts had examined his patient during her illness; he knew myelitis when he saw it, and she was not hysterical.[100]

Faulty logic was caught by the postulants in the cause of Maria Domenica Mazzarello. In 1937, an expert physician claimed (quite wrongly at the time) that X-ray-proven tuberculosis was "axiomatically fatal" in the face of any treatment, natural or supernatural. He pointed to the patient's 1926 recovery to insist that the treating physician's diagnosis of tuberculosis must have been wrong in the first place.[101] Apparently, his objections were rejected, because the beatification took place the following year.

Age could sometimes be a factor in medical disagreements. In 1902, two graduates of the Paris faculty, separated by more than fifty years, held widely diverging views on the same case. The eighty-six-year-old attending physician dismissed his thirty-three-year-old consultant's confident opinion that their patient, a thirty-year-old nun, was hysterical. The younger doctor admitted that he had not systematically looked for signs of hysteria; his evidence derived from the fact that her left-sided paralysis stubbornly refused to respond to his treatment of electrical stimulation. Indeed, he insisted, she had been most uncooperative and had "exaggerated" the pain of his therapy to such an extent that she had to be held down to receive it. He believed that she was deliberately mimicking an illness that she had observed a year earlier in a child. The octogenarian physician, who had attended the ailing nun for several months, testified that her illness was physical. He was not at all religious, he said, having spent several years of his youth estranged from the Church, and he had never given credence to miracles in the past. Nevertheless, he had encouraged the nun in her own idea to pray to her founder; he happily admitted that he could offer no scientific explanation for the recovery.[102] This case was not the final miracle in the process.

Inevitably, and without necessarily knowing what others had testified, doctors disagreed. Some would refuse to acknowledge that a miracle had occurred, because their therapies were effective and, in their opinions, miracles never happen. They fretted that cooperation made them appear to condone the process, and their replies would be guarded. Others were compelled to go out of their way to offer the truth as they saw it, even if it would displease the miraculé. They were especially defiant when they learned that their diagnoses or treatments had been attacked.

For example, in 1867, a Belgian physician, who was a practicing Catholic, wrote a long, eloquent analysis of the case of a married woman supposedly cured of Bright's disease of the kidney in the postpartum setting. Although not asked to do so specifically, his consultant had called her recovery a "miracle." But the treating physician claimed that he knew the case better, having seen the woman daily, and that the so-called cure of urinary protein loss was "hardly miraculous," as it had not completely resolved. "I regret," he wrote, "to find myself in contradiction with such an eminent authority, but I owe you the truth." His opponent retaliated with an affidavit signed by several professors of the Louvain faculty of medicine, who, having read the opponent's summary, deemed the case "extraordinary."[103] But it is not clear if any of the professors had examined the patient. The cause waited for another miracle.

Hysteria provided a special point of contention by the late nineteenth century, as was shown in several cases above and in chapter 3. Especially it was the expert doctors uninvolved with treatment who might suspect a patient of having been hysterical. This suspicion not only tilted toward accusing the patients of "faking" the disease and its cure, it also conveyed the embedded insinuation that the treating physician had made the wrong diagnosis. Aside from its religious significance, recognition of the miracle might have been professionally satisfying to a doctor because it affirmed the original diagnosis.

For example, in 1899, a controversy ensued over the diagnosis of a twenty-two-year-old Corsican woman who had been lame since age nine. The experts were convinced that she was "certainly neuropathic if not hysterical." But one of the treating doctors had been so impressed with the physical nature of her ailment that he had proposed surgery to fix it.[104] The Church authorities seem to have taken sides with the treating doctor because this case was the last of at least seven examined in the cause.

As noted in the examples above, when a clinical story was laden with medical controversy, it rarely became the final miracle in a process. Disagreement among the doctors was sufficient to weaken the case. The office of the devil's advocate relied heavily on the expert criticisms for arguments against the miracle. Except on rare occasions, more evidence would be needed for canonization to proceed.

When medically controversial miracles were the only ones in a successful cause, they were usually attached to the files of martyrs. To illustrate this point, take the example of the dubious testimony given in Quebec in 1930 concerning two separate healings from peritoneal tuberculosis in two Canadian nuns in 1926 and 1927, respectively. The sisters attributed their cures to the intercession of the French Jesuits martyred in Canada in 1649. In the first case, the treating doctor came to doubt his own original diagnosis, because he had not ordered an exploratory laparotomy and biopsy during the acute illness. In the second, the finding of anatomical sequelae suggested that the cure had not been "perfect."[105] But—following the rules for canonization—a martyr need not have worked a miracle to be canonized; if those healings were "soft," medically speaking, a certain indulgence could be allowed.

Doctors Avoiding the Inquiry

Occasionally, doctors were suspicious or resentful, not only of each other but of the entire process. They responded with condescension, impatience, and undisguised irritation. Hopeful postulants and the miraculés may have worried about what the men of science would say, or if they would show up.

A guarded reaction was expressed by a doctor whom I was astonished to recognize in these files, because a painting of him performing surgery already adorned the cover of one of my books. Dr. William Hingston of Montreal testified as an expert in 1902 on the 1890 cure of a twenty-five-year-old nun from rectal bleeding and anemia. With evident irritation, he responded to the questions: "I know nothing at all of [the patient's] illness nor of that which is called her cure. I can only repeat that her present condition is healthy."[106]

No such irritation colors the responses of a doctor to a summons in 1910, but the cooperation was demanding of time and effort. He supplied a certificate, testified in person, received special questions, answered in writing, received still more questions, and replied in writing again.[107] The delicacy in obtaining medical commentary is evident again in 1867: an American surgeon responded guardedly, saying that he had not seen the miraculée in question for several years and that she had not followed his advice; his experience and attitude may have been known to the priest who had doubted that he would even agree to testify.[108]

In 1891, an English man, cured of leg ulcers seven years earlier, told the tribunal not to bother summoning his own doctor, "For he is an unbeliever in miracles," and it would be "useless to appeal to him."[109] Perhaps because the case was in a cause for martyrs, the authorities seem not to have insisted; however, the canonization did not take place until 1970. Two physician brothers in Normandy were hard pressed to respond to the summons in 1917: one had been called up to war, while the other usually saw more than sixty patients daily and thought that he should not be expected to recall details about the bizarre case of a young woman who maintained that her chronic headache had been cured by the miraculous closure of her fontanel—at age eighteen.[110]

As members of a scientific tradition that had been defined in opposition to the concept of "sacred" diseases, physicians may have doubted the wisdom of responding to a summons to testify. In the last two hundred years, some must have declined, but if doctors absolutely refused to cooperate, then the would-be miracle could not proceed and is not to be found in these records. Postulants whom I have interviewed indicate that these refusals happen, but I am unable to estimate their frequency. Postulants also explain that miracles from developing nations are more difficult to put forward because those countries lack facilities for documentation and up-to-date medical care. Indeed, African saints have been canonized on the basis of miracles worked in Europe. Doctors enjoy a great deal of power over these proceedings.

Even within the extant files, a few doctors ignored the initial summons and left testimony to others. Many replied only in writing. For example, a doctor refused to testify in 1907 on the healing of a woman's knee from traumatic synovitis two years earlier; he sent a certificate instead.[111] In 1918, a doctor wrote to explain his refusal to testify on the death of a child miraculée, because he had already said all that he could at an earlier process in 1902.[112] He wished to alter nothing twenty-two years after her cure and seventeen years after her death. In 1931, another doctor did not appear as a witness, although he was said to have prematurely completed the death certificate of a seven-year-old boy who recovered from typhoid fever in 1927; he, too, sent a written statement.[113]

A certificate could help when distance or death, rather than unwillingness, prevented the doctor from appearing in person. A surgeon who seems to have been cooperating with the process provided a certificate describing a conversation that told a tale on himself. When his patient claimed that she had been miraculously cured of the fistula that he had treated surgically, he replied that "there's no miracle if there's a scar." Smiling, she invited him to look, but he found no scar.[114]

Offering a written certificate also provided a polite way to avoid what the medic might anticipate as an uncomfortable confrontation. For example, in 1946, a surgeon sent a statement about an Irish nun whom he had treated with what he considered effective surgery three years earlier. He recalled the case but would not comment on her cure. Although he did not ask in so many words, he clearly wondered, how can a woman, treated surgically with a bone graft, have been cured by a saint?[115]

Occasionally, a repeat request from the inquiry brought a response, even an apology and an explanation. Thus a Brussels radiologist, pleading overwork, apologized in 1905 for his original refusal to comment on a watchmaker's recovery from a leg injury of the previous year. Nevertheless, he dismissed the case as a charade, contending that the first X-ray revealed no bony lesion; consequently, the second, which was also normal, could not reveal a cure.[116] Did he relent and reply because the refusal might jeopardize his standing? His negative opinion meant that the postulants had to go trolling for another miracle, which, eventually, they found in the Netherlands.[117]

Dead Doctors and History

Often, as in the 1834 example of bleeding used above, standards of diagnosis and care had changed in the interval between the cure and the testimony. On at least seventeen occasions, ranging from one to twenty-nine years after the cures, treating physicians had died before the inquiry took place. An early example of this difficulty is found in testimony given in 1796 on the 1778 cure of a woman with an abscess; only one doctor testified, because three of the four treating physicians had died.[118] Another doctor had died before 1822 when testimony was given on the 1810 cure of his patient.[119] Two other doctors, involved in two different cures in the cause of Bernadette Soubirous of Lourdes, had died by the time of the testimony less than three years later.[120]

As a result of physician deaths, medical witnesses would find themselves retrospectively justifying or criticizing courses of action taken by others in a remote past. In this situation, a sense of history was essential to fully contextualize the medical analysis; the intent was to show that the correct decisions had been made *at the time* of the cure.

These historically sensitive judgments seem to become more frequent. I have found at least thirty examples, almost all from the twentieth century. For example, in 1901, a treating physician justified his 1889 diagnosis of a case of paralysis by saying that it had been investigated "without all the rigor on which we are accustomed to insist today."[121] In 1921, a seventy-three-year-old teaching nun looked back on her cure in 1881 of what was thought to have been pulmonary tuberculosis, saying that "the thermometer did not exist."[122] A fifty-year lag, between a cure in 1937 and testimony in 1987, resulted in a number of delicate historical judgments.[123] Similar problems arose with the sixty-eight-year lag, between the 1922 cure of a stomach ailment in a woman, who died in 1957, and the 1990 testimony on her case.[124] In the cause for Mary MacKillop, an Australian woman recovered from leukemia in 1962; commenting a full decade later, an official said, "Today, the treatment administered ten years ago would be considered inadequate."[125]

Unlike the doctor who criticized bleeding in 1834, or the young consultant who decried the absence of a tuberculosis culture in 1885, these observers made allowances for changes in medical practice. For example, medical witnesses calmly situated in the antibiotic era look back on fevers cured prior to penicillin and mollify their opinions of management that would now be considered negligent. It is not clear why. Do these historically sensitive judgments represent a heightened sophistication in the witnesses? It is probably too much to hope that they reveal an effect of the rise of medical history as a professional discipline. Do they simply reflect the increasingly rapid change in practice, together with health-care professionals' greater awareness of it? Or, more plausibly, could it be that this apparent rise in historical sensitivity is merely a reflection of religious indulgence and of the general willingness to see more saints recognized in our time? I have no answers. These questions are for others to consider.

Doctors and Their Religious Faith

The inquiries explored the religious faith of all witnesses; doctors were not excused from responding. The earliest records insisted on detail, not only on faith but also on the frequency and nature of devotions. Because most miracles until the twentieth century were worked in the European countries of Italy, France, and Spain, it is scarcely surprising that most attending doctors professed to be observant Roman Catholics who regularly attended Mass and confession. In one exceptional case, two witnesses were student priests in a Jesuit seminary having been doctors in their secular lives.[126]

But most doctors are not and have never been known for religious fervor. Some admitted that they kept Easter only and were otherwise negligent. Once or twice they confessed to shirking Easter rites as well; yet the testimony

proceeded.[127] Two doctors even acknowledged that they had been excommunicated in the past. One had hit a cleric in a rowdy game, but by 1758, he had been
pardoned.[128] The other was a repeat offender who, by 1847, had thrice been
excommunicated for dissecting unclaimed bodies.[129] Even then, it seemed that
laxity in Christian duty did not disqualify those physicians as witnesses.

The questions about faith became all the more pressing as the canonization process extended to nations on other continents. Sometimes only Protestant doctors could be found to testify, but they, at least, would swear on the
Bible. In 1997, much media attention was focused on Dr. Ronald Kleinman,
a Jewish attending physician who went from Harvard to Rome to testify about
a girl's recovery from a drug overdose attributed to the intercession of Catholic convert Edith Stein.[130] But, as has been shown, Jewish physicians have
long been involved in these cases, even in medieval times.[131] In the sixteenth
century, two of the three doctors who examined the corpse of Diego d'Alcalá
were "Hebrews."[132] Summaries of causes from Lebanon include names that
suggest some physicians might have been Muslim, but the original files are
still sealed.[133] In recent cases, some doctors openly profess no religion and
"affirm" their statements according to "personal criteria."[134] The investigations
proceed.

The earliest example that I have found of actual testimony from Jewish doctors was from Memphis, Tennessee, in 1917. Doctors B. Herman and
Alphonse Meyer had been the only physicians treating a nun in 1913, when
she inexplicably recovered from several life-threatening conditions. At the
inquiry four years later, the oath to tell the truth and keep the proceedings a
secret posed a problem. Aware that a precedent might be established, the clerical scribe wrote, "Dr. Meyer, being a Jew, objected to making an oath on the
Gospels and was allowed to swear on the Old Testament. He made the oath
kneeling, with his hand on the Old Testament." The doctor's exact words were
carefully copied into the record. For his part, Dr. Herman was unable to appear
because of his own illness, for which he was residing in a warmer climate. But
he sent a letter describing the case, in which he wrote, "I had not entertained
the slightest hope of her recovery, and I must admit that this was in mw [sic]
opinion simply miraculous." He closed by expressing his "deepest regards."[135]
Neither Jew seemed to be offended by the request of his patient and her entourage to account for his medical actions; nor was he troubled by a happy outcome for which he took no credit.

Clearly it has always been more important that the attending doctor give a
"scientific" account than that he be a devotee of the faith that had generated the
process. Herman volunteered his opinion that the recovery was "miraculous,"
but doctors were never required to make that judgment; they were invited to

explain the cure with science. When they could not, a miracle was not established, but it might be possible.

Diagnosing Miracles: Speed Is of the Essence

From the foregoing, it is clear that medicine, science, and doctors are key to the
Vatican's process of investigating miracles (figure 4.5). When asked to define
a miracle, doctors usually replied that it was an event "beyond the bounds of
nature" or "exceeding expectations." Together with many uneducated people,
some physicians admitted that they did not know how to define a miracle,
nor could they easily distinguish between a miracle and an act of grace.[136] But
the process never requires doctors to detect miracles. Instead, it asks them to
explain the events scientifically. When such an explanation can be found, it
will end the process by a form of falsification.[137] Consequently, doctors serve as
essential witnesses from science—the polar opposite of religion.

By early twentieth century, the gold standard of a miracle cure entrenched
three specific characteristics often recurring in the reports of the Consulta
Medica: the healing must be complete, durable, and instantaneous. These three
words enter into the conclusions of the final reports like a form of liturgical
chant. Minor deviation from each of the three was tolerated.

Cures could be "complete" even if scars or deformities remained. "Durable"
could accommodate the startling possibility that the patient in whom the miracle had been worked might already be dead by the time the investigation took
place. In those situations, discussed in chapter 2, the onus was on the inquiry to
establish that death resulted from another disease; consequently, new medical
witnesses would be summoned. "Instantaneous" healings were interpreted to
be unusually rapid. It was in this last area that doctors were most comfortable
pronouncing on the "extraordinary" nature of cures.

The speed at which patients recovered occasioned many comments of
astonishment. When asked if such a cure might have taken place naturally, the
doctor would reply, "Perhaps, but not so quickly." More than a hundred examples
can be found. A few cases exemplify the workings of this comfort zone for
physicians. In 1797, a Roman doctor emphasized the rapidity of healing in the
1786 cure of an arthritic knee in a five-year-old boy.[138] In 1877, a French doctor
was presented with a cure of a ten-year-old boy from a serious lung ailment,
possibly tuberculosis; at least, he said, there could be no doubt that a very sick
child had recovered. As far as he could tell, three causes might explain it: a
supernatural intervention, a medication, or nature. The drugs had been ineffec-
tive; nature might possibly produce a cure, but not in such a short time. Having

FIGURE 4.5. Two doctors treat four-year-old Marius Tassy for a deep abdominal wound sustained when he fell on a bottle. His mother appeals successfully to the Virgin. Ex-voto painted by deaf-mute Eusèbe Nicolas, 1875, Chapel of Le Beausset Vieux. Cousin, *La vie au village*, 2006.

eliminated two possibilities, he continued, "It is not for me to decide if the healing was a miracle"; however, his reasoning left only one explanation for those who would decide.[139] In 1908, the rapidity of a nun's recovery from tuberculosis was one point of agreement between skeptical doctors: some saw it as evidence of a miracle; others used it to reassess the original diagnosis, believing tuberculosis was always incurable.[140] The most recent example of speed of healing was found in the previously cited 1989 cure of a physician attributed to Zdislava de Lemberk.[141]

Similarly, in 1939, a doctor reasoned his way through the inexplicable healing of a nun from an obscure condition that might have been inflammatory or malignant. He said, "Had her problem been a simple inflammation of the pelvis involving microbes and lymphatics, it could heal naturally, whether there was a tumor or not, but what is not easily explained from the medical point of view is the immediacy [*instantaneità*] of her cure."[142]

Gradually, I began to understand that the process cannot normally proceed without the testimony of a physician. The doctor need not believe in miracles; the doctor need not be Roman Catholic, or even a Christian. But the doctor has to fill two absolutely essential roles.

The first role is to declare the hopeless prognosis even with the best of the art. Without best treatment, the process cannot know if the cure might have taken place by nature or medical intervention. As for the dire prognosis, Catholic tradition itself subtends this task: it obliges physicians to announce impending death by telling the family to summon the priest. This rigorous duty is built into the drama of every final illness. Many miracle healings occurred in people who had already received the last rites. No doctor—religious or atheist—takes that decision lightly; nor can it be taken in private. As a result, it becomes a public admission of medical failure, available for corroboration in a distant future. Its credibility resides on trust in the physician's acumen: the diagnosis and prognosis must have been correct; the learning and experience, solid. Treating physicians who happened to be academics held great sway over the proceedings, because their expertise was not in doubt. A doctor is a good witness, not for being a good Catholic, or a believer in miracles, but for being demonstrably skilled in medical science.

The second role, which is equally if not more important to the recognition of a miracle, is to express surprise at the outcome. And here's the rub—although the doctors must have used the best scientific medicine available, they can take no credit for the cure. A religious miracle defies explanation by science. Traditionally arrogant, medicine must confess its ignorance. In so many different languages and more than a hundred cases, the treating physicians, one after another, proclaimed their wonder at the recovery of their patients: *sorpresa, meraviglia, merveille, surpris, stupefait, incredulo, con stupore, obstupescentibus,* amazed.

Urged on by patients and by postulants, Church authorities nevertheless withhold declaration of their own surprise until they have heard from the doctors. For the canonization process, miracles occur when the patient recovers from certain death or permanent disability following excellent, up-to-date medical care, which the doctor claims had nothing to do with the cure. To turn a familiar phrase on its head, the doctor must say, "The operation was a failure, but the patient lived." And only the doctor can say it. Therefore, the Vatican prepares to define and "diagnose" a miracle when the doctor is surprised.

5

The Cure as Drama

*Gestures of Invocation and
the Context of Healing*

The doctors refused to give any more treatment, saying that the infant's death was only moments away. After three weeks of excruciating dysentery, tiny Berengarius had grown progressively pale, weak, and flaccid; some said he was already dead. In desperation, his mother picked him up and ran to the nearby church, where she gently laid his lifeless, little body on the ancient tomb. Then she fell on her knees, sobbing and praying fervently to the spirit of the man inside, asking him to intercede with God to spare the child's life. Anxious neighbors and family slowly gathered too; some mumbling softly, some simply watching. An hour or two later, the baby began to stir, his fever gone, his color improved, and all gave joyful thanks with words and offerings.

Llot, *Laudabili . . . Raymundi Penia Forti,* 1595, 97.

This resuscitation from fourteenth-century Barcelona was cited in the 1600 canonization process of Ramón of Penyafort. Over the centuries, many desperate parents have placed their dying children on cold, stone tombs. The practice may have been borrowed from shrines to ancient heroes, the Virgin, and established saints.[1] The actual number is unknown, but it must be very large indeed, because in this collection alone, from 1588 to 1986, at least twenty families witnessed an astonishing recovery under similar circumstances.

Gestures of appeal to divine help are just one of many modalities that people employ for relief of suffering. Often they begin at the onset of illness and continue throughout in tandem with the efforts of physicians. The plurality of these practices has been explored for medieval and early modern times;[2] however, the canonization files of the modern era imply that it is timeless and universal. Appeals for divine intervention are not the only sources of comfort, but they are all that remains when the doctors give up. The vast majority of people who turn to religion have also consulted medicine, and they do both simultaneously. In the previous two chapters, the medical aspects of the healings were explored; in this chapter, we turn to the religious gestures of invocation and experience of healing. For the miraculées, these actions are embedded in the stories of recovery told to friends and family long before they are told to the inquiries. In narrative resides the social and spiritual drama of every miracle.[3]

Invocation

Invocation establishes a connection between the venerated one, who is already dead, and a sick human being, who is still alive, if only barely. Recall that according to the religious tenets, only God can work miracles. Invoking the spirits of not-yet-saints by prayer and other gestures is to invite them to intercede with God. The success of an appeal can become a sign that the saint must be with God. Simple prayer is all that is necessary, but it is usually accompanied by other actions or rituals. Nevertheless, in some settings, especially emergencies, a prayer is all that can transpire.

Emergency Invocations

In a crisis, no additional gestures are possible. Thus, in 1596, a nineteen-year-old farmer called out to Ramón of Penyafort when he saw his friend suddenly buried under a pile of earth.[4] Similarly, a father and two sons were spared injury, in 1644, having invoked Tomás de Villanueva just as the house they were building collapsed around them.[5] In 1611, ten-year-old Francesco cried the name of Alessandro Sauli from the well in which he had fallen, and was saved.[6] Not long after, a mother appealed to François de Sales when her little girl tumbled into the rushing Thioux River at Annecy.[7] In 1647, Maria Maddalena de'Pazzi was called by a fifteen-year-old lad who had slipped from his small boat into the sea;[8] and, in 1661, she was said to have prevented two ships colliding on a foggy night.[9] In 1662, a seven-year-old boy, also on the point of drowning, prayed to Pasqual Baylón.[10] In 1702, two young fishermen, caught in a flash flood of the River Orba, prayed to Pope Pius V, as described in chapter 3.[11] A man riding across the river near Spoleto was thrown in the water when his horse was startled by a bull; he cried out to Chiara of Montefalco and the torrent slowed, allowing him to climb out, weak and vomiting but alive.[12] Two saints were summoned to rein in stampeding mules: once in a remote past to save an entire crowd;[13] once, in 1669, to save a three-year-old boy.[14] At least four saints were engaged successfully to fight blazing fires.[15]

Another emergency miracle, in which the miraculé and all others were oblivious of the inadvertent appeal, was the 1683 story of a thirty-five-year-old Italian *capitano* from Civita Capellana, just north of Rome. While on an after-dinner stroll in the piazza with three companions, he was seized with the mundane urge to blow his nose and raised his right arm. In that instant and without warning, he was shot by another man standing just thirteen paces away and wielding an arquebus. Hearing the "huge explosion like fireworks," a crowd came running to carry the bleeding capitano to his home and summon the surgeon. The shot had passed through his right elbow and into the middle chest; everyone feared for his life. Gingerly, the surgeon probed the chest wound, finding it more superficial than expected. In the bottom lay a small religious medal of "bone and crystal," with an "Agnus Dei on one side and Pope Pius V on the other." Long accustomed to wearing the medal around his neck, the capitano had forgotten it was there; lucky for him, it had stopped the shot, and equally strange, it did not break. Testimony on this memorable tale came twenty-one-years later from many eyewitnesses, including the surgeon, two friends, and the capitano himself. Everyone mentioned the nose blowing, the medal, the arquebus, and the ignominious shooter. The last, however, did not testify, and the reason for discharging his weapon in such a public place was never disclosed. The miracle was ascribed to Pope Pius V.[16]

Stories of emergency invocations, like the ones described above, were included in summaries published at the time of canonization; however, they seem to decline in frequency and authority. Only one spontaneous appeal ever formed the final miracle in its cause (for beatification); it was also the most recent: the 1940 prayer of a mountaineer to Marguerite Bays mentioned in chapter 3.[17] The remainder of emergency appeals were included in larger collections dominated by the much more frequent miracles of healing.

Other Invocations

The depositions make it clear that the prayer had to be especially sincere and given with value-added devotion, whether in a crisis or not. Not just any prayer would do; quality counted, too, as if the hoped-for favor relies on the prior miracle of faith. Attention was given to the setting. Supplicants would arrange themselves in a special manner, most often on their knees in chapels or bedrooms,

prostrate;[18] supine,[19] or standing by open windows.[20] Words emphasizing passion and intensity recur: the prayer was given with "tears," "fervor," "great faith,"
"deep devotion," and "heart"—especially when the invocation was offered on
behalf of someone else, such as a mother for her child or a husband for his wife.
Several miracles in the collection for Pasqual Baylón emphasize the power of
prayers charged with the energy of maternal tenderness, weeping, and sighs.[21]
In May 1930, a mother who had already lost two children kept a waking vigil by
her four-year-old son writhing in abdominal pain; exhausted and fully clothed,
she lay down beside him, continuing her invocation and unwilling to "allow
herself to be conquered by sleep." When the boy fell asleep, she panicked and
needed reassurance that he was not dead.[22]

The generally understood requirement for powerful prayer may have inhib-
ited simple folk who felt incapable of the necessary elegance, erudition, and
faith to formulate an articulate and convincing plea. For example, in 1881, Anna,
a poor fishmonger of Lucca, was dying of fever, possibly typhoid, having just
given birth to her *seventh* child. Urged by her priest to appeal to the *Seven*
Founders, she believed herself unworthy of making such a request. But the
priest told her to pray "not with words but with her heart."[23] This same inhib-
ition was compounded many-fold for those miraculés and their attendants,
who, like Anna the fishmonger, later admitted that they had never heard of the
prospective saint until someone else suggested an appeal.[24]

Religious observers and family members played an important role in
steering the supplicants to potential saints. The choices were often a result of
circumstance rather than a long-standing conviction about the sanctity of the
prospective saint. The hiker mentioned in chapter 2 would never have selected
Roberto Bellarmino had not he fallen gravely ill near a Jesuit sanctuary.[25] The
father mentioned in chapter 3, who blamed the doctor for omitting a house call,
was inspired to pray to Pompilio Pirrotti by his own brother and sister; he
offered a gold watch, his only valuable possession.[26] Similarly, a fourteen-year-
old boy with chronic osteomyelitis of the hip was sent to visit an aunt in Turin
for a cheerful distraction. She urged him to pray to Giuseppe Cafasso. The lad
did so out of obedience, but he was miserably homesick and his heart was not
in it. Once he was back home, he and his poor widowed mother continued the
nightly appeals that had been stimulated by the visit to Turin.[27]

Prayers sometimes came with a bargain or promise to be kept, should the
favor be granted: hopeful miraculés would offer a Mass, a votive, or a pilgrimage. Keeping the promise would entail some trouble, financial contribution,
and public display. These arrangements seem to subscribe to vogue of time and
place. In invocations made between 1601 and 1605, five different people promised Masses to Andrea Corsini.[28] One of these and three others promised silver

votives of eyes and hearts to be left near his tomb.[29] Yet another in 1789 invoked Giovanni Giuseppe della Cruce (Calosinto) with the promise of a silver lamp.[30] In the early seventeenth century, a man prayed to Girolamo Miani on behalf of his sister-in-law who lay dying in obstructed labor; he promised a costly gift should her life be spared.[31] Six people vowed to make pilgrimages to saints' tombs. One of these occurred in 1645 in the Florentine convent where Maria Maddalena de'Pazzi had been buried four decades earlier; a nun promised a year of nightly visits to the tomb should her mental affliction be relieved.[32] The most recent of these promises to visit a tomb after a cure was made in the 1890s.[33] Several parents vowed to give their children to religion should they be allowed to live.[34]

Testimony on this type of invocation always includes evidence that the promises were kept, sealing the deal, and closing the circle of the story. Failure to do so could be disastrous. In 1702, a Spaniard suffered from severe headache and fever; in his invocation, he promised a special act of devotion. After his recovery, he failed to perform the act and was punished with a relapse. When he eventually fulfilled the promise, he enjoyed another return to health.[35] In the same cause, a nun rejoicing over her recovery rushed out without her veil; for this transgression she was punished with a relapse, the cure of which formed another miracle.[36]

Taunts were occasionally incorporated in the bargaining prayers for intercession. Tossed off as challenges, they hint at a jocular cheekiness and familiarity that could scarcely be imagined in a conversation with God. Perhaps they were intended to irritate the saints and provoke them to action as proof of their sanctity. In 1587, a Milanese nobleman prayed on his knees to the recently deceased Carlo Borromeo, saying, "If you are a saint in the city, please heal my leg."[37] In 1771, Elena, a sixty-six-year-old midwife who claimed kinship with the recently deceased candidate for sainthood begged him to help a woman in obstructed labor with a transverse lie; she draped her uncle's scapular over the tumid belly and said, "O my uncle who never did anything for me during your life, at least do me some good after your death; help us."[38] In Sardinia in 1853, the lame girl Francesca was healed enough to walk with a limp; like a dissatisfied customer, her mother returned to the tomb with "lively faith" to request a perfect cure, which was granted.[39] In 1866, a woman with severely infected eczema invoked Francis Xavier Maria Bianchi, saying, "I won't call you a saint, if you do not heal my leg."[40] In the same year in the United States, a young woman made a plea with a similar taunt: "If it is true that you can work miracles, I wish you would do something for me. If not, I will not believe in you."[41] In 1899, a woman with sores on her club foot was directed to Alessandro Sauli by her confessor, who said, "Now here's a saint who needs a miracle in order to be canonized;

I thought of you."[42] Surely, between two needy individuals a mutually beneficial outcome could be arranged. And in 1929, parents prayed to Pompilio Pirrotti on behalf of their infant son saying, "If you are a saint, grant this request."[43]

On a few occasions, supplicants seemed to have been inviting saints and would-be saints to a contest. In 1602, a nun was cured after appealing to Carlo Borromeo, but she had already tried the recently canonized saints Jacek Odrowaz (Hyacinthe) and Ramón of Penyafort. Carlo's success where they had failed strengthened the argument for equal, if not greater, recognition.[44] In 1899, a forty-two-year-old Canadian member of the Christian Brothers with a penchant for purple prose described his long search for a cure: "Because St. Joseph refused to heal me, I turned to his august spouse the very holy Virgin." He also applied to Jesus "the Sacred Heart and the Precious Blood," but all these appeals ended in "failure." Then on the feast day of his founder Jean-Baptiste de la Salle, the brother dragged himself to the chapel altar, his "swollen legs" covered in painful sores "oozing pus," and said, "You could heal me if you wish." Then suddenly, "after Mass, I heard a voice say 'Get up and walk,' and under the empire of gentle force, I left my crutches, rose with my brothers—with them and like them—I genuflected, and with a fairly steady gait, returned to my place." Several faces "glistened with tears."[45]

Invocations beyond Prayer

Prayer has always been the basis of every invocation, and it is used throughout the Christian world. But prayer *alone* is one of the least frequently reported forms of appeal in the files for canonization. Except in emergencies, as described above, other gestures are added to incorporate rituals of behavior and formalized use of objects. Concentrating on the correct performance of these acts provides an opportunity for self-help when all other avenues have been exhausted. Like the careful taking of medicine or the following of a strict diet, rituals of invocation are said to provide patients, families, and friends "something to do," even in hopeless situations when nothing else can be done.[46] Furthermore, unlike a simple, solitary prayer, the ritualized gestures could be witnessed, timed, and documented for future evidence. The modifications of Urban VIII had emphasized the demand for corroboration; as a result, the canonization process itself encouraged the extension of private prayers into public and participatory acts. Since the mid-seventeenth century, the process seems to have preferred invocations that are fleshy, sensual, and tangible: gestures that are visible to others.[47] First among the documentable gestures adopted by the faithful was prayer near the body of the dead saint.

Invocations at the Tomb

In its earliest form, touching or kissing the actual corpse of the saint established a connection, as if a direct body contact would arouse a saint's attention. Ancient hagiographies show that pilgrimages to burial sites were well established prior to Christianity itself. Invocations at the tombs of prospective saints flourished before and following the procedures laid down in the late 1580s; they constituted the single most frequent gesture of appeal for three hundred years and were not displaced until after 1900[48] (figure 5.1).

An example comes from the process for the first saint canonized within the Tridentine reforms, although the practice began long before. The final resting place of the illiterate Franciscan, Diego d'Alcalá, was a well-recognized site of pilgrimage following his death in 1463. The corpse had emitted a sweet odor and did not decay; many people came to seek his intercession through contact with these remains. For the process, authorities were presented with evidence consisting of "duly sworn testimony" in which Diego had been invoked through his body to cure 130 people and one costly mule.[49] Some pilgrims called him "Doctor Diego."[50] As noted in chapter 1, among the earliest miraculés was King Henry IV of Castile and his small daughter.[51] For royalty and the wealthy, severe infirmity posed no obstacle to a journey or an expensive gift. Thus in May 1555, the young noblewoman Donna Maria, who had suffered for a year from an "atrocious illness" of paralysis and seizures, was carried on her bed to Diego's corpse accompanied by her parents and companions. She heard him say, "Arise, Maria, and come with me," and, to the astonishment of her doctors and everyone else, she was suddenly healed. No fewer than eighty witnesses testified in her case.[52]

The fame of Diego's incorrupt body spread further. In 1562, seventeen-year-old Prince Carlos of Spain, son of Philip II and grandson of Holy Roman Emperor Charles V, tripped on a staircase, hit his head, and slipped into a coma. The "useless" doctors judged the boy too sick to be moved. His royal father had Diego's one-hundred-year-old corpse conveyed from the chapel to the sickroom, where the lad recovered in "the briefest of moments." The following year, Philip II used his considerable influence to press for the canonization out of gratitude and in a shrewd attempt to mend fences: a rift with the church had opened in 1527 when his own father, Charles V, had allowed his troops to sack Rome.[53] In 1588, Diego became the first saint canonized under the rules set down that very year. The miracles described above and many more formed part of the process.

In the cause of Ramón of Penyafort, whose trial Ditchfield called the "first mature expression" under the new rules, at least three miracles took place at the

FIGURE 5.1. Pilgrims pray for healing at the tomb of St. Sebastian, by Josse Lieferinxe, circa 1497, Galleria Nazionale d'Arte Antica, Palazzo Barberini, Rome. Photo courtesy Nimatallah/Art Resource, NY ART16074.

tomb, including the one that opens this chapter; another miraculé visited the tomb in thanks.[54]

For certain saints, the majority of miracles cited in the cause took place at the tomb. Immediately after a burial and on the feast day, which is the anniversary of a saint's death, crowds would appear seeking intercession. Sometimes a cluster of favors occurred within a short interval after the death. Infants and children could be carried in a state of grave illness and even apparent death, as described above. For most adults, however, especially those who lived in poverty, a visit to the tomb required a modicum of mobility and financial resources. Perhaps as a result, the majority of adult ailments cured after this gesture were chronic diseases or deformities, rather than acute illnesses. In the case of martyrs, a burial site was not always identified or accessible, but sometimes cures were effected at the place of death. Four cures of six from the early 1720s in the cause of Portuguese Jesuit João de Brito were healings of people who had been carried to the spot where he had died in India thirty years before.[55]

Supplicants carefully placed their infirm body parts in direct contact with the tomb or the corpse. For example, in 1594, a weaver with a swollen neck went to the tomb of Andrea Corsini; adopting a posture, difficult to imagine, he brought his swollen neck into contact with the saintly feet.[56] Similarly, a seventeenth-century mother and her young son both kissed the tomb of François de Sales.[57] In 1686, a man with fever touched the hands and feet of Giacomo della Marca.[58] A widow afflicted with severe pains in her abdomen twice "threw" her stomach against the tomb of Pietro Orseolo.[59] In 1761, a pharmacist (*speziale*) took his paralyzed arm with his good hand and draped it over the tomb of Serafino of Monte Granario.[60] In 1853, a mother carried her mute and motionless little boy to the church and inserted his leg into the tomb of Ignazio of Laconi; the child soon spoke and walked.[61]

Prayer at a tomb could be effective even for people who were neither religious nor aware of the possible saint. A thirty-six-year-old Belgian watchmaker had been indifferent to religious devotion until he was treated for an accidental leg injury. His doctors had suspected an underlying tuberculosis or syphilis and were considering amputation. He reported that several novenas had already been said without success when a nun "conducted" him into a "cellar, where there appeared to be a tomb," and ordered him to pray. He replied, "'Oui, oui madame' and pretended to pray with bowed head." Suddenly, he was seized with a glacial sensation and turned to see if somebody was pouring ice water on his leg. Overcome with the urge to sleep, he went home and rested comfortably for several hours, where previously he could not bear the weight of blankets on his sore limb. When he awoke the leg was completely healed, and on the third day, he danced until three o'clock in the morning.[62]

Pilgrimages in Invocations

For their expense and attendant trappings, distant pilgrimages were considered ostentatious and the Counter-Reformation Church did not encourage them; faith should be sufficient without display.[63] They persisted, nevertheless, and increased into the nineteenth century, perhaps because they satisfied that urge to "do something," filling time and supplying an offering of sacrifice. In 1905, a fifty-eight-year-old nun, Sister Antoinette, longed to go to the tomb of Jean Vianney to seek his intercession for her variceal ulcers. Her Mother Superior resisted the plan, calling it "madness." But she relented in the face of Antoinette's persistence, and the nun began "counting the days that separated [her] from the departure." She was accompanied by the local baker and two sisters. After the invocation, the sores healed rapidly over four days.[64]

MIRACLES AT A TOMB IN SOUTHERN FRANCE. The tomb of Germaine Cousin in Pibrac near Toulouse has been the site of many miracles and many more appeals. A description of this group typifies appeals at a tomb. A poverty-stricken and sickly shepherdess, Germaine, died in 1601, at age twenty-two, having been ridiculed by neighbors and beaten by her family. Her corpse was observed to be incorrupt on two occasions: at an accidental disinterment in 1644, and again, more remarkably, after it had been desecrated and reburied with quicklime in 1793. The ASV holds files on seven miracles attributed to Germaine, five of which took place at her tomb between 1828 and 1856. Like the saint, most miraculés were poor laypeople in modest occupations such as farming and sewing; they all suffered from chronic ailments and had seen up to five doctors before making their pilgrimages. Distances traveled were small, perhaps no more than the twelve kilometers from Toulouse; however, in every case the trip posed physical and logistical difficulties. Indeed, the arduous journey was part of the prayer. A brief summary of each case reveals that the saint seemed to specialize in chronic complaints of working youth, and that these unrelated stories of recovery follow a similar structure—a structure that may be generated by peculiarities of the site, by the previous miracles, and by the process itself.

In 1828, seven-year-old Jacquette was cured suddenly of rickets on her third trip to Pibrac. In the moment of cure, the astonished congregation heard the sound of bones cracking as she wrestled out of her brother's grasp to join her mother praying near the altar. Twenty years later, testimony of both parents emphasized Jacquette's difficult birth, her suffering, and their wonder at the events in Pibrac. Medical experts had not examined the child before her cure, but they certified that she had grown into an able-bodied woman who, among other emblems of her good health, experienced regular menstruation.[65]

In 1837, twenty-four-year-old Marie, a draper (*mercière*), had been sick for four years, ever since she entered into service of a cruel master. Doctors imposed the chic new diagnosis of "enlarged heart" and predicted a fatal outcome. Marie went in a carriage with her mother and aunt to Pibrac, where she prayed on her knees for three hours and immediately felt well. The little group paused in the shelter of a wall for a picnic of bread, fruits, and water drawn from a nearby spring; she found an appetite that she had never known. In truly catholic inclusiveness, one of the witnesses for this inquiry was the wife of the cruel employer herself.[66]

In 1844, a twenty-six-year-old dressmaker, Ursula, had suffered for two years from pain and swelling of her knee, so severe that she needed a cane; at the height of her infirmity, a priest took her in his carriage to Pibrac, where she was healed.[67] In 1847, sixteen-year-old Philippe with tuberculous fistulae in his hip bones had considered doctors' orders of a stay at thermal baths in the mountains, but he could not afford it. Instead, he walked on his crutches to Pibrac and was cured.[68] In 1854, thirty-five-year-old Anna Maria had a dislocated hip; her legs were in the form of an X, and she could stand only with assistance. Two trips to Sette for sea bathing had been to no avail, but when she prayed at Pibrac, she felt herself healed and exclaimed for all too hear, "*Je marche! Je marche!*"[69]

Two other miracles added to these healings, demonstrating the spread of the saint's fame: a feat of multiplication in a convent at Bourges in 1845,[70] and the final miracle worked at Langres in a nun healed of a spinal cord disease. Rather than making a journey, she and her sisters said a novena.[71]

PILGRIMAGES OF INVOCATION IN THE TWENTIETH CENTURY. In the twentieth century, the causes of Jeanne de Valois and Ignazio of Laconi, canonized in 1950 and 1951, respectively, featured numerous miracles worked after invocations made at their tombs; however, the practice was waning. Testimony for the former was from 1632; for the latter, from 1853 and 1930. Nevertheless, pilgrimages for invocation have not disappeared altogether.

The most recent example of such an invocation took place in Chile in 1990, when a family went to the grave of Alberto Hurtado Cruchaga to invoke his intercession for their daughter who lay comatose in hospital having had brain surgery for a ruptured aneurysm.[72] The most recent in-person (rather than proxy) pilgrimage seems to have been that of Maureen, an American woman with chronic lymphedema of her leg; in 1981 she journeyed to the tomb of Maria Faustina Kowalska in Cracow and was cured.[73] Air travel has altered the dimensions of invocation.

In another long-distance pilgrimage, it was not the tomb, but the Roman rituals of the process itself that provided the destination. Forty-eight-year-old

Beatriz of Quito attributed her cure from myasthenia gravis to the intercession of a countryman, Miguel Febres Codera of Ecuador. Wife of an orthodontist, Beatriz had been ill for seven years, and neurologists managed her symptoms with prostigmine therapy. When news came that the beloved Miguel was to be beatified in August 1978, Beatriz's sister arranged their trip to Rome to attend the ceremony and appeal for healing. "As soon as I reached Rome," Beatriz said, "I was better." Her illness resolved completely. Like all the other cases, it entailed the best medicine that contemporary science could muster: a full neurological examination complete with visual fields, electromyography, nerve conduction studies, and blood tests. Miguel was canonized in 1984, barely seven years after (and perhaps because) the journey to his beatification blessed Beatriz with a cure.[74]

Votive Objects

The practice of leaving votive body parts—arms, legs, heads, breasts, hearts—at sacred places extends back to Greco-Roman antiquity and pervades Catholic tradition. The object lingers at the holy site as a permanent invocation, perhaps reminding the saint of the problem and prolonging the supplicant's contact. But this practice is little apparent in these files. Between 1600 and 1602, visitors to the tomb of Andrea Corsini left cardboard votives: a leg, a head, and an arm.[75] In 1632, most of the thirty-one witnesses in the cause of Jeanne de Valois reported on the large number of wax body parts at her tomb, but none of the eleven miraculés actually deposed (or described) in her cause claimed to have used such objects themselves.[76] Similar items were also left after favors, as offerings of thanks. In the early eighteenth century, a woman cured of fiery erysipelas and severe headache left a wax head at the shrine of Juan de la Cruz, but it was for thanks, not supplication.[77] More on the use of votives in thanksgiving appears below.

Relics in Invocation

Gestures of appeal at the tomb of a saint never completely disappeared from the miracle files, but they declined in relative frequency over the four centuries (table 5.1). Vauchez detected a relative decline in the practice in the late Middle Ages in favor of invocations at a distance.[78] On one hand, this observation may be explained by the geographic extension of canonization to other nations—a journey to the tomb was not always possible. On the other hand, different rituals were adopted and preferred. Contact between the saint and the appellant could be accomplished through intermediary objects reminiscent of the saint through

TABLE 5.1 Forms of Invocations by Century of Canonization

	16th C.	17th C.	18th C.	19th C.	20th C.
Tomb of saint	19	59	20	29	45
Dust/wood from tomb	1	0	1	2	6
Children carried/ placed on tomb	3	3	4	2	6
Corpse (includes intermediate objects)	3	6	7	0	1
Relics	3	34	36	28	91
Applied	0	10	13	8	9
Image	0	20	16	21	45
Clothing	2	7	15	2	7
Prayer[a]	3	17	11	17	72
Novena	0	5	6	28	129
Unspecified appeal	0	19	13	4	6
Water	0	13	2	3	4
Swallowed	0	2	2	1	5
Oil	0	13	12	2	5
Lamp	0	4	9	2	2
Promise	0	8	3	4	3
Pilgrimage[b]	2	5	2	6	14
Vigil	2	5	3	1	5
Church/chapel	11	4	7	2	2
All	9	369	244	185	503

[a]Excludes prayer at the tomb.

[b]Includes four pilgrimages promised if a cure was granted.

the long-established practice of disseminating "relics." According to Ward, the first compendium of miracles at a Christian shrine was written by St. Augustine about the arrival in Hippo of the relics of St. Stephen in 416.[79]

In my collection, witnesses sometimes indicated that they had applied the relic directly to a painful part, or laid it on the forehead, mouth, or chest of the sick person, who, often enough, was oblivious. Sometimes, the words of a prayer uttered during the impromptu ceremony would be included in the testimony. Gradually, these intermediary objects took the place of graveside appeals.

The most direct relics were taken from the saint's corpse—hair, bones, fingers, heart, or dust from the tomb—in anticipation of future veneration. As with Marie Euphrasie Pelletier's rescue of the good nun's heart, told in chapter 2, organic relics must be collected soon after a person dies "in the odor of sanctity."[80] Embalming by removal of organs was known in Catholic tradition from the thirteenth century.[81] The twelfth-century Hugh of Lincoln was alleged to have gathered relics on his pilgrimages by biting or slicing fragments from venerated corpses.[82] The preservation of remains is still familiar and various body parts are kept in prominent places in ornate reliquaries. Sometimes physicians were summoned to retrieve organs. Sallman told the story of an eighteenth-century surgeon from Ravello who was asked to cut off the nipple of a prospective saint.[83]

Examples of the use of relics in this collection occur early and throughout all four centuries. Among miracles worked between the 1595 death of Filippo Neri and his rapid canonization in 1622, a midwife revived a stillborn baby by stroking it with hairs from the corpse.[84] A *Vita* on this saint classified his miracles after death according to the different relics or modes of invocation: hair, cap, reading the life, votive offerings, visiting the tomb, images, etc.[85] In most other instances, however, the exact nature of the "relics" was not specified. Moreover, people often selected several modalities for their invocations and used them simultaneously with the recommendations of doctors, surgeons, apothecaries, and neighbors.

In these records, relics, more frequently identified than body parts, consisted of pieces of the saint's clothing and other belongings, or bits of fabric that had touched the corpse. In the cause cited above, thirteen people invoked Filippo Neri with cloth that had been dipped in his blood; fourteen others used his cap; seven visited the tomb.[86] The skeletal corpse of Francesca Romana was visited—as it still is today in its glass coffin—by most of the eleven pilgrims whose stories contributed to her canonization in 1608; however, at least three of these early miraculés used intermediary cloths that had touched the corpse.[87]

Precious relics were known to reside in certain convents or chapels for use in times of need. In 1603, a poverty-stricken mother wrapped her sickly baby in the habit of Andrea Corsini of Fiesole.[88] Similarly, as part of his invocation, a twelve-year-old boy wore the habit of Giacomo della Marca for a year; when he recovered, the parents left an offering of gold.[89] During 1703 and 1704, three female supplicants from a town near Florence—a widow with fever, a nun with cancer, and a girl with convulsions—were healed following invocations in which they had been touched "from head to toe" with a piece of cotton that had also touched the corpse of Agnes of Montepulciano.[90] The saint had died four centuries earlier and her incorrupt remains lay in Orvieto, nearly one hundred kilometers away. It is likely that the same cloth was used in every case and that it had been carried to these sick people by a member of the convent where it was kept. In 1927, a mother used the good offices of a concerned nun to press for access to the living quarters of the possible saint; once inside, she touched the infirm foot of her child to a "host of objects" in the holy man's room.[91]

As described in chapter 2, the Austrian-born Jesuit Francis Xavier Weninger brought unspecified "relics" of Pedro Claver to America. Between 1858 and 1863, he urged their use on at least six people in five cities, all with good results.[92]

The famous power of certain relics meant that local people might "call for" them, as they would a doctor or a priest. In 1603, a birthing mother and her midwife "called for" the relics of Andrea Corsini.[93] The veil of Maria Maddelena de'Pazzi was used for nuns in at least four of the many miracles cited in her cause between 1638 and 1652.[94] The relics of the body of Juan de la Cruz were kept in the Carmelite monastery at Ubeda, Spain, where he died in 1591. Until 1703, through his beatification in 1675 and the partial translation to Segovia in 1677, local people in distress would summon the Ubeda relics, and a monk would come to place them on the affected parts.[95] Thus, in 1699 a doctor suffering from sore throat laid relics of Juan de la Cruz directly on his neck.[96]

Relics of Caterina de'Ricci, including pieces of brocade and linen clothing, as well as a small carafe of her blood, were held by her kinsman Bartholomeo Ricci, nephew of the archbishop of Arezzo. He told how he traveled from Gubbio to her grave in Prato, Tuscany, to collect these objects in the summer of 1655. On at least twenty occasions, he brought them when requested, sometimes moving them three times over the ailing person in the sign of a cross. On other occasions, it appears that people borrowed them. For example, a man dying of a lengthy fever and sore throat was attended by his aunt, who placed a drop of the saint's blood directly on his neck. From 1655, Ricci kept a journal describing more than fifty of these "prodigies." He wrote, "I have seen with mine own eyes . . . manifest signs and palpable effects of her greatness [in the] . . . healings of sick people abandoned by their doctors." Many of these stories were endorsed by signatures of the beneficiaries to enhance their credibility. This journal is not the record of a process of inquiry, but it is kept together with those documents.[97]

In several other causes, priests and family members "brought relics" to assist invocations for ailing people.[98] Some people kept them for future use. For example, in 1597, a surgeon suffered painful headache and visual problems so severe that his colleagues planned removal of an eye. He applied unspecified relics of Ignatius Loyola and was cured. Thereafter, he kept the same relics in his room for use again whenever he felt ill.[99] A woman who had been attended by many physicians, including her father and brother, was brought a relic that her "sister had kept for many years in her house"; she placed it over her heart.[100]

As alluded to above, desire for intimacy with the would-be saint subtended the direct application of the relic to the sick body. Extending their reach and durability, substitutes for the actual relics were prepared, including oil or water in which bits of clothing or other objects had been immersed. Anointing the sufferer with oil from lamps was associated with eighteen different saints and appeared steadily in causes from all four centuries from 1606 to 1947. Typifying such a recovery was the 1781 tale of a twenty-nine-year-old nun from Brescia with dense right-sided paralysis, aphonia, and convulsions; she was anointed on arms and legs with oil from the lamp of Angela Merici and instantly recovered both movement and sensation. Her prioress came running into the room calling others to witness the wondrous event.[101] The *olio multiplicato*, in the file of Maria Maddalena de' Pazzi, was itself the product of a miracle described in chapter 3; subsequently, it was used several times to anoint sick people, thereby generating more miracles for the cause.[102] In at least two cases it had been carried some distance.[103]

The yearning for contact extended to actual ingestion of relics. Several people drank water altered by a drop of the saint's blood or a thread from the garment.[104] At least two children, both Italian schoolboys—one in 1816, the other in 1927—were urged by their parents to swallow bits of clothing immersed in water.[105] At least five blesseds were linked to wells: Isidro Labrador, Maria Maddelena de' Pazzi, Pierre Fourier de Notre Dame, and Teresia and Sancia of Portugal; water from their fountains was conveyed great distances for consumption by either anointing or drinking.

As mentioned above, gestures of invocation could be multiple and they often coincided with medical care. For example, a nursing nun suffered from tuberculous meningitis and had been tended by no fewer than seven doctors, three of whom testified in 1935. But she also had been the subject of two novenas, offered by her sister nuns together with her biological mother, at the tomb of the would-be saint Louis Grignon de Montfort. She swallowed water in which a sliver from the coffin had been immersed, a bony relic was placed on her chest, and she was covered by a flannel shirt that had lain on his tomb. Meanwhile the nuns and her mother kept up steady offerings of prayer. The testimony does not specify which of these many gestures was considered the most important; it was evidence of the appeal that mattered.[106]

Sometimes flowers were carried from the tomb of the saint to a sick person by a family member. This delicate practice seems rare but persistent: three such invocations occurred in the seventeenth century and one in the twentieth.[107] Floral appeals were adopted by both women and men. In the most recent example, a Sicilian man, Salvatore, described in chapter 2, was healed of Pott's disease in 1938 after an appeal to Giuseppe Benedetti Dusmet; the invocation entailed a little flower from the tomb conveyed by his brother-in-law.[108] These supplicants also used an image.

Images as Relics

Pictures of the would-be saint with various attributes were also considered relics. The accuracy of the portrayal was often debatable; in many cases, they were based on the flimsiest of physical descriptions handed down over centuries. But they were always pleasing, and with the advent of printing, they became more affordable. As Simon Ditchfield has shown, images and their wide dissemination were an important but costly part of a Tridentine cause.[109] Images were not intended for worship but as reminders, stimuli to devotion, and aids to prayer. They could, however, provoke controversy, because they risked offending doctrine in the ancient commandment against idols. Nevertheless, images were quickly reconciled with Church dogma, absorbed into the machinery of evangelism, and established as a routine of devotional ritual.

In my collection, images first appear with certainty as part of the invocation for five of the earliest healings, two in the cause of Ignatius Loyola worked in 1599 and 1601, and three for Carlo Borromeo, from 1601 to 1604.[110] Intriguingly, the events of these same miracles attributed to Carlo were soon depicted in engravings that appeared in the year of canonization (figure 3.4).[111] Evidence of the use of images increases steadily in canonizations, to peak in the nineteenth century when they were used in 10 percent or more of invocations. They remained important during the twentieth century. It is possible that many of the unspecified "relics" were images (table 5.2). Most images seem to have been small woodcuts or other engravings; later, they were reproductions of colorful paintings, often with a prayer or a short biography printed on the back. Only once was a photograph of a saint specifically mentioned in an invocation, together with one of her socks.[112]

Like the other relics, images were applied directly to afflicted body parts. In 1601, a miraculée in the cause of Loyola placed his picture directly on her stomach.[113] Images were also laid on foreheads, mouths, chests, knees, tumors, sores, and wounds. They were made as gifts, hung on walls, placed on beds, clasped in hands, suspended from belts, worn next to the skin, and, yes, even prayed to. They lingered as physical evidence of the invocation. Once in a while the reputation of an image for helping in a specific circumstance invested it with power for the future; an additional narrative about the object could do the same. For example, a woman whose paralyzed arm had not been helped by the

TABLE 5.2 Images in Invocations by Century of Canonization and as a Percentage of All Miracles and of Miracles for Which Information about the Invocation Was Provided

	16th C.	17th C.	18th C.	19th C.	20th C.
Images	0	20	16	21	45
No. files with information on invocation	44	250	195	128	437
Percent images in invocations	0	8	8.2	16.4	10.3

"ministrations of surgeons or the herbs of pharmacists" was healed instantly as she moved to snatch an image of Pierre Fourier de Notre Dame from a blazing fire. This same image was used in future invocations.[114] Similarly, sometime prior to 1853, a birthing mother survived a difficult labor while holding an image of Ignazio of Laconi in her hand. Thereafter, according to witnesses, all parturient women of Cagliari would hold that image or some other relic of the saint, whether they were in difficulty or not.[115]

Some images that had been instrumental in healings actually found their way into the depositions held in the Vatican archive, where, with their color and form, they provoke startled reactions of immediacy and wonder in even the weariest of scholars.[116] The most recent application of an image occurred in the 1990 healing of an eight-year-old Polish boy who had suffered a fracture to the base of his skull with multiple neurological problems. The family used a picture and a novena to invoke Angela Salawa; she was beatified the following year.[117]

Novenas

By the twentieth century, prayer at the tomb of a saint was superseded by the novena as the most frequent form of invocation in these files. This nine-day series of prayers has ancient roots, reaching back to Roman times, if not earlier. In Catholic tradition, novenas were originally offered for mourning, especially of popes, and later, for other specific reasons, such as appealing to saints. The novena of invocation originated in France, but the Church did not encourage it until the nineteenth century. Even today it is not a formal part of the liturgy.[118]

Novenas offered certain advantages for invocation of future saints. They could be given far from the place of burial, and they were documented in that they usually involved a religious figure who later could attest to the fact of the appeal. Prospero Lambertini conceded that novenas had been used in successful invocations, but he was suspicious of their magical and numerological overtones: "We do not wish to discourage Novenas, or to scoff at them . . . [but] we are anxious to make it clear, lest superstition should arise, that there is no particular virtue about precisely nine days or precisely three . . . God heeds prayers whenever He wills."[119]

By the mid-nineteenth century, opinion was changing, especially among the teaching orders such as the Ursulines. It was felt that the spiritual preparation associated with nine days of prayer prior to a feast day or to consolidate a request gave results that were sometimes more effective and always more meaningful. In America, a novena was associated with a famous miracle of Ann Mattingly of 1824, and novenas were included in prayer books by the 1840s.[120]

In this collection, novenas rise steadily through time to become the single most frequent form of appeal in the late twentieth century. Traces appear in the earliest records without the word *novena*: a *Vita* of 1622 noted that nine days of prayer had been offered for Francis Xavier, but the report of the accompanying incantations seems brusque, and possibly embarrassed.[121] Novenas, named as such, were confined at first to France and Spain; then they spread into other Catholic nations throughout the world (table 5.3). Of the three earliest novenas resulting in miracles, two were from France with testimony given in 1628 for the cause of François de Sales; the other was from Spain with testimony from 1673 in the cause of Pasqual Baylón.[122] The first Italian saint in this collection to have been invoked by a novena was the tenth-century doge of Venice Pietro Orseolo, canonized in 1731. Tellingly, his tomb was at Cuxa in the Pyrenees on the border between France and Spain. The novena was offered by a pharmacist's wife who had been blind for four months, despite the best efforts of her surgeons. Perhaps she doubted the reliability or acceptability of a novena, because she also held a familiar relic, a crystal globe, the "Sacro Cristallo." Possibly it was an ampoule of the true blood of Christ held earlier in the treasure of San Marco or an object that had once belonged to the doge and left in the monastery of Cuxa where he died. The "Cristallo" was used by two other miraculés whose stories formed part of the process.[123] Given this juxtaposition, novenas would seem no more or less superstitious than crystal balls.

Novenas can be given in private, but they invite participation. Aside from their potential to increase the number of witnesses to an act of supplication and

TABLE 5.3 Novenas Used in Miracle Depositions by Country of Origin of the Saint and Century of Canonization

Nationality	17th C.	18th C.	19th C.	20th C.
France[a]	2	2	20	49
Spain	3	2	4	13
Italy		2	2	35
Belgium			1	3
Holland			1	3
Poland				9
Germany				7
Canada				2
Sudan				1
Other[b]				7
Total	5	6	28	129

[a]Includes Corsica.
[b]Chile, Croatia, England, Hercegovina, Denmark, Lithuania, Madagascar.

a possible cure, they are comforting and pleasing, especially for religious communities whose members can expect to be available every day. With regular, dramatic recurrence over a sustained period, novenas allow for the problem and its solution to be shared. The repetitious ritual can be awaited with eager anticipation. In this collection, fifty-six novenas were offered for nuns usually by their sister nuns, although sometimes a mother or other family member would participate too. Only three were offered for ailing male clerics, one an Irish priest on whose behalf the novena was made to the English martyrs by nuns at St. Mary's, York, in 1878. Among those given for laypeople, a smaller preponderance of women miraculées was noticed (67 vs. 37).

Like the Hippocratic physicians of old, who relied on theories of coction (a form of ripening), crisis, and critical days to measure the duration of illness, the supplicants set much store by counting the days of the novena. In most situations, the patient's condition continued to worsen until the final day, when suddenly all symptoms would resolve. For example, on November 8, 1923, a nun, whose seven-year illness with pulmonary tuberculosis had caused her to travel all over Spain, found healing at midnight on the last hour of the last day of her novena to the Spanish priest Enrique de Ossó y Cervelló.[124] But cures could take place even on the first day, in which case the complete novena would be offered out of thanks. They also happened on any of the other days, the next most frequent of which was the fourth. In one of its older forms, a novena would begin nine days before a feast; as a result, the best opportunity might present itself only once a year. However, other significant dates were chosen to commence the series: anniversaries, festivals, New Year's Day, Easter, and Christmas. When the first novena did not produce results, the devout, undaunted, would start another.

Thus, a thirty-six-year-old Belgian spinster, Thérèse, found healing for a mysterious, festering stab wound in her hip on the night of August 3–4, 1852, the last night of her second novena to Gerardo Majella. Living as a housekeeper in her brother's home and working for a noblewoman, Thérèse had concealed her wound for two years out of "the modesty of a good Christian woman" and "for fear that her father or brother would harm the person who did it." When the sore began to affect her gait, the lady employer urged Thérèse to tell her confessor, but the priest ordered her to the doctors. For another year, three physicians tried to heal her wound without success; they and two experts were surprised by the cure and the absence of a crisis. On that day, she had completed a second novena, during each day of which she and a companion had also repeated nine Our Fathers and nine Ave Marias and attended Mass.[125]

In 1922, a Jesuit brother, Peter, became one of the three male clerics to have resorted to a novena. His cure of septic endocarditis came at the end of his second novena to Peter Kanis.[126] Similarly, in 1951, a fifty-six-year-old Genoese nun, Sister Domenica, was expected to die of tuberculous meningitis that had been investigated by lumbar puncture and treated with penicillin and strepto-mycin, all to no avail. No sooner had her community completed the first novena to Virginia Bracelli than they launched another while her condition grew steadily worse. On the eighth day of the second novena, her symptoms quickly resolved. She was reexamined three decades later, at age eighty-seven, and found to be well.[127]

In a variation on this theme of multiple novenas, an 1868 cure, attributed to Jean-Baptiste de la Salle, followed novenas offered to other candidates for canonization, including Pedro Claver.[128]

Bringing home the theme of multiple simultaneous gestures of appeal is the story of Eugenie, a working class mother from Hull, Quebec. In May 1947, she was horrified when her baby boy tumbled from his carriage over a nine-foot wall; the child catapulted onto his head, sustaining a black eye and many bruises. She rushed him to hospital, where the doctors and nursing sisters feared that he would be blind for the rest of his life. Eugenie resolved to travel to Notre Dame du Cap, a shrine to the Virgin near Trois Rivières; she went door-to-door with her babe in arms to raise money for their tickets. The journey was miserable, the boy sick and vomiting, but she recited her rosary all the way. At the shrine, she washed his eyes, but nothing happened. Then an "Oblate father took pity" and directed her to a relic of Charles-Joseph-Eugène de Maze-nod left by a wealthy woman. (Notice the similar name.) Eugenie touched the relic to her baby's eyes and began a novena, which she continued from home in Hull. At its completion, she and her daughter excitedly devised a "test" of the baby's vision by waving a bottle of milk to see if he would reach for it. He did, and doctors confirmed his full recovery within the week.[129]

These demanding gestures have long been a vital part of the illness experi-ence for devout Roman Catholics. They are usually combined with relics, images, or other gestures of devotion. For example, in 1935, Honorine, a twenty-two-year-old French nun with peritonitis and an abdominal abscess, was treated by sev-eral physicians; her Mother Superior brought a "true relic" of Marie-Euphrasie Pelletier, had her kiss it, and then laid it upon her belly. The abscess soon opened and "began to flow like a tap." This hopeful sign fostered another form of appeal: the sisters "decided," said Honorine, "with good heart and great faith" to start a novena involving the "entire convent" in praise of the candidate for sainthood. Honorine passed dreadful days and nights, until the excruciating pains reached a peak just before her cure. When she wanted to leave her bed, the Mother Superior urged caution, but later reported, ironically, that it was "impossible to reason with this dying person."[130]

Sometimes novenas were instigated at the onset of the illness and overlapped with medical care; they simply continued when the doctors gave up.

Invocations by Others

The chronically ill could make appeals on their own behalf; however, those who were acutely ill, or unconscious, left prayers to members of their biological or religious families. As proxy appellants, women outnumbered men nearly three to one in every century (table 5.4).

Mothers most frequently sought intercession on behalf of their ailing children, be they infant or adult, but sisters and aunts could also be instrumental in appeals, sometimes over the opposition of closer relatives. Wives also prayed for husbands ailing from a wide variety of acute ailments. As a result, testimony from these key female witnesses was always important to the process.

Male relatives also participated in appeals to would-be saints. In eight of the ten cases in which husbands sought intercession, the illness was related to obstetrical complications involving pregnancy and labor. Fathers were more

TABLE 5.4 Invocations in Which a Familial Appellant Is Identified by Century of Canonization

	16th C.	17th C.	18th C.	19th C.	20th C.
Mother alone	1	31	20	7	28
Father alone	1	2	1	5	4
Both parents	2	9	7	6	13
Wife	0	7	6	2	5
Husband	0	5	2	0	2
Son	0	0	0	0	1
Daughter	0	0	0	0	0
Brother[a]	0	1	2	0	0
Sister[b]	0	7	3	3	10
Aunt	0	0	1	0	4
Total female	3	54	37	18	60
Total male	3	17	12	11	19
All miracles	89	382	248	185	506

[a]Includes brothers in-law.
[b]Includes religious sisters.

likely to pray in the company of their wives, but they also prayed alone for children, both boys and girls, and with increasing frequency through time.

Seasons of Healing

Many of the invocations and cures were given a precise date by the witnesses. As a result, it is possible to explore the time of year in which they took place. Sickness demands immediate attention whenever it occurs, but the timing of an appeal suggests that the date may influence the choice of saint. Several successful invocations or cures coincided with the anniversary of death (usually the feast day) or beatification of candidates for sainthood. At least eight miracles in the many collected for the cause of Maria Maddelena de'Pazzi occurred during her feast of May 25 or the night before.[131] Many other examples were found.[132]

In each century under study, almost every month saw a successful appeal (table 5.5). However, comparison of the absolute number of miracles in each month with the monthly average for every century suggests that late spring (May) and late summer (August) usually saw the most successful appeals, whereas late winter (January and February) saw the least. These observations may correlate with the seasonal incidence of important religious ceremonies, such as Easter, Christmas, and All Saints' Day. But they also imply that fair weather offers favorable conditions for a *documentable* gesture of appeal.

TABLE 5.5 Datable Invocations by Month and Century of Canonization

	16th C.	17th C.	18th C.	19th C.	20th C.
Jan.	0	1	4	1	26
Feb.	0	0	2	1	25
Mar.	0	2	3	4	31[a]
Apr.	0	5[a]	7[a]	1	23
May	1[a]	10[a]	4	5[a]	37[a]
Jun.	0	1	4	6[a]	28[a]
Jul.	0	3	8[a]	5[a]	23
Aug.	0	2	13[a]	4	30[a]
Sep.	0	2	3	4	26
Oct.	0	2	5[a]	3	26
Nov.	0	4[a]	3	1	21
Dec.	0	2	3	4	14
Total dated	1	34	59	49	310
Av./month	.08	2.83	4.9	4.1	25.8

[a]Number of miracles in the month exceeds monthly average for century.

The Context of Healing

People still suffer and die in exactly the same ways as in the prehistoric past. The diagnostic labels may change, but illness, death, and dying do not. As these records suggest, unexpected recovery—like the arc of a theatrical performance—also follows several constant forms.

Looking over the rich tapestry of these remarkable personal stories from several centuries and six continents, many features recur in established patterns: the sickroom, medical consultation, desperate prognosis, identifiable acts of supplication, night vigils, incubation, the peak of symptoms, visions, dreams, a sudden datable cure, and the corroboration of witnesses. If the event is not an emergency, then it usually occurs in the most intimate spaces—the bedchamber or the church—and it frequently happens at night with candles burning. Like a dramatic setting for a stage, the constancy, even the *sameness* of these conditions through time, reminds us that the enacting of a miracle always takes place within a stable context of illness and anticipated death. These trajectories may be a feature of biological reality, or they may be constructed by the process itself.

Incubation

Incubation is a response to illness that entails a vigil or sleeping in a divine sanctuary. It has been studied as a carryover from Aesculapian temple medicine into the realm of Christianity.[133] Incubation was among the treatments of the wandering Aelius Aristides: sleeping in temples, where he hoped for therapeutic dreams.[134] The practice also occurs in Christian churches. For example, the most famous miracle of the doctor saints, Cosmas and Damian, is the "transplantation" mentioned in chapter 3. But it also entailed incubation: a man with a diseased leg slept in their basilica; the saints appeared in a dream and replaced his leg with the freshly dead but "unused" leg of a "moor," who had been buried the same day in the nearby cemetery.[135] Having allowed incubation to blur the boundary between pagan religious practices and early Christianity, historians of the ritual tend to stop in antiquity. Yet, healings of our own time can also be viewed as incubation, although, as Risse has noticed, the "temple" is often a hospital or a home.[136]

Because severely ill people are recumbent, descriptions of their circumstances necessarily include their beds, which are mentioned frequently throughout the records in all four centuries. The numerous references to beds also imply incubation whether or not the testimony indicates sleep. In other cases, sleep was not a means of cure so much as a manifestation of health after the fact, when a patient sank into restorative slumber.

For at least nine cases in this collection, incubation is specifically linked to the context of invocation and recovery, in the form of sleep and dreams. The earliest occurred in the miracles of Ramón of Penyafort, canonized in 1600: a Spanish woman was healed in her sleep of paralyzed hands and feet.[137] Similarly, in 1749, an Italian novice, Maria Angela, suffered from a chronic illness and acute joint pain, fever, and convulsions. She invoked Jan Berchmans, through a novena given on her knees, and then she fell into a deep sleep, from which she awoke to absolute relief from all her ailments. The mystery worked during her slumber was only one of the unfathomable aspects of her case. Her acute illness was deemed to be an incurable form of rheumatic fever, but the chronic illness was more sinister: she was one of the people in whom doctors had detected venereal disease, contracted "in her mother's womb" (see chapter 3). Sister Maria Angela may never have been told her diagnosis.[138] All the better that she was healed during sleep.

Peak of Symptoms before a Cure

Many other miraculés experienced the transcendent moment in bed at the peak of grave illness. A certain logic would imply that the worst of an illness inevitably precedes a cure; however, the exacerbation of symptoms at the transcendent moment appears so frequently that it constitutes a standard feature of the healing process itself. It is as if saintly intervention requires things to get much worse before they can be better. This phenomenon appeared in tales from all centuries under examination.

In 1756, a forty-six-year-old woman suffered for several years from what her numerous, up-to-date doctors, including her own brother, called a "polyp in the heart." When she was thought to be dying, she placed a relic of Giuseppe of Cupertino on her chest. Immediately, a sudden pain arose from inside her heart as if "something was being torn out." She thought it was "a sign that [she] would die." The pains increased until the moment of cure.[139]

Similarly, a doctor testifying in 1877 reasoned that his medicine could not have been responsible for the recovery of a schoolboy, because his condition had steadily worsened after the start of a novena.[140] In 1880 a group of nuns and even their doctors were longing for death to end the agony of thirty-three-year-old Sister Clementina. Having been adopted into the convent at age four, she herself supervised orphans, but now she was coughing blood and in great pain. Forty years after her abrupt recovery, she emphasized the doctors' mistaken prognosis and told how her suffering grew worse during the novena until her sudden cure.[141] In 1924, a mother and her five-year-old daughter instigated a novena to Giuseppe Cafasso, hoping for the child's recovery from tuberculosis of the hip; the symptoms increased after the start of the novena and steadily worsened until her abrupt cure on the final day.[142]

Dreams

Dreams in which the saint appears or speaks to the sufferer are another vivid reminder of incubation. Some of the most dramatic stories in the collection entail dream content. Two inquiries from the nineteenth century explored the nature of dreams, but they are most apparent in the records of the twentieth century, inviting speculation about the cultural impact of Sigmund Freud although he was never named (table 5.6).

The earliest dream described in detail was in the 1864 testimony of a forty-year-old Roman woman, Maria, who suffered for many years from severe abdominal distress with pain and vomiting. During this time, she gave birth to three babies; however, she resorted to wet nurses because her milk was insufficient and her infirmity was aggravated by breastfeeding. Maria's complicated story of steadily worsening illness emphasized how it was the doctors at Santo Spirito Hospital who suggested an appeal to the would-be saint Giovanni Battista Rossi. At the peak of her illness, on the night of his feast, May 23, she received extreme unction and made her appeal, holding his image in her hand. She soon fell asleep and dreamed that a priest in a long robe appeared, saying, "I am Giovanni Battista Rossi," and promising a cure. Three days later, she had "milk in abundance," and went to Rossi's chapel in the church of Santa Maria in Cosmedin "to express her gratitude."[143]

In 1894, twelve-year-old Enrichetta, daughter of a widowed physician of Salerno, described her memory of a serious illness, diagnosed as nephritis following a bout of scarlatina six years earlier. The distressed father had held "relics" and vowed, should she recover, to journey to the tomb of the prospective saint Gerardo Majella, patron of children. He lay down in exhaustion, expecting

TABLE 5.6 Context of Healing by Century of Canonization

	16th C.	17th C.	18th C.	19th C.	20th C.
Heard voice	3	3	2	1	6
Saw vision	2	7	6	3	14
Dream	0	0	0	1	8
All miracles	89	382	248	185	506

her death that night. In a dream, the child felt a hand on her mouth and saw, standing at her bedside, a "small brother holding a crucifix," who said, "Little one, you have been healed ... you must get up." She slipped out of her room dressed in her nightgown and roused her doctor-father; not realizing that she was well, the drowsy man ordered her back to bed. In the morning, he and the servants were astonished at the recovery; and the promise was kept. The role of family in establishing this narrative was considerable and extended well beyond what had likely been the oft-repeated story of her cure: the father and postulator shared the same last name, while Enrichetta's brother was a seminarian with the monk whose cure formed the second miracle investigated in the same process.[144] As for the child's clear memory of these events, the saint's attributes must have been familiar since her birth; repetition of the tale would have engraved its elements on her mind and perhaps suggested a few too. But the dream had been her own.

In the twentieth century, dream content was more consistently reported. In May 1936, eighteen-year-old Maria of Barcelona fractured and dislocated her left elbow while playing ball with other young people; she was awaiting surgical repair. At the inquiry six years later, she told how she had fallen asleep with an image of the young Domenico Savio on her injured arm. In her vivid dream, she was descending a staircase, where she met a man in a white robe who said that he had heard that she possessed relics, but very little faith. He asked pointedly if she believed in Savio as a saint. She admitted that she did not, but believed in his mentor, Giovanni Bosco. The vision told her to make a novena to Savio with as much faith as she could muster. The following morning, she began the novena; four days later, she was cured without an operation.[145]

In 1938, a thirty-six-year-old Lebanese woman, Elisabetta, was diagnosed with cancer of the uterus detected when she miscarried at three months' gestation. Consultations in Beirut led to treatment with radium, but the disease was unresponsive, and she suffered continuous discharge and bleeding. The doctors sent her home to die. Too weak to walk, she was carried on a stretcher. The little group stopped at the tomb of Rafqa al Rayes. That night, Elisabetta dreamed that the saint appeared saying that she was cured. She awoke free of symptoms. Six weeks later, Elisabetta returned to the tomb to give thanks. Her cure was medically confirmed as late as 1952, and she died of kidney failure in 1966 at age sixty-four.[146]

Healing dreams could entail prophecies of cure, although they might not represent the moment of cure itself. Like Elisabetta above, two unrelated women–one in Warsaw and another in Padua—were sent home from hospitals to die, both in 1946. In the first, a thirty-two-year-old Polish nun, Magdalena, suffered from high fever, joint pain, and rectal bleeding; she was diagnosed with pancytopenia, a decrease in all blood cells. In a dream, she heard Ursola Ledochówska promise that she would be healed on the last day of a novena. She awoke and began the nine-day ritual, but her condition steadily worsened. On the final day, she was suddenly symptom-free and continued well until at least 1969 when her gall bladder was successfully removed.[147]

The second woman who dreamed a prophecy of cure was twenty-four-year-old Elsa. She had been operated for abdominal pain and suspected appendicitis, but the surgeons found disseminated tuberculosis. They closed her up and sent her home. Beginning in July, her appeal to the Dalmatian brother Leopold Bogdan Mandic included a novena and intense prayer while holding his image. In her dream, the future saint appeared, promising a recovery on September 12. Her doctor and sister described the continued aggravation of all her symptoms until the morning of September 12 when, over their objections, Elsa insisted on going to church, where she was instantly cured.[148] A remarkably similar story, also from 1946, involved a dream and cure of abdominal tuberculosis in an Italian woman; it was used in the cause for beatification of Maria Margherita Caiani.[149]

Miraculés seem to have experienced dreams as an integral part of the transcendent moment, an important aspect of the miracle itself. The dreams of "innocent" children are perhaps the most compelling. It seems, however, that clerics tended to downplay their content and significance; as evidence, dreams were considered weak. Unlike the other gestures of appeal, which are corroborated by the testimony of multiple witnesses, dreams fall into a special category: that of a single witness. Authorities were also aware that retrospective suggestion could play a role, especially in the young. Perhaps for this lack of corroboration, cures related to sleeping and dreaming were considered no more remarkable than those without. When, in June 1927, a nineteen-year-old Neapolitan nun claimed that her chronic, purulent ear infection had been healed following a dream of Jeanne Thouret, both the physicians and the clerics were skeptical. One expert doctor was particularly scathing, arguing that she did not "decide" that her cure had been a miracle until a full month had elapsed.[150] This doubt spilled over into the reception of her dream.

Visions

Visions, unlike dreams, belong to a waking state. As a result, additional witnesses could be found to comment on the appearance of the sufferer during the experience, without necessarily sharing it. For example, in 1709 an epileptic nun was observed to change during the transcendent moment of her healing as she cried, "O how beautiful!"[151] Similarly nuns keeping vigil at the bedside of a sister dying of stomach cancer noticed an alteration in her appearance as she uttered the words, "Look how beautiful are the eyes of this servant of God!"[152]

In these records, visions appear earlier and more frequently than dreams and across all time periods (table 5.6). Some seem to typify the modus operandi of certain saints. For example, at least four of forty-three miracles for Alessandro Sauli entailed visions in 1610 and 1611.[153] Interestingly, only one miracle involving a vision occurs in my collection after 1918.[154] This finding invites speculation that the apparent rise in dreams into the twentieth century, described above, is a false distinction that represents a simple shift in semantic convention. Is it possible that what a person in the seventeenth century might have labeled a "vision" could be recognized, in the twentieth, as a "dream"? Sometimes distinguishing between the two is difficult. For example, newspaper reports of the miracle used in the recent canonization of Padre Pio recount the story of a seven-year-old son of a doctor who recovered from meningitic coma, during which he "saw" a man with a white beard and a long robe who promised that he would be cured.[155] Was the lad's unconscious experience a vision or a dream?

Visions also entail senses other than sight. In 1604, a woman with a fractured arm keeping vigil at the tomb of Andrea Corsini in Fiesole felt something touch her arm and heard a voice promise her cure.[156] Testifying in the cause of Giacomo della Marca in 1699, a Salerno physician reported that one of his patients recovered as light filled his hospital room.[157] In 1703, a nun was cured of both cancer and sciatica when a voice commanded her to "get up quickly, dress yourself, and go to Mass."[158] Another nun, at the moment of her cure in 1923, saw Enrique de Ossó y Cervelló at the foot of her bed; she asked if she would be cured, and he replied that she already was.[159]

In 1890, a twenty-six-year-old Canadian nun, Soeur St. Louis de Gonzague, endured a three-year illness characterized by abdominal pain, stubborn constipation, bleeding hemorrhoids, general malaise, and increasing prostration that forced her to abandon teaching and keep to her bed. At the process twelve years later, she described a candlelight vigil on the night of June 6, during which Mère Marguerite Bourgeoys appeared saying, "If only my daughters had more confidence in me!" The sick nun "understood immediately, begged for forgiveness, and asked for healing." She heard the saint promise, "You will be cured." The night nurse stood nearby holding dust from the tomb of Marguerite; although the nun did not share the vision, she was startled by the immediate transformation in her patient and exclaimed, "Can it be that this cadaver is returning to life?"[160]

In these visions, potential saints appear, speak, promise, command, or perform gestures of benediction and touch. In 1807, a forty-six-year-old Corsican widow told how, six years earlier, she had been carrying a heavy load down stairs, when she stumbled and twisted her foot to such an extent that the "heel was facing forward." During the night, she went to the tomb of Theophilus of Corte, where she saw the saint making the sign of the cross over her leg. The following day she was cured and working in her shop.[161] The testimony from New Orleans by and about the novice Mary, described in chapter 2, entailed a vision of Jan Berchmans and the sensation of his placing a finger in her mouth.[162]

Some visions were actually shared by others. In April 1754, twenty-two-year-old Elisabetta of Venice was suffering from nephritic colic; her doctors predicted death, and a priest administered last rites. While lying on her bed surrounded by family, Elisabetta saw Girolamo Miani; before she could speak, a small child exclaimed, "O che bel vecchio!" When the doctor returned to complete the death certificate, he found her cured.[163] Similarly, two nuns shared a vision of Theophilus of Corte in 1905. In the opinion of her nephew-physician, forty-nine-year-old Sister Maria Domenica was dying of tuberculosis with pleural effusions. At the height of her suffering, she received the last rites and felt profound joy. In this state, she was being helped to change her damp clothes by another sister; just as the habit was passed over her head, both women saw the saint, standing at the altar of the infirmary. Three years later, they described the moment to the inquisitors, the flash of healing, and how they both fell on their knees "weeping hot tears."[164]

At the Moment of Cure

Even without dreams or visions, patients recall, and are remembered for, the events at the instant of recovery. These memories may serve to condition a much later decision that a miracle has been worked. In 1891, an English man described the context of his cure seven years earlier: keeping watch from his bed with a candle in hand, he roused the "missus" to stare with him in amazement at the rapid resolution of the exquisitely painful ulcers ringed by "proud flesh" on his shins.[165] In 1934, a nursing nun who had been dying of tuberculous meningitis awoke with a sensation of well-being and announced, "I feel better; I feel that Père de Montfort will cure me."[166]

Exact words, such as these, appear often in testimony on miracles, although various witnesses remember them differently. At Easter 1898, a young priest shouted "Sono guarito; sono guarito!" in the moment of his sudden recovery from what had been diagnosed as pulmonary tuberculosis. As other witnesses told it, he had been given the last rites at eight o'clock in the morning, and by eleven, he was exclaiming over his cure. But the "exact words" are debatable: some said that he cried, "Mamma mia!"; others, that he shouted news of "una granda grazie."[167] We can be confident that in his excitement the young priest did utter something, but–quotation marks notwithstanding—what he said will never be known.

The ambiguity in tiny details confidently supplied occurs in many of the stories told and retold by countless witnesses. Another example is found in the postcure picnic for Marie at Pibrac—was it in the shade of a "wall," as her mother said, or was it under "a tree"?[168] Might it have been both? The seductiveness of these tiny imprecisions reminds us of the near impossibility of writing "history as it really was" and suggests the difficulties with precise evidence required by the cause. Minor contradictions are tolerable; others are not.

Narrative in Signs of Health and Disease

Although doctors "label," or name, the problem from which a person is suffering, it is the patients themselves who are custodians of the symptoms and signs of health and disease. These personal "clues" are of interest for what they tell of the experience of illness and well-being in time and place. They also indicate that what the supplicant seeks to cure does not necessarily correspond to the doctor's diagnosis. Narrative applies to causes of disease, as well as their symptoms, and signs of recovery.

In terms of disease causation, psychic stress and physical hardship loomed large. Symptoms engendered by these factors could not be fully relieved until harmony was restored. Thus, Marie, the draper, described above, related her broken health to four unhappy years in service of a cruel employer; a doctor warned that she would die if she did not quit.[169] In the mid-eighteenth century, Elisabetta was convinced that her illness arose when she was denied entry to a convent because she "did not know how to read"; however, the doctors, fully admitting that they did not know the cause, diagnosed kidney stones and bled her.[170] Another woman, aged fifty-six, believed that her painful knee had been "sent from heaven to test her soul," notwithstanding the fact that it began after she tripped in the dark over a bucket left by a careless servant.[171] Testifying in 1937, family members of a widow were convinced that her heart condition had grown abruptly worse after the death of her husband.[172] Several women related their ill health to marriage through coincidental or even causal links to bearing children either too early or too late in life.[173]

Narrative as cause and nature of disease was especially apparent in the story of thirty-nine-year-old Sinforosa, whose horribly ulcerated legs had been under the care of doctors for three long years. With her first husband, she had borne thirteen babies, but only one survived; then her husband died too. She remarried a much younger man who was now in trouble with the police. On the last day of Christmas 1786, the new husband was shot in the head and carried home. His scalp had only been grazed, but he was bleeding profusely. "Imagine my consternation," said Sinforosa. "I thought that they had murdered my husband." Then, ulcers began attacking her legs: first the right, then the left, eroding to the bone and oozing pus. To the great surprise of the doctors, the sores healed rapidly after she made a pilgrimage to the tomb of Leonardo of Porto Maurizio in 1789. But it is difficult to "imagine" that this articulate storyteller had seen an end to all her woes with the physical cure.[174]

These tales and their etiological frameworks were familiar not only to the miraculés, but also to family and friends. In the early nineteenth century, a feverish woman and all the other witnesses connected her illness to the death of her first baby, a daughter. The doctors also recognized the "emotional" factors in her illness, but advised her not to have any more children, and they bled her too. The injunction against future pregnancies seems to have motivated her "poor husband" to urge her to seek divine help for her fever and "tired blood" that had been further aggravated by the doctors' treatment. Cured following an appeal to Leonardo of Porto Maurizio, she was fit to walk, but she ordered a carriage for her thanksgiving journey to church because the situation demanded more "pomp."[175]

Narrative also reveals indicators of health and recovery cited by the lay witnesses in these records. First among the recurring signs of health are sleep, as described above, and appetite. Many patients reported unaccustomed hunger in the aftermath of illness, as did Marie, who ate so well at the little picnic in Pibrac. In 1913, an American nun, Sister Magdalen, weighed only ninety-nine pounds following a long illness with gastric bleeding and jaundice; she was nursed in the convent school, where she was custodian of the girls' clothing. She testified that she had to argue about her recovery. On that morning, Sister Teresa brought toast and coffee and prepared to bargain with the chronic anorectic by offering to eat the toast "if she would at least drink the coffee." Magdalen recalled, "When I drank it," I said, 'I wonder if Sister Teresa has put anything in this coffee?' I drank all of it and all of a sudden I felt cured . . . I got up, and Sister said, 'Don't get up, Magdalen.' I said, 'Let me alone . . . I am well!'" Sister retorted, "You are not well!" Magdalen declared, "I am hungry!"[176]

Similarly, Sister Clementina, mentioned above, had been delirious the night of her healing, but upon awakening, she announced, "I am cured . . . I am hungry," and she took the midday meal in the convent refectory.[177] In 1844, a thirty-two-year-old laywoman was ecstatic at her sudden recovery from a chest illness diagnosed as pericarditis; she immediately asked for bouillon, cheese, and chocolate.[178]

Other cardinal signs of health include the return of menstruation or lactation for women and procreation for both men and women. Like the Roman woman Maria, who found that her recovery coincided with abundant milk, other mothers in the records identified signs of health in their ability to nurse.[179] These physiological functions were cited as evidence of complete recovery. For example, from the nineteenth century, attention was paid to the irregular menstrual cycle and its restoration, even when the problem had nothing to do with the generative organs or reproduction.[180] Menstrual disturbance was a recognized feature of any chronic illness. Similarly, the Sicilian man who had been healed of a back problem after the invocation of the little flower, described above, was already dead when testimony was given fifty years later. His wife, brother-in-law, and two nieces both nuns, all pointed to the fact that he became a father soon after his cure. To emphasize the point, family photographs were included in the file.[181]

Other patients recognized well being in recovered ability to perform religious acts, such as making the sign of the cross (at least two), kneeling, genuflecting, and walking to church.

Recognizing Miracles

Just as the doctors' surprise is crucial to the process, the patient's surprise at recovery also seems to be an important element of every miracle story. The devout do not presume: they pray in hope but without anticipation of intercession; they are humbled should they become beneficiaries of unexpected acts of grace. Therein lies the surprise. On November 12, 1617, Antonia suffered a uterine hemorrhage and lost consciousness; she was given the last rites. Her confessor stood near the bed, holding relics of Majorcan Jesuit Alfonso Rodriguez; he later reported the moment of her brisk recovery: "'Good Jesu!' the woman exclaimed in a clear voice, 'Alfonso has already interceded. I am cured!'"[182] More than three centuries later in 1958, a twenty-six-year-old Chilean nun realized that she had been suddenly cured of a nine-year ordeal of respiratory insufficiency and bronchiectasis; she cried out, "Chitas! No me mori!"[183] Similarly, a five-year-old boy with tuberculous hip disease was prayed over by his mother, who held a packet of dust from the tomb of Ignazio of Laconi. When his fistulous wound closed rapidly on August 22, 1923, the mother exclaimed, "My baby is cured!" And the little boy declared, "Brother Ignazio has cured me!"[184]

Whether "miracle" is defined as an event against nature or within the laws of nature, it must defy human expectations. Long before the Vatican becomes involved with these tales, the miraculés and the people around them must have concluded for themselves that the event was indeed extraordinary enough to merit special attention. Sometimes, as in the examples above, the designation is made immediately; often, it takes time.

Indeed, most miracle designations are neither obvious nor sudden. Contrary to expectation, the realization may dawn slowly in the aftermath of a recovery. Unless the fellow observers are convinced that a miracle has occurred, the story will never be told outside a narrow range of friends. As noted above, the request and hope for healing does not include the expectation of a cure; in praying, the sick and their families are also preparing for death. When a recovery takes place, the realization may emerge gradually, both for the patient and the caregivers. That the cure could have been of a transcendent nature is only rarely appreciated in the first instance, when fear of relapse looms large. Some people need time to reflect on what transpired; still others, who had been overcome with illness, were unaware of appeals made on their behalf.

In short, a miracle must be labeled as extraordinary, not only by the patient, but also by the companions, and long before it is brought to the Vatican officials for consideration. Without collective enthusiasm for the idea, patients will hesitate to come forward and, in some cases, may never even suspect that such an interpretation is possible. Furthermore, the miraculé may not be the first person to suggest that the cure is miraculous.

Both doctors and clerics were annoyed with the woman, described above, who "decided" a month after her cure that she had been the beneficiary of a miracle. The delay in her case was indeed lengthy, but delay itself may not have been unusual. The relative absence of miracle cures in the late eighteenth and early nineteenth centuries likely had more to do with macroscopic Church history—the suppression of monasteries in Europe and reticence in the Vatican toward making more saints—than it did to any paucity of transcendent experiences on the microscopic (or individual) level. An absence of nuns and monks—both to encourage invocations of not-yet saints and to convey news of happy outcomes to the attention of clerical authorities—would result in a lack of miracles for the canonization process. Disinterest in the authorities designated to receive said testimony would have the same effect. Active postulants, who are prepared to guide and instruct, not only shape the process; they maintain it too.

Sometimes the post hoc decision that a miracle had occurred was owing to unsuspecting physicians who remarked, perhaps casually, that a recovery was "miraculous." They would find that the unwitting comment had launched ecclesiastical investigations, in which their figurative words of wonder were widely reported and repeated back as literal statements of fact. Other doctors would deliberately explain their reasons for using the word *miracle*. For example, an elderly French physician adamantly rejected the miraculous nature of most cures, but he readily applied the word *miracle* to a healing that he witnessed in 1900, and for "three reasons" that, by now, are familiar to us: the desperate symptoms, the failure of his medicine, and the speed.[185] Usually, however, doctors hesitated to make such pronouncements, and, as we have seen in chapter 4, they were never required to do so. When they did, the patient might feel prompted, or even obliged, to proceed to a process out of gratitude, duty, and respect.

For example, in 1889, fifteen-year-old Leopold, a student in a French boarding school, told how he had been so delirious that—"extraordinary thing!"—he failed to recognize his mother. He awoke to discover that he had been the object of an appeal to Jean-Baptiste de la Salle that had involved his entire school. Testifying two years later, the lad waxed eloquent about his early illness, but could recall nothing after he lapsed into unconsciousness. Nor could he say if he had prayed himself or the invocation had been made by others if at all. He remembered only his incomprehension when he awoke to find his mother standing at the foot of his bed. Testimony on the invocation and the grave danger of his illness had to come from others, including his mother and doctors, all of whom were convinced of a miracle. The lad accepted their judgments, but did not pretend to have decided. In this case, the doctor readily agreed and provided a signed statement describing the moments of recovery: "How we were astonished to learn that our moribund had come to his senses, recognized his mother and those taking care of him, and asked for something to drink . . . We crowded round, as he took some bouillon, swallowed a few spoonfuls of wine, replied perfectly well to our questions, and then fell into a peaceful sleep . . . These are the extraordinary things that passed before my eyes."[186]

Occasionally the testimony includes the disbelief of close family members, especially fathers. In 1868, Nancy, an eleven-year-old American girl with a chronic hip problem, called out, "Mama, Mama! I am cured." Her Scottish-born father was skeptical and had to be convinced.[187] The father of lame Pierina, described in chapter 2, refused to believe that his two-year-old baby had suddenly recovered until he saw her walking with his own eyes; his surprise then matched that of the midwife and doctors caring for her.[188] During the 1927 novena made near Poitiers by a mother and a nun on behalf of two-year-old Lucienne with rickets, the father repeatedly asked—perhaps skeptically—if she had been cured yet; he was convinced only after the child ran to him.[189] In 1930, another disbelieving father in Turin, who happened to be a physician, needed persuading of his little son's recovery from appendicitis without surgery.[190] These successful searches for validation were incorporated into the stories in which they increased the evidentiary weight of the miracle.

Thanksgiving

The final act in the drama of healing entails a gesture of thanks. It seals the process, acknowledges the transaction, and links the mortal supplicant with the future saint. It may be a simple profession of joy and gratitude in the hearts and minds of the miraculés and their loved ones. The backdrop of medical wonder, as discussed in chapter 4, is a component of the scene. If a promise was made during the invocation, then it must be kept, as described above.

Others who did not make promises were often motivated to personal and financial sacrifice following the cure. Tangible signs could be left at the shrine or tomb: silver and gold offerings, tablets or wall plaques, images, and votive objects in the form of body parts or reminders of the saint. Unless they are specifically labeled and dated, however, they are indistinguishable from the left objects that had been used in invocations.

Like artifacts of material proof, the gifts of thanks join with the prayers ongoing to become additional evidence for the causes, memorials of the healing, inspiration to future supplicants, and a form of embellishment that proclaims power stemming from sanctity long after the beneficiaries have died. Sometimes they become relics in their own right and are applied to future invocations. They transform the brief moment of cure into a static and enduring object that argues silently for the cause. They are familiar to visitors at Catholic sites all over the globe, and they are unfailingly present in this collection in all four centuries under study.

In the sixteenth century, as noted above, King Henry of Castile recovered from an ailment and his daughter from an acute illness after they had appealed to Diego d'Alcalá; in gratitude, the king built a splendid chapel.[191] In 1627, a man who had been so lame that he had to travel on horseback to make his invocation ran out of the church in joy at the sudden cure, and expressed his gratitude by returning daily on foot.[192] Other young people marked the wonder of their recoveries by entering a life of religion.[193]

From the seventeenth century to the nineteenth, images of the saint, or of the healing itself, were commissioned and hung conspicuously at the shrines, where they have become a special genre worthy of study in their own right. Images were published as votive engravings in the cause of Carlo Borromeo in 1610, and they were left as offerings of thanks at the shrines of Alessandro

Sauli in 1611 and of Caterina Ricci prior to 1657. [194] Enormous collections of votive objects became subjects of discussion in the early processes for miracles; more recently, they are separated from the investigations of miracles to be analyzed as part of the *fama,* or a "confirmation of cult," establishing a reputation for heroic virtue in any would-be saint.

Thus, in 1632, local worthies of Bourges—most elderly male clerics or notables with the occasional widow—were summoned to describe the objects left at the tomb of Jeanne de Valois. These people had little specific knowledge of cures, but they were confident that the numerous objects signified many favors granted.[195] Votives were especially important in causes of long-dead saints being considered through the "equivalent" process as *casi excepti.* In 1628, the cause of Humility heard the testimony of four nuns, two priests and two nobles, all of whom commented on the vast assemblage of silver votives as evidence for her many miracles.[196] Such objects were itemized and classified by location in a 1649 *Dubio* for Jan of Dukla,[197] and in 1892, an analytical list of votives left between 1519 and 1719 was incorporated into the cause for beatification of the hermit Falco.[198]

Myriad and dazzling variations upon the themes discussed in this chapter are played out in the records of the four centuries of healings. Incubation may have moved from the temple to the hospital, but it still provides a dominant structure to the healing experience. Likewise, beds, dreams, despair, an effort to help one's self, and the validation of others in witnessing illness and recovery are elements of the therapeutic experience that have persisted for millennia.

In the end—and unlike the diagnoses of doctors—these many variations are suspended from a solid structure of suffering, invocation, healing, and thanksgiving: a structure that is static through time. When it comes to recovery from illness, human experience follows a constant arc, a shape, a form. Is that stability an illusion, constructed by religion and the process of inquiry? Or could it be that suffering and the wonder of an unexpected recovery are timeless aspects of human existence itself? These questions are mostly for others to answer, but I offer some preliminary thoughts of a nonexpert in the final chapter.

Conclusion

Religion, Medicine, and Miracles

Do you believe in miracles? I am often asked that question when I speak about my work. After years of hesitating, now I answer comfortably, "Yes, I do." It is a historian's belief, and it challenges my medical identity.

I believe in the goodwill and honesty of these witnesses, be they educated or illiterate, religious or atheist. I believe in the accuracy of the scribes and translators. I believe in the plausible wonder that these tales meant to the players and the people involved in their collection, transmission, preservation, and use as evidence. I believe in the remarkably careful scrutiny conducted by the Church officials with the help of the best science and medicine available at the time. These stories are true. As a result, they are indeed miracles. Rather than appealing to an abstract philosophical definition in answer to "What is a miracle?" this ensemble defines the concept pragmatically: these events *were* miracles for the people involved.

The sheer number of healing miracles and their relentless stability command respect in this bottom-up approach to the definition. But I do not contend that these miracles represent all miracles imaginable. Far from it. They are mostly of one kind gathered for the specific purpose of serving the Roman Catholic process of canonization. The need for credible evidence has always pushed the selection process toward healings, by virtue of the witnesses, including doctors. The presence of an objective, educated, "nonpartisan" witness in the person of a physician was one factor that would favor healings over other wondrous events. The evidence was compelling.

In this conclusion, I will explore the remarkable stability of the healings and relate it to parallels in both the "nature" and the "doing" of medicine and religion. I am not the first to recognize these parallels, but my work on the miracle tales for this book brought the message home in a vivid way.

The Stability of Healing Miracles and the Nature of Medicine and Religion

Traditionally, historians look for change through time. Analysis of more than 1,400 miracles deriving from the sixteenth century to the end of the twentieth revealed some important changes in form (chapter 1), in diagnoses (chapter 3), in numbers of physicians involved (chapter 4), and in modalities of appeal (chapter 5). But the most remarkable feature of this survey is not change, but stability. The structure of the healing narratives and the investigative impulse, with its commitment to science, are remarkably constant in many different times and places. As shown in chapter 5, a dramatic "arc" defines each tale. Why should this be so? Two contradictory reasons can be considered.

On the one hand, as shown in chapter 5, the narratives are shaped by the formal questions. The stability, nature, and sequence of those questions generate an organized set of replies that tends to mold the story to a prescribed form. The questions might increase or decrease in number with time and place, but they were always directed at the same information; they were clearly delineated and usually compiled in a list in every complete file. The more files that I examined, the more familiar became the questions and the easier it was for me to ferret out the particular material that I sought. Regardless of the century in which they were written, I could count on these records to "deliver" in a reliable way through those numbered questions. Gradually I realized that the questions were "ordering" the story itself, even as they elicited its details. (In a similar manner, doctors "order" patient histories to make them amenable to their canons of knowledge—a point to which I will return in the "doing" section below.) This observation implies that the stability of miraculous experience was a product of the process, more apparent than real.

On the other hand, consider the opposite possibility that these narratives reflect a certain timelessness in human suffering and transcendence. Could the intrinsic nature of human experience have generated the questions that shape the records and the process? This explanation invites the possibility that religious and medical traditions are constructed in response to the perennial, inevitable challenges of suffering and death. Three surprising and telling elements of these files tend to support this second explanation.

First, the most constant aspect of medical (and religious) reality is the subliminal intelligence that we all must die. As a wag teacher used to quip, "Life is the only 'disease' that has one hundred percent mortality." In the many tales of "lives saved" resides a surprising irony: almost all witness who testified—be they miraculés, clerics, caregivers, or family—are now dead; if not, they will die soon. Sometimes, as discussed in chapter 2, the person who had been miraculously healed had already died before the investigation took place. As a result, the "miracle"—the thing of wonder—had nothing to do with breaking natural law by replacing death with immortality; rather, it lay in the *contemporary inability to explain* the recovery. All healings, natural or miraculous, are not about "lives saved"; rather they are tales of death delayed.

The second surprising feature of the records is their deep commitment to scientific evidence and the essential ingredient of medical surprise. The extent to which the religious observers relied on scientific skepticism came to me as a genuine shock. In the process of canonization, religion draws from and is instructed by science—and not just any random science, but the best available. Daniel Dennett, a famous atheist, labels this process a form of going "through the motions."[1] But it is far more sincere, deliberate, and committed than his grudging words would suggest. With the exception of ignoring the events altogether, no other "motions" or methods are available to us mortals. Even Dennett must admit that there is no science other than that which is known today, and he overstates his premise that the process does not challenge its witnesses.[2]

As this analysis of four centuries of inquiries has shown, the clerics question every witness and they readily defer to the opinion of scientists. They withhold a judgment of supernatural agency until they are convinced that the diagnoses are accurate, the investigations and treatments up-to-date, and the experts prepared to label the events inexplicable. In this sense, religion celebrates and endorses medical science, and it appears to have no need to refute it. Religion relies on the best of human wisdom before it imposes a judgment from inspired doctrine. When science provides a plausible explanation, religion will wait.

A corollary arises to this observation: religion sits more comfortably with medical science than vice versa. Of course, one advantage is that the process itself emerges from religion; the clerics are "at home," the medics are not. However, medical discomfiture stems not so much from the details of individual cases, but from the heart of medical identity. As shown in chapter 4, some treating physicians expressed doubts about the entire process; similarly, a few experts hesitated to pronounce on the cures, as if cooperation would constitute a betrayal of their own belief systems. Their skepticism originates in the built-in commitment of Western medicine to the idea that diseases and their cures are not, and can never be, of divine origin.

In the fifth century B.C., the Hippocratic author wrote the following on the "sacred disease," or what we call epilepsy: "It is not, in my opinion, any more divine or more sacred than other diseases, but has a natural cause, and its supposed divine origin is due to men's inexperience and to their wonder at its peculiar character."[3] In Western medical tradition, all diseases are natural; therefore, all cures must be natural too, even if we cannot explain them yet, or ever. This objection is not new. Absence of an explanation does not automatically turn an event into a miracle, a position strongly argued in debates between Protestants and Catholics during the nineteenth century.[4] A hematologist colleague insists that "we may never find the natural explanation, but one *must* exist." This recognition that people are not to be blamed (too much) for their ailments has consequently pervaded Occidental medicine. I will return to this essential trait of medical science below.

The third surprising feature of these records is the fact that history is relevant to the interpreters. Religion little cares if an explanation may come along in the future; medicine confidently expects that it will, and if it does, the explanation may disqualify the miracle retroactively. In this sense, religion proves more tolerant than does medicine of the human plight, anchored in time and space.

In the eighteenth century, Prospero Lambertini seemed to reckon with the possibility that perceived miracles might find natural explanations in an unforeseen future. With his insistence on heroic virtue as a necessary condition before considering miracles, a canonization would nonetheless remain justified, as it was for martyrs whose recognition did not require miracles. Saints were human, and like us they were once confined to time and space; invocations are similarly anchored in physicality. For all its emphasis on the eternal, in the domain of saint making, religion displays a surprising comfort with temporal relativism. Science does not, and the gap counts in this process.

These three surprising features of the miracle records suggest that the regularity of human experience in confrontation with suffering and death have shaped the questions and the process. This possibility is unimagined by skeptics, including many of my medical colleagues who are baffled by this research. They simply assume that all the healings must have been produced by autosuggestion, as described in the section on hysteria (chapter 3), or worse, by deception. Their discomfort stems from the idea that I, together with the doctors in the past, and perhaps also the miraculés themselves, have been duped by well-intentioned, wishful thinking. They are confident that modern techniques of examination would have exposed the majority of the diagnoses as honest mistakes or frauds. They may be right, but their objections are metahistorical, even presentist. Medical scientists are uncomfortable with relative truth; for them, somebody must be lying or misled. This posture flows from the commitment to natural if unknown explanations cited above, and it has been a characteristic of medicine since antiquity.[5]

These concrete attitudes about truth and demonstration inform the recent randomized controlled trials on the effectiveness of intercessory prayer for healing. Attempts to gauge the effectiveness of prayer stretch back at least to the nineteenth century.[6] In these studies, people are prayed for at a distance by collectivities of strangers or friends; the outcomes are assessed together with those of controls who ostensibly suffered without the benefit of prayer. Improved outcomes in the prayed-for group are construed as evidence for the effectiveness of prayer and the immanence of transcendence in our lives. Equal or worse outcomes are construed as evidence in favor of atheism and futility. Skeptics often refer to these studies and their failures as "proof" that appeals for divine help do not "work" and never will.

But the so-called evidence-based method cannot really address the questions that are most pressing. On the one hand, as the Vatican's chief medical expert explained, the miracle is in the particular, in the exceptional; statistics cannot prove or disprove that singular cause-and-effect relationship.[7] Furthermore, neither God nor the elusive and as-yet-unknown natural explanations, which my medical colleagues are convinced must exist, can be falsified. The possibility of falsification is used to design experiments and is considered a hallmark of the scientific method.[8] Both are beliefs, and they fall outside the realm of scientific method as we know it. Because the one belief utterly pervades the scientific community, it seems not to be a belief but a "fact."

Our predecessors, both medical and religious, lived within their own eras, and were obliged to reckon with problems by applying the best wisdom available, just as we are obliged to dwell within the limitations of our own time. One such limitation seems to be the tautological argument of positivist medics that wonder is impossible, because a natural explanation must exist and that it might eventually be found. Therefore, if something strikes us as wondrous, we must either ignore it or reject it as illusion, lying, posturing, or naiveté, because nothing can really be wondrous. Ironically, as explained above, this confidence in the existence of an unseen and unfathomable natural explanation is a belief masquerading as fact, which cannot be falsified any more than the proposition that God exists. In this context, Woodward wrote, "to assert that miracles cannot occur is no more rational—and no less an act of faith—than to assert that they can and do happen."[9]

Somehow, doctors have trouble accepting that claim. I understand the problem; in the clinic, I always behave according to that belief. As a physician, I must. But I do not lose anything by admitting it is a "truth" on the order of belief. Nor do I lose anything by respecting and acknowledging my patient's belief in God and the "enduring appeal of the miraculous," not only of the distant past, but also in our present.[10]

Yes, I believe that these stories are miracles. And through them, I have come to reconsider the *nature* of medical thinking as another form of faith, a system of belief. That is one parallel with religion. Another parallel emerges in the functioning, or the *doing* of both medicine and religion: the reading of signs.

Medicine and Religion as Semiotic Endeavors

Everyone—devout and skeptic alike—knows that their hour will come. If we are unlucky, death will be a deliberate or accidental killing. If we are lucky, the best possible end will be to die of illness in old age under the care of wise and kindly people.

These healing narratives, which the subjects chose to call "miraculous," are temporary postponements of the inevitable; as described above, they are stories of life improved and death delayed. They bespeak a *longue durée* that could serve as the very definition of medical practice: medicine, like life, has always been (and may always remain) a noble but losing struggle against our mortality. Many medical practitioners are uncomfortable with that definition too; they gloss over it when they claim to "save lives."

The *processi* reveal striking similarities between the actual performance of both religion and medicine on the personal level. Clerics and doctors together are tasked with bringing their elaborate systems of knowledge to bear upon an individual problem of suffering. Confronted with a sick person, both doctors and saint makers must observe each situation carefully, gathering evidence, reading "signs" that connect the particular to the established canons of wisdom from their respective disciplines. The evidence is the same; the method is the same; it is the interpretation that differs.

In the symptoms and the physical examination, the doctor searches for signs to confirm the diagnosis and the prognosis, and for signs of recovery and decline. To elicit the patient's history, the doctor asks a set of routine questions and performs physical manouvers in a specific way that allows the tale to be ordered and the body explored according to the demands of the diagnostic process. The resulting evidence can more easily be juxtaposed to prevailing wisdom about disease, investing the particular with interpretive power, turning observations into signs. This practice used to be called medical semiology in English, as it still is in many other European languages. Similarly through their formal approach and rigorous questions, the clerics look for signs of sanctity to be found in evidence that the case was truly desperate, that the best medicine was given, that an appeal was indeed made, and that no scientific explanation can be found. Beyond passive observation, the examinations in both medicine and religion are active: the canonical wisdom of both traditions participates in the process, directing the inquiry and investing the particular circumstances with meaning, transforming them into signifiers for deeper interpretation.

The difference between these two perspectives does not require us to discredit any of the testimony as lying or wishful thinking. Rather, it resides in the interpretation of the evidence. For doctors, the medical canon is immersed in an antideistic tradition, as described above: only nature—not God—can ever be the cause or cure of diseases. For religion, all plausible scientific explanations, be they human or natural, must first be eliminated before the case becomes a contender as a reliable sign of transcendence or holiness. In both cases, what is left is that which is unknown; religious observers are prepared to call it God. They accept divine agency within their interpretive framework through belief in God and the inspirational nature of scripture; such faith is often described as a miracle itself. It is the source of a burgeoning, hoary literature of theological explication on such questions as "Why does God send plague?"[11]

But medical scientists are not prepared to attribute the unknown to God. As described above, their discomfort also arises from a kind of faith—the absolute belief in the nontranscendence of earthly events. Like those who believe in God, they *believe in* the existence of a natural explanation, as yet unknown but open for discovery. A commitment to this article of secular faith is found in the popular writing of atheists, who strive to contrast religion with reason.[12] But as Mark Corner wrote, "there can be no certainty (since we obviously cannot anticipate what medical science will know in a century's time) that a miracle has taken place. At the same time, however, there is no certainty that a miracle has *not* taken place."[13] As outlined above, only another form of belief sustains that interpretation.

Although these miracle stories emerged through the Roman Catholic tradition, I think that they also represent human response to illness everywhere, and assimilating this message could be useful to doctors. Sick people from many times and places consult physicians and carefully follow their advice. But they simultaneously look for other ways out of their predicaments. They may see doctors as instruments of healing, but they are equally comfortable with, if not more inclined to, the opinion that cures are effected by ourselves, by nature, or by deities with help from saints and long-lost predecessors. Getting better is directly connected to gestures of personal history, lifestyle, sacrifice, supplication, penance, and worship. The Lord helps those who help themselves.

It is these personal gestures of appeal to medicine and beyond that link the illness and healing experiences of all people, whenever or wherever they may have lived and whether they are religious or not. Those who eat tofu, run marathons, practice yoga, quit smoking, avoid the sun, watch their weight, curb their alcohol, play sports, make sacrifices—or swallow aspirin, multivitamins, antioxidants, and hormones—are also pilgrims and penitents actively hedging their bets against the inevitable. Those gestures may have nothing to do with religion, but they have everything to do with interpretation and faith; they instill and enrich our existence with meaning because they are connected to beliefs about how the world works. This struggle for continuity in the face of death marks our lives. The Roman Catholic process of inquiry is shaped by it. I believe that the static structure of the healing stories reflects this timeless and pervasive reality of human experience.

In these remarkable files, two ancient, human-built traditions of knowledge confront each other on the mysterious terrain of human suffering. Medicine has been elaborated to prevent or relieve suffering; religion, to reconcile us to it. Departing from radically different premises, both are positioned to confront the inevitability of death: medicine trying to postpone it; religion, to console us. In their confraternation around the stories of death delayed and life restored, we learn more about their striking operative similarities.

In order to pronounce, religion and medicine are obliged to gather, order and assess the evidence emerging from a single locus of human misery before they can connect it to their respective and elaborate bodies of wisdom, each of which relies on a commitment to what must govern the unknown.[14] Therefore, medicine and religion emerge as remarkably similar belief systems and semiotic endeavors—applying their ever-evolving canons of wisdom to locate meaning in the careful observation and interpretation of signs, of diagnosis, of healing, and of wonder.

Appendix A

Note on Sources and Method

The Vatican Secret Archives is a remarkable place. From my first naïve foray as an academic tourist, I was given a polite welcome and generous access to the canonization files (Riti Processi) up to and including 1922. All files covering the years of the six most recent papacies are sealed. With the death of Pope John Paul II, seventeen more years of records were opened through to the end of the papacy of Pius XI in 1939. I was able to consult them in my last visit. Superb finding aids to the Riti Processi, prepared by Father Yvon Beaudoin, help with the search, and never was any requested file reported missing.[1] Once or twice in many weeks of work, the wrong file arrived, but the clerks rectified it promptly with an apology even when the mistake had been mine.

With such accessibility, efficiency, and courtesy, the ASV is a scholar's dream. But its limitations are familiar to anyone who has worked there: one can request only three files in any given day. Some scholars toil on the same file for months on end. Not me. With a goal of covering as much miracle ground as possible, I began to view each bundle brought from the depths as a kind of complicated, seamless nut that I must crack in short order—a Houdini-esque challenge. Logistics were an issue.

The archive opens six days a week until 1:30 P.M. It is located next door to the Vatican Library, which holds many printed depositions on the miracles and remains open in the afternoon. Working in both places, I could have a continuous supply of either manuscript or printed records to feed my frenzy from dawn till evening when the library doors shut too. Forget lunch. The fascination of the testimony kept me ever more motivated, but my execrable Italian and the demanding pace over four increasingly long visits taxed the patience, good humor, and stamina of the kind *signori* who fetched the files. By the end, however, they began to find me more of a joke than an annoyance.

On the eve of my departure for Canada, in the last hour of the last open day before Christmas, they handed me an unprecedented fourth requisition, as a *regalo di Natale*.

As explained in the preface, each *positio*—or deposition—is the record of an inquiry run like a court of inquest and usually including the testimony of many witnesses: clerical, medical, and laypeople. Every witness to a miracle is asked the same questions, which are based on the mid-eighteenth-century codification of Prospero Lambertini. The questions usually appear as a list at the beginning or end of each file. The oaths and testimony are recorded verbatim in the vernacular by religious scribes. For inquiries held outside Italy, a Latin or Italian translation is often kept with the original. Usually a summary in numbered "articles" accompanies the testimony, and witnesses are sometimes invited to endorse or refute each article in the summary. Tape recorders are now used to gather testimony. The evidence is then transcribed into a fair copy and sent to the Vatican for consideration. The earliest typewritten record that I examined was from 1904;[2] however, many records were handwritten after that date. Only rarely do the records enjoy an index or a list of witnesses. Some *positiones* were printed and bound, like the one given to me in 1990. Being books, they might also be placed in the Vatican and other libraries where they are more accessible than those in the archives.

As physical objects, each archival *positio* is a bundle of papers or parchment, running from fifty pages to more than a thousand. They are gathered by laces, envelopes, boxes, or file folders. Some are illuminated with colored or gilded ornaments; a few have large wax seals that dangle from cords or are protected with cotton wool. Once in a while, the ink had crystallized into metallic granules that eventually covered my desk, paper, fingers, and face. Scripts can be difficult to decipher, but only one file proved to be absolutely illegible, owing as much to my lack of skill as a paleographer as to inadequacies of the hand and pallor of the ink.[3] The most unusual file that I examined was from the cause of Ferdinand: bound as a supple, sewn codex, it contained more than five thousand eight-by-eleven-inch pages; lying flat on the desk, it towered nearly thirty-six inches high.[4] Heads turned in the reading room as the *signori* helped bring it to my place.

Given these difficulties, familiarity with the questions and their sequence offers an indispensable guide to each file. For example, Question 2 asks each witness for a name, age, birthplace, parentage, occupation, and income. Question 3 asks each witness to describe her own religious practices. Another question asks for a definition of "miracle"; yet another, for an account of the events under consideration. Subtle variations emerge in versions of the same miracle when told by several witnesses, one of many enticing aspects of this work.

The records are classified by saint. Each saint's collection may contain separate files for the biography (*vita*), reputation (*fama*), the doubts of the devil's advocate (*dubio*), and the miracle or miracles (*miro* or *miris*). The files that had been used in the beatification may also be included. In the archival documents of saints canonized in the seventeenth century, sometimes all these elements were gathered into a single file; alternatively, testimony on many miracles could be assembled into a single inquiry designated as "that which happened after death."[5] These characteristics are carefully identified in Father Beaudoin's finding aids.

In my first visit, it quickly became clear that the collections for some saints contained many files on miracles—up to a dozen and generated over the course of a century or more—each representing a separate investigation. Notwithstanding the traditional requirement of two miracles for beatification and another two for canonization, it seemed that some miracles might have been relatively unconvincing. Of course, factors other than miracles influence the decision to canonize: the time must be ripe, politically and socially, for a canonization to proceed. More miracles will flow during the wait.[6]

Given the wealth of the files and the logistical constraints of opening times, some selection became necessary. I began by examining one miracle—preferably the final miracle—in the records of every canonization since 1800. The year of the final miracle may bear little correspondence to that of canonization: a twentieth-century canonization could cite a miracle cure from the eighteenth. In making this selection, I reasoned that the miracle closest to the decision to canonize must have been convincing; at least it could not have been unconvincing. Initially I focused on the last two hundred years, because that was the era of my previous historical interests and ability. This systematic restriction resulted in a set of 158 cures (30 for beatifications) scattered unevenly across three centuries. Few of these miracles were generated between 1750 and 1850 when canonizations were rare.

To compensate for the unevenness and wondering about what transcendent experiences, if any, may have been reported during that period, I extended the search to include nonfinal miracles for each saint, concentrating whenever possible on testimony generated in the early nineteenth century. Also I decided to roll back the chronological parameters to seek information on the miracles of saints who had been canonized before 1800. Initially, I had suspected that these records would prove more difficult to read, but they were often better organized and more legible than those of the twentieth century.

Finally, I attempted to collect at least one miracle for every canonization from 1588 to 1999, if the saint's collection contained miracles. To the best of my ability, that is what I have done. In figure A.1, the top of the bars displays the 1,409 miracles collected in this study by year of canonization; the two lower portions of the bars represent the *final* miracles for canonizations (N = 521) or beatification. Nine hundred miracles of the total provided a date for the invocation or testimony. Figure A.1 shows their distribution by year of cure, invocation, or testimony.

A conservative estimate suggests that I have examined a third to a half of the total number of files on miracles in the ASV (table A.1). This number is amplified by the supplementary information described below. As can be seen in the two figures, even with the broadened criteria, early-nineteenth-century miracles are relatively scarce.

For more than 500 miracles, my information came from examination of the actual *positiones*, verbatim transcripts of the inquiry, usually in the form of manuscripts, in the ASV (table A.2). Another 144 were derived from detailed testimony in the printed *Positiones* that are held in the Vatican Library. For the most recent fifty years, the ASV records are inaccessible and the books of Andrea Resch concerning both beatifications and canonizations were indispensible sources;[7] another 14 miracles were retold by Dario Composta.[8] Both authors relied on privileged access to the *Positiones*.

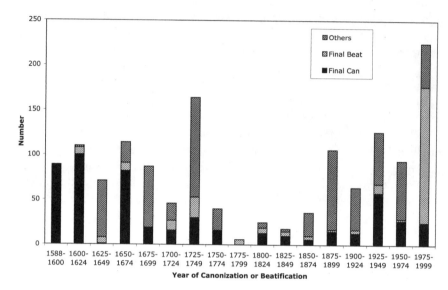

FIGURE A.1. Final miracles and other miracles by year of canonization or beatification
(*N* = 1,409).

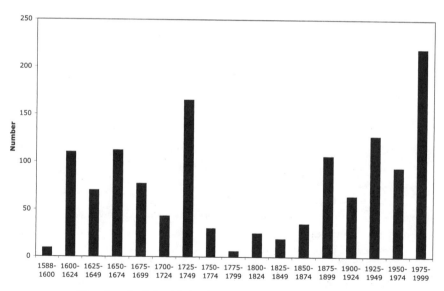

FIGURE A.2. Nine hundred datable healing miracles examined in the study by year
of cure.

TABLE A.I. Estimate of Unexamined Miracles ($N = 486$ files with at least 571 miracles)

From year to year	1600 1649	1650 1699	1700 1749	1750 1799	1800 1849	1850 1899	1900 1949	1950 1999
No. files unexamined	3	2	20	17	12	22	150	249
*Av. no. miracles per file	26.3	11.1	6.9 (3.7)[a]	3	2.3	3.1 (1.2)[b]	1.5	2 (1)[c]
Estimated number unseen miracles	79	22	138 (74)[a]	51	28	68 (26)[b]	225	(248)[c]

*See Figure 1.2. Estimated total of unseen miracles in ASV: maximum 1,107; medium 753; minimum 571. Therefore, proportion of all miracles in ASV files seen ranges from 563 of 1,671 (33.8 %) to 563 of 1,317 (43%) to best possible 563 of 1,134 (50%). Optimistic estimate 50% of the miracles records in ASV. Pessimistic estimate 33%. Realistic estimate approximately 40%.

[a]Correction by elimination of one file, Catarina Riccis: testimony of 1637 with 55 miracles; not a process but a list kept by a descendant and filed with the canonization records.

[b]Correction by exclusion of an ASV file on testimony from 1682 applied to the nineteenth-century canonization of Pierre Fourier.

[c]Correction by exclusion of an ASV file on testimony from 1632 applied to the twentieth-century canonization of Jeanne de Valois.

For 393 of the miracles, however, information is less detailed and comes from the *Vitae* or *Compendia,* the pamphlet-sized summaries of the process published by the Vatican at the time of each canonization. These documents are especially important when original records are missing or inaccessible. For example, the ASV holds no archival documents pertaining to investigations for several of the saints canonized between 1588 and 1700. Similarly, these printed summaries are important for the most recent canonizations, because the archival files after 1939 are sealed. In five summaries, the miracle was described only as an unspecified "healing"; however, the majority identify the diagnoses, the sufferers, and their doctors, often with names, dates, and places of cure.

TABLE A.2. Sources on Miracles in This Study

	Canonization	Beatification	Total
Complete			
ASV manuscript	529	18	547
Published *Positio*	118	26	144
Subtotal	647	44	691
Summary			
Compendia	226	54	280
Vitae	92	6	98
Resch	20	131	151
Other	178	11	189
Subtotal	516	202	718
Total	1,163	246	1,409

As the work proceeded, I entered information from the miracles into an electronic database using Filemaker Pro © (now in version 7). Elements of each miracle were transferred into a record with up to forty-five fields that offered calculation possibilities and could be searched and sorted alphabetically, numerically, or by date. This electronic record was no substitute for my detailed notes in penciled scrawl, but it proved to be a fabulously pliable index that generated many observations which I would otherwise have missed. In the future, I plan to make essential portions of this database available through a central data archive, hoping that my fallible efforts will prove useful to others.

Unless otherwise indicated, all translations are my own.

Appendix B

Saints, Blesseds, Venerables,
and the Sources on Their Miracles

Birth and death dates are sometimes approximate.

Collective canonizations, especially of martyrs, have only one entry in this list.

Except in cases of well known saints, the names are given in the common usage for the saint's homeland. For example, "John" could be Jan, Jean, Juan, Giovanni, Joannes, Iohannes, or Johann. The ASV archive and most *Compendia* identify saints with the Latin version of their names. As a result, the Latin version is used in the reference notes with the ASV Riti Processi call number. Saints for whom no sources on miracles were found were most often canonized as *casi excepti*.

Printed sources appear in the bibliography only if they were specifically cited in this book. They can be found in either the BAV or the Archives of the CCS. Some, especially multiple volumes of printed *Positiones and Compendia*, are not in the online catalogue, but library staff are invariably helpful in tracing them quickly. With the wide array or languages, names, and numbers, making errors is all too easy. I would be grateful for corrections to these lists.

Abbreviations used in these appendices appear on pages 207 and 213.

Some blesseds in table B.2 have been canonized since 1999.

TABLE B.I. Saints Canonized between 1588 and 1999 and Sources Examined on Their Miracles

Name	Born	Died	Can.	M/F	Nation (city or region)	Printed Source	ASV RP File No.
Agnes of Prague	1211	1282	1989	F	Czechoslovakia (Bohemia)	CV	
Agnes Segni of Montepulciano	1268	1317	1726	F	Italy (Tuscany)		1801
Agostina Pietrantoni	1864	1894	1999	F	Italy	CV	
Albert Chmielowski	1845	1916	1989	M	Poland (Cracow)	R	
Albertus Magnus	1206	1280	1931	M	Germany		
Alessandro Sauli	1534	1592	1904	M	Italy	CV	1163, 3764
Alfonso Maria of Liguori	1696	1787	1839	M	Italy	CV	2080, 2083
Alfonso Rodriguez	1532	1617	1888	M	Spain (Majorca)	D, P	1624, 1625
André Hubert Fournet	1753	1834	1933	M	France		4321, 4322
Andrea Avellino	1521	1608	1712	M	Italy	D	1993
Andrea Corsini	1302	1374	1629	M	Italy (Florence)	CV	
Andrzej Bobola, martyr	1592	1657	1938	M	Poland	CV, P	762
Angela Merici	1470	1540	1807	F	Italy	CV	344
Antonio Gianelli	1789	1846	1951	M	Italy (Cortona)	CV	
Antonio Maria Claret	1807	1870	1950	M	Catalonia	CV	4390
Antonio Maria Pucci	1819	1892	1962	M	Italy	CV	
Antonio Maria Zaccaria, doctor	1502	1539	1897	M	Italy		
Bartholomea Capitanio	1807	1833	1950	F	Italy (Brescia)	CV, P	3857
Beatrice da Silva Meneses	1424	1492	1976	F	Portugal	CV	
Benedetto Menni	1841	1914	1999	M	Italy (Milan)	CV	
Benedetto of S. Philadelpho (Manassari)	1526	1589	1807	M	Italy (Sicily)	CV	
Benilde Romançon	1805	1862	1967	M	France	CV	
Benoit Joseph Labré	1748	1783	1881	M	France		
Bernadette Soubirous	1844	1879	1933	F	France	P	2392–93, 2397

(continued)

Name							
Bernardino Realino	1530	1616	1947	M	Italy (Capri)	CV	
Bruno	1030	1101	1623	M	France	CV	
Camillo de Lellis	1550	1614	1746	M	Italy (Naples)	CV	1681
Carlo Borromeo	1538	1584	1610	M	Italy	CV	
Carlo da Sezze	1613	1670	1959	M	Italy	P	
Caterina of Bologna	1413	1463	1712	F	Italy (Bologna)	D	262
Caterina de' Ricci	1522	1590	1746	F	Italy (Florence)	CV	793
Caterina of Genoa (Fieschi Adorno)	1447	1510	1737	F	Italy (Genoa)	CV	
Caterina Thomas of Palma	1533	1574	1930	F	Spain (Majorca)	P	4518
Catherine Labouré	1806	1876	1947	F	France	P	
Charbel Makhlouf	1828	1898	1977	M	Lebanon		
Charles-Joseph-Eugène de Mazenod	1782	1861	1995	M	France	Co, R	2930
Chiara of Montefalco	1268	1308	1881	F	Italy	P	
Claude de la Colombière	1641	1682	1992	M	France (Dauphiné)	R	
Clelia Barbieri	1847	1870	1989	F	Italy (Bologna)	CV, R	
Clement Maria Hofbauer (Dvorak)	1751	1821	1909	M	Moravia	CV	3861
Colette Boylet de Corbie	1381	1447	1807	F	Belgium	P	1021
Conrad of Parzham	1818	1894	1934	M	Germany (Bavaria)	CV	
Crispin of Viterbo	1668	1750	1982	M	Italy	CV	
Diego d'Alcalá (Didacus)	1400	1463	1588	M	Spain	P	
Domenico Savio	1842	1857	1954	M	Italy (Turin)		
Egidio Maria di San Giuseppe (Pontillo)	1729	1812	1996	M	Italy (Puglia)	CV	
Elisabeth Ann Seton	1774	1821	1975	F	USA	CV	
Elizabeth of Portugal Lusitania	1271	1336	1625	F	Portugal		
Emilie de Rodat	1787	1852	1950	F	France		4292
Emilie de Vialar	1797	1856	1951	F	France	P	

Name	Born	Died	Can.	M/F	Nation (city or region)	Printed Source	ASV RP File No.
English & Welsh Martyrs (Cuthbert Mayne et al.)		1679	1970	M	England/Wales	CV	5112
Enrique de Ossó y Cervelló	1840	1896	1993	M	Spain	Co, R	
Eustochia Calafato	1434	1491	1988	F	Italy (Sicily)	R	
Ezeqiel Moreno y Díaz	1848	1906	1992	M	Spain/Philippines	R	
Felice of Cantalice	1515	1587	1712	M	Italy	CV	
Felix of Valois*	1127	1212	1666	M	France	CV	
Felmo (Pedro Gonzales)	1190	1246	1741	M	Spain		3257
Fernando, King of Castile	1198	1252	1671	M	Spain		1111
Fidelis of Sigmaringen	1577	1622	1746	M	Prussia		
Filippo Benizi, doctor	1233	1285	1671	M	Italy	CV	
Filippo Neri	1515	1595	1622	M	Italy (Florence)	CV	
Frances Xavier Cabrini	1850	1917	1946	F	USA	CV	
Francesca Romana (Ponziani)	1384	1440	1608	F	Italy	CV	
Francesco Antonio Fasani	1681	1742	1985	M	Italy	R	
Francesco Caracciolo	1563	1608	1807	M	Italy	CV	1897
Francesco Maria of Camporubeo	1804	1866	1962	M	Italy	CV	
Francesco of Girolamo	1641	1716	1839	M	Italy	CV	
Francis Xavier	1506	1552	1622	M	Spain (Basque)	CV	
Francis Xavier Maria Bianchi	1743	1815	1951	M	Italy (Naples)		1921, 3724
Francisco Borgias	1510	1572	1670	M	Spain	CV	
Francisco Solano	1549	1610	1726	M	Spain		1333
François de Sales	1567	1622	1665	M	France		991
Gabriel of Our Lady of Sorrows (Possenti)	1838	1862	1920	M	Italy		4610

Name				Sex	Place	Type	Reference
Gaetano of Thiene	1480	1547	1671	M	Italy (Vincenza)	CV	
Gaspare Bertoni	1777	1835	1989	M	Italy (Verona)	R	
Gaspari del Bufalo	1786	1837	1954	M	Italy	CV	4613
Gemma Galgani	1878	1903	1940	F	Italy (Lucca)	CV	3842, 4622
Gerardo Majella	1725	1755	1904	M	Italy		3283–86
Germaine Cousin	1579	1601	1867	F	France (Toulouse)	CV	
Gery of Monte Santo*		13C	1742	M	France (Provence)		3588, 3595
Giacinta Marescotti	1585	1640	1807	F	Italy	CV	2009
Giacomo della Marca	1394	1476	1726	M	Italy	CV, D	
Giovanni da Capistrano	1386	1456	1690	M	Italy	CV	2548–49
Giovanni Battista Rossi	1698	1764	1881	M	Italy	P	
Giovanni Bosco	1815	1888	1934	M	Italy	CV	
Giovanni Calabria	1873	1954	1999	M	Italy	CV	1944–47
Giovanni Giuseppe (Calosinto)	1654	1739	1839	M	Italy (Ischia)	CV	1481, 5661
Giovanni Leonardi	1543	1609	1938	M	Italy (Lucca)	CV	3507
Girolamo Miani	1481	1537	1767	M	Italy	CV	
Giuliana Falconieri	1270	1341	1737	F	Italy	CV	
Giuseppe Desideri of Leonissa	1556	1612	1746	M	Italy		4798
Giuseppe Benedetto Cottolengo	1786	1842	1934	M	Italy		4799, 4801
Giuseppe Cafasso	1811	1860	1947	M	Italy (Asti)	P	
Giuseppe Maria Pignatelli	1737	1811	1954	M	Spain	CV, R	
Giuseppe Maria Tomasi	1649	1713	1986	M	Italy (Sicily)	CV, R	
Giuseppe Moscati, doctor	1880	1927	1987	M	Italy (Benevento)	CV	
Giuseppe of Cupertino (Desa)	1603	1663	1767	M	Italy	CV	
Gregorio Barbarigo	1625	1697	1960	M	Italy (Venice)	CV	5404
Hedwig	1371	1399	1997	F	Poland		
Herman, Joseph*	1150	1241	1958	M	Germany	M	
Humility	1226	1310	1720	F	Italy	F	712
Hyacinthe (Jacek Odrowacz)	1185	1257	1594	M	Poland	CV	

(continued)

TABLE B.I. (continued)

Name	Born	Died	Can.	M/F	Nation (city or region)	Printed Source	ASV RP File No.
Ignatius of Loyola	1491	1556	1622	M	Spain	CV	
Ignazio of Laconi	1701	1781	1951	M	Italy (Sardinia)	CV, P	414
Isidro Labrador (Agricola)	1080	1130	1622	M	Spain	CV	
Jan Berchmans	1599	1621	1888	M	Belgium (Brabant)		2324, 2327, 2329, 3716
Jan Dukla	1414	1484	1997	M	Ukraine	D	
Jan Kanty (John Cantius)	1390	1473	1767	M	Poland	CV	633
Jan Nepomuk	1340	1393	1729	M	Czech	CV	
Jan Sarkander	1576	1620	1995	M	Silesia	R	
Jean-Baptiste de la Salle	1651	1719	1900	M	France		3886, 3889, 3890, 3892
Jean-Baptiste Vianney	1786	1859	1925	M	France		4713
Jean Eudes	1601	1680	1925	M	France		4764
Jean-François Régis	1597	1640	1737	M	France	CV	
Jean-Gabriel Perboyre, martyr	1802	1840	1996	M	France		4766, 4768
Jeanne Antide Thouret	1765	1826	1934	F	France	P	
Jeanne de Lestonnac	1556	1640	1949	F	France	Co, CV	
Jeanne de Valois	1461	1504	1950	F	France	CV	
Jeanne Delanoue	1666	1736	1982	F	France	CV	
Jeanne Elisabeth Bichier des Ages	1773	1838	1947	F	France	CV	252
Jeanne Françoise Fremiot de Chantal	1572	1641	1767	F	France	CV	
Joan of Arc	1412	1431	1920	F	France	CV	883
João de Brito	1647	1693	1947	M	Portugal	D, P	5682
Joaquina Vedruna de Mas	1783	1854	1959	F	Spain	P	
John Fisher, martyr	1469	1535	1935	M	England	CV	
John Nepomucene Neumann	1811	1860	1977	M	Bohemia/USA	CV	

John of God	1495	1550	1690	M	Portugal	CV	
John of Matha*	1160	1223	1666	M	France	CV	
John Ogilvie, martyr	1579	1615	1976	M	Scotland	CV	
Josaphat Kuncevic, martyr	1580	1623	1876	M	Ukraine/Lithuania	CV	2707
José de Calasanz	1556	1648	1767	M	Spain (Aragon)	CV	4089
José Orioli	1650	1702	1909	M	Spain (Barcelona)	CV	
Juan Bautista de la Concepción	1561	1613	1975	M	Spain	CV	
Juan de la Cruz	1542	1591	1726	M	Spain	CV	
Juan de Ribera	1532	1611	1960	M	Spain	CV	2828
Juan de S. Facondo de Sahagún	1430	1479	1690	M	Spain	CV	
Juan Grande Roman	1546	1600	1996	M	Spain	Co	
Juan Macias	1585	1645	1975	M	Spain/Peru		3172
Juan of Avila	1500	1569	1970	M	Spain	CV	
Julie Billiart	1751	1816	1969	F	France	CV	
Julien Eymard	1811	1868	1962	M	France	CV	
Justin de Jacobis	1800	1860	1975	M	Italy (Naples)	CV	
Kinga	1234	1292	1999	F	Hungary/Poland	CV	
Leonardo Murialdo	1828	1900	1970	M	Italy	CV	
Leonardo of Porto Maurizio	1676	1751	1867	M	Italy	Co, R	2497, 2499, 2502, 2503
Leopold Bogdan Mandic	1866	1942	1983	M	Croatia	CV	
Lorenzo Giustiniani	1381	1455	1690	M	Italy (Venice)	CV	381
Lorenzo of Brindisi	1559	1619	1881	M	Italy		
Louis-Marie Grignon de Montfort	1673	1716	1947	M	France		4116, 4894
Louise de Marillac	1591	1660	1934	F	France	P	
Lucia Filippini	1672	1732	1930	F	Italy		4862, 4865
Luigi Gonzaga	1568	1591	1726	M	Italy	CV	
Luis Bertran	1526	1581	1671	M	Spain	CV	
Maddalena of Canossa	1774	1835	1988	F	Italy (Verona)	R	

(continued)

TABLE B.I. (continued)

Name	Born	Died	Can.	M/F	Nation (city or region)	Printed Source	ASV RP File No.
Madeleine Sophie Barat	1779	1865	1925	F	France		4912, 4917
Marcellin Champagnat	1789	1840	1999	M	France	CV	
Margaret of Hungary	1242	1271	1943	F	Hungary	CV	
Margherita of Cortona	1247	1297	1728	F	Italy		550
Marguerite Bourgeoys	1620	1700	1982	F	France/Canada	CV	4927
Marguerite Marie Alacoque	1647	1690	1920	F	France		4933
Maria Anna of Jesus de Paredes	1618	1645	1950	F	Ecuador	CV	
Maria Bertilla Boscardin	1888	1922	1961	F	Italy	P	
Maria Crocifissa di Rosa	1813	1855	1954	F	Italy	PV	
Maria Domenica Mazzarello	1837	1881	1951	F	Italy	P	
Maria Francesca of the Five Wounds (Gallo)	1715	1791	1867	F	Italy (Naples)	CV	1959
Maria Giuseppa Rossello	1811	1880	1949	M	Italy (Liguria)	P	
Maria Goretti	1890	1902	1950	F	Italy	CV	
Maria Maddelena de' Pazzi	1566	1604	1669	F	Italy (Florence)		770, 771
Maria Michaela de San Sacramento (Desmaisieres)	1809	1865	1934	F	Spain		5074, 5085
Maria of Providence Eugenie Smet	1825	1871	1957	F	French		
Maria Rosa Molas y Vallvé	1815	1876	1988	F	Spain (Tarragon)	R	
Maria Soledad della Dolorato Torres Acosta	1826	1887	1970	F	Spain	CV	
Marie-Euphrasie Pelletier	1796	1868	1940	F	France	F	4971, 4974
Marie de St Ignatius (Claudine Thévenet)	1774	1837	1993	F	France		
Marie-Madeleine Postel	1756	1846	1925	F	France	R	5073

Name				Sex	Country		
Marie-Marguerite de Youville	1701	1771	1990	F	Canada	P, R	
Marie-Victoire-Thérèse Couderc	1805	1885	1970	F	France	P	
Martin de Porres, doctor	1579	1639	1962	M	Peru	CV	
Martyrs of Astoria (9), Cirilo Bertrán et al.		1934	1999	M	Spain		
Martyrs of Canada (8): Jean de Brébeuf, I. Jogues, R. Goupil (doctor) et al.		1649	1930	M	France/Canada	P	
Martyrs of Gorkum (18), Nicholas Pieck et al.		1572	1867	M	Holland	CV, D	
Martyrs of Japan (15), Lorenzo Ruiz et al.		1630	1987	M, F	Japan		
Martyrs of Japan (26), Paul Miki, Peter Baptiste et al.		1597	1862	M	Japan/Spain	CV	
Martyrs of Kosice (3)		1619	1995	M	Croatia/Hungary		
Martyrs of Paraguay (3), Rocco Gonzalez et al.		1628	1988	M	Paraguay	CV	
Martyrs of Uganda (21), Charles Lwanga et al.	1865	1885	1964	M	Uganda	CV	
Martyrs of Vietnam (117)			1988	M, F	Vietnam	CV	
Maximilian Kolbe	1894	1941	1982	M	Poland	D, P	5137
Michael Garicoits	1797	1863	1947	M	France (Basque)	CV	3435
Miguel de los Santos (Argemir)	1591	1625	1862	M	Spain	CV	
Miguel Febres Codero	1854	1910	1984	M	Ecuador	P, R	
Mutien Marie (Louis Wiaux)	1841	1917	1989	M	Belgium (Namur)	R	4209
Nicholas de Flue	1417	1487	1947	M	Switzerland		
Oliver Plunkett	1629	1681	1975	M	Ireland	Co, CV	
Pacífico de San Severino	1653	1721	1839	M	Italy	CV	2945
Paola Frassinetti	1809	1882	1984	F	Italy	R	

(continued)

TABLE B.I. (continued)

Name	Born	Died	Can.	M/F	Nation (city or region)	Printed Source	ASV RP File No.
Paolo della Croce (Danei)	1694	1775	1867	M	Italy (Piedmont)		2355–56, 2360
Pasqual Baylón	1540	1592	1690	M	Spain	CV	3407
Pedro Arbués, martyr	1442	1485	1867	M	Spain	CV	
Pedro Claver	1581	1654	1888	M	Spain		1183, 1189, 1190
Pedro de Alcántara	1499	1562	1669	M	Spain	CV	10, 14b
Pedro Regalado	1390	1456	1746	M	Spain	CV	2138
Pellegrino Laziosi	1260	1345	1726	M	Italy	CV	
Peter Kanis	1521	1597	1925	M	Holland	P	5166
Peter Nolasco*	1182	1258	1628	M	France		
Pierre Fourier de Notre Dame	1565	1640	1897	M	France	D, P	3008, 4119
Pierre-Louis Chanel, martyr	1803	1841	1954	M	France		5162
Pietro Orseolo	928	987	1731	M	Italy (Venice)	CV	
Pompilio Maria Pirrotti	1710	1756	1934	M	Italy		5258, 5262
Pope Gregory VII (Hildebrand)	1004	1085	1606	M	Italy	CV	
Pope Pius V	1504	1572	1712	M	Italy	CV	2553, 2554
Pope Pius X	1835	1914	1954	M	Italy (Venice)	CV	
Raffaela Maria Porras	1850	1925	1977	F	Spain	CV	
Ramón de Penyafort	1185	1276	1600	M	Spain	CV	
Raphael Kalinowski	1835	1907	1991	M	Lithuania/Poland	R	221
Raymond Nonnatus*		1240	1657	M	Spain		
Riccardo Pampuri, doctor	1897	1930	1989	M	Italy (Pavia)	R	
Rita of Cascia	1386	1457	1900	F	Italy		4022, 4023
Roberto Bellarmino	1542	1621	1930	M	Italy	CV	5266
Rosa of Lima	1586	1617	1671	F	Peru	CV	
Rose Philippine Duschesne	1769	1852	1988	F	France/USA	R	
Salvador de Horta	1520	1567	1938	M	Spain	CV	
Serafino of Monte Granario	1540	1604	1767	M	Italy	CV	95
Seven Founders		1310	1888	M	Italy		3850

Name			Sex	Place		
Simon de Rojas	1552	1624	M	Spain (Valladolid)	R	
Stanislaus Kostka	1550	1568	M	Poland	CV	
Teresa Benedicta (Edith Stein)	1891	1942	F	Germany	CV, N, W	
Teresa de Jesús (Jornet y Ibars)	1843	1897	F	Spain	CV	
Teresa de los Andes	1900	1920	F	Chile	R R1	
Teresa Margerita Redi	1747	1770	F	Italy (Florence)		5652, 5656
Teresa of Avila	1515	1582	F	Spain	CV	
Teresia & Sancia of Portugal		1250	F	Portugal	D	
Theophilus of Corte	1676	1740	M	Corsica		1829, 5292, 5294, 6215i
Thérèse of Lisieux	1873	1897	F	France		7002
Thomas More, martyr	1478	1535	M	England	CV	
Tomás de Villanueva	1488	1555	M	Spain		3641
Tomasso of Cori	1655	1729	M	Italy	CV	
Turibio Alfonso Mogrovejo	1538	1606	M	Spain		1605
Veronica Giuliani	1660	1727	F	Italy (Umbria)		3170
Vincent de Paul	1581	1660	M	France	CV	
Vincentia Maria Lopez y Vicuña	1847	1896	F	Spain	P	
Vincenza Gerosa	1784	1847	F	Italy (Brescia)	CV	
Vincenzo Pallotti	1795	1850	M	Italy	CV	
Vincenzo Strambi	1745	1824	M	Italy	CV, R	
Zdislava of Lemberk	1220	1252	F	Czech (Moravia)		5357
Zita	1218	1272	F	Italy	CV	

ASV Archivio Segreto del Vaticano, Riti Processi Call Number

b   Beatification
Co   Composta, Il miracolo, 1981
CV   Compendium or Vita
D   Positio super dubio (or Animadversiones)
F   Positio super fama
N   Newspaper

P   Positio super miraculo (or miraculis)
PV   Positio super validitate
R   Resch, Miracoli dei Santi, 2002
R1   Resch, Miracoli dei Beati, 1983–1990, 2002
R2   Resch, Miracoli dei Beati, 1991–1995, 2002
v   Venerable
W   Woodward, Making Saints, 1990

* Casi excepti

TABLE B.2. Some Blesseds and Venerables Recognized between 1588 and 1999 and Sources Examined on Their Miracles

Name	Born	Died	Year Beat./Ven.	M/F	Nation (city or region)	Printed Source	ASV File No.
Adolph Kolping	1813	1865	1991 b	M	Germany (Cologne)	R2	
Agnès de Jésus de Langeac	1602	1634	1994 b	F	France	R2	
Agostino Roscelli	1818	1902	1995 b	M	Italy	R2	
Albert Chimielowski	1845	1916	1983 b	M	Poland	R1	
Alberto Hurtado Cruchaga	1901	1952	1994 b	M	Chile	R2	
Alfred Pampalon‡	1867	1896	1991 v	M	Canada		
Alfonsa of the Immaculate Conception (Muttathupadathu)	1910	1946	1986 b	F	India	R1	4059
Andrea Carlo Ferrari	1850	1921	1987 b	M	Italy	R1	
Andrea of Burgio	1705	1772	1873 v	M	Italy (Sicily)		
Angela Salawa	1881	1922	1991 b	F	Poland	R2	
Angela Truszkowska	1825	1899	1993 b	F	Poland	R2	
Anne de Xainctonge‡	1567	1621	1900 v	F	France	R1	
Annibale Maria di Franci	1851	1927	1990 b	M	Italy	R1	
Annunciata Cochette	1800	1876	1991 b	F	Italy (Brescia)	R2	
Antoine Chevrier	1826	1879	1986 b	M	France (Lyon)	R1	
Antonio Lucci	1682	1752	1989 b	M	Italy	R1	
Arnold Rèche	1838	1890	1987 b	M	France	R1	
Benedetta Cambiago Frassinello	1791	1858	1987 b	F	Italy	R1	
Benedetto Menni	1841	1914	1985 b	M	Italy (Milan)	R1	
Benvenutus Bombozzi‡	1809	1875	1987 v	M			
Bernardo Maria Silvestrelli	1831	1911	1988 b	M	Italy (Rome)	R1	
Blandina Merten	1883	1918	1987 b	F	Germany	R1	
Boleslava Maria Lament	1862	1946	1991 b	F	Poland	R2	
Bonaventura Gran	1620	1684	1906 b	M	Spain (Barcelona)	R2	2459

Name					Country	Code	
Caecilia Eusepi	1910	1928	1987 v	F	Italy (Viterbo)	R1	
Caterina Troiani	1813	1887	1985 b	F	Italy	R1	
Charles of Mount Argus (Houben)	1821	1893	1988 b	M	Holland	R2	
Chiara Dina Bosatta da Pianello	1858	1887	1991 b	F	Italy (Como)	R2	
Claudio Granzotto	1900	1947	1994 b	M	Italy	R2	
Clemente Marchisio	1833	1903	1984 b	M	Italy	R1	
Colomba Janina Gabril	1858	1926	1993 b	F	Ukraine	R2	
Damiano (Joseph Veuster)	1840	1889	1995 b	M	Belgium	R2	
Daniel Brottier	1876	1936	1984 b	M	France	R1	
Dominic of Jesus and Mary	1559	1630	1907 v	M	Austria (Vienna)	D	
Edoardo Guiseppe Rosaz	1830	1903	1991 b	M	Italy	R2	
Elisabetta Canori Mora	1774	1825	1994 b	F	Italy (Rome)	R2	
Elisabetta Renzi	1786	1859	1989 b	F	Italy	R1	
Elisabetta Vendramin	1790	1860	1990 b	F	Italy	R1	
Elizabeth of the Trinity (Catez)	1880	1906	1984 b	F	France	R1	
Emmanuele Domingo y Sol	1836	1909	1987 b	M	Spain	R1	
Enrichetta Domenici	1829	1894	1978 b	F	Italy (Torino)	Co	
Eugenie Joubert	1876	1904	1994 b	F	France	R2	
Falco	1440		1893b	M	Italy (Abruzzi)		3769
Federico Albert	1820	1876	1984 b	M	Italy (Torino)	R1	2067
Felice of Nicosia	1715	1787	1888 b	M	Italy (Sicily)		
Filippo Rinaldi	1856	1931	1990 b	M	Italy	R1	
Florida Cevoli	1685	1767	1993 b	F	Italy	R2	
Francesco Faà di Bruno	1825	1888	1988 b	M	Italy	R1	
Francesco Spinelli	1853	1913	1992 b	M	Italy	R2	
Francisca Ana Cirer y Carbonell	1781	1855	1989 b	F	Spain	R1	
Francisco Gárate	1857	1929	1985 b	M	Spain	R1	
Francisco Coll	1812	1875	1979 b	M	Spain (Catalan)	Co	
Francisco Palau y Quer	1811	1872	1988 b	M	Spain	R1	

(continued)

TABLE B.2. (continued)

Name	Born	Died	Year Beat./Ven.	M/F	Nation (city or region)	Printed Source	ASV File No.
Françoise de Sales Aviat	1844	1914	1992 b	F	France	R2	
Frédéric Janssoone	1838	1916	1988 b	M	France/Canada	R1	
Genoveva Torres Morales	1870	1956	1995 b	F	Spain	R2	
George Matulaitis	1871	1927	1987 b	M	Lithuania	R1	
Gertrude Comensoli	1847	1903	1989 b	F	Italy	R1	
Gianna Beretta Molla, doctor	1922	1962	1994 b	F	Italy	R2	
Giovanna Maria of the Cross	1603	1673	1891 v	F	Italy (Trento)	D	
Giuseppe Allamano	1851	1926	1990 b	M	Italy	R1	
Giuseppe Baldo	1843	1915	1989 b	M	Italy	R1	
Giuseppe Benedetto Dusmet	1818	1894	1988 b	M	Italy (Palermo)	P R	
Giuseppe Marello	1844	1895	1993 b	M	Italy	R2	
Giuseppe Nascimbeni	1851	1922	1988 b	M	Italy	R1	
Giuseppina Gabriella Bonino	1843	1906	1995 b	F	Italy	R2	
Giuseppina Vannini	1859	1911	1994 b	F	Italy	R2	
Grimoaldo Santamaria	1883	1902	1995 b	M	Italy	R2	
Honoratus Kozminski	1829	1916	1988 b	M	Poland	R1	
Hyacinthe Marie Cormier	1832	1916	1994 b	M	France	R2	
Isidore de St. Joseph (de Loor)	1881	1916	1984 b	M	Belgium	R1	
Jacques Désiré Laval	1802	1864	1979 b	M	France (Evreux)	Co	
Jan Nepomuk von Tschiderer	1777	1860	1995 b	M	Italy	R2	
Jeanne Jugan	1792	1879	1982 b	F	France	F	
José Maria de Yermo y Parres	1851	1904	1990 b	M	Mexico	R1	
José Maria Rubio y Peralta	1864	1929	1985 b	M	Spain (Madrid)	R1	
José Mayanet y Vives	1833	1901	1984 b	M	Spain	R1	
Josefa Naval Girbés	1820	1893	1988 b	F	Spain	R1	
Josemaria Escriva de Balaguer	1902	1975	1992 b	M	Spain	R2	

Joseph Gérard	1831	1988 b	France	M	R1
Joseph Vaz	1651	1995 b	India	M	R2
Josephine Bakhita	1869	1992 b	Sudan	F	R2
Jozef Sebastian Pelczar	1858	1991 b	Poland	M	R2
Junipero Serra	1713	1988 b	Majorca	M	R1
Karl Steeb	1773	1975 b	Germany (Tubingen)	M	Co
Kaspar Stanggassinger	1871	1988 b	Germany	M	R1
Katharine Mary Drexel	1858	1988 b	USA (Philadelphia)	F	R1
Kuriakose Elias Chavara	1805	1986 b	India	M	R1
Laura Vicuña	1891	1988 b	Chile	F	P R
Lorenzo Salvi	1782	1989 b	Italy	M	R1
Louis-Zéfiran Moreau	1824	1987 b	Canada	M	R1
Louise Thérèse de Montaignac de Chauvance	1820	1990 b	France	F	R1
Ludovico of Casoria (Palmentieri)	1814	1993 b	Italy	M	R2
Maddalena Caterina Morano	1847	1994 b	Italy	F	R2
Marcello Spinola y Maestre	1835	1987 b	Spain	M	R1
Marguerite Bays	1815	1995 b	Switzerland	F	R2
Maria a Jesu Crucifixio Baouardy‡	1846	1983 b	Palestine	F	R1
Maria Alvarado Cordozo	1875	1995 b	Venezuela	F	R2
Maria Bernarda Butler	1848	1995 b	Switzerland	F	R2
Maria Crocifissa Satellico	1706	1993 b	Italy	F	R2
Maria Domenica Brun Barbantini	1789	1995 b	Italy (Lucca)	F	R2
Maria Faustina Kowalska	1905	1993 b	Poland	F	R2
Maria Francesca Rubatto	1844	1993 b	Italy	F	R2
Maria Gabriela Sagheddu	1914	1983 b	Italy (Sardinia)	F	
Maria Helena Stollenwerk	1852	1995 b	Germany	F	R2
Maria Josefa Sancho de Guerra	1842	1992 b	Spain	F	R2
Maria Margherita Caiani	1863	1989 b	Italy	F	R1

(continued)

TABLE B.2. (continued)

Name	Born	Died	Year Beat./Ven.	M/F	Nation (city or region)	Printed Source	ASV File No.
Maria of Jesus Martiny	1841	1884	1989 b	F	France	R1	
Maria of Jesus Siedliska	1842	1902	1989 b	F	Poland	R1	
Maria Rafols	1781	1853	1992 b	F	Spain	R2	
Maria Schinina	1844	1910	1990 b	F	Italy	R1	
Maria Theresa Scherer	1825	1888	1995 b	F	Switzerland	R2	
Maria Theresia Gerhardinger	1797	1879	1985 b	F	Germany	R1	
Maria Venegas de la Torre	1868	1959	1992 b	F	Mexico	R2	
Marie Catherine de St Augustin (Longpré)	1632	1668	1989 b	F	France/Canada	R1	
Marie de l'Incarnation Guyart	1599	1672	1980 b	F	Canada	D	
Marie de Ste Cécile (Dina Bélanger)	1897	1929	1993 b	F	Canada (Quebec)	R2	
Marie-Leonie Paradis	1840	1912	1984 b	F	Canada (Acadia)	R1	
Marie-Louise Trichet	1684	1759	1993 b	F	France	R2	
Marie Poussepin	1653	1744	1994 b	F	France	R2	
Marthe Thérèse Haze	1782	1876	1991 b	F	Belgium	P R	
Marthe Aimée le Bouteillier	1816	1883	1990 b	F	France	R1	
Martyrs of Korea (103)		1839	1984 b	M, F	Korea	CV	
Mary MacKillop	1842	1909	1995 b	F	Australia	R2 W	
Mercedes de Jesús Molina	1828	1883	1985 b	F	Ecuador	R1	
Modestino Mazzarella	1802	1854	1995 b	M	Italy	R2	
Narcissa Martillo Morán	1832	1869	1992 b	F	Ecuador	R2	
Nazaria Ignacia March Mesa	1889	1943	1992 b	F	Spain	R2	
Nicolas Roland	1642	1678	1994 b	M	France	R2	
Niels Stensen, doctor	1638	1686	1988 b	M	Denmark	R1	
Padre Pio da Pietralcina	1887	1968	1999 b	M	Italy	N	
Paul Montal Fornés	1799	1889	1993 b	F	Spain	R2	

Name	Call Number	Year	Positio	Sex	Country	Status	ASV
Paulina Visintainer	1865	1942	1991 b	F	Italy/Brazil	R2	
Pauline von Mallinckrodt	1817	1887	1985 b	F	Germany	R1	
Peter Friedhofen	1819	1860	1985 b	M	Germany	R1	
Petra Pérez Florida	1845	1906	1994 b	F	Spain	R2	
Pier Giorgio Frassati	1901	1925	1990 b	M	Italy	R1	
Pierre François Jamet	1762	1845	1987 b	M	France	R1	
Pietro Bonilli	1841	1935	1988 b	M	Italy	R1	
Pietro Casani	1572	1647	1995 b	M	Italy	R2	
Pio di San Luigi (Campidelli)	1868	1889	1985 b	M	Italy	R1	
Pope Gregory X	1210	1276	1713 b	M	Italy	CV	2153
Rafael Arnáiz Barón	1911	1938	1992 b	M	Spain	R2	
Rafael Chylinski	1694	1741	1991 b	M	Poland	R2	
Rafaela Ybarra da Vilalonga‡	1843	1900	1984 b	F	Spain (Bilbao)		
Raffaele Guizar Valencia	1878	1938	1995 b	M	Mexico	R2	
Rafqa al Rayes	1832	1914	1985 b	F	Lebanon	R1	
Savina Petrilli	1851	1923	1988 b	F	Italy	R1	
Scubilion Rousseau	1797	1867	1989 b	M	France (Réunion)	R1	
Teresa Maria della Croce (Manetti)	1846	1910	1986 b	F	Italy	R1	
Timoteo Giaccardo	1896	1948	1989 b	M	Italy	R1	
Ulrika Franziska Nisch	1882	1913	1987 b	F	Germany	R1	
Ursula Ledóchowska	1865	1939	1983 b	F	Austria/Poland	R1	
Virginia Centurione Bracelli	1587	1651	1985 b	F	Italy (Genoa)	R1	
Vittoria Rasoamanari	1848	1894	1989 b	F	Madagascar	R1	

ASV Archivio Segreto del Vaticano, Riti Processi Call Number
b   Beatification
Co   Composta, Il miracolo, 1981
CV   Compendium or Vita
D   Positio super dubio (or Animadversiones)
F   Positio super fama
N   Newspaper

P   Positio super miraculo (or miraculis)
PV   Positio super validitate
R   Resch, Miracoli dei Santi, 2002
R1   Resch, Miracoli dei Beati, 1983–1990, 2002
R2   Resch, Miracoli dei Beati, 1991–1995, 2002
v   Venerable
W   Woodward, Making Saints, 1990

‡ ASV files identified but not yet seen

Appendix C

Canonizations and Beatifications Used in This Study by Year of Celebration

1588	Diego d'Alcalá (Didacus)
1594	Jacek Odrowaz (Hyacinthe)
1600	Ramón de Penyaforte
1606	Pope Gregory VII (Hildebrand)
1608	Francesca Romana (Ponziani)
1610	Carlo Borromeo
1622	Filippo Neri
1622	Francis Xavier
1622	Ignatius of Loyola
1622	Isidro Labrador (Agricola)
1622	Teresa of Avila
1623	Bruno
1629	Andrea Corsini
1658	Tomás de Villanueva
1665	François de Sales
1666	Felix of Valois
1666	John of Matha
1669	Maria Maddelena de' Pazzi
1669	Pedro de Alcántara
1670	Francisco Borgias
1671	Fernando, King of Castile
1671	Filippo Benizi, doctor
1671	Gaetano Thiene
1671	Luis Bertran

1671	Rosa of Lima
1690	Giovanni da Capistrano
1690	John of God
1690	Juan de S. Facondo de Sahagún
1690	Lorenzo Giustiniani
1690	Pasqual Baylón
1696	Zita
1705	Teresia & Sancia of Portugal
1712	Andrea Avellino
1712	Caterina of Bologna
1712	Felice of Cantalice
1712	Pope Pius V
1713	Pope Gregory X
1720	Humility
1726	Agnes Segni of Montepulciano
1726	Francisco Solano
1726	Giacomo della Marca
1726	Juan de la Cruz
1726	Luigi Gonzaga
1726	Pellegrino Laziosi
1726	Stanislaus Kostka
1726	Turibio Alfonso Mogrovejo
1728	Margherita of Cortona
1729	Jan Nepomuk
1731	Pietro Orseolo
1737	Caterina of Genoa (Fieschi Adorno)
1737	Giuliana Falconieri
1737	Jean François Regis
1737	Vincent de Paul
1741	Felmo (Pedro Gonzales)
1746	Camillo de Lellis
1746	Caterina de' Ricci
1746	Fidelis of Sigmaringen
1746	Giuseppe Desideri of Leonissa
1746	Pedro Regalado
1767	Girolamo Miani
1767	Giuseppe of Cupertino (Desa)
1767	Jan Kanty (John Cantius)
1767	Jeanne Françoise Fremiot de Chantal
1767	José de Calasanz

1767	Serafino of Monte Granario
1807	Angela Merici
1807	Benedetto of S. Philadelpho (Manassari)
1807	Colette Boylet de Corbie
1807	Francesco Caracciolo
1807	Giacinta Marescotti
1839	Alfonso Maria of Liguori
1839	Francesco of Girolamo
1839	Giovanni Giuseppe of the Cross (Calosinto)
1839	Pacifico de San Severino
1839	Veronica Giuliani
1862	Martyrs of Japan (26), Paul Miki, Peter Baptiste, etc
1862	Miguel de los Santos (Argemir)
1867	Germaine Cousin
1867	Leonardo of Porto Maurizio
1867	Maria Francesca of the Five Wounds (Gallo)
1867	Martyrs of Gorkum (18), Nicholas Pieck et al
1867	Paolo della Croce (Danei)
1867	Pedro Arbués, martyr
1873v	Andrea of Burgio
1876	Josaphat Kuncevic, martyr
1881	Benoit Joseph Labré
1881	Chiara of Montefalco
1881	Giovanni Battista Rossi
1881	Lorenzo of Brindisi
1888	Alfonso Rodriguez
1888	Jan Berchmans
1888	Pedro Claver
1888	Seven Founders
1888b	Felice of Nicosia
1891v	Giovanna Maria of the Cross
1893	Falco
1897	Antonio Maria Zaccaria, doctor
1897	Pierre Fourier de Notre Dame
1900	Jean Baptiste de la Salle
1900	Rita of Cascia
1904	Alessandro Sauli
1904	Gerardo Majella
1906b	Bonaventura Gran
1907v	Dominic of Jesus and Mary

1909   Clement Maria Hofbauer (Jan Dvorak)

1909   José Orioli

1920   Gabriel of Our Lady of Sorrows (Possenti)

1920   Joan of Arc

1920   Marguerite Marie Alacoque

1925   Jean Baptiste Vianney (le curé d'Ars)

1925   Jean Eudes

1925   Madeleine Sophie Barat

1925   Marie Madeleine Postel

1925   Peter Kanis

1925   Thérèse of Lisieux

1930   Caterina Thomas of Palma

1930   Martyrs of Canada, René Goupil, doctor, Jean de Brebeuf, Isaac Jogues

1930   Lucia Filippini

1930   Theophilus of Corte

1933   André Hubert Fournet

1933   Bernadette Soubirous

1934   Conrad of Parzham

1934   Giovanni Bosco

1934   Giuseppe Benedetto Cottolengo

1934   Jeanne Antide Thouret

1934   Louise de Marillac

1934   Maria Michaela de San Sacremento (Desmasières)

1934   Pompilio Maria Pirrotti

1934   Teresa Margherita Redi

1935   John Fisher, martyr

1935   Thomas More, martyr

1938   Andrzej Bobola, martyr

1938   Giovanni Leonardi

1938   Salvador de Horta

1940   Gemma Galgani

1940   Marie Euphrasie Pelletier

1943   Margaret of Hungary

1946   Frances Xavier Cabrini

1947   Bernardino Realino

1947   Catherine Labouré

1947   Giuseppe Cafasso

1947   Jeanne Elisabeth Bichier des Ages

1947   João de Brito

1947   Louis-Marie Grignon de Montfort

1947   Michael Garicoits
1947   Nicholas de Flue
1949   Jeanne de Lestonnac
1949   Maria Giuseppe Rossello
1950   Emilie de Rodat
1950   Antonio Maria Claret
1950   Bartholomea Capitanio
1950   Jeanne de Valois
1950   Maria Anna of Jesus de Paredes
1950   Maria Goretti
1950   Vincenza Gerosa
1950   Vincenzo Strambi
1951   Antonio Gianelli
1951   Emilie de Vialar
1951   Francis Xavier Maria Bianchi
1951   Ignazio of Laconi
1951   Maria Domenica Mazzarello
1954   Domenico Savio
1954   Gaspare del Bufalo
1954   Giuseppe Maria Pignatelli
1954   Maria Crocifissa di Rosa
1954   Pierre Louis Chanel, martyr
1954   Pope Pius X
1959   Carlo da Sezze
1959   Joaquina Vedruna de Mas
1960   Gregorio Barbarigo
1961   Maria Bertilla Boscardin
1962   Antonio Maria Pucci
1962   Francesco Maria of Camporubeo
1962   Julien Eymard
1962   Martin de Porres, doctor
1963   Vincenzo Pallotti
1967   Benilde Romaçon
1969   Julie Billiart
1970   English Welsh Martyrs (Cuthbert Mayne et al.)
1970   Juan of Avila
1970   Leonardo Murialdo
1970   Maria Soledad della Dolorato Torres Acosta
1970   Marie Victoire Thérèse Couderc
1974   Teresa de Jesús (Jornet y Ibars)

1975	Elisabeth Ann Seton
1975	Juan Bautista de la Concepción
1975	Juan Macias
1975	Justin de Jacobis
1975	Oliver Plunkett
1975	Vincentia Maria Lopez y Vicuña
1975b	Karl Steeb
1976	Beatrice da Silva Meneses
1976	John Ogilvie, martyr
1977	Charbel Makhlouf
1977	John Nepomucene Neuman
1977	Raffaela Maria Porras
1978b	Enrichetta Domenici
1979b	Francisco Coll
1979b	Jacques Désiré Laval
1980b	Marie de l'Incarnation Guyart
1982	Crispin of Viterbo
1982	Jeanne Delanoue
1982	Marguerite Bourgeoys
1982	Maximilian Kolbe
1982b	Jeanne Jugan
1983	Leopold Bogdan Mandic
1983b	Albert Chimielowski
1983b	Ursola Ledóchowska
1984	Martyrs of Korea (103)
1984	Miguel Febres Codero
1984	Paola Frassinetti
1984b	Clemente Marchisio
1984b	Daniel Brottier
1984b	Elizabeth of the Trinity (Catez)
1984b	Federico Albert
1984b	Isidore de St. Joseph (de Loor)
1984b	José Mayanet y Vives
1984b	Marie Leonie Paradis
1985	Francesco Antonio Fasani
1985b	Benedetto Menni
1985b	Caterina Troiani
1985b	Francisco Gárate
1985b	José Maria Rubio y Peralta
1985b	Maria Theresia Gerhardinger

1985b	Mercedes di Gesu Molina
1985b	Pauline von Mallinckrodt
1985b	Peter Friedhofen
1985b	Pio di San Luigi (Campidelli)
1985b	Rafqa al Rayes
1985b	Virginia Centurione Bracelli
1986	Giuseppe Maria Tomasi
1986b	Alfonsa of the Immaculate Conception (Muttathupadathu)
1986b	Antoine Chevrier
1986b	Kuriakose Elias Chavara
1986b	Teresa Maria della Croce (Manetti)
1987	Giuseppe Moscati, doctor
1987b	Andrea Carlo Ferrari
1987b	Arnold (Rèche)
1987b	Benedetta Cambiago Frassinello
1987b	Blandina Merten
1987b	Emmanuele Domingo y Sol
1987b	George Matulaitis
1987b	Louis-Zéfiran Moreau
1987b	Marcello Spinola y Maestre
1987b	Pierre François Jamet
1987b	Ulrika Franziska Nisch
1988	Eustochia Calafato
1988	Maddalena of Canossa
1988	Maria Rosa Molas y Vallvé
1988	Martyrs of Paraguay (3), Rocco Gonzalez et al
1988	Martyrs of Vietnam (117)
1988	Rose Philippine Duschesne
1988	Simon de Rojas
1988b	Bernardo Maria Silvestrelli
1988b	Charles of Mount Argus (Houben)
1988b	Francesco Faà di Bruno
1988b	Francisco Palau y Quer
1988b	Frédéric Janssoone
1988b	Giuseppe Benedetto Dusmet
1988b	Giuseppe Nascimbeni
1988b	Honoratus Kozminski
1988b	Josefa Naval Girbés
1988b	Joseph Gérard
1988b	Junipero Serra

1988b   Kaspar Stanggassinger
1988b   Katharine Mary Drexel
1988b   Laura Vicuña
1988b   Niels Stensen, doctor
1988b   Pietro Bonilli
1988b   Savina Petrilli
1989   Agnes of Prague
1989   Albert Chmielowski
1989   Clelia Barbieri
1989   Gaspare Bertoni
1989   Mutien Marie (Louis Wiaux)
1989   Riccardo Pampuri, doctor
1989b   Antonio Lucci
1989b   Elisabetta Renzi
1989b   Francisca Ana Cirer y Carbonell
1989b   Gertrude Comensoli
1989b   Giuseppe Baldo
1989b   Lorenzo Salvi
1989b   Maria Margherita Caiani
1989b   Maria of Jesus Martiny
1989b   Maria of Jesus Siedliska
1989b   Marie Catherine de St Augustin (Longpré)
1989b   Scubilion Rousseau
1989b   Timoteo Giaccardo
1989b   Vittoria Rasoamanari
1990   Marie Marguerite d'Youville
1990b   Annibale Maria di Franci
1990b   Elisabetta Vendramin
1990b   Filippo Rinaldi
1990b   Giuseppe Allamano
1990b   José Maria de Yermo y Parres
1990b   Louise Thérèse de Montaignac de Chauvance
1990b   Maria Schinina
1990b   Marthe Aimée le Bouteillier
1990b   Pier Giorgio Frassati
1991   Raphael Kalinowski
1991b   Adolph Kolping
1991b   Angela Salawa
1991b   Annunciata Cochette
1991b   Boleslava Maria Lament

1991b	Chiara Dina Bosatta da Pianello
1991b	Edoardo Guiseppe Rosaz
1991b	Jozef Sebastian Pelczar
1991b	Marie Thérèse Haze
1991b	Paulina Visintainer
1991b	Rafael Chylinski
1992	Claude de la Colombière
1992	Ezeqiel Moreno y Díaz
1992b	Francesco Spinelli
1992b	Françoise de Sales Aviat
1992b	Josemaria Escriva de Balaguer
1992b	Josephine Bakhita
1992b	Maria Josefa Sancho de Guerra
1992b	Maria Rafols
1992b	Maria Venegas de la Torre
1992b	Narcissa Martillo Morán
1992b	Nazaria Ignacia March Mesa
1992b	Rafael Arnáiz Barón
1993	Enrique de Ossó y Cervelló
1993	Marie de St Ignatius (Claudine Thévenet)
1993	Teresa de los Andes
1993b	Angela Truszkowska
1993b	Colomba Janina Gabril
1993b	Florida Cevoli
1993b	Giuseppe Marello
1993b	Ludovico of Casoria (Palmentieri)
1993b	Maria Crocifissa Satellico
1993b	Maria Faustina Kowalska
1993b	Maria Francesca Rubatto
1993b	Marie de Ste Cécile (Dina Bélanger)
1993b	Marie Louise Trichet
1993b	Paul Montal Fornés
1994b	Agnès de Jésus de Langeac
1994b	Alberto Hurtado Cruchaga
1994b	Claudio Granzotto
1994b	Elisabetta Canori Mora
1994b	Eugenie Joubert
1994b	Gianna Beretta Molla, doctor
1994b	Giuseppina Vannini
1994b	Hyacinthe Marie Cormier

1994b	Maddalena Caterina Morano
1994b	Marie Poussepin
1994b	Nicolas Roland
1994b	Petra Pérez Florida
1995	Charles-Joseph-Eugène de Mazenod
1995	Jan Sarkander
1995	Zdislava of Lemberk
1995b	Agostino Roscelli
1995b	Damiano (Joseph Veuster)
1995b	Genoveva Torres Morales
1995b	Giuseppina Gabriella Bonino
1995b	Grimoaldo Santamaria
1995b	Jan Nepomuk von Tschiderer
1995b	Joseph Vaz
1995b	Marguerite Bays
1995b	Maria Alvarado Cordozo
1995b	Maria Bernarda Bütler
1995b	Maria Domenica Brun Barbantin
1995b	Maria Helena Stollenwerk
1995b	Maria Teresa Scherer
1995b	Mary MacKillop
1995b	Modestino Mazzarella
1995b	Pietro Casani
1995b	Raffaele Guizar Valencia
1996	Egidio Maria di San Giuseppe (Pontillo)
1996	Jean Gabriel Perboyre, martyr
1997	Jan of Dukla
1998	Teresa Benedicta (Edith Stein)
1999	Agostina Pietrantoni
1999	Benedetto Menni
1999	Giovanni Calabria
1999	Kinga
1999	Marcellin Champagnat
1999	Tomasso of Cori
1999b	Padre Pio da Pietralcina

Notes

INTRODUCTION

1. Duffin, "Medical Miracle," 1997.

2. For the view of Catholic theology, see T. G. Pater, "Miracles (Theology of)," in Mathaler, ed., *New Catholic Encylopedia*, 9: 664–70.

3. For philosophical discussions, see Larmer, *Water into Wine*, 1988, 3–15; Larmer, *Questions of Miracle*, 1996; Mullin, *Miracles*, 1996; Ward, "Monks," 1999; Woodward, *Book of Miracles*, 2000, 28.

4. For recent arguments against religion, see Harris, *End of Faith*, 2004; Dennett, *Breaking the Spell*, 2006; Dawkins, *The God Delusion*, 2006.

5. Duffin, "Medical Miracles: Absence and Prevalence," 2002.

6. Ladurie, *Montaillou*, 1979; Ginzburg, *Cheese and the Worms*, 1980; Goodich, *Voices from the Bench*, 2006.

7. Cavadini, *Miracles*, 1999; Finucane, *Rescue*, 1997; Boesch Gaejano and Michetti, *Europa Sacra*, 2002; Goodich, *Violence and Miracle*, 1995; Sigal, *L'homme*, 1985; Vauchez, *Sainteté*, 1981; Ward, *Miracles*, 1982.

8. Andric, *Miracles of St. John of Capistrano*, 2000; Neyrey, "Miracles," 1999; Schlauch, *Medieval Narrative*, 1934; Van Dam, *Saints*, 1993; Yarrow, *Saints and Their Communities*, 2006.

9. Beaujard, *La culte*, 2000; Darricau, "Une source sur l'histoire des miracles," 1983; Finucane, *Rescue*, 1997; Boesch Gajano, "Dalla storiografia alla storia," 1999; Vauchez, "Les procès de canonisation médiévaux," 1979; Wilson, *Saints and Their Cults*, 1983.

10. Ziegler, "Practitioners and Saints," 1999.

11. Park, "Criminal and the Saintly Body," 1994; Park, *Secrets of Women*, 2006.

12. Bynum, *Holy Feast and Holy Fast,* 1987; Bynum, "Bodily Miracles," 1991.

13. Gentilcore, *Healers and Healing,* 1998, 177–202.

14. Boesch Gajano and Modica, *Miracoli dai segni alla storia,* 1999; Sodano, "Miracoli e canonizzazione," 1999; Sallman, *Naples et ses saints,* 1994.

15. Schutte, *Aspiring Saints,* 2001.

16. Burkardt, *Les clients des saints,* 2004; Smoller, "A Case of Demonic Possession," 2006.

17. Turchini, *La Fabbrica,* 1984.

18. Ditchfield, *Liturgy, Sanctity, and History,* 2002.

19. Delooz, *Sociologie et canonisations,* 1969.

20. Burke, "How to Be a Counter-Reformation Saint," 1987.

21. Composta, *Il miracolo,* 1981; Resch, *Miracoli dei Santi,* 2002; Resch, *Miracoli dei Beati,* 2 vols., 2002; Sabourin, *Divine Miracles,* 1977. Later editions of Resch exclude medical details on the miracles to focus on the saints and blesseds.

22. Antonelli, *De inquisitione medico-legale,* 1962; Blouin, *Vatican Archives,* 1998, 92–94; Boyle, *Survey of the Vatican Archives,* 2001, 87; Higgins, *Stalking the Holy,* 2006; Woodward, *Making Saints,* 1990; Woodward, *Book of Miracles,* 2000.

23. Harris, *Lourdes,* 1999, 288–319; Kaufman, *Consuming Visions,* 2005, 95–134; Kselman, "Miracles and Prophecies," 1978; Mangiapan, "Le contrôle médical," 1983; O'Connell, "The Roman Catholic Tradition," 1986; Risse, *Mending Bodies,* 1999; Szabo, "Seeing Is Believing?" 2002.

CHAPTER 1

1. Cavadini, *Miracles in Jewish and Christian Antiquity,* 1999; Anon., *Saints: Christianity, and Other Religions,* 1986; Woodward, *Book of Miracles,* 2000.

2. Ditchfield, *Liturgy, Sanctity, and History,* 2002, 214–20; Higgins, *Stalking the Holy,* 2006; Woodward, *Making Saints,* 1990; Wyshogrod, *Saints and Postmodernism,* 1990.

3. Ferngren, "Early Christianity," 1992; Amundsen and Ferngren, "The Early Christian Tradition," 1986; Brown, *Cult of the Saints,* 1981; Temkin, *Hippocrates in a World of Pagans and Christians,* 1991; Delehaye, *Legends of the Saints,* 1962; Jackson, *Doctors and Diseases,* 1988; Hamilton, *Incubation,* 1906.

4. Delooz, *Sociologie et canonisations,* 1969; Vauchez, *Sainteté,* 1981.

5. Goodich, *Lives and Miracles,* 2004.

6. Menesto, *Il processo di canonizzazione,* 1984.

7. Porterfield, *Healing in the History of Christianity,* 2005, 96–100.

8. The first published work on the new mechanism is the 1601 treatise by Fr. Angelo Rocca, *De canonizatione sanctorum commentarium,* reprinted in 2004.

9. Urban VIII, *Decreta servanda in canonizatione et beatificatione sanctorum,* 1642. On the early history of the process, see Burke, "How to Be a Counter-Reformation Saint," 1987; Ditchfield, *Liturgy, Sanctity, and History,* 2002, 212–20; Schutte, *Aspiring Saints,* 2001, 77–78.

10. Pope Benedict XIV (Prospero Lambertini), *De servorum Dei beatificatione et beatorum canonizatione,* 1734–38. Miracles are discussed in thirty chapters of Liber

quartus, Pars I. In the sixteen-volume Naples edition, published by Paci in 1773–75, the miracle discussion entails 7 (1774): 151–257 and 8 (1774): 3–184. On Benedict XIV, see Baudeau, "Analyse," 1865; Guarino, "Benedict XIV," 2002; Haynes, *Philosopher King*, 1970; M. L. Shay, "Benedict XIV," in Mathaler, ed., *New Catholic Encyclopedia*, 2: 247–48; Woodward, *Making Saints*, 1990, 76.

11. Benedict XIV, *Nuova tassa e riforma*, 1741; Benedict XIV, *Nota dei medici e chirurgi*, 1743.

12. For example, see Ratzinger and Bertone, *Istruzione circa le preghiere per ottenere da Dio la guarigione*, 2000.

13. The following Popes were canonized: Gregory VII, called "Hildebrand" (1606), Pius V (1712), and Pius X (1954). Ongoing *processi* include the cause for Gregory X (beatified in 1713) and John XXIII (beatified in 2000). On papal saints, see Benedict XIV, *Heroic Virtue*, 1851, 2: 60–94; Woodward, *Making Saints*, 1990, 188–89.

14. For a history and guide to the canonization process, including changes since 1983, see Veraja, *Le cause di canonizzazione dei Santi*, 1992; Woodward, *Making Saints*, 1990, 90–95.

15. Burke, "Rituals of Healing," 1987. On the Inquisition, see E. Peters, "Inquisition," in Mathaler, ed., *New Catholic Encyclopedia*, 7: 485–92. On parallels of canonization with the Inquisition, see Schutte, *Aspiring Saints*, 2001, 76–79.

16. Ditchfield, *Liturgy, Sanctity, and History*, 2002, 12–13, 273–360; De Renzi, "Witnesses of the Body," 2002.

17. Castellano, *De inquistione miraculorum in SS martyrum canonizatione*, 1629.

18. SRC, *Viennen. Beat. . . . Dominici a Iesu Maria. Positio super dubio*, 1677.

19. Vauchez, *La sainteté en occident*, 1981, 544–58, esp. 547.

20. Micheli, *L'Isola Tiberina*, 1995, 28; Russotto, "La constituzione," 1964.

21. Saintly physicians in this study include Filippo Benizi, can. 1671; Antonio Maria Zaccaria, can. 1897; René Goupil, can. 1930; Martini de Porres, can. 1962; Niels Stenson, beat. 1988; Giuseppe Moscati, can. 1987; Riccardo Pampuri, can. 1989; Gianna Beretta Molla, beat. 1994.

22. Bracciolini, *Compendio . . . di San Diego*, 1598; Gallesini, *Vita . . . di San Diego*, 1589. At least thirteen of the miracles appear in both summaries. Details on the remaining seventy-three miracles differ between the two books making it difficult to determine other examples of overlap.

23. Bracciolini, *Compendio . . . di San Diego*, 1598, 45.

24. Case, "The Year 1588 and San Diego," 1988; Bracciolini, *Compendio . . . di San Diego*, 1598, 46–48; Gallesini, *Vita . . . di San Diego*, 1589, 107, 138–43.

25. Bracciolini, *Compendio . . . di San Diego*, 1598, 39.

26. Bracciolini, *Compendio . . . di San Diego*, 1598, 40.

27. A young woman found healing through use of a card with Arabic letters, Gallesini, *Vita . . . di San Diego*, 1589, 117. Francis Xavier's miracles were attested by Muslims and Christians alike. Bourbon del Monte, *Relatio facta . . . super vita, Beati Francisci Xavieri*, 1622, 49.

28. Fernando III of Castile, Zita, Juan de San Facondo de Sahagún, and Pedro de Alcántara. Clusters appear in the 1881 canonization of Chiara of Montefalco, but the

evidence in her cause derived from the seventeenth century and earlier. See Menesto, *Il processo di canonizzazione*, 1984.

29. Bailey et al., *Hope and Healing*, 2005.

30. Turchini, *La fabbrica*, 1984.

31. Carolus Borromaeus, ASV RP 1681 (1604), 238v–40. On donations from the tomb, see Turchini, *La fabbrica*, 1984, 17. For more on costs, see Delooz, *Sociologie et canonisations*, 1969, 435–39; Ditchfield, *Liturgy, Sanctity, and History*, 2002, 223, 233–40.

32. Cited in Ditchfield, *Liturgy, Sanctity, and History*, 2002, 257.

33. Andrea Corsini, ASV RP 762 (1606).

34. SRC, *Suffragia in canonizatione S. Andreae Corsini*, 1629; Torres, *Predica per la canonizzazione di S. Andrea Corsini*, 1629.

35. SRC. *Positio super dubio . . . Beato Ioanne patratis* [de Capistrano], 1664; SRC, *Harlemen. Canonizationis . . . Martyrum Gorgomiensum*, 1674; SRC, *B. Andreae Avellini. Positio super dubio*, 1695.

36. Andrea Corsini, ASV RP 762 (1606); Catharina de Ricciis, ASV RP, 793 (ca. 1657); Ferdinandus III Castiliae, ASV RP 1111 (1656); Maria Magdalena de Pazzis, ASV RP 770 (ca. 1666) and 771 (ca. 1663); Petrus Forerius, ASV RP 3008 (1682).

37. See for example, Margarita, second miracle, cured in 1618, in SRC, *Majoricen . . . Alphonsi Rodriguez. Novissima positio*, 1824, 7.

38. Paulus Zacchias, "Testamento," Notaio Antonio Franciscus Maria Simi, Cura del Vicario, Officio 32, Rome. Archivio di Stato, 662–84v. A description of Zacchia's death and burial prepared by his confessor, Dominicus Arnolphinus Curatus, accompanies the will (p. 663).

39. Cardano, *Book of My Life*, 1931, 10. On Cardano and miracles, see Siraisi, *Clock*, 1997, 149–73.

40. Zacchia, *Beseelung des menschlichen Fötus*, ed. Spitzer, 2002.

41. Colombero, "Contributo," 1982; Vallon and Genil-Perrin, *La psychiatrie médico-légale*, 1912.

42. Boari and Froldi, "Paolo Zacchia," 1987; Pierini, *Venefici*, 2001.

43. De Renzi, "Witnesses of the Body," 2002.

44. Laugier, *Paul Zacchias*, 2006; Karplus, "Medical Ethics," 1973; Mahier, *Les questions médico-légales*, 1872.

45. Maeder, "Die Frau im 17. Jahrhundert," 1981.

46. Bajada, *Sexual Impotence*, 1988.

47. Colombero, "Il medico," 1986.

48. In mid-2007, Google Scholar reported more than thirty references to Zacchia in writings of the last two decades, most are single-sentence allusions to his greatness as a "founding father" of medical jurisprudence. Few authors have actually attempted to read his work.

49. Bajada, *Sexual Impotence*, 1988, 161–3.

50. Zacchia, *Quaestionum*, 1725, tome 2, 685–707, esp. 703–4. This chapter first appeared in the posthumous edition of 1661. For a translation and discussion, see Zacchia, *Beseelung des menschlichen Fötus*, ed. Spitzer, 2002, 21–26.

51. De Renzi, "Witnesses of the Body," 2002, 226–29.

52. Zacchia, *Quaestiones*, 1657, 197–247 (Liber 4, titulus 1), esp. 223–33 (question 8).

53. Zacchia, *Quaestiones*, 1657, 224, 235, 238, 240, 659–75 (Liber 9, Consilia I-VIII [miracles ascribed to Lorenzo Giustiniani]), 675–80 (Consilia IX and X [miracle ascribed to Gregory X]), 725–26 and 728–29, and 753 (Consilia XXX, XXXII, and XLV [miracles ascribed to Felice]).

54. Zacchia, *Quaestiones*, 1657, 224.

55. See for example Zacchia, *Quaestionum*, 1725, Tome 3, 126–29 (Consilia LXXIX [resurrection of boy] and LXXX [boy with epilepsy]).

56. Antonelli, *De inquisitione medico-legale*, 1962, p. 31.

57. Findlen, "Science as a Career," 1993.

58. Haynes, *Philosopher King*, 91–92, 160, 220–21; Palazzini, "La perfettibilità," 1988, 67.

59. Addleshaw, "Benedict XIV," 1935; Allen, "Upholding Tradition," 1994.

60. Addelshaw, "Benedict XIV," 1935, 94.

61. Haynes, *Philosopher King*, 1970, 178–82.

62. SRC, *Bononien. Can. B. Catharinae . . . Positio super dubio*, 1681. An archival file includes testimony on the same eight miracles. Catharina a Bononia, ASV RP 262 (ca. 1674). On the corpse of Caterina, see Pomata, "Malphighi and the Holy Body," 2007.

63. Haynes, *Philosopher King*, 1970, 33.

64. Benedict XIV, *Heroic Virtue*, 2: Chapter 3.

65. SRC, *Compendium . . . Pii V*, 1712.

66. Anon., *Relazione del miracolo*, 1713.

67. Amadori, *Relatio vitae . . . Felicis a Cantalicio*, 1712.

68. Andrea Avellino, ASV RP 1993 (1681); SRC, *B. Andreae Avellini. Positio super dubio*, 1695.

69. SRC, *Tullen. Beat. . . . Petri Forerii*, 1703; 1710; 1726; 1729; SRC. *Leopolien. Can. . . . B. Ioannis de Dukla. Positio super dubio*, 1732; SRC, *Tridentina. Beatificationis . . . Positio super dubio Ioannae Mariae a Cruce*, 1737.

70. Petrus Forerius, ASV RP 3008 (1682), 208, article number 325; and first miracle in SRC, *Tullen. Beat. et Can, . . . Petri Forerii*, 1726 and 1729. See also Haynes, *Philosopher King*, 1970, 130–31.

71. The votes of Cardinals on a Portuguese cause from 1724 were recorded by hand. SRC. *Positio . . . Theresiae et Sanciae*, 1709, on the last page, opposite the title page of the next item bound with it in Vatican Library code Barberini LL.VII.33 (13)–(14). See also SRC, *Tullen. Beat. et can. . . . Petri Forerii*, 1710, 46–7 (votes of cardinals).

72. Iohannes Berchmans, ASV 2327 (1749), 35–44.

73. See, for example, Margarita de Cortona, ASV RP 550 (1726), and Agnes Segni de Montepulciano, ASV RP 1801 (1719).

74. Benedict's 1737 memoir on "La Notomia" [sic] was reprinted by Martinotti, "Sopra la Notomia," 1911, 147–78. See also Gorce, "L'oeuvre medicale," 1915.

75. Cited and translated in Haynes, *Philosopher King*, 1970, 80.

76. Benedict XIV, *Heroic Virtue*, 1850–52.

77. Baudeau, "Analyse [1759]," 1865.

78. Haynes, *Philosopher King*, 1970, 78–150.

79. Caraccioli, *La vie*, 1783. The correspondence was first published in French, then in Italian. Benedict XIV, *Correspondance*, 1912; Benedict XIV. *Le lettere*, 1955–1984. On the papal radio address, see Palazzini, "La perfettibilità," 1988.

80. Benedict XIV. *De servorum Dei beatificatione et beatorum canonizatione in synopsim redacta*, 1840, 250.

81. Benedict XIV, *Heroic Virtue*, 1: 352–77, esp. 372–73.

82. Haynes, *Philosopher King*, 1970, 65.

83. Haynes, *Philosopher King*, 1970, 78, 126, 138–50.

84. Haynes, *Philosopher King*, 1970, 150.

85. Haynes, *Philosopher King*, 1970, 29–30.

86. Haynes, *Philosopher King*, 1970, 32–33.

87. Haynes, *Philosopher King*, 1970, 33–34. I have found no records pertaining to miracles of Imelda Lambertini.

88. Micheli, *L'Isola Tiberina*, 1995, 99.

89. Haynes, *Philosopher King*, 1970, 76; Marini, *Degli archiatri*, 1784, vol. 1, xiviii.

90. De Buck, *Suppression*, 1873; J. F. Broderick and V. A. Lapomarda, "Jesuits: Suppression and Restoration," and J. Rippinger, "Monasticism: Modern: Secularisation," in Mathaler, ed., *New Catholic Encylopedia*, 7: 786–87; 9: 794–95.

91. Ludovicus Maria Grignion de Montfort, ASV RP 4894 (1935), 36.

92. Files with handwritten annotations, possibly by the office of the postulator fidei or by postulants, include "punto oscuro" in Michaelis Garicoïts, ASV RP 5137 (1939), 143; "una forma funzionale" (suggesting hysteria) in Lucia Filippini, ASV RP 4862 (1927), 150v; and penciled exclamation marks, etc., in Nicolaus de Flue, ASV RP 4209 (1892), 600 et seq.

93. Antonelli, *De inquisitione medico-legale*, 1962, esp. xxiv-xxviii (list of printed Positiones from 1666 to 1957), 207–19 (articles of Consulta Medica).

94. Blouin, *Vatican Archives*, 1998, 92–94; Woodward, *Making Saints*, 1990, 194–201, 205–7. For the rules of service, see SCCS, *Regolamento per il Collegio dei medici periti*, 1976.

95. Giunchi, "L'esame del miracolo," 1988.

96. Woodward, *Making Saints*, 1990, 194–201.

97. Haynes, *Philosopher King*, 1970, 79–80, 92.

98. Haynes, *Philosopher King*, 1970, 150.

CHAPTER 2

1. Porter, "Patient's View," 1985; Sharpe, "History from Below," 1991.

2. Behr, *Aelius Aristides*, 1968, 143–47; Lloyd, *Magic, Reason*, 1979, 40–41; Risse, *Mending Bodies*, 1999, 15–20, 33–38; Temkin, *Hippocrates*, 1991, 183–84.

3. Sallman, "Sainteté et société," 1997; Vauchez, *Sainteté*, 1981; Wilson, *Saints and Their Cults*, 1983; Goodich, *Lives and Miracles*, 2004; Goodich, "Mirabilis Deus,"

2005, 135–56; Goodich, *Other Middle Ages*, 1998; Goodich, *Vita Perfecta*, 1982; Goodich, *Voices from the Bench*, 2006.

4. Yarrow, *Saints and Their Communities*, 2006; Ashley and Sheingorn, *Interpreting Cultural Symbols*, 1990; Brown, *Cult of the Saints*, 1981; Halkin, *Saints de Byzance*, 1981; Horden, "Saints and Doctors," 1982; Huddard, "I miracoli del re," 1999.

5. Burkardt, *Les clients des saints*, 2004; Andric, *Miracles of St. John of Capistrano*, 2000; Sallman, *Naples et ses saints*, 1994; Sodano, "Miracoli e canonizzazione," 1999; Lappin, "Miracles in Spanishness," 2005.

6. Burke, "How to Be a Counter-Reformation Saint," 1987; Delooz, *Sociologie et canonisations*, 1969; Delooz, "Towards a Sociological Study," 1983; Schutte, *Aspiring Saints*, 2001; Neyrey, "Miracles," 1999.

7. Bourbon del Monte, *Relatio facta . . . Isidori Agricolae*, 1622, 21.

8. Case, "The Year 1588," 1988; Bracciolini, *Compendio . . . di San Diego*, 1598, 46–48; Gallesini, *Vita . . . di San Diego*, 1589, 107, 138–43.

9. On Mother Mary MacKillop, see, for example, Fletcher, "Australian Spirituality," 1995; McCreanor, *Sainthood in Australia*, 2001; Gardiner, *Mary MacKillop, Extraordinary Australian*, 2007; Woodward, *Book of Miracles*, 2000, 368–69. See also the following Web sites accessed in April 2008:

http://www.sosj.org.au/mary/index.html

http://www.southaustralianhistory.com.au/mackillop.htm

10. Bourbon del Monte, *Relatio facta . . . B. Theresiae a Iesu de Avila*, 1622, 23–24.

11. SRC, *Compendium . . . Aloysii Gonzagae*, 1726, second miracle.

12. SRC, *Compendium . . . Ioannis de Deo*, 1690, 9.

13. SRC, *Compendium . . . Gemmae Galgani*, 1939; Sabourin, *Divine Miracles*, 1977, 169–70.

14. Resch, *Miracoli dei Santi*, 2002, 155–60.

15. BBC News, http://news.bbc.co.uk/2/hi/europe/6504233.stm, accessed July 12, 2008.

16. Burke, "How to Be a Counter-Reformation Saint," 1987.

17. SRC, *Brevissimum Compendium*, 1671, 19, fourth miracle.

18. Bourbon del Monte, *Relatio facta . . . Francisci Xavieri*, 1622, 49–54; SRC, *Beat. . . . Joannis de Britto. Novissima positio*, 1941.

19. Iohannes Baptista de la Salle, ASV RP 3890 (1892), 98–131 (miraculé).

20. SRC, *Compendium . . . Antonii Mariae Pucci*, 1962, 9, second miracle.

21. Resch, *Miracoli dei Beati*, 1983–1990, 2002, 155–61.

22. Resch, *Miracoli dei Santi*, 2002, 97–103.

23. Iohannes Berchmans, ASV RP 2327 (1749), 38.

24. Robertus Bellarmino, ASV RP 5266 (1926), 71–78 (miraculé), 61–65v (doctor). See also SRC, *Compendium . . . Roberti Card. Bellarmino*, 1930, 10.

25. Carolus Borromaeus, ASV RP 1681 (1604), 155v; Peña, *Relatione . . . S. Caroli Borromei*, 1625, 72. In the same summary, another woman had also tried diverse other saints (p. 80). Bonino, *Nonnulla praeclara*, 1610. See also Turchini, *La Fabbrica*, 1984, 145, 147.

26. Baby Carlo in Franciscus Salesius, ASV RP 991 (1628), 45.

27. Gaetano in Maria Francisca a Vulneribus, ASV RP 1959 (1851), 48–69, esp. 65v. See also SRC, *Compendium . . . M.F. Vulneribus,* 1867, 14; SRC, *Commentarium,* 1868, 57.

28. Maria Angela in Iohannes Berchmans, ASV RP 2324 (1751), 174v–193, esp. 181v, 184.

29. Louis S. in Magdalena Sophia Barat, ASV RP 4917 (1917), 77–87 (miraculé).

30. Cardano, *Book of My Life,* 1931, 10.

31. Carolus Borromaeus, ASV RP 1681 (1604), 112; Bonino, *Nonnulla praeclara gesta,* 1610; Peña, *Relatione,* 1625, 68. See also Turchini, *La fabbrica,* 1984, 147.

32. Iohannes Cantii, ASV RP 633 (1753), 11–11v.

33. SRC, *Compendium . . . Iohannae de Valois,* 1949, 10–11, first and second miracles.

34. Alphonsus Rodriguez, ASV RP 1625 (1866), 37–42 (summary).

35. Marie Madeline, in Maria Magdalena Postel, ASV RP 5073 (1917), 81, 220–33.

36. SRC, *Compendium . . . Angelae Mericiae,* 1807, xvii.

37. Petrus Canisius, ASV RP 5166 (1922), 63–85 (Sor. Ignatia).

38. Surius, *Vita,* 1621, 162–63. The "Probatica piscina" alludes to a venerated site in Jerusalem in which Christ healed a lame man (John 5, 2–8).

39. The concept of a social network generated around a miracle is developed in an intriguing essay on twentieth-century Spain. Christian, "Storia di una guarigione," 1999, esp. 209–11.

40. Fifth miracle in Andrea Corsini, ASV RP 762 (1606), 21v–25, 126v–127, 219 (Pucetti and his wife, miracles 30 to 32), 176–79 (Cresci's wife, miracles number 45 and 46).

41. Andrea Corsini, ASV RP 762 (1606), 18v–21v.

42. Maria Magdalena de Pazzis, ASV RP 771 (ca. 1663) and ASV RP 770 (ca. 1666).

43. Maria Magdalena de Pazzis, ASV RP 771 (ca. 1663), 444–59.

44. Petrus Forerius, ASV RP 3008 (1682), 197 (article 293) and 208 (article 325). See also first and sixth miracles in SRC, *Tullen. Beat. et Canonizationis . . . Petri Forerii,* 1726, and 1729.

45. Petrus Forerius, ASV RP 4119 (1885).

46. See, for example, the overlapping testimony and names in one file concerning two miracles for Theophilus a Corte, ASV RP 1829 (1807). See also two miracles involving a father and his daughter in the cause of Gemma Galgani. SRC, *Compendium . . . Gemmae Galgani,* 1939; Sabourin, *Divine Miracles,* 1977, 169–70.

47. Germana Cousin, ASV RP 3283 (1856); RP 3284 (1859); RP 3285 (1846), RP 3286 (1847).

48. Theophilus a Corte, ASV RP 5294 (1908), 72–76. In another file, an expert witness shared the patient's surname (Loy; also Loi). See second miracle in SRC, *Calaritana. . . . Ignatii a Laconi. Positio,* 1937, 17–27.

49. Margareta C. and Joanna C., miracles II and III (alias IV) in SRC, *Majoricen . . . Alphonsi Rodriguez,* 1822, 1823, 1824; SRC, *Matriten. . . . Vincentiae Mariae Lopez Vicuña. Positio,* 1949, and *Nova positio,* 1949, first miracle (Agnes) and second miracle (Joseph).

50. Catharina de Ricciis, ASV RP 793 (ca. 1657), n.p., esp. title page and approx. 23–25 (1655 journey to collect relics).

51. Salvatoris Pagnani, ASV RP 2522 (1773), 234–44 (Angela), 246–52 (Elena), 301–7 (Nicoletta).

52. Ignatius a Laconi, ASV RP 414 (1852), 49 (item #116, Suor Agnesa).

53. Theophilus a Corte, ASV RP 5294 (1908), 42–54, esp. 43.

54. Petrus Chanel, ASV RP 5162 (1907), 70–85 (Rosalie). Dr. Boissarie's attestation is at the end of the file. On Lourdes and Boissarie, see Harris, *Lourdes*, 1999, 339–42; Szabo, "Seeing Is Believing?" 2002. See also Mangiapan, "Contrôle," 1983.

55. Martyri Inglesi, ASV RP 5112 (1891), 74–99 (Joseph, first miracle).

56. Iohanna de Valois, ASV RP 252 (1632).

57. Iohanna de Valois, ASV RP 252 (1632), 83, 100v, 121v, 148, 159v.

58. Iosephus a Cupertino, ASV RP 2048 (1758), 181–217, 221–39, 350–71, 379–89.

59. Maria Magdalena de Pazzis, ASV RP 771 (ca. 1663), 262r–v.

60. Leonardus a Porto Mauritio, ASV RP 2499 (1790), 208v (Angela A.).

61. Felix a Nicosia, ASV RP 2067 (1870).

62. For example, a carpenter described an event as having happened "seventeen years ago" when his thirty-six-year-old son "had been six years old"; others said thirty years had passed. Petrus Alcantara, ASV RP 10 (1616), 321, 322, 331.

63. Delooz, *Sociologie et canonisations*, 1969, 255–77.

64. See, for example, Bynum, *Fragmentation*, 1991; Ferguson, *Women and Religion*, 1995, 234–6; Kselman, "Miracles and Prophecies," 1978, 79–81; Orsi, "He Keeps," 1991.

65. Bynum, "Bodily Miracles," 1991; Bynum, *Holy Feast*, 1987; Ferguson, *Women and Religion*, 1995.

66. Bynum, *Holy Feast*, 137–38, 257; Bynum, "Female Body," 1989, 161; Park, "Criminal and Saintly Body," 1994; Park, *Secrets of Women*, 2006, 39–49.

67. SRC, *Andegaven. Beat . . . Mariae Euphrasiae Pelletier. Fama*, 1901, 153–54.

68. Gennaro, first miracle in Seraphinus a Montegranario, ASV RP 95 (1762), 21–25 (summary), 45v–56v. See also SRC, *Compendium . . . Seraphino ab Asculo*, 1767, xxiii.

69. SRC, *Bononien. Can. . . . B. Catharinae . . . Positio super dubio*, 1681, 362–64.

70. Michaelis de Sancti, ASV RP 3435 (1833), 51r–87v. See also SRC, *Compendium . . . Michaelis de Sanctis*, 1862, 14.

71. Resch, *Miracoli dei Beati*, 1983–1990, 2002, 46–49.

72. Trambusti, *Vita . . . Rossi*, 1861, 84.

73. SRC, *Nivernen . . . Bernardae Soubirous. Positio*, 1932, *Nova positio*, 1933, *Novissima Positio*, 1933 (Rev. Alexii L., first miracle).

74. Germana Cousin, ASV RP 3286 (1847), esp. 40–47 (summary), 389 (baker) and 503 (carpenter).

75. Angela Merici, ASV RP 344 (1782), entire file, esp. 26 (list of witnesses). See also SRC, *Compendium . . . Angelae Mericiae*, 1807, xvii.

76. Germana Cousin, ASV RP 3284, 1859, entire file on Francesca. See also SRC, *Compendium . . . Germanae Cousin*, 1867, 9.

77. Petrus Forerius, ASV RP 4119 (1885), 71–74 (Mère Maria Alexandra).

78. Falconieri, *Storia della vita,* 1726, 197–98 (Soror Mericia).

79. Andrea Fournet, ASV RP 4321 (1921), n.p., quire #4, second miracle Soeur Maria G.

80. Soeur Marie Cécile on healing of Mathilde R. in Iohannes Baptista Maria Vianney, ASV RP 4713 (1919), variable pagination, 131–37 (also 191–97), esp. 136 (196).

81. Garraghan, *Jesuits of the Middle United States,* 1938, 2: 53–65, and portrait facing p. 98. See also Taves, *Household,* 1986, 11–12, 58; Weninger, "Interesting Letter," 1886.

82. Petrus Claver, ASV RP 1183 (1867), 79–80 (Weninger on Margareta S.).

83. Petrus Claver, ASV RP 1190 (1866), 90–99.

84. Petrus Claver, ASV RP 1189 (1867), 129.

85. Petrus Claver, ASV RP 1190 (1866), 92.

86. CCS, *Marianopolitana. . . . Mariae Margaritae . . . (v. Youville). Positio,* 5 (chronology), 17, 28–29.

87. Maria Euphrasia Pelletier, ASV RP 4971 (1917), 102–3.

88. Alphonsus Maria de Ligorio, ASV RP 2080 (1827), 44v–57v (doctor), 127–43 (miraculé). See also SRC, *Compendium, . . . Alphonsi Mariae de Ligorio,* 1839, 19, second miracle.

89. Andrea Fournet, ASV RP 4321 (1921).

90. CCS, *Viedmen. Can. . . . Laurae Vicuña . . . Positio,* 1988, 1–28, 163; see also Resch, *Miracoli dei Beati,* 1983–1990, 2002, 330–34.

91. O'Connell, "Roman Catholic Tradition," 1986, 125.

92. Ariès, *Centuries of Childhood,* 1962, 128; Cunningham, *Children and Childhood,* 2005, 40–80, esp. 50; Finucane, *Rescue,* 1997, 151–58; Hanawalt, "Medievalists," 2002; Stone, *Family, Sex and Marriage,* 1979, 88, 409.

93. A survey of canonizations from 1900 to 1970 reported 17 percent of miraculés were children. Sabourin, *Divine Miracles,* 1977, 167.

94. SRC, *Compendium . . . Aloysii Gonzagae,* 1726, miracles number 7, 10, 11, and 12.

95. SRC, *Asten . . . Domenici Savio. Positio,* 1946, esp. 16–17 (first miracle, Sabatini A.) and 49 (doctor's declaration, 1931).

96. SRC, *Aquen . . . B. M.D. Mazzarello. Novissima positio,* 1938 (first miracle, Ercolina).

97. SRC, *Aquen . . . B. M.D. Mazzarello. Positio,* 1950, 80–135 (second miracle, Giancarla).

98. Lucia Filippino, ASV RP 4865 (1921), 60–65v (miraculée).

99. SRC, *Aquen . . . B. M.D. Mazzarello. Novissima positio,* 1938 (second miracle, Rosa); *Aquen . . . B. M.D. Mazzarello. Positio,* 1950, 1–79 (first miracle, Sor. Maiorina).

100. CCS, *Compendium . . . Zdislavae de Lemberk,* 1995, 4; Resch, *Miracoli dei Santi,* 186–92.

101. Bracciolini, *Compendio . . . di San Diego,* 1598, 35; Gallesini, *Vita . . . di San Diego,* 1589, 115–16.

102. Laurentius a Brundusio, ASV RP 381 (1797), 44v–51 (summary), esp. 48r–v.

103. Maria Magdalena Postel, ASV RP 5073 (1917), 220–33.

104. SRC, *Passavien . . . Conradi a Parzham. Positio*, 1930 (second miracle, Elisa [also Elisabetta]). See also Composta, *Il miracolo*, 1981, 15–25.

105. SRC, *Passavien . . . Conradi a Parzham. Positio*, 1933 (Augusta).

106. Laurentius a Brundusio, ASV RP 381 (1797), 314–23v (Pietro Paolo).

107. Paulus a Cruce Danei, ASV RP 2355 (1819), 61–64.

108. SRC, *Aquen . . . B. M.D. Mazzarello. Positio*, 1950, 80–135 (second miracle, Giancarla).

109. Finucane, *Rescue*, 1997, 141–47.

110. SRC, *Compendium . . . Ios. Calasanctii*, 1767, xxxiv.

111. Andrea a Burgio, ASV RP 4059 (1878), 174–95 (miraculée), 334–41 (doctor).

112. SRC, *Vicen . . . Ioachimae de Vedruna. Positio*, 1936 (first miracle).

113. SRC, *Vicen . . . Ioachimae de Vedruna. Positio*, 1955.

114. SRC, *Tarvisina. Beat. Can. . . . Mariae Bertillae Boscardin. Positio*, 1951 (second miracle).

115. Iosephus Calasanctius, ASV RP 2707 (1761), 33–35 (summary), 64–74v (widow miraculée), 135 (servant). See also SRC, *Compendium . . . Ios. Calasanctii*, 1767, xxxi–xxxiii.

116. Iosephus Cafasso, ASV RP 4801 (1918), 364 (Lucia's statement).

117. Seraphinus a Montegranario, ASV RP 95 (1762), 25–30v (summary), 62–66 (miraculé Ugo), 45v–61, 82v–85v, and 110–133 (doctors).

118. Maria Francisca a Vulneribus, ASV RP 1959 (1851), 72 (Fortunata), 99v–108 (doctor), 109 (daughter), 199 (servant), 205 (son), 283–85 (doctor). See also SRC, *Commentarium*, 1868, 57; SRC, *Compendium . . . M.F. Vulneribus*, 1867, 14.

119. Alexander Sauli, ASV RP 1163 (1745), 47v, 67v, 166–79 (priests); 143–55 (doctor).

120. SRC, *Lausanen. Beat. . . . Petri Canisii*, 1860 (fourth miracle, Maria Anna).

121. Theophile a Corte, ASV RP 6215i (1919), unnumbered pages (testimony on Flora's whereabouts from Maria Domenica, a seventy-six-year-old *cucitrice*).

122. For example the miraculé, Margareta S., was listed as the third witness, but her testimony is not in the file. Petrus Claver, ASV RP 1183 (1867), 79–80 (list).

123. The causes included four canonizations and twenty-eight beatifications described in the three volumes by Andreas Resch. For the stories of dead miraculés in the four canonizations, see Resch, *Miracoli dei Santi*, 2002, 47–55, 84–89, 129–34, 182–85.

124. Pius V, ASV RP 2553 (1704), 70–75 (summary), 94v–110v (husband). See also SRC, *Compendium . . . Pii V*, 1712, last miracle.

125. The testimony on the case of Father Francesco S. appears in four files all from 1802 to 1803. For summaries, see Ioannes Iosephi a Cruce, ASV RP 1944, 35v–39; RP 1945, 54v–63v; RP 1946, 27–30, RP 1947, 77–80v. See also, SRC, *Compendium . . . Ioannis Iosephi a Cruce*, 1839, 21–22.

126. The testimony on the case of Father Mariano A. appears in two files. For summaries, see Ioannes Iosephus a Cruce, ASV RP 1945 (1802-3), 30; RP 1946 (1802-3), 59–61.

127. SRC, *Parisien. Canonizationis . . . B. Catharinae Labouré. Positio*, 1944, and *Nova positio*, 1945 (first miracle).

128. Iosephus Cafasso, ASV RP 4801 (1918), 62–63 (summary), 363 (death certificate), 364 (Lucia's statement of 1902), 371–72 (her letter of 1906).

129. CCS, *Catanen. Can. . . . Dusmet. Positio*, 1988, 41 (photograph). See also Resch, *Miracoli dei Beati*, 1983–1990, 2002, 346–49.

130. Antonia N. in *Catharina Thomas of Palma*, ASV RP 4518 (1920), 22 (doctor), 25–26 (sister), 27 (death certificate).

131. Iosephus Cafasso, ASV RP 4801 (1918), 50–54 (Pierina).

132. Iohannes Berchmans, ASV RP 3716 (1886), 409–10 (vision), 428–29 (autobiography), 422–27 (letters).

CHAPTER 3

1. Amundsen, "Medieval Christian Tradition," 1986; Amundsen and Ferngren, "Early Christian Tradition," 1986; Ferngren, "Early Christianity," 1992; Numbers and Amundsen, *Caring and Curing*, 1986; Porterfield, *Healing*, 2005; Van Dam, *Saints*, 1983, 82–115.

2. Sigal, *L'homme*, 1985, 227, 255; Vauchez, *Sainteté*, 1981, 544–58.

3. Bull, *Miracles*, 1999, 99–100, 139–40, 179.

4. Kunstmann, *Treize miracles*, 1981, 12–13, 19–21.

5. Andric, *Miracles*, 2000, 193–279, esp. 211–12.

6. Vauchez, *Sainteté*, 1981, 547.

7. Sodano, "Miracoli," 1999, 188–89.

8. An Irish student nurse recovered from multiple sclerosis in 1946; a German nun, in 1955. SRC, *Massilen. Can. . . . B. Aemiliae de Vialar. Positio*, 1950, 35–75. Resch, *Miracoli dei Beati*, 1983–1990, 2002, 102–10.

9. SCCS, *Quiten . . . B. Fratris Michäelis. Positio*, 1983. See also Resch, *Miracoli dei Santi*, 2002, 40–46.

10. Resch, *Miracoli dei Beati*, 1991–1995, 2002, 158–62 (lymphoma), 350–54 (leukemia). See also Woodward, *Book of Miracles*, 2000, 368–69.

11. Sigal, *L'homme*, 1985, 228–65.

12. William D. Johnston, "Tuberculosis," in Kiple, ed., *World History of Human Disease*, 1993, 1059–68.

13. See, for example, Duffin, *Better Eye*, 1998, 96–100.

14. Resch, *Miracoli dei Beati*, 1983–1990, 2002, 312–16.

15. Resch, *Miracoli dei Beati*, 1983–1990, 2002, 225–28, 466–69.

16. Antonius Maria Claret, ASV RP 4390 (1910), entire file, esp. 22–28v (summary), 37v–49v (doctor), 127–28 (on vaccination).

17. Frederick L. Dunn, "Malaria," in Kiple, ed., *World History of Human Disease*, 1993, 855–62.

18. Leonardus a Porto Mauritio, ASV RP 2503 (1834), 54–84v, esp. 63v (doctor).

19. Pius V, ASV RP 2553 (1704), esp. 70–71, 96r–v. See also SRC, *Compendium . . . Pii V*, 1712, last miracle. On the history of Jesuit bark, see Jarcho, *Quinine's Predecessor*, 1993.

20. Zacchia, *Quaestiones*, 1657, 717–19, esp. 718 (Consilium XXVII).

21. On the 1656 epidemic, see Bertolasi, "Peste Romana," 1969; Henderson, "Historians and Plagues," 2003; Risse, *Mending Bodies*, 1999, 190–214.

22. Catharina de Ricciis, ASV RP 793 (ca. 1657), n.p., copy of letter from Francesco Maria Falucci of Naples, May 5, 1657. See also in same file healings from August 1656, "morto resuscitato."

23. Charles W. LeBaron and David W. Taylor, "Typhoid Fever: History," in Kiple, ed., *World History of Human Disease*, 1993, 1075–76.

24. Gentilcore, *Healers and Healings*, 1998, 179–80.

25. Iohannes Berchmans, ASV RP 2324 (1751), entire file, esp. 36–47v (summary), 174v–93 (her testimony, 176 [wicked disease]).

26. Testimony referred to examination of a nun upon her arrival at the convent a few years earlier. Ludovicus Maria Grignion de Montfort, ASV RP 4894 (1935), 25v–30v.

27. Maria Micaela a San Sacremento, ASV RP 5047 (1928), entire file, esp. 51, 85.

28. Resch, *Miracoli dei Beati, 1983–1990*, 2002, 94–101.

29. Resch, *Miracoli dei Beati, 1983–1990*, 2002, 447–50.

30. Maria Francisca a Vulneribus, ASV RP 1959 (1851), 25v–29 (summary), 43–69v (miraculé). See also SRC, *Compendium . . . M.F. Vulneribus*, 1867, 14; SRC, *Commentarium*, 1868, 57.

31. Iohannes Berchmans, ASV RP 2324 (1751), 155 r–v (doctor).

32. On the case of a boy with *cachexia scorbutica*, both the promotor fidei and the postulants cited numerous distinguished authors including Boerhaave, Hoffman, Sennert, Bonet, Boissier des Sauvages and James's *Dictionary*, SRC, *Polona. . . . Andreae Bobola. Animadversiones*, 1830, 17–18, and *Responsio*, 137–57 (fifth miracle).

33. Bracciolini, *Compendio . . . di San Diego*, 1598, 34–37; Gallesini, *Vita . . . di San Diego*, 1589, 113.

34. SRC, *Brevissimum Compendium*, 1671, 12 (seventh miracle of Philip Benitius).

35. Petrus Forerius, ASV RP 3008 (1682), 208; SRC, *Tullen. Beat. et can, . . . Petri Forerii*, 1726 and 1729 (article number 325; first miracle). See also Haynes, *Philosopher King*, 1970, 130–31.

36. Zacchia, *Quaestionum*, 1725, Tome 3, 126–28 (Consilium LXXIX [resurrection of boy]).

37. Andrea Avellino, ASV RP 1993 (1681), esp. 107 r–v (doctor).

38. Boothbyer, "Gospel Miracles," 1964, 33; Mullin, "Science, Miracles," 2003, 205.

39. Gallesini, *Vita . . . di San Diego*, 1589, 113 (pain); Petrus Alcantara, ASV RP 10 (1616), 293 (pain) and 347 (palpitations).

40. Fourth miracle in SRC, *Polona. . . . Andreae Bobola. Animadversiones*, 1830, 15–16; *Responsio*, 110–38.

41. Duffin, *Better Eye*, 1998, 176–79, 368n8.

42. Iohannes Leonardi, ASV RP 1481 (1822), entire file, esp. 123–33 (doctor).

43. Franciscus Xavierus Maria Bianchi, ASV RP 1921 (1827), 168v (undulation), 255v-276 (doctor), 593r–v (digitalis).

44. On the history of pleurisy, see Maulitz, "In the Clinic," 1990; Wilson, "Disease Concepts," 2000.

45. Franciscus Carraciolo, ASV RP 1897 (1780), 34–43v (Agata).

46. Duffin, "Pneumonia," in Kiple, ed., *World History of Human Disease*, 1993, 938–41.

47. Petrus Forerius, ASV RP 3008 (1682), 217 (Maria Hyacintha).

48. Resch, *Miracoli dei Beati, 1983–1990*, 2002, 218–22.

49. SRC, *Romana . . . Pignatelli. Positio*, [1933], second miracle.

50. Iohannes Berchmans, ASV RP 2329 (1867), entire file. On the history of kidney disease, see Peitzman, "Bright's Disease," 1992.

51. Resch, *Miracoli dei Beati, 1991–1995*, 2002, 312–16.

52. SRC, *Parisien. . . . Catharinae Labouré. Positio*, 1944 and 1945 (Josephine); Resch, *Miracoli dei Beati, 1991–1995*, 2002, 125–29.

53. Maria Euphrasia Pelletier, ASV RP 4971 (1917), 20–45 (Mother Superior on Sister Mary). On the history of floating kidney, see Moss, "Floating Kidneys," 2005.

54. On the history of liver disease, see Duffin, *Lovers and Livers*, 2005, 82–88.

55. Resch, *Miracoli dei Beati, 1983–1990*, 2002, 272–78 (German woman); 295–301, esp. 299 (Liborio); 407–13 (policeman). See also CCS, *Compendium . . . Ioannis Calabria*, 1994, 10 (Liborio).

56. SRC, *Calaritana. . . . Ignatii Laconi. Positio*, 1937, 17–27 (cyst); Woodward, *Book of Miracles*, 2000, 370. CCS, *Compendium . . . Theresiae Benedictae a Cruce (Edith Stein)*, 1997, 8–9.

57. Duffin, *Better Eye*, 1998, 277, 376n84.

58. Alphonsus Rodriguez, ASV RP 1624 (1833), entire file (Joaquina).

59. On the history of peritonitis, see Duffin, *Better Eye*, 36; Duffin, "Great Debate," 1987.

60. Duffin, "Great Debate," 1987.

61. First of two miracles, SRC, *Compendium . . . Antonii Gianelli*, 1951.

62. Vauchez, *Sainteté*, 1981, 520, 549–52.

63. SRC, *Compendium . . . Io. Francisci Regis*, 1737, xxix.

64. Resch, *Miracoli dei Beati, 1991–1995*, 2002, 59–62; Resch, *Miracoli dei Santi*, 2002, 129–34.

65. On the history of the neurological examination, see a series of essays in *Seminars in Neurology*, 2002, volume 22, number 4.

66. Resch, *Miracoli dei Beati, 1991–1995*, 2002, 335–38.

67. Resch, *Miracoli dei Beati, 1983–1990*, 2002, 424–27 and *Miracoli dei Beati, 1991–1995*, 2002, 150–53; Anon., *Sommario . . . Alessandro Sauli*, 1638, 63.

68. Wilson, *Making Man-Midwifery*, 1995, 49–53.

69. Zacchia, *Quaestiones*, 1657, 675–80 (Consilia IX and X). See also Ditchfield, *Liturgy, Sanctity, and History*, 2002, 235.

70. Salvatoris Pagnani, ASV RP 2522 (1773), 112v article 143, 301–3v (miraculée).

71. Anon. *Sommario . . . Alessandro Sauli*, 1638, 78; Resch, *Miracoli dei Beati, 1983–1990*, 2002, 424–27.

72. Wilson, *Making Man-Midwifery*, 1995, 22, 65–106.

73. Falconieri, *Storia . . . Giovanni della Croce*, 1726, 221–22; Zacchia, *Quaestiones*, 1657, 739 (Consilium XXXIX).

74. CCS, *Compendium . . . Aegidii Mariae*, 1994, 6 (Signora Angela).

75. Wilson, *Making Man-Midwifery*, 1995, 1–7.

76. Bracciolini, *Compendio . . . di San Diego*, 1598, 38; Ramirez, *Relatione . . . Isidoro Agricola*, 1622, 57; Fuligatti, *Compendio . . . Francesco Saviero*, 1637, 156; Petrus Forerus, ASV RP 3008 (1682), 213.

77. Andrea Corsini, ASV RP 762 (1606), 135 (mother), 180 (sixteenth miracle), 231 (surgeon).

78. Alphonsus Ligorio, ASV RP 2083 (1826), 49–52v (miraculée), 54–57v (doctor), 73–75v (surgeon). See also SRC, *Compendium . . . Alphonsi Mariae Ligorio*, 1839, 21.

79. Germana Cousin, ASV RP 3283 (1856), 26v–31v (summary), 58–59, 72–86v (doctors), 114–30v (miraculée). See also SRC, *Compendium . . . Germanae Cousin*, 1867, 9.

80. Resch, *Miracoli dei Santi*, 2002, 141–47.

81. Barkan, "Cosmas and Damian," 1996; Lehrman, "Miracle," 1994; Schlich, "Gods and Saints," 1995; Zimmerman, *One Leg in the Grave*, 1998.

82. SRC, *Passavien . . . Conradi a Parzham. Positio*, 1933, 5–48 (summary of first miracle).

83. Resch, *Miracoli dei Beati, 1991–1995*, 2002, 385–90.

84. On Daria, see Maria Magdalena de Pazzis, ASV RP 771 (ca. 1663), 324–25, 329v-332v, 337v-338. See also ASV RP 770 (ca. 1666), 14 (number 8).

85. On Colomba, see Maria Magdalena de Pazzis, ASV RP 771 (ca. 1663), 101v–106v. See also ASV RP 770 (ca. 1666), 13 (number 13).

86. On monk with *"estrema maninconia"* [sic], see Maria Magdalena de Pazzis, ASV RP 771 (ca. 1663), 444–59, 450–52.

87. On Lucretia, see Maria Magdalena de Pazzis, ASV RP 771 (ca. 1663), 322–26, esp. 324r–v.

88. SRC, *Taurinen. Beat. Ioannis Bosco. Positio*, 1907, 986–1020 (Miraculis postobit.), esp. 1010–11 (Angelina).

89. SRC, *Compendium . . . Aloysii Gonzagae*, 1726, fourteenth miracle.

90. SRC, *Compendium . . . Iulianae Falconeriae*, 1738, 18.

91. Gorce, "L'oeuvre medicale," 1915, 113; Colombero, "Un contributo," 1982; Foucault, *Madness*, 1973, 94n9, 102–5; Haynes, *Philosopher King*, 1970, 126, 138–50; Zacchia, *Quaestiones*, 1657, 94–95 (Liber 2, Titulus 3, Question 3 [animi vitiis]); 149–70 (Liber 3, Titulus 2 [de morborum simulatione]); 582–85 (Liber 8, Titulus 1, Question 2 [irregularitate spirituale]). Zacchia used the word "histericae" to refer to uterine disorders that excused women from conjugal obligation. Zacchia, *Quaestiones*, 1657, 545 and 547, item 10 (in Liber 7, Titulus 3, question 3).

92. Petrus Forerius, ASV RP 3008 (1682), 223–26 (article numbers 366–73); SRC, *Tullen. Beat. et can., . . . Petri Forerii*, 1726, 3 (fourth miracle).

93. Alphonsus Rodriguez, ASV RP 1624 (1833), entire file, esp. 37v, 55v.

94. Alphonsus Rodriguez, ASV RP 1625 (1866), entire file, 37–42 (summary), 177–95 (miraculée), 197–223 (doctor).

95. Maria Guilelma Aemilia de Rodat, ASV RP 4292 (1902), 57–76, 249–55.

96. SRC, *Beat. . . . Joannis de Britto. Novissima positio*, 1941 (first miracle, Dr. Cabral on Gloria). Several healing miracles in this cause may have been gathered after João's martyrdom was contested in a *Dubio* of 1851.

97. Composta, *Il miracolo*, 1981, 165–74. See also second miracle in SCCS, *Compendium . . . Raphaëlae Mariae a SS Corde Jesu. Positio*, 1976.

98. Iohannes Baptista de la Salle, ASV RP 3886 (1846), entire file, esp. 65–75v (miraculée), 176 (Lallemand), 179v (Recamier).

99. Iohanna Francisca Fremiot de Chantal, ASV RP 883 (1757). See also SRC, *Compendium . . . Iohannae Franciscae Fremiot de Chantal*, 1767, xxx–xxxii.

100. Resch, *Miracoli dei Beati, 1983-1990*, 2002, 453–57.

101. SRC, *Polona . . . Andreae Bobola. Positio*, 1936 (first miracle, Ida).

102. Christian, "Storia," 1999.

103. Bracciolini, *Compendio . . . di San Diego*, 1598, 64. The author related the recovery to two established saints: St. Jerome's report on St. Hillarion's ability to calm madness in animals.

104. Park, *Secrets of Women*, 2006, 50. See also Bynum, "Bodily Miracles," 1991; Pomata, "Malpighi and the Holy Body," 2007.

105. For example, see numerous anatomical citations in the first two miracles of eight (from a total of more than a hundred) in SRC, *Spoletana. Can. B. Clarae a Cruce de Montefalco. . . . Positio*, 1881, 39–49, 74–80, 93, 63–134. See also SRC, *Bononien. Can. B. Catharinae . . . Positio super dubio*, 1681, 343–72; SRC, *Compendium . . . Iosephi a Leonissa*, 1746, 20–21; Iacobus de Marchia, ASV RP 2009 (1700), 450–56, 483r–v, 486–506 (six doctors on the corpse).

106. Haynes, *Philosopher King*, 1970, 70–77. On incorruptibility, see Liber quarto, Pars I, Cap. XXX, in Benedict XIV, *De servorum Dei* (Naples ed.), 8 (1774): 246–64; Cruz, *Incorruptibles*, 1977; Guida, *Caterina Labouré*, 1997; Park, "Criminal and Saintly Body," 1994; Thomas, *Le cadavre*, 1980, 39–45; Woodward, *Making Saints*, 1990, 83–84, and Woodward, *Book of Miracles*, 2000, 163–65.

107. Clara a Montefalco, ASV RP 2930 (1726), 23–25, 27v–30. For more on the corpse of Chiara of Montefalco, see Menesto, *Il processo*, 1984, xxxix, xlv; Park, "Criminal and Saintly Body," 1994; Park, *Secrets of Women*, 2006, 39–49.

108. O'Connell, "Roman Catholic Tradition," 1986, 115, 138–9.

109. See, for example, http://members.chello.nl/~l.de.bondt/IncorruptBodies. htm, accessed April 2008.

110. Gemma Galgani, ASV RP 4613 (1921), 26 pages in front of file.

111. Gemma Galgani, ASV RP 4613 (1909), 41 pages in back of file; SRC, *Compendium . . . Gemmae Galgani*, 1939. See also Sabourin, *Divine Miracles*, 1977, 169–70.

112. Andrea Corsini, ASV RP 762 (1606), 179, 279 (eighth miracle, Elisabetta).

113. Llot, *Laudabili . . . Raymundi Penia Forti*, 1595, 83 (Bartolomeus); Anon., *Sommario . . . Sauli*, 1638, 55 (Anna Aurelia).

114. SRC, *Compendium . . . Aloysii Gonzagae*, 1726 (sixth miracle, Joanna).

115. See, for example, Marcus "maligno vexatus spiritu," in SRC, *Positio super dubio . . . Ioanne patratis* [de Capistrano], 1664, 7; Federighi, *Vita . . . Zita*, 1582, 89–91.

116. Elisabetta eighth miracle and Menia "malis spiritibus obsessa," 57th miracle in Andrea Corsini, ASV RP 762 (1606), 185, 238 (on Menia), and 279 (Elisabetta).

117. On Daria, Maria Magdalena de Pazzis, ASV RP 771 (ca. 1663), 324–25 ("mente molesta"), 329v–32v, 337v–38 ("pazza"); ASV RP 770 (ca. 1666), 14 (number eight, "demens" "furore").

118. Cardano, *Book of My Life*, 1931, 10.

119. Zacchia, *Quaestiones*, 1657, 225–27 (Liber 4, Titulus 1, question 8).

120. Goodich, *Other Middle Ages*, 1998, 152–7. See also Smoller, "Case of Demonic Possession," 2006.

121. Turchini, *La fabbrica*, 1984, 146.

122. Macdonald, "Religion, Social Change," 1982, 123–24.

123. Charuty, *Couvent des fous*, 1985, 251–364.

124. Robbins, *Encyclopedia*, 1959, 195–96.

125. Van der Hart et al., "Jeanne Fery," 1996; Ferracuti et al., "Dissociative Trance Disorder," 1996.

126. Asch, "Depression and Demonic Possession," 1985.

127. Klaniczay, "Miracoli di punizione," 1999.

128. Bracciolini, *Compendio . . . di San Diego*, 1598, 33.

129. Gretser, *Commentarius . . . Vita Gregorii VII*, 1610.

130. Valenzuela, *Historia*, 1729, 59–64.

131. Ramirez, *Relatione . . . Isidoro Agricola*, 1622, 58.

132. Falconieri, *Storia . . . Giovanni della Croce*, 1726, 219–20.

133. Valauri, *Vita . . . Giovanni da San Facondo*, 1690, 166–70. A prison escape is also mentioned in early seventeenth-century documents in the cause of Jerome Emiliani. Pellegrini, *Acta et processus*, 1980, 60.

134. Iulii, third miracle in Paschalis Bailon, ASV RP 3407 (1673), 13; Ramirez, *Relatione . . . Isidoro Agricola*, 1622, 42; Bourbon del Monte, *Relatio facta . . . Isidori Agricolae*, 1622, 19; Maria Magdalena de Pazzis, ASV RP 771 (ca. 1663), 246–53 (ships).

135. Pius V, ASV RP 2553 (1704), 71v–74 (summary flood), 269–77v (Pietro), 285–94 (father). The two other miracles were the Capitano, shot in 1683 (see chapter 5), and Isabella, the doctor's wife cured in 1678 (see chapter 2 and at n119 above). Of these miracles only Isabella appeared in the *Compendium*. SRC, *Compendium . . . Pii V*, 1712, last miracle.

136. Seraphinus a Montegranario, ASV RP 95 (1762), 27v–29r, 86v–100v.

137. Paschalis Bailon, ASV RP 3407 (1673), 14 (fourth miracle); Salvatoris Pagnani, ASV RP 2522 (1773), 494–611 (Fra Michele).

138. Ramirez, *Relatione . . . Isidoro Agricola*, 1622, 37; Bourbon del Monte, *Relatio facta . . . Isidori Agricolae*, 1622, 17.

139. Stories of Caterina, Alfonso, Hilario, and Agostino in Bourbon del Monte, *Relatio facta . . . Isidori Agricolae*, 1622, 16, 17, 20; and in Ramirez, *Relatione . . . Isidoro Agricola*, 1622, 34, 26, 39, 46.

140. Maria Magdalena de Pazzis, ASV RP 771 (ca. 1663), 148–64 (summary), 495–499 (Sor. Eugenia on oil). See also ASV RP 770 (ca. 1666), 13v (number 7, oil).

141. Maria Magdalena de Pazzis, ASV RP 771 (ca. 1663), 428v–437v, esp. 433 (Sor. Reparata on oil).

142. Maria Magdalena de Pazzis, ASV RP 771 (ca. 1663), 386r–87v (M. Minima on sisters M. Margarita, Angela, and Eufrasia), 480–86 (Antonio on Diacinto and Margarita T.), 486v–89v (Pietro C.). See also ASV RP 770 (ca. 1666), 14v, 191–96 (number 16, Petrus).

143. SRC, *Harlemen. Canonizationis . . . Martyrum Gorgomiensum,* 1674, 2 (first miracle); SRC, *Polona. . . . Andreae Bobola. Animadversiones,* 1830, 12–13, and *Responsio,* 86–109 (third miracle).

144. SRC, *Compendium . . . Mariae Goretti,* 1950, 13, 15; Young, "Imperishable," 1989.

145. Resch, *Miracoli dei Beati,* 1991–1995, 2002, 474–79.

146. Composta, *Il miracolo,* 1981, 133–41.

147. See, for example, Ferdinandus III Castiliae, ASV RP 1111 (1656); Pope Gregorius X, ASV RP 2153 (1627); Petrus Gonzales (Felmo), ASV RP 3257 (ca. 1731); Falco, ASV RP 3769 (1892). Two of these four files were nearly illegible, and I may have missed evidence of physician involvement.

148. Germana Cousin, ASV RP 3286 (1847).

CHAPTER 4

1. Skinner, *Health and Medicine,* 1996, 41–42, 91–98, 104–6; Occhioni, *Il processo,* 1984, 489–90, 578–79, 598–99; Vauchez, *Sainteté,* 1981, 549n82.

2. Menesto, *Il processo,* 1984, 264, 306–7, 395, 590, 624; Federighi, *Vita . . . Zita,* 1582, 73–74 (Pietro, cured in 1272), 75–79 (Andrea, cured in 1320); SRC, *Positio super dubio . . . Ioanne patratis* [de Capistrano], 1664, 3 (cured in 1435, attended by surgeons and doctors, summ. 10); Andric, *Miracles,* 2000, 238.

3. Many records in the cause of Carlo Borromeo reside in Milan, suggesting that others may be found in the host cities of the inquiries. Turchini, *La Fabbrica,* 1984.

4. Bracciolini, *Compendio . . . di San Diego,* 1598, 29, 31.

5. Bracciolini, *Compendio . . . di San Diego,* 1598, 37, 38, 40, 45, 46, 47; Gallesini, *Vita . . . di San Diego,* 1589, 109, 111, 114, 128, 134, 137–43.

6. Maria Magdalena de Pazzis, ASV RP 771 (ca. 1663), 475v–80 (Dr. Tiberio Gaci); 485v–89v (Dr. P. B. Cervieri), 490–94v (Dr. G. B. Signi).

7. Maria Magdalena de Pazzis, ASV RP 770 (ca 1666), 297–300v.

8. Catharina a Bononia, ASV RP 262 (1674), 60–61 (list), 178v–88 (Dr. Galeazzo Manzi), 201v–210v (Dr. Pasi), 213v–21 (Dr. Bonio). One doctor seems not to have testified: Vincentis de Caradoris.

9. SRC, *Vicen . . . Ioachimae de Vedruna, viduae de Mas,* 1936 (second miracle, Joseph).

10. Turchini, *La fabbrica,* 1984, 116–27, 141–47.

11. Carolus Borromaeus, ASV RP 1681 (1604).

12. McVaugh, "Bedside Manners," 1997; García Ballester, *Medicine in Multicultural Society,* 2001; McVaugh, *Medicine before the Plague,* 1993, 143–44.

13. Falconieri, *Vita . . . Giovanni della Croce,* 1726, 213–16.

14. Ignatius a Laconi, ASV RP 414 (1853), 49v (article number 117).

15. Vauchez, *Sainteté,* 1981, 545, 549.

16. Carolus Borromaeus, ASV RP 1681 (1604), 116v, 202–3 (Dr. Augustus Tergus), 169, 199, 297 (medici); Andrea Corsini, ASV RP 762 (1606), 230–32v (Dr. Claudius Anselmi Cocchi).

17. Ramsey, *Professional and Popular Medicine*, 1988; Gentilcore, *Healers and Healing*, 1998, 1–28.

18. Falco, ASV RP 3769 (1892).

19. Franciscus Solanus, ASV RP 1333 (1697), 155. A physician testified as the first witness in each of the following: Laurentius a Brundusio, ASV RP 381 (1797), 65v–96v; Leonardus a Porto Mauritio, ASV RP 2502 (1809), 65v–99; Alphonsus Maria Ligorio, ASV RP 2080 (1827), 65v–99; Alphonsus Rodriguez, ASV RP 1624 (1833), 34v–43; Paulus a Cruce Danei, ASV RP 2355 (1819), 53v–60 and ASV RP 2356 (1846), n.p.; Iohannes Gabrielus Perboyre, ASV RP 4766 (1892), 75–90; Iohannes Eudes, ASV RP 4764 (1920), 16–26; SRC, *Vicen . . . Ioachimae de Vedruna*, 1936, 70.

20. Pompilius Pirrotti, ASV RP 5262 (1906), 3v–14v; Iacobus de Marchia, ASV RP 2009 (1700), 476–85, esp. 478 (Dr. C. Prudente on a man with broken hip); Hyacintha Marescotti, ASV RP 3588 (1711), 176–94v (Dr. B. Stella on 3 miraculés; for two he is the only witness: case of Giuseppe M. and himself); Iohannes Baptista de la Salle, ASV RP 3889 (1877), 51–60 and 71–91 (Dr. L. Simon); 35–50 and 63–69 (Dr. H. Colombel).

21. For early examples of expert testimony, see Andrea Corsini, ASV RP 762 (1606), 149 (Dr. Angelus Bonnellus and Dr. Ios. Paulus Alegney on corpse of saint); Maria Magdalena de Pazzis, ASV RP 771 (ca 1663), 486v–489v (Dr. Pietro Cervieri on Sor. Angela's knee); Franciscus Solanus, ASV RP 1333 (1697), n.p. end of file (reports of experts, Dr. Angelo Modio and Dr. Antonius Placentin on Joanna's breast).

22. Zacchia, *Quaestiones*, 1657, Liber 9, 659–75 (Consilia I–VIII, miracles ascribed to Lorenzo Giustiniani), 675–80 (Consilia IX and X, miracle ascribed to Gregory X), 725–26 and 728–29, 753–55 (Consilia XXX, XXXII, and XLV, miracles ascribed to Felice). See also Giustiniani, *Vita*, 1690, 73–79 (boy Hieronymo [Cons. I]), and n.p. following p. 79 (Soror Lucia [Cons. III] and Marina [Cons. VIII]).

23. Dr. Lorenzo Sympa appears to have traveled for inquiries to Spain in 1925 and France in 1935. Robertus Bellarmino, ASV RP 5266 (1926); Ludovicus Maria Grignion de Montfort, ASV RP 4894 (1936), 42v, 49.

24. Wilson, *Making Man-Midwifery*, 1995, 1–7.

25. Andrea Corsini, ASV RP 762 (1606), 181v–182 (list), 116 (case 27, Dionara, midwife), 155-7 (cases 25 and 40 Menica midwife), 228 (midwife), 231 (surgeon Cocchius), 301–3v (parents). A midwife (*ostetrica*) also appears to have testified in 1613 in the cause of Girolamo Miani. Pellegrini, *Acta et processus*, 1980, 20–21.

26. SRC, *Majoricen . . . Alphonsi Rodriguez. Novissima positio*, 1824, 42, 67 (second miracle, Margarita).

27. Iohanna Francisca Fremiot de Chantal, ASV RP 883 (1757), 149–253, esp. 258v–59 (miraculée), 266–307, 381–97, 399–417 (nurses).

28. Lucia Filippini, ASV RP 4865 (1921), 76–143.

29. SRC, *Passavien. . . . Conradi a Parzham. Positio*, 1930, 71–74. See also Composta, *Il miracolo*, 1981, 15–25.

30. For example, Pompilius Pirrotti, ASV RP 5258 (1930), 165 (Dr. V. Polito).

31. Leonardus a Porto Mauritio, ASV RP 2502 (1809), 207–211v.

32. For example, Andrea Avellino, ASV RP 1993 (1681), 97 (Dr. Gio. Domenico La Bollita).

33. For example, Johannes Berchmans, ASV RP 2327 (1749), 271 (Dr. Diotellecci).

34. Leonardus a Porto Mauritio, ASV RP 2502 (1809), 65v–99 (Dr. D. Buto); Maria Euphrasia Pelletier, ASV RP 4971 (1917), 83 (Dr. Alphonse Meyer).

35. Ignatius a Laconi, ASV RP 414 (1853), 50, article 119 (Antonio P.). See also Ramirez, *Relatione . . . Isidoro Agricola*, 1622, 41, and Bourbon del Monte, *Relatio facta . . . Isidori Agricolae*, 1622, 18 (boy "absque alia medicamento"); Andrea Corsini, ASV RP 762 (1606), 124–126v (boy Octavianus), 181 (Elisabetta); CCS, *Compendium . . . Ioannis Calabria*, 1994, 11 ("senza ricorso alla medicina").

36. Andrea Corsini, ASV RP 762 (1606), 124–26 (Octavius).

37. Germana Cousin, ASV RP 3285 (1846), 660–62 (mother of Philippe); Elisa (also Elisabetta) in Composta, *Il miracolo*, 1981, 15–25. On Elisa, see also SRC, *Passavien . . . Conradi a Parzham. Positio*, 1930 (second miracle).

38. Iohannes Berchmans, ASV RP 2324 (1751), 174v (Sor. Maria Angela).

39. Valladier, *Speculum . . . Franciscae Romanae*, 1609, 78 (Antonius de Palumbaria).

40. Bourbon del Monte, *Relatio facta . . . Francisci Xavieri*, 1622, 51–53.

41. SRC, *Bononien. . . . Catharinae a Bononia. Positio super dubio*, 1681, 140–44, 360.

42. Falconieri, *Storia . . . Giovanni della Croce*, 1726, 219–20 (Dr. B. Molino).

43. Resch, *Miracoli dei Santi*, 2002, 112–16.

44. Resch, *Miracoli dei Santi*, 2002, 176–79.

45. CCS, *Compendium . . . Zdislavae de Lemberk*, 1995, 4. On the same case, see also Resch, *Miracoli dei Santi*, 2002, 188–92.

46. Llot, *Laudabili . . . Raymundi Penia Forti*, 1595, 89–90.

47. SRC, *Matriten. . . . Vincentiae Mariae Lopez Vicuña. Positio* and *Nova Positio*, 1949 (second miracle, Joseph).

48. Andrea Fournet, ASV RP 4322 (1928), 60–64, esp. 62 (Dr. P. Loisseau).

49. Pompilius Pirrotti, ASV RP 5258 (1930), 97–135, esp. 119 (father), 138–61, esp. 143 (mother), 204–29, esp. 206 (uncle), 165–88, esp. 169–70 (Dr. Polito).

50. Composta, *Il miracolo*, 1981, 77–91.

51. Zacchia, *Quaestionum*, 1725, Tome 3, 126–28, esp. 127 (Consilium LXXIX). See also Pomata, "Malphighi and the Holy Body," 2007.

52. Ludovicus Maria Grignion de Montfort, ASV RP 4894 (1935), 25v–30v (summary); certificates unnumbered in back of file.

53. Germana Cousin, ASV RP 3286 (1847), 40–47 (summary).

54. Leonardus a Porto Mauritio, ASV RP 2503 (1834), 406 ("normale"), 407 ("naturale"). On "normal" and the rise of medical numbers, see Warner, *Therapeutic Perspective*, 1986, 89–91.

55. Germana Cousin, ASV RP 3285 (1846), 60–62, 227–43.

56. Iohannes Baptista de la Salle, ASV RP 3886 (1846), 179v (Recamier), 181v–82v (Dr. James).

57. Septem Fundatores, ASV RP 3850 (1884), 58v ("temperatura").

58. Pompilius Pirrotti, ASV RP 5262 (1906), 11 (cure of 1892); Antonius Maria Claret, ASV RP 4390 (1910), 22v (cure of 1897).

59. Nicolaus de Flüe, ASV RP 4209 (1892), 600.

60. SRC, *Andegaven. Mariae Euphrasiae Pelletier. Fama,* 1901, 153–66, esp. 158–59.

61. Theresia Margarita Redi, ASV RP 5652 (1907), 162–64.

62. Magdalena Sophia Barat, ASV RP 4917 (1906), 259.

63. Maria Euphrasia Pelletier, ASV RP 4971 (1917), 126–27.

64. Maria Micaela a San Sacremento, ASV RP 5074 (1928), 75v (doctor complained that the Wassermann test was not done). On the "fact" of the Wassermann test, see Fleck, *Genesis,* 1979.

65. Lucia Filippini, ASV RP 4862 (1928), 257v. For other instances of typhoid serology, see Resch, *Miracoli dei Beati, 1982–1990,* 2002, 323–27, esp. 325 (1933) and *Miracoli dei Beati, 1991–1995,* 328–32, esp. 330 (1911).

66. Resch, *Miracoli dei Beati, 1982–1990,* 2002, 88–93; *Miracoli dei Santi,* 2002, 33–39.

67. Iosephus Cafasso, ASV RP 4801 (1918), 352–56 (hospital notes and drawing of a chest X-ray). See also Lucy Filippini, ASV RP 4865 (1921), 136–39; SRC, *Tarvisina. . . . Mariae Bertillae Boscardin. Positio,* 1951, 83.

68. Iohannes Baptista de la Salle, ASV RP 3886 (1846), 179v.

69. Maria Guilelma Aemilia Rodat, ASV RP 4292 (1902), 249–55, esp. 253.

70. For cardioversion, see CCS, *Compendium . . . Zdislavae de Lemberk,* 1995, 4; Resch, *Miracoli dei Santi,* 2002, 141–47, 186–92; *Miracoli dei Beati, 1991–1995,* 2002, 217–21.

71. Resch, *Miracoli dei Beati, 1991–1995,* 2002, 165–69.

72. Resch, *Miracoli dei Santi,* 2002, 56–62, 84–89; *Miracoli dei Beati, 1991–1995,* 2002, 134–38.

73. Seraphinus a Montegranario, ASV RP 95 (1762), 25–26v.

74. Franciscus Xavierus Maria Bianchi, ASV RP 1921 (1827), 157–202, esp. 167v (Dr. N. Corsi).

75. SRC, *Savonen. . . . .Mariae Josephae Rossello. Positio,* 1946 (first miracle, Rachaela).

76. Resch, *Miracoli dei Beati, 1983–1990,* 2002, 63–67.

77. Maria Micaela a San Sacremento, ASV RP 5074 (1928), 84–87, 117–21 (Dr. Coll).

78. Composta, *Il miracolo,* 1981, 92–105.

79. Resch, *Miracoli dei Beati, 1983–1990,* 2002, 78–81.

80. Resch, *Miracoli dei Beati, 1983–1990,* 2002, 127–33 (nun); *Miracoli dei Beati, 1991–1995,* 2002, 459–63 (baby).

81. Resch, *Miracoli dei Beati, 1983–1990,* 2002, 157–61.

82. Iohannes Leonardi, ASV RP 5661 (1934), part 3, 25.

83. Resch, *Miracoli dei Santi,* 2002, 150–54.

84. Similarly, evidence from investigations of saintly bodies shows that anatomy was accepted in Renaissance Italy. Park, "Criminal and Saintly Body," 1994; Park, *Secrets of Women,* 2006; Siraisi, *Medicine and the Italian Universities,* 2001, 356–80.

85. Hyacintha Marescotti, ASV RP 3588 (1711), 177–94 (Dr. Bernardino Stella).

86. Michaelis Garicoïts, ASV RP 5137 (1939), 168.

87. Andrea Fournet, ASV RP 4321 (1921), quire 4, n.p. (Dr. Michiels quoted in summary on first miracle, Sor. Clementina).

88. For more on the medico-legal context, see De Renzi, "Witnesses," 2002.

89. Iohannes a Cruce, ASV RP 2852 (1723), 43–43v (Dr. Vaugien), 133–39 (Vaugien's testimony). See also Falconieri, *Storia . . . Giovanni della Croce*, 1726, 217–19.

90. Rita a Cassia, ASV RP 4023 (1775), 48v–51, esp. 51 (surgeon Lori and Drs. Giorgi and Lauri).

91. Theophilus a Corte, ASV RP 5292 (1925), 18v–22 (summary), 43–51 (Dr. Anghinelli).

92. Theophilus a Corte, ASV RP 5294 (1908), 86–89v, 110–19, 155r–56v.

93. Theophilus a Corte, ASV RP 6215i (1919), n.p.

94. SRC, *Savonen. Beat. et can. . . . Mariae Josephae Rossello. Positio*, 1946, 83–157, esp. 126.

95. Iosephus a Cupertino, ASV RP 2048 (1758), 422–39, esp. 426.

96. Lucia Filippini, ASV RP 4862 (1927), 14–19 (summary), 147–51 (Dr. R. Salvatucci).

97. SRC, *Romana . . . Caroli a Setia. Positio*, 1956 (second miracle, Dr. Pappalardo on Luisa).

98. Leonardus a Porto Mauritio, ASV RP 2503 (1834), 405–6.

99. Nicolaus de Flüe, ASV RP 4209 (1892), esp. 89–95 (summary), 175–230 (miraculée, Justine), 383–419 (Dr. Genoud citing Dr. Miniat, "poitrinaire"), 589–96, esp. 593 (Dr. Röllin "hystérique").

100. Iohannes Gabrielus Perboyre, ASV RP 4766 (1892), 7–9; RP 4768 (1892), 75–90, 304–6, 307–9.

101. SRC, *Aquen. Beat. . . . Mariae Domenicae Mazzarello. Novissima positio*, 1938 (Dr. Vecchi comments on Rosa, second miracle, and response, March 24).

102. Maria Guilelma Aemilia Rodat, ASV RP 4292 (1902), 57–76, 249–55.

103. Iohannes Berchmans, ASV RP 2329 (1867), entire file, esp. 47v–74v (Dr. van Brussel), 218v–238v (Dr. Elewant). An extra folder of unnumbered pages contains the affidavit of the professors, signed January 10, 1868, item number 35, and Elewant's letter of December 7, 1867, item number 36.

104. Alexander Sauli, ASV RP 3764 (1899), 31–40 (summary), 151–61 (surgeon Dr. Vincent), 363–67 (Dr. A. St. George, "neuropathique").

105. SRC, *Quebecen. Can. . . . Beatorum Martyrum Ioannis de Brebeuf, ... Novissima positio*, 1930, 2, 10–12, 15.

106. Margarita de Bourgeoys, ASV RP 4927 (1902), 307–10, esp. 310.

107. Iosephus a Cottolengo, ASV RP 4798 (1910), 202–23 (Dr. Rossetti).

108. Petrus Claver, ASV RP 1183 (1867), 235 (priest), 275–79 (Dr. H. H. Smith [also Schmidt]).

109. Martyri Inglesi, ASV RP 5112 (1891), 74–99, esp.93.

110. Maria Magdalena Postel, ASV RP 5073 (1917), 332–35.

111. Clemens Maria Hofbauer (Jan Dvorak), ASV RP 3861 (1907), 110v.

112. Iosephus Cafasso, ASV RP 4801 (1918), 50–57 (summary), 327–28 (certificates Dr. Ferrare).

113. SRC, *Asten . . . Domenico Savio. Positio*, 1946, 49.

114. Gerardus Maiella, ASV RP 3842 (1875), n.p. (letter from Dr. Daubiol, August 23, 1852).

115. SRC, *Massilen . . . Aemiliae de Vialar. Positio*, 1950, 113, 145 (second miracle, surgeon Robert de Vernejoul on Sister Maria).

116. Magdalena Sophia Barat, ASV RP 4917 (1906), 85, 244, 263 (Dr. Henraud?).

117. Magdalena Sophia Barat, ASV RP 4914 (1912–13), process of Buscoducen.

118. Iohannes de Avila, ASV RP 3172 (1796), 77–131.

119. Iohannes Leonardi, ASV RP 1481 (1822), 123–24.

120. SRC, *Nivernen . . . Bernardae Soubirous. Positio*, 1932 (first miracle, Dr. Petit; second miracle, Dr. Darmand).

121. Iohannes Gabrielus Perboyre, ASV RP 4768 (1901), 4–5.

122. Andrea Fournet, ASV RP 4321 (1921), 4–5.

123. CCS, *Catanen. Can. . . . Josephi Benedicti Dusmet. Positio*, 1988, 42.

124. CCS, *Leodien. Can . . . Mariae Theresiae Haze. Positio*, 1990. See also, Resch, *Miracoli dei Beati, 1991–1995*, 2002, 27–33.

125. Woodward, *Book of Miracles*, 2000, 368–69; Resch, *Miracoli dei Beati, 1991–1995*, 2002, 350–54. For other examples of historical contextualization, see Resch, *Miracoli dei Beati, 1983–1990*, 2002, 346–49, 447–50, 507–11, 515–19, 550–54, 563–66, 557–60; and *Miracoli dei Beati, 1991–1995*, 2002, 27–33, 240–44.

126. Petrus Canisius, ASV RP 5166 (1922), 366–75 (B. Hapig), 402–8 (J. B. Nöthen).

127. Iohanna Arcensis, ASV RP 5682 (1911), 305 (Dr. Touche).

128. Iosephus a Cupertino, ASV RP 2048 (1758), 83–104, esp. 83v (Dr. Antonio Battista Contini).

129. Benedictus Iosephus Labré, ASV RP 2393 (1847), 75v-104v, esp.76 (Dr. Giovanni Castelli).

130. Robin Estrin, "Vatican: Girl's recovery a miracle," Associated Press, April 20, 1997. http://archive.southcoasttoday.com/daily/04-97/04-20-97/a03sr015.htm (accessed April 2008).

131. García Ballester, *Medicine in Multicultural Society*, 2001, esp. essay iv; Ziegler, "Practitioners and Saints," 1999, 208.

132. Bracciolini, *Compendio . . . di San Diego*, 1598, 29, 31.

133. See, for example, physician names cited in two recent Lebanese causes: SRC, *Antiochena . . . Sarbelli Makhlouf. . . . Novissima positio*, 1965; Resch, *Miracoli dei Beati, 1983-1990*, 2002, 162–68.

134. SCCS, *Barcinonen . . . Fratris Michaëlis. Positio*, 1977, 16, 28.

135. Maria Euphrasia Pelletier, ASV RP 4971 (1917), 82–83, 113–14.

136. Most witnesses attempted an explanation, but one miraculée stated "I do not know how to distinguish between a miracle and an act of grace." Maria Francisca a Vulneribus, ASV RP 1959 (1851), 72v. See also Gentilcore, *Healers and Healing*, 1998, 188.

137. According to Karl Popper, falsifiability demarcates scientific knowledge from other forms. For a concise summary, see Popper, *Conjectures and Refutations*, 1963, 33–39, esp. 36–37.

138. Laurentius a Brundusio, ASV RP 381 (1797), 65v–96v, esp. 70.

139. Iohannes Baptista de la Salle, ASV RP 3889 (1877), 21–23.

140. Theophilus of Corte, ASV RP 5294 (1908), 89v, 155v, 156v.

141. Resch, *Miracoli dei Santi*, 2002, 186–92; See also CCS, *Compendium* . . . *Zdislavae de Lemberk*, 1995, 4.

142. Michaelis Garicoïts, ASV RP 5137 (1939), 212.

CHAPTER 5

1. Ehrstine, "Motherhood," 2001, 125n13 and n14.

2. On the plurality of healing rituals, see Burke, "Rituals," 1987; Skinner, *Health and Medicine*, 1996, 143.

3. On narrative in miracles, see Andric, *Miracles*, 2000, 228–34; Gentilcore, *Healers and Healing*, 1998, 179–86; Goodich, *Violence*, 1995; Goodich, *Voices*, 2006; Kselman, *Miracles*, 1978, 62–79; Schlauch, *Medieval Narrative*, 1934.

4. Raimundus de Peniafort, ASV RP 221 (1596), 109v (miraculé).

5. Thomas a Villanova, ASV RP 3641 (1653), 12.

6. Anon. *Sommario* . . . *Alessandro Sauli*, 1638, 65.

7. Anon. *Contextus actorum* . . . *Francisci de Sales*, 1665, 130–31.

8. Maria Magdalena de Pazzis, ASV RP 770 (ca. 1666), 89v–116v (miraculé Gaspare).

9. Maria Magdalena de Pazzis, ASV RP 771 (ca. 1663), 246v–53.

10. Paschalis Bailon, ASV RP 3407 (1673), 17–18 (sixth miracle, Pasqualis).

11. Pius V, ASV RP 2553 (1704), 71v–74 (summary), 269–77v (miraculé), 285–94 (father).

12. Clara a Cruce de Montefalco, ASV RP 2930 (1726), 19v–22 (son of miraculé).

13. Bourbon del Monte, *Relatio facta* . . . *Isidori Agricolae*, 1622, 19; Ramirez, *Relatione* . . . *Isidoro Agricola*, 1622, 42.

14. Paschalis Bailon, ASV RP 3407 (1673), 13 (third miracle, Julio).

15. Pellegrini, *Acta* . . . *Hieronymi Aemiliani*, 1980, 60 (seventeenth-century process of Treviso); SRC, *Compendium* . . . *Fidelis a Sigmaringa*, 1746, 21; Valauri, *Vita* . . . *Giovanni da San Facondo*, 1690, 166–69; Petrus Forerius, ASV RP 3008 (1682), 220–21.

16. Pius V, ASV RP 2554 (1704), 45–49, 80, 99. Traditionally made of wax, Agnus Dei medals are often placed inside a metal locket. Pope Pius V is said to have used one during his life when he calmed the Tiber River.

17. Resch, *Miracoli dei Beati, 1991–1995*, 2002, 474–79.

18. Agatha in Franciscus Caracciolo, ASV RP 1897 (1780), 34–43v, esp. 39; Composta, *Il miracolo*, 1981, 26–38; Leone, *Ristretto*, 1690, 56 (Juan de Sahagún); Bourbon del Monte, *Relatio* . . . *Francisci Xavieri*, 1622, 51, 54.

19. Petrus Forerius, ASV RP 3008 (1682), 219 (article number 356).

20. Michaelis de Sancti (Miguel Argemir), ASV RP 3435 (1833), 51–87, esp. 62r–v (miraculé); Iosephus Calasanctius, ASV RP 2707 (1761), 64–75v, esp. 65v (miraculée).

21. Leone, *Ristretto*, 1690, 94 (Pasqual Baylón).

22. Theresia Margarita Redi, ASV RP 5656 (1933), 49–52 (summary), 71–85 (father), 102–16 (mother).

23. Septem Fundatores, ASV RP 3850 (1884), 118r–v, 124.

24. See, for example, Andrea a Burgio, ASV RP 4059 (1878), 334–41, esp. 335 (doctor); Leonardus a Porto Mauritio, ASV RP 2497 (1863), 44–51v, esp. 44v (miraculée).

25. Robertus Bellarmino, ASV RP 5266 (1926), 71–78 (miraculé), 61v–65v (doctor). See also SRC, *Compendium . . . Roberti Card. Bellarmino*, 1930, 10.

26. Pompilius Pirrotti, ASV RP 5258 (1930), 97–135, esp. 118–19 (father).

27. Iosephus Cafasso, ASV RP 4799 (1934), 127–48 (miraculé).

28. Andrea Corsini, ASV RP 762 (1606), 181v–86 (miracles by number: 25 [Dionora], 33 [Angelus], 34 [Matthias], 36 [Seta], 46 [Julia], 61 [Magdalena]). From these summaries, cross references to full testimony can be found.

29. Andrea Corsini, ASV RP 762 (1606), 182v–185 (miracles by number: 33 [Angelus], 52 [boy Cosimus], 55 [Marcus], 56 [Maria]). From these summaries, cross references to full testimony can be found.

30. Priest Francesco S. in Iohannes Iosephus a Cruce, ASV RP 1947 (1802), 77–80v (summary), esp. 78v (lamp). On this same healing, see ASV RP 1944 (1802), 35v–39 (summary); ASV RP 1945, (1802), 27–30 (summary); ASV RP 1946, (1802-3), 54v–63v (summary); and SRC, *Compendium. Ioannis Iosephi a Cruce*, 1839, 21–22.

31. Pellegrini, *Acta . . . Hieronymi Aemiliani*, 1980, 20–21.

32. Maria Magdalena de Pazzis, ASV RP 771 (ca. 1663), 322–26v (Lucretia).

33. Gerardus Maiella, ASV RP 4622 (1900), 29v. For other promises to visit tombs, see Leone, *Ristretto*, 1690, 94 (blind boy, Pasqual Baylón); Petrus Forerius, ASV RP 3008 (1682), 203 (article number 310).

34. For example, but perhaps only symbolically, a boy was dressed in a religious habit after being healed by Juan de Sahagún. Leone, *Ristretto*, 1690, 56.

35. Falconieri, *Storia . . . Giovanni della Croce*, 1726, 219–20.

36. Falconieri, *Storia . . . Giovanni della Croce*, 1726, 213–16.

37. Carolus Borromaeus, ASV RP 1681 (1604), 116v–17v, sixth miracle Lomatio. See also, Peña, *Relatione . . . Carlo Borromeo*, 1625, 71; Turchini, *La fabbrica*, 1984, 135.

38. Salvatoris Pagnani, ASV RP 2522 (1773), 27.

39. Ignatius a Laconi, ASV RP 414 (1853), 48r–v (article number 114, Francesca).

40. Franciscus Xavierus Maria Bianchi, ASV RP 3724 (1874), 40–55 (miraculée).

41. Iohannes Berchmans, ASV RP 3716 (1886), 410.

42. Alexander Sauli, ASV RP 3764 (1899), 31–40, esp. 37 (summary).

43. Pompilius Pirrotti, ASV RP 5258 (1930), 97–135 (father), 138–61, esp. 144 (mother).

44. Sister Angelica in Peña, *Relatione . . . Carlo Borromeo*, 1625, 72. See also the same healing, Carlo Borromeo, ASV RP 1681 (1604), 117v, 155v–56 (seventh miracle).

45. Iohannes Baptista de la Salle, ASV RP 3890 (1892), 101–2. For other examples of miraculés who had first appealed to other saints, see Maria Francisca a Vulneribus, ASV RP 1959 (1851), 65v; Composta, *Il miracolo*, 1981, 125–32.

46. Orsi, "He Keeps Me Going," 1991.

47. O'Connell, "Roman Catholic Tradition," 1986, 115.

48. Beaujard, *Le culte*, 335–37, 363–65; Vauchez, *La sainteté*, 1981, 519–29; Ward, *Miracles*, 1982; Ward-Perkins, "Memoria," 1966.

49. Bracciolini, *Compendio . . . di San Diego*, 1598, 39.

50. Bracciolini, *Compendio . . . di San Diego*, 1598, 37.

51. Henry IV of Castile (called Enrico Impotente, b. 1425–1474), and his daughter (b. ca. 1462). Bracciolini, *Compendio . . . di San Diego*, 1598, 46; Gallesini, *Vita . . . di San Diego*, 1589, 106–7.

52. Bracciolini, *Compendio . . . di San Diego*, 1598, 40–45, esp. 45; Gallesini, *Vita . . . di San Diego*, 1589, 137–38.

53. Case, "Year 1588," 1988. Bracciolini, *Compendio . . . di San Diego*, 1598, 47; Gallesini, *Vita . . . di San Diego*, 1589, 138–43.

54. Raimundus de Peniafort, ASV RP 221 (1596), 110v–11 (miraculé); Llot, *Laudabili . . . Raymundi Penia Forti*, 1595, 91–93, 97. See also Ditchfield, *Liturgy, Sanctity, and History*, 2002, 218; McVaugh, *Medicine before the Plague*, 1993, 139–43.

55. SRC, *Beat. . . . Joannis de Britto, Positio super dubio*, 1851, 94–109 (four miraculés: Ignatius, boy Gasparis, and two girls, both Joanna).

56. Andrea Corsini, ASV RP 762 (1606), 180, 164–67, esp. 166 (miracle number 13, Laurenti).

57. Anon. *Contextus actorum . . . Francisci de Sales*, 1665, 130.

58. Iacobus de Marchia, ASV RP 2009 (1700), 49v–56v, esp. 50v (Nicola).

59. Grandi, *Vita . . . Pietro Orseolo*, 1733, 108 (item vi, Maria).

60. Seraphinus a Montegranario, ASV RP 95 (1762), 25–27, esp. 26v (summary on Ugo); SRC, *Compendium . . . Seraphini ab Asculo*, 1767, xxiv.

61. Ignatius a Laconi, ASV RP 414 (1853), 49v–50 (article number 118, Antonio).

62. Magdalena Sophia Barat, ASV RP 4917 (1917), 77–87, esp. 83–84 (miraculé).

63. O'Connell, "The Roman Catholic Tradition," 1986, 132, 141–42. O'Connell finds it ironic that great pilgrimage sites rose just as medicine began its nineteenth-century advancement.

64. Iohannes Vianney, ASV RP 4713 (1919), esp. 104–6.

65. Germana Cousin, ASV RP 3285 (1846), 49–53 (summary), 110 (mother), 138 (father), 791 and 795 (doctors).

66. Germana Cousin, ASV RP 3285 (1846), esp. 59–66, 273, 392.

67. Germana Cousin, ASV RP 3285 (1846), 428–39 (summary), 466–83 (miraculée).

68. Germana Cousin, ASV RP 3285 (1846), 619–30 (summary), 633–46 (miraculé).

69. Germana Cousin, ASV RP 3283 (1856), 26v–31v, esp. 29v (summary), 114–130v (miraculée). See also SRC, *Compendium . . . Germanae Cousin*, 1867, 9 (Anna Lucie).

70. Germana Cousin, ASV RP 3286 (1847), 40–47 (summary on multiplication).

71. Germana Cousin, ASV RP 3284 (1859), 17v–50v (miraculée). See also SRC, *Compendium . . . Germanae Cousin*, 1867, 9 (Francesca).

72. Resch, *Miracoli dei Beati, 1991–1995*, 2002, 276–79.

73. Resch, *Miracoli dei Beati, 1991–1995*, 2002, 202–5.

74. SCCS, *Quiten . . . B. Fratris Michäelis. Positio*, 1983. See also Resch, *Miracoli dei Santi*, 2002, 40–46. The beatification miracle was the 1937 cure of a nun from biliary lithiasis. SCCS, *Barcinonen . . . B. Fratris Michäelis. Positio*, 1977.

75. Andrea Corsini, ASV RP 762 (1606), 182v–83v (miracles: 36 [Merica], 37 [Andrea], 45 [Julia]). From these summaries references to full testimony can be found.

76. Iohanna de Valois, ASV RP 252 (1632), entire file.

77. Falconieri, Storia . . . Giovanni della Croce, 1726, 222–24.

78. Vauchez, Sainteté, 1981, 519–30.

79. Ward, "Monks," 1999, 133.

80. SRC, Andegaven. Beat . . . Mariae Euphrasiae Pelletier. Fama, 1901, 153–54.

81. Siraisi, Medicine and the Italian Universities, 2001, 356–80; Park, Secrets of Women, 2006, 39–50, 163–65, 170–80.

82. Ward, "Monks," 1999, 134–35.

83. Sallman, Naples et ses saints, 1994, 302–3.

84. Bourbon del Monte, Relatio facta . . . Philippi Neri, 1622, 11. See also Bacci, Vita di Filippo Neri, 1625, 406–7.

85. Bacci, Vita di Filippo Neri, 1625, liber 6, esp. chapters II to IX (hair, cap, fabric dipped in his blood, etc.), and index "miracoli."

86. Bourbon del Monte, Relatio facta . . . Philippi Neri, 1622, 10; Bacci, Vita di Filippo Neri, 1625, liber 6, chapters IV, V, and XI.

87. Valladier, Speculum . . . Franciscae Romanae, 1609, 78 (Augustina, surgeon Antonius, and Antonia).

88. Andrea Corsini, ASV RP 762 (1606), 182, 124–26v (miracle number 29, son of Octavianus).

89. Iacobus de Marchia, ASV RP 2009 (1700), 185–86 (priest on son of Salvatore).

90. Agnes Segni de Montepulciano, ASV RP 1801 (1719), 66r–v (nun), 71v–72 (Lucia widow), 74r–v (Caterina).

91. Andrea Fournet, ASV RP 4322 (1928), 1–5, esp. 5 (summary), 40–60 (mother).

92. Petrus Claver, ASV RP 1183 (1867), 79–80; RP 1190 (1866), 90–99; RP 1189 (1867), 129; Weninger, "Interesting Letter," 1886.

93. Andrea Corsini, ASV RP 762 (1606), 183, 155–57 (miracle number 40, Margarita).

94. Maria Magdalena de Pazzis, ASV RP 771 (ca. 1663), 344–45 (Maddalena Angela), 350v–51 (Maria Elisabetta, Maria Ansilla, Maddalena Angela [again]), 355–60 (Madre Maria).

95. Falconieri, Storia . . . Giovanni della Croce, 1726, 194, 197, 198, 217, 219–20.

96. Falconieri, Storia . . . Giovanni della Croce, 1726, 219.

97. Catharina de Ricciis, ASV RP 793 (ca. 1657), n.p., approx. 23–25 (journey).

98. For example, see Franciscus Xaverius Maria Bianchi, ASV RP 1921 (1827), 25–34, esp. 30v (summary, article number 16), 52–156 (miraculée), 507–34 (priest).

99. Bourbon del Monte, Relatio facta . . . Ignatii, 1622, 51–53.

100. Iosephus a Cupertino, ASV RP 2048 (1758), 422–39, esp. 424–26 (Catherina on cure of her sister Benedetta, with relic of her other sister Maddalena).

101. Maria in Angela Merici, ASV RP 344 (1781), 26v–29. See also SRC, Compendium . . . Angelae Mericiae, 1807, xvii (second miracle).

102. Maria Magdalena de Pazzis, ASV RP 771 (ca. 1663), 386r–87v (M. Minima on sisters M. Margarita, Angela, and Eufrasia), 480–86 (Antonio on Diacinto and Margarita T.).

103. Maria Magdalena de Pazzis, ASV RP 771 (ca. 1663), 486v–89v; RP 770 (ca. 1666), 14v, 191–96 (miracle number 16, Petrus of Naples).

104. Anon. *Contextus actorum . . . Francisci de Sales*, 1665, 128–30 (Maria Juditha).

105. Paul a Cruce Danei, ASV RP 2355 (1819), 29–36v (summary), 61–64 (miraculé); SRC, *Asten . . . Domenici Savio. Positio*, 1946, esp. 16 (first miracle, Sabato).

106. Ludovicus Maria Grignion de Montfort, ASV RP 4894 (1935), 25v–30v (summary).

107. Maria Magdalena de Pazzis, ASV RP 771 (ca. 1663), 226–35 (Lorenzo on Maria Costanza), 293 (Ugolino on boy); Catharina de Ricciis, ASV RP 793 (ca. 1657), n.p. (Francesca P.).

108. CCS, *Catanen . . . Josephi B. Dusmet. Positio*, 1988, 33. See also Resch, *Miracoli dei Beati, 1983–1990*, 2002, 346–49.

109. Ditchfield, *Liturgy, Sanctity, and History*, 2002, 237–38.

110. Candida, Angela, Anna, and Anastasia, in Carolus Borromaeus, ASV RP 1681 (1604), 115v–116, 124–v, 158v; Peña, *Relatione . . . Carlo Borromeo*, 1625, 67, 75, 80, 82; Bourbon del Monte, *Relatio facta . . . Ignatii*, 1622, 47, 55.

111. Turchini, *La fabbrica*, 1984, 46–53, and figures 15 to 22.

112. SRC, *Andegaven. Beat . . . Mariae Euphrasiae Pelletier. Fama*, 1901, 157.

113. Bourbon del Monte, *Relatio facta . . . Ignatii*, 1622, 47.

114. Petrus Forerius, ASV RP 3008 (1682), 199–200.

115. Ignatius a Laconi, ASV RP 414 (1853), 48v–49 (wife of Pietro), 49 (Angela).

116. Robertus Bellarmino, ASV RP 5266 (1926), 76v; Antonius Maria Zaccaria (a physician), ASV RP 3857 (1883), 143 (linen that had touched bones); Iohannis Leonardi, ASV RP 5661 (1936), pt. 2, vellum envelope containing card with color image of the saint, dated Sept. 26, 1936; Iosephus Cafasso, ASV RP 4799 (1934), between 260 and 261 (image of saint).

117. Resch, *Miracoli dei Beati, 1991–1995*, 2002, 80–84.

118. On the history of the novena, see Taves, *Household of Faith*, 1986, 41, 53.

119. Haynes, *Philosopher King*, 1970, 150.

120. Taves, *Household of Faith*, 1986, 41, 52, 55; Schultz, *Capital Miracle*, forthcoming.

121. Bourbon del Monte, *Relatio facta . . . Francisci Xavieri*, 1622, 50–51.

122. Novenas for two of three miraculés (Giovanna and infant Carlo), both healed before 1628, in Franciscus Salesius, ASV RP 991 (1628), 38, 46. On infant Carlo, see also Anon., *Contextus actorum . . . Francisci de Sales*, 1665, 131; Paschalis Bailon, ASV RP 3407 (1673), 11 (boy Dionysius).

123. Grandi, *Vita . . . Pietro Orseolo*, 1733, 107 (item v, Francesca). On the cristallo, see also 106 ("*un globo di cristallo tondo*"), 107 (items iii and iv). See also Mariani, *Storia*, 2002.

124. Composta, *Il miracolo*, 1981, 39–53.

125. Gerardus Maiella, ASV RP 3842 (1875), 147–54, esp. 148, 153.

126. Petrus Canisius, ASV RP 5166 (1922), 280–90, 368–69.

127. Resch, *Miracoli dei Beati, 1983–1990*, 2002, 125–33.

128. Iohannes Baptista de la Salle, ASV RP 3889 (1877), 75.

129. Composta, *Il miracolo*, 1981, 106–17.

130. Maria Euphrasia Pelletier, ASV RP 4974 (1936), 36v–40, 144–45.

131. Maria Magdalena de Pazzis, ASV RP 770 (ca. 1666), 14 (Daria and Agnes), 14v (Colomba and Ludovicus), 254 (Domenico); RP 771 (ca. 1663), 101–2 (Colomba), 221v (Don Gervasio on Giacopo), 339 (on Daria), 366 (Angela Maria).

132. See, for example, Lucia Filippini, ASV RP 4862 (1927), 168–70v (on day of beatification); Falconieri, *Storia . . . Giovanni della Croce*, 1726, 213–16 (on day of beatification); CCS, *Compendium . . . Laurentii Ruiz . . . Martyrum in Japonica*, 1987, baby Cecilia, cured in 1983 (on the second anniversary of beatification).

133. Hamilton, *Incubation*, 1906; Harrison, "Survival," 1908; Delehaye, *Legends*, 1962, 121–22; Jackson, *Doctor and Diseases*, 1988, 145–69; Risse, *Mending Bodies*, 1999, 56–58.

134. Behr, *Aelius Aristides*, 1968, 143–47; Risse, *Mending Bodies*, 1999, 33–38.

135. Barkan, "Cosmas and Damian," 1996; Lehrman, "Miracle," 1994; Schlich, "Gods and Saints," 1995; Voragine, *Légende dorée*, 1997, 913–17; Zimmerman, *One Leg in the Grave*, 1998.

136. Risse, *Mending Bodies*, 1999, 675–79.

137. Llot, *Laudabili . . . Raymundi Penia Forti*, 1595, 92.

138. Iohannes Berchmans, ASV RP 2324 (1751), 174v–93, esp. 181v–85 (Maria Angela).

139. Iosephus a Cupertino, ASV RP 2048 (1758), 210.

140. Iohannes Baptista de la Salle, ASV RP 3889 (1877), 21–23 (report of Dr. Leon Simon, March 10, 1869).

141. Andrea Fournet, ASV RP 4321 (1921), quire number 4, n.p. (summary on Sister Clementina); quire 5, 2–11 (her testimony).

142. Iosephus Cafasso, ASV RP 4799 (1934), 86–93 (summary).

143. Iohannes Baptista de Rossi, ASV RP 2548 (1864), 27–36 (summary, esp. 33), 60v–94v (miraculée, esp. 61).

144. Gerardus Maiella, ASV RP 4622 (1900), 87–93v, esp. 88v–89 (Enrichetta on her dream).

145. SRC, *Asten . . . Domenici Savio. Positio*, 1946, second miracle, esp. 66–67.

146. Resch, *Miracoli dei Beati, 1983–1990*, 2002, 162–68.

147. Resch, *Miracoli dei Beati, 1983–1990*, 2002, 33–36.

148. Composta, *Il miracolo*, 1981, 92–105.

149. Resch, *Miracoli dei Beati, 1983–1990*, 2002, 430–34.

150. SRC, *Beat. can. . . . Joannae Antidae Thouret. Nova positio*, 1933, first expert (Vidau) on first miracle (Sor. Cecilia).

151. Hyacintha Marescotti, ASV RP 3588 (1711), 351–62, esp. 355 (sister Mathilde on miraculée Virginia). See also SRC, *Compendium . . . Hyacinthae Mariscottae*, 1807, xxiv (Virginia).

152. Iohannes Berchmans, ASV RP 2327 (1749), 35–44 (summary).

153. Anon. *Sommario . . . Alessandro Sauli*, 1638, 53, 56, 64, 66.

154. Resch, *Miracoli dei Beati, 1983–1990*, 2002, 125–33.

155. Patron Saints Index: "Padre Pio," http://saints.sqpn.com/saintp27.htm, accessed April 2008.

156. Andrea Corsini, ASV RP 762 (1606), 184, 188–91 (miracle 49, Flametta).

157. Iacobus de Marchia, ASV RP 2009 (1700), 476–85, esp. 478v–v (Dr. Carlo Prudente on man with fractured hip).

158. Agnes Segni de Montpulciano, ASV RP 1801 (1719), 64–76, esp. 67v (summary).

159. Composta, *Il miracolo*, 1981, 39–53.

160. Margarita Bourgeoys, ASV RP 4927 (1902), 80–113.

161. Theophilus a Corte, ASV RP 1829 (1807), 27v–31, esp. 29v (miraculée).

162. Iohannes Berchmans, ASV RP 3716 (1886), 410.

163. Hieronymus Aemiliani, ASV RP 3507 (1762), 75v–80v (Elisabetta of Venice). See also SRC, *Compendium . . . Hieronymi Aemiliani*, 1767, xix (Elizabetha).

164. Theophile a Corte, ASV RP 5294 (1908), 42–54, esp. 44v–45 (miraculée).

165. Martyri Inglesi, ASV RP 5112 (1891), 74–99, esp. 77–86 (miraculé).

166. Ludovicus Maria Grignion de Montfort, ASV RP 4894 (1935), 25–30v (summary).

167. Testimony of miraculé and three priests in Gregorius Barbarigo, ASV RP 5404 (1923), 30–63, esp. 34–36 (miraculé), 96–105, 112–20, and 129–37.

168. Germana Cousin, ASV RP 3285 (1846), 66, 273.

169. Germana Cousin, ASV RP 3285 (1846), 59–66, esp. 59 (summary), 248–63, esp. 249 (miraculée), 269–83, esp. 270 (mother), 290–91 (aunt).

170. Hieronymus Aemiliani, ASV RP 3507 (1762), 75v–80v (summary), 96–124 (miraculée, esp. 101 [illiteracy]), 134–62 (doctor), 221–40 (doctor, esp. 224v [cause]). See also SRC, *Compendium . . . Hieronymi Aemiliani*, 1767, xix.

171. Clemens Maria Hofbauer (Jan Dvorak), ASV RP 3861 (1907), 40v–65 (miraculée), esp. 41 ("del cielo"), 43v (bucket).

172. SRC, *Parisien. Canonizationis . . . B. Catharinae Labouré. Positio*, 1944 (first miracle).

173. Septem Fundatores, ASV RP 3850 (1884), 118r–v; Franciscus Carraciolo, ASV RP 1897 (1780), 49v–55; Composta, *Il miracolo*, 1981, 142–50. On the last case, see also SCCS, *Compendium . . . Oliver Plunket*, 1975, 8.

174. Leonardus a Porto Mauritio, ASV RP 2499 (1790), 65–98v (miraculée).

175. Leonardus a Porto Mauritio, ASV RP 2503 (1834), 90–134, esp. 80–80v, 98 (miraculée).

176. Maria Euphrasia Pelletier, ASV RP 4971 (1917), 102–3.

177. Andrea Fournet, ASV RP 4321 (1921), quire number 4, n.p., summary re Sister Clementina; quire 5, 2–11 (her testimony).

178. Iohannes Baptista de la Salle, ASV RP 3886 (1846), 65–75v, esp. 74 (miraculée).

179. For example, Andrea Corsini, ASV RP 762 (1606), 181, 84–86v (miracle 21, Donna Ginevra).

180. See, for example, Iohannes Baptista de la Salle, ASV RP 3886 (1846), 39v, 111v; Maria Micaela a San Sacramento, ASV RP 5085 (1919), 64v–80v (summary) and RP 5086 (1919), 239–58 (doctor on same case); Petrus Forerius, ASV RP 4119 (1885), 230–32 (Dr. Gingeot); Petrus Chanel, ASV RP 5162 (1907), 70–71.

181. CCS, *Catanen . . . Josephi Benedicti Dusmet. Positio*, 1988, 33; Resch, *Miracoli dei Beati, 1983–1990*, 2002, 346–49.

182. SRC, *Majoricen . . . Alphonsi Rodriguez. Novissima positio*, 1824, 2, 8 (first miracle, Antonia [b. 1617]).

183. CCS, *Viedmen. Can. . . . Laurae Vicuña. Positio*, 1988, 1–28, 168, esp. 22.

184. SRC, *Calaritana. Beat. Can. . . . Ignatii a Laconi. Positio*, 1937, 3–16, esp. 14 (first miracle).

185. Maria Guilelma Aemilia Rodat, ASV RP 4292 (1902), 58, 73.

186. Iohannes Baptista de la Salle, ASV RP 3892 (1891), 89–102, esp. 91, 95 (miraculé), 123–45, esp. 124–6 (doctor).

187. Magdalena Sophia Barat, ASV RP 4912 (1888), 36–40 (summary), 75–86 (miraculée), 87–100 (father).

188. Iosephus Cafasso, ASV RP 4801 (1918), 50–54.

189. Andrea Fournet, ASV RP 4322 (1928), 1–5, esp. 5 (summary), 33v–39 (father), 40–60 (mother).

190. Theresia Margarita Redi, ASV RP 5656 (1933), 49–52 (summary), 102–16 (mother).

191. Bracciolini, *Compendio . . . di San Diego*, 1598, 46; Gallesini, *Vita . . . di San Diego*, 1589, 106–7.

192. Anon., *Compendio . . . Pietro d'Alcantara*, 1666, 76–80.

193. For a few examples, Antonia, cured at age 18, became a nun in Franciscus Xavierus Maria Bianchi, ASV RP 1921 (1827), 25–34 (summary), 52 (miraculée); after her cure, a doctor's daughter became a nun, Humilitas, ASV RP 712 (1628), 20–28, esp. 25–26.

194. Turchini, *La fabbrica*, 1984, 40–53. Anon., *Sommario . . . Alessandro Sauli*, 1638, 64; Catharina de Ricciis, ASV RP 793 (ca. 1657), n.p., on behalf of a Capuchin nun and a child Violante. On votive objects, see Cousin, *Ex voto*, 1981; Lindars and Nordquist, *Gifts to the Gods*, 1987.

195. Iohanna de Valois, ASV RP 252 (1773).

196. Humilitas, ASV RP 712 (1628), esp. 25–26, 31v, 37–38v, 49v, 57v–v, 60 (commentary on article number 2).

197. SRC, *Leopolien. Canonizationis . . . B. Ioannis de Dukla. Positio super dubio*, 1732, 20–21.

198. Falco, ASV RP 3769 (1892), 33–38.

CONCLUSION

1. Dennett, *Breaking the Spell*, 2006, 21, 26.

2. Dennett, *Breaking the Spell*, 2006, 325.

3. Hippocrates, "The Sacred Disease," 1923, esp. 139, 183.

4. Mullin, "Science, Miracles," 2003, 209–11.

5. Van Dam, *Saints and Their Miracles*, 1990, 83–86.

6. On the debate over intercessory prayer, see Benson et al., "Study," 2005; Hobbins, "Step," 2006; Koenig et al., "Religion, Spirituality," 1999; Lilly, "Step," 2006; Matthews, "Religious Commitment," 1998; Matthews, "Prayer and Spirituality," 2000; Matthews and Larson, "Faith and Medicine," 1997; Peschel and Peschel, "Medical Miracles," 1998; Sloan, "Religion, Spirituality," 1999. On the nineteenth-century "prayer gauge," see Mullin, *Miracles*, 1996, 40–46; Mullin, "Science, Miracles," 2003, 211–12.

7. Giunchi, "L'esame," 1988.

8. On falsification, see Popper, *Conjectures*, 1963, 33–39. See also Larmer, *Water into Wine*, 1988, 83–92; Ramsey, *Miracles*, 1964.

9. Woodward, *Making Saints*, 1990, 200.

10. Ditchfield, *Liturgy, Sanctity*, 2002, 129.

11. For an example from a plague year, see Binetti, *Sovrani et efficaci rimedi*, 1656.

12. See, for example, Harris, *The End of Faith*, 2004.

13. On this subject, see Corner, *Signs of God*, 2005, 198.

14. Elsewhere, and inspired by Carlo Ginzburg, I have used the semiotic notion of evidence to connect the practice of medicine not with religion, but with history. Duffin, "A Hippocratic Triangle," 2004; Ginzburg, "Clues," 1989.

APPENDIX A

1. Yvon Beaudoin, *Indice dei processi*, Vaticano: typescript, ASV Indice 1047 covers files call numbers RP 1–4255 (1588–1920); ASV Indice 1147 covers call numbers RP 4256–7030 (1920–1982).

2. José Oriol, ASV RP 4089 (1904) from Barcelona.

3. Johannes de San Facondo da Sahagún, ASV RP 2828 (1608).

4. Ferdinand, ASV RP 1111 (1656).

5. The designation "his quae supervenerunt post obitum" occurs in files for Andrea Avellino, Juan de la Cruz, Margerita of Cortona, and Pasqual Baylón, among others.

6. On local politics and Vatican priorities in canonization, see Higgins, *Stalking the Holy*, 2006, 27–107; Woodward, *Making Saints*, 1990, 21–49, 114–21.

7. Resch, *Miracoli dei Santi*, 2002, *Miracoli dei Beati*, 1983–1990, 2002, and *Miracoli dei Beati*, 1991–1995, 2002.

8. Composta, *Il miraculo*, 1981.

Bibliography

Addleshaw, G. W. O. "Benedict XIV (1740–1758): His Contribution to the Problem of Church Government." *Church Quarterly Review* 120 (April 1935): 74–94.

Allen, David F. "Upholding Tradition: Benedict XIV and the Hospitaller Order of St. John of Jerusalem at Malta, 1740–1758." *The Catholic Historical Review* 80 (January 1994): 18–35.

Amadori, Vincenzo Maria. *Relatio vitae, virtutum, et miraculorum B. Felicis a Cantalicio*. Rome: Joannis Francisci Chracas, 1712. BAV R. G. Miscell. B.5(8)

Amundsen, Darrel W. "The Medieval Christian Tradition." In *Caring and Curing. Health and Medicine in the Western Religious Traditions*, ed. Ronald L. Numbers and Darrel W. Amundsen, 65–107. New York: Macmillan, 1986.

Amundsen, Darrel W., and Gary B. Ferngren. "The Early Christian Tradition." In *Caring and Curing. Health and Medicine in the Western Religious Traditions*, ed. Ronald L. Numbers and Darrel W. Amundsen, 40–60. New York: Macmillan, 1986.

Andric, Stanko. *The Miracles of St. John of Capistrano*. Budapest: Central European University Press, 2000.

Anonymous. *Compendio della vita e miracoli del B. Pietro d'Alcantara*. Trans. from Spanish to Italian. Rome: Nicol'Angelo Tinassi, 1666. BAV Barb. T.IV.145

———. *Contextus actorum omnien in beatificatione & canonizatione S. Francisci de Sales*. Rome: Jacobi Dragondelli, 1665. BAV Barb.HH.II.44

———. *Relazione del miracolo operato nella città di Roma dal glorioso pontifice S. Pio Quinto*. Rome: Francesco Gonzaga, 1713. BAV Miscell. H.67(23)

Anonymous. *Saints: Christianity and Other Religions.* Rome: Gregorian University Press, 1986.

———. *Sommario de processi fatti d'ordine della Sacra Congregatione dei Riti di Roma per la canonizatione del venerabile servo di Dio Alessandro Sauli.* Milan: Pacifico Pontio e Piccaglia, 1638. BAV Barb.U.XIII.90

Antonelli, Francesco. *De inquisitione medico-legale super miraculis in causis beatificationis et canonizationis.* Rome: P. Athenaeum Antoniarum, 1962.

Ariès, Philippe. *Centuries of Childhood: A Social History of Family Life.* Trans. Robert Baldick. New York: Vintage Books, 1962.

Asch, S S. "Depression and Demonic Possession: The Analyst as Exorcist." *Hillside Journal of Clinical Psychiatry* 7, no. 2 (1985): 149–64.

Ashley, Kathleen, and Pamela Sheingorn, eds. *Interpreting Cultural Symbols: Saint Anne in Late Medieval Society.* Athens: University of Georgia Press, 1990.

Bacci, Pietro Giacomo. *Vita di Filippo Neri Fiorentino.* Rome: Mascardi, 1625. BAV Barb.T.II.42

Bailey, Gauvin Alexander, Pamela M. Jones, Franco Mormando, and Thomas W. Worcester, eds. *Hope and Healing: Painting in Italy in a Time of Plague, 1500–1800.* Worcester, MA, and Chicago: Clark University, College of the Holy Cross, and Worcester Art Museum; University of Chicago Press, 2005.

Bajada, Joseph. *Sexual Impotence: The Contributions of Paolo Zacchia (1584–1659).* Analecta Gregoriana 252. Rome: Pontificia Università Gregoriana, 1988.

Barkan, Leonard. "Cosmas and Damian: of Medicine, Miracles and the Economies of the Body." In *Organ Transplantation: Meanings and Realities,* ed. Stuart J. Younger, Renée C. Fox and Laurence J. O'Connell, 221–51. Madison: University of Wisconsin Press, 1996.

Baudeau, Nicolas. "Analyse de l'ouvrage du Pape Benoît XIV sur les béatifications et les canonisations [1759]." In *Theologiae Cursus Completus,* columns 854–940. Paris: J. P. Migne, 1865.

Beaujard, Brigitte. *Le culte des saints en Gaule. Les premiers temps d'Hilaire de Poitiers à la fin du VIe siècle.* Paris: Cerf, 2000.

Behr, C. A. *Aelius Aristides and the Sacred Tales.* Amsterdam: A. M. Hakkert, 1968.

Benedict XIV, Pope. *Correspondance de Benoît XIV, précédée d'une introduction, et accompagnée de notes et tables,* ed. Émile de Heeckeren. Paris: Plon-Nourrit, 1912.

———. *Heroic Virtue: a Portion of the Treatise of Benedict XIV on the Beatification and Canonization of the Servants of God.* 3 vols. London: T. Richardson and Son, 1850–52.

———. *Le lettere di Benedetto XIV al Card. de Tencin ai testi originali,* ed. Emilia Morelli. 3 vols. Storia e Letteratura. Racolta di studi e testi. Rome: Edizioni di Storia e Letturatura, 1955–84.

———. *Nota dei medici e chirurghi destinati a scrivere nelle cause di beatificazione e canonizatione sopra i miracoli.* Rome: Rev. Camera Apostolica, 1743.

———. *Nuova tassa e riforme delle spese per le cause delle beatificazione e canonizatione.* Rome: Rev. Camera Apostolica, 1741.

———. *De servorum Dei beatificatione et beatorum canonizatione . . .* 4 vols. Bononiae (Bologna): Formis Longhi, 1734–38.

——. *De servorum Dei beatificatione et beatorum canonizatione* . . . 16 vols. Neapoli: Paci, 1773–75.

——. *De servorum Dei beatificatione et beatorum canonizatione in synopsim redacta.* Brussels: Typis Societatis Belgicae, 1840.

——. "Sopra la Notomia da farsi nelle pubbliche scuole. Prospero Lambertini (Benedetto XIV) e lo studio dell'anatomia in Bologna [1737]." In *Studi e Memorie per la Storia dell'Università di Bologna,* 2 vols. ed. Giovanni Martinotti, 2: 147–78. Bologna: Cooperativa Tipografica Azzoguidi, 1911.

Benson, Herbert, et al. "Study of the Therapeutic Effects of Intercessory Prayer (STEP) in Cardiac Bypass Patients: A Multicenter Randomized Trial of Uncertainty and Certainty of Receiving Intercessory Prayer." *American Heart Journal* 151, no. 4 (2005): 934–42.

Bertolaso, Bartolo. "La peste Romana del 1656–1657 dalle lettere inedite di S. Gregorio Barbarigo." *Fonte e ricerche di storia ecclestiastica padovana* (1969): 223–269 (estratto).

Binetti, Stefano [Etienne Binet]. *Sovrani et efficaci rimedi contro la peste.* Rome: Ignazio Lazaii, 1656. BAV Chigi.VI.47

Blouin, Francis X. *Vatican Archives; An Inventory and Guide to Historical Documents of the Holy See.* New York: Oxford University Press, 1998.

Boari, Marco, and Rino Froldi. "Paolo Zacchia, il concetto di veleno e i fondamenti della tossicologia forense." *Zacchia: Rivista di medicina legale* 60, no. 1–2 (1987): 1–14.

Boesch Gajano, Sofia. "Dalla storiografia alla storia." In *Miracoli dai segni alla storia,* ed. Sofia Boesch Gajano and Marilena Modica, 215–33. Rome: Viella, 1999.

Boesch Gajano, Sofia, and Raimondo Michetti, eds. *Europa Sacra: Raccolte agiografiche e identità politiche in Europa fra Medioevo ed Età moderna.* Rome: Carocci, 2002.

Bonino, Cesare. *Nonnulla praeclara gesta Beati Caroli Borromaei.* Milano, 1610.

Boobyer, G. H. "The Gospel Miracles: Views Past and Present." In *The Miracles and the Resurrection; Some Recent Studies,* Theological Collections 3, ed. Ian T. Ramsey, G. H. Boobyer, F. N. Davey, M. C. Perry, Henry J. Cadbury, 31–49. London: S.P.C.K., 1964.

Bourbon del Monte Sta Maria, Francesco Maria. *Relatio facta . . . super vita, sanctitate actis canonizationis et miraculis beati Isidori Agricolae de Matrito.* Rome: Zannetti, 1622. BAV Barb.LL.7(1)

——. *Relatio facta . . . super vita, sanctitate actis canonizationis et miraculis b. Theresiae a Iesu de Avila.* Rome: Zannetti, 1622. BAV Barb.LL.III.7(5)

——. *Relatio facta . . . super vita, sanctitate actis canonizationis et miraculis beati Francisci Xavieri Societate Iesu.* Rome: Zannetti, 1622. BAV Barb.LL.III.7(3)

——. *Relatio facta . . . super vita, sanctitate actis canonizationis et miraculis beati Ignatii fundatoris Societatis Iesu.* Rome: Zannetti, 1622. BAV Barb.LL.III.7(2)

——. *Relatio facta . . . super vita, sanctitate actis canonizationis et miraculis beati Philippi Nerii Florentini congregationis oratorii fundatoris.* Rome: Zannetti, 1622. BAV Barb.LL.III.7(4)

Boyle, Leonard E. *A Survey of the Vatican Archives and of Its Medieval Holdings.* rev. ed. Toronto: Pontifical Institute of Medieval Studies, 2001.

Bracciolini, Francesco. *Compendio della vita, morte, et miracoli di San Diego*. Milano: Gratidio Ferioli, 1598. BAV Barb.T.V.64

Brown, Peter Robert Lamont. *The Cult of the Saints: Its Rise and Function in Latin Christianity*. Chicago: University of Chicago Press, 1981.

Bull, Marcus. *The Miracles of Our Lady of Rocamadour*. Woodbridge, U.K.: Boydell Press, 1999.

Burkardt, Albrecht. *Les clients des saints. Maladie et quête du miracle à travers les procès de canonisation de la première moitié du XVII siècle en France*. Rome: Ecole française de Rome, 2004.

Burke, Peter. "How to Be a Counter-Reformation Saint." In *The Historical Anthropology of Early Modern Italy: Essays on Perception and Communication*, ed. Peter Burke, 48–62. Cambridge: Cambridge University Press, 1987.

———. "Rituals of Healing in Early Modern Italy." In *The Historical Anthropology of Early Modern Italy. Essays on Perception and Communication*, ed. Peter Burke, 207–20. Cambridge: Cambridge University Press, 1987.

Bynum, Caroline Walker. "Bodily Miracles and the Resurrection of the Body." In *Belief in History: Innovative Approaches to European and American Religion*, ed. Thomas Kselman, 68–106. Notre Dame, IN: University of Notre Dame Press, 1991.

———. "Female Body and Religious Practice." In *Fragments for a History of the Body*, ed. Michel Feher, Ramona Naddaff and Nadia Tazi, 161–219. New York: Zone Books, 1989.

———. *Fragmentation and Redemption: Essays on Gender and the Human Body in Medieval Religion*. New York City: Zone Books, 1991.

———. *Holy Feast and Holy Fast. The Religious Significance of Food to Medieval Women*. Berkeley: University of California Press, 1987.

Cannon, Joanna, and André Vauchez. *Margherita of Cortona and the Lorenzetti*. University Park: Pennsylvania State University Press, 1999.

Caraccioli, Louis-Antoine. *La vie du pape Benoît XIV*. Paris: Hotel Serpente, 1783.

Cardano, Girolamo. *The Book of My Life (De vita propria liber)*. Trans. Jean Stoner. London and Toronto: J. M. Dent and Sons, 1931.

Carpentieri, Toti, ed. *Per grazia ricevuta: ex voto artistici conservati nel Monastero di Santa Rita da Cascia*. Terni: Umbriagraf 1992.

Case, Thomas. "The Year 1588 and San Diego de Alcalá." *The Journal of San Diego History* 34, no. 1 (1988), http://www.sandiegohistory.org/journal/88winter/index.htm (accessed May 2008).

Castellini, Luca. *De inquisitione miraculorum in sanctorum martyrum canonizatione*. Rome: Iacobum Mascardum, 1629. BAV Barb.HH.II.47

Cavadini, John, ed. *Miracles in Jewish and Christian Antiquity: Imagining Truth*. Notre Dame, Ind.: University of Notre Dame Press, 1999.

Charuty, Giordana. *Le couvent des fous. L'internement et ses usages en Languedoc aux XIXe et XXe siècles*. Paris: Flammarion, 1985.

Christian, William A., Jr. "Storia di una guarigione straordinaria nella Spagna contemporanea." In *Miracoli dai segni alla storia*, ed. Sofia Boesch Gajano and Marilena Modica, 197–214. Rome: Viella, 1999.

Colombero, C. "Il medico e il giudice." *Materiali per una storia della cultura giuridica* 16 (1986): 386–81.

———. "Un contributo alla formazione della nozione di malattia mentale: le 'Quaestioni medico-legali' di Paolo Zacchia." In *Follia psichiatriae società: isituzioni manicomiali, scienza psichiatrica e classi sociali nell'Italia moderna e contemporanea*, ed. Alberto De Bernardi, 317–29. Milano: F. Angeli, 1982.

Composta, Dario. *Il miracolo: realtà o suggestione? Rassegna documentata di fatti staordinari nel cinquentennio, 1920–1970*. Rome: Città Nuova Editrice, 1981.

Congregatio pro Causis Sanctorum (CCS). *Catanen. Canonizationis ven. servi. Dei Josephi Benedicti Dusmet. Positio super miraculo*. Rome: Guerra, 1988. BAV R. G. Riti.III.42

———. *Compendium vitae virtutum et miraculorum . . .* [hereinafter *Compendium . . .*] *ven. serv. Dei Aegidii Mariae a Sancto Joseph*. Rome: Guerra, 1994. Archive of CCS A5a/23.

———. *Compendium . . . Beatorum Andreae Dung-Lac, sacerdotis, Thomae Thien et Emmanuelis Phung, Laicorum, Hieronymi Hermosilla, Valentini Berrio Ochoa et aliorum VI episcoporum necnon Theophani Venard, sacerdotis et CV sociorum martyrum*. Rome: Guerra, 1987. BAV R. G. Miscell.III.1076(9)

———. *Compendium . . . Ioannis Calabria*. Rome: Guerra, 1994. Archive of CCS J12^b/11

———. *Compendium . . . Laurentii Ruiz . . . Martyrum in Japonia*. Rome: Guerra, 1987. BAV R. G. Miscell.III.1076(10)

———. *Compendium . . . Theresiae Benedictae a Cruce (Edith Stein)*. Rome: Guerra, 1997. Archive of CCS H67^b/8

———. *Compendium . . . Zdislavae de Lemberk*. Rome: Guerra, 1995. Archive of CCS F20^b/5

———. *Index ac status causarum*. Città del Vaticano: Guerra, 1999.

———. *Leodien. Canonizationis ven. serv. Dei Mariae Theresiae Haze. Positio super miraculo*. Rome: Guerra, 1990. BAV R. G. Riti.II.730

———. *Marianopolitana. Canonizationis . . . Mariae Margaritae Dufrost de Lajemmerais (viduae Youville). Positio super miraculo*. Rome: Guerra, 1989.

———. *Viedmen. Canonizationis . . . Laurae Vicuña virginis saecularis. Positio super miraculo*. Rome: Guerra, 1988. BAV R. G. Riti.II.734

Corner, Mark. *Signs of God: Miracles and Their Interpretation*. Aldershot, U.K.: Ashgate, 2005.

Cousin, Bernard. *Ex-voto de Provence: Images de la religion populaire et de la vie d'autrefois*. Bruges: Desclée de Brouwer, 1981.

———. "La vie au village figurée et transfigurée." *Imageson.org* 10 (February 2006), http://www.imageson.org/document687.html (accessed May 2008).

Cruz, Joan Carroll. *The Incorruptibles: A Study of the Incorruption of the Bodies of Various Catholic Saints and Beati*. Rockford, Ill.: Tan Books and Publishers, 1977.

Cunningham, Hugh. *Children and Childhood in Western Society since 1500*. Harlow, U.K.: Pearson, 2005.

Darricau, Raymond. "Une source sur l'histoire des miracles: 'positio super miraculis.'" In *Histoire des miracles. Actes de la sixième rencontre d'histoire religieuse, 8–9 octobre 1982*, 165–72. Angers, France: Presses de l'Université d'Angers, 1983.

Davey, F. N. "Healing in the New Testament." In *The Miracles and the Resurrection; Some Recent Studies*, Theological Collections 3, ed. Ian T. Ramsey, G. H. Boobyer, F. N. Davey, M. C. Perry, Henry J. Cadbury, 50–63. London: S.P.C.K, 1964.

Dawkins, Richard. *The God Delusion*. Boston: Houghton Mifflin, 2006.

De Buck, Victor, ed. *Suppression of Religious Orders in Rome*. London: Burns and Oates, 1873.

Delehaye, Hippolyte. *The Legends of the Saints*. Trans. Donald Attwater. New York: Fordham University Press, 1962.

Delooz, Pierre. *Sociologie et canonisations*. Liège and La Haye: Faculté de Droit Liège and Martinus Nijhoff, 1969.

———. "Towards a Sociological Study of Canonized Sainthood in the Catholic Church [1962]." In *Saints and Their Cults: Studies in Religious Sociology, Folklore, and History*, ed. Stephen Wilson, 189–216. Cambridge: Cambridge University Press, 1983.

Dennett, Daniel. *Breaking the Spell: Religion as a Natural Phenomenon*. New York: Viking, 2006.

De Renzi, Silvia. "Witnesses of the Body: Medico-Legal Cases in Seventeenth-Century Rome." *Studies in the History and Philosophy of Science* 33, no. 2 (2002): 219–42.

Ditchfield, Simon. *Liturgy, Sanctity, and History in Tridentine Italy: Pietro Maria Campi and the Preservation of the Particular*. Cambridge: Cambridge University Press, 2002.

Duffin, Jacalyn. "The Great Canadian Peritonitis Debate, 1844–47." *Histoire Sociale-Social History* XIX, no. 38 (1987): 407–24.

———. "A Hippocratic Triangle: History, Clinician-Historians, and Future Doctors." In *Locating Medical History: the Stories and their Meaning*, ed. Frank Huisman and John Harley Warner. Baltimore, MD: Johns Hopkins University Press, 2004.

———. *Lovers and Livers: Disease Concepts in History*. Toronto: University of Toronto Press, 2005.

———. "Medical Miracle." *Saturday Night* (December 1997): 28–42.

———. "Medical Miracles: Absence and Prevalence in Our Recent Past." In *Mystics, Visions, and Miracles, St. Michael's College Symposium, 2001*, ed. J. Goering, F. Guardiani and G. Silano, 149–160. New York: Legas, 2002.

———. *To See with a Better Eye: A Life of R. T. H. Laennec*. Princeton, NJ: Princeton University Press, 1998.

Ehrstine, Glenn. "Motherhood and Protestant Polemics: Stillbirth in Hans von Rüte's Abgotterei (1531)." In *Maternal Measures: Figuring Caregiving in the Early Modern Period*, ed. Naomi J. Miller and Naomi Yavneh, 121–34. Brookfield, VT: Ashgate, 2001.

Falconieri, Alessandro. *Storia della vita, virtu, doni e miracoli di S. Giovanni della Croce*. Rome: Ferri, 1726. BAV T.II.15

Federighi, Giovanni, trans. *Vita e miracoli della vergine Beata Zita*. Lucca: Vincenzo Busdraghi, 1582. BAV Barb R.I.IV.1542

Ferguson, Marianne. *Women and Religion*. Englewood Cliffs, NJ: Prentice Hall, 1995.

Ferngren, Gary B. "Early Christianity as a Religion of Healing." *Bulletin of the History of Medicine* 66 (1992): 1–15.

Ferracuti, S., R. Sacco, and R. Lazzari. "Dissociative Trance Disorder: Clinical and Rorschach Findings in Ten Persons Reporting Demon Possession and Treated by Exorcism." *Journal of Personality Assessment* 66, no. 3 (1996): 525–39.

Findlen, Paula. "Science as a Career in Enlightenment Italy: the Strategies of Laura Bassi." *Isis* 84 (September 1993): 441–69.

Finucane, R. C. *Rescue of the Innocents: Endangered Children in Medieval Miracles.* New York: St. Martin's Press, 1997.

Fleck, Ludwik. *Genesis and Development of a Scientific Fact [1935].* Trans. Frederick Bradley. Chicago: University of Chicago Press, 1979.

Fletcher, Frank. "Australian Spirituality and Mary MacKillop." *Compass Theology Review* 29 (1995): 1–5.

Foucault, Michel. *Madness and Civilization: A History of Insanity in the Age of Reason.* Trans. Richard Howard. New York: Vintage; Random House, 1973.

Fuligatti, Giacomo. *Compendio della vita dell'Apostolo dell'India S. Francesco Saverio.* Rome: Bernardino Tani, 1637. BAV R. G. Vite.V.297

Gallesini, Pietro. *La vita, i miracoli, e la canonizatione di San Diego d'Alcala d'Henares. Divisa in tre parti.* Rome: Domenico Busi, 1589. BAV R.I.V.276(1)

García Ballester, Luis. *Medicine in a Multicultural Society; Christian, Jewish and Muslim Practitioners in the Spanish Kingdoms, 1222–1610.* Aldershot, UK: Ashgate, 2001.

Gardiner, Paul. *Mary MacKillop: An Extraordinary Australian. The Authorised Biography.* 2nd ed. North Sydney: E. J. Dwyer, David Ell Press, and the Trustees of the Sisters of St. Joseph, 1994.

Garraghan, Gilbert J. *Jesuits of the Middle United States.* 3 vols. New York: American Press, 1938.

Gentilcore, David. *Healers and Healing in Early Modern Italy.* Manchester: Manchester University Press, 1998.

Ginzburg, Carlo. *The Cheese and the Worms. The Cosmos of a Sixteenth-Century Miller.* Trans. John and Anne Tedeschi. Baltimore, MD: Johns Hopkins University Press, 1980.

———. "Clues: Roots of an Evidential Paradigm [1986]." In *Clues, Myths, and the Historical Method,* trans. John and Anne Tedeschi, 96–125. Baltimore, MD: Johns Hopkins University Press, 1989.

Giunchi, Giuseppe. "L'esame del miracolo sotto il profilo medico-scientifico: Esper-ienze di un perito della Consulta Medica per le Cause dei Santi." In *Miscellanea in occasione de IV Centenario della Congregazione per le cause dei santi (1588–1988),* ed. CCS, 211–20. Città del Vaticano: Guerra, 1988.

Giustiniani, Barnardo. *Vita b. Laurentii Iustiniani.* Rome: Rev. Camera Apostolica, 1690. BAV Barb.T.II.73

Goodich, Michael. *Lives and Miracles of the Saints: Studies in Medieval Latin Hagiogra-phy.* Aldershot, UK: Ashgate/Variorum, 2004.

———. "Mirabilis Deus in Sanctis Suis: Social History and Medieval Miracles." In *Signs, Wonders, and Miracles. Representations of Divine Power in the Life of the Church,* ed. Kate Cooper and Jeremy Gregory, 135–56. Woodbridge, Suffolk, UK: Boydell Press, 2005.

Goodich, Michael. *Other Middle Ages: Witnesses at the Margins of Medieval Society*. Philadelphia: University of Pennsylvania Press, 1998.

———. *Violence and Miracle in the Fourteenth Century. Private Grief and Public Salvation*. Chicago: University of Chicago Press, 1995.

———. *Vita Perfecta: The Ideal of Sainthood in the Thirteenth Century*. Stuttgart: Anton Hiersemann, 1982.

Gorce, Denys. "L'oeuvre médicale de Prospero Lambertini, le Pape Benoît XIV, 1675–1758." Thèse de médecine, Université de Bordeaux, 1915.

Grandi, Guido. *Vita del glorioso prencipe S. Pietro Orseolo, doge di Venezia*. Venice: Giuseppe Bettinelli, 1733. BAV R. G. Vite.III.41

Gretser, Jacob. *Commentarius Pauli Bernriedensis . . . Vita Gregorii VII*. Ingolstadt: Adam Sartorii, 1610. BAV Barb.U.I.58

Guarino, John B. "Benedict XIV: 'Third Party' Pope (1740–1758)." In *The Great Popes through History: An Encyclopedia*, ed. Frank J. Coppa, 405–14. Westport, CT: Greenwood, 2002.

Guida, Palmarita. *Caterina Labouré e le apparizioni della Vergine alla Rue du Bac per una rilettura del messaggio della Medaglia Miraculosa*. Torino: San Paolo, 1997.

Halkin, François. *Saints de Byzance et du Proche Orient*. Cahiers d'orientalisme 13. Génève: Patrick Cramer, 1981.

Hamilton, Mary. *Incubation, or the Cure of Disease in Pagan Temples and Christian Churches*. London: W.C. Henderson, 1906.

Hanawalt, Barbara A. "Medievalists and the Study of Childhood." *Speculum* 77 (2002): 440–60.

Harris, Ruth. *Lourdes: Body and Spirit in the Secular Age*. New York: Viking Penguin, 1999.

Harris, Sam. *The End of Faith: Religion, Terror and the Future of Reason*. New York and London: Norton, 2004.

Harrison, Marian C. "A Survival of Incubation." *Folk-Lore* 19 (1908): 313–15.

Haynes, Renée. *Philosopher King: The Humanist Pope, Benedict XIV*. London: Weidenfeld and Nicolson, 1970.

Henderson, John. "Historians and Plagues in Pre-Industrial Italy." *History and Philosophy of the Life Sciences* 25 (2003): 481–99.

Higgins, Michael W. *Stalking the Holy: The Pursuit of Saint-Making*. Toronto: Anansi, 2006.

Hippocrates. "The Sacred Disease." In *Hippocrates with an English Translation*, vol. 2, ed. W. H. S. Jones, 139–183. Loeb Classical Library 148. London: Heinemann, 1923.

Hobbins, Peter. "A Step Towards More Ethical Prayer Studies." *American Heart Journal* 152, no. 4 (2006): e33.

Horden, Peregrine. "Saints and Doctors in the Early Byzantine Empire: The Case of Theodore of Sykeon." In *The Church and Healing: Studies in Church History*, vol. 19, ed. W. J. Sheils, 1–13. Oxford: Basil Blackwell for the Ecclesiastical History Society, 1982.

Huddard, Sophie. "I miracoli del re: una lezione di semiologia politica nella Francia del XVI secolo." In *Miracoli dai segni alla storia*, ed. Sofia Boesch Gajano and Marilena Modica. Rome: Viella, 1999.

Jackson, Ralph. *Doctors and Diseases in the Roman Empire*. Norman: University of Oklahoma Press, 1988.

Jarcho, Saul. *Quinine's Predecessor: Francesco Torti and the Early History of Cinchona*. Baltimore, MD: Johns Hopkins University Press, 1993.

Jones, Terry, *Patron Saints Index*. http://saints.sqpn.com/indexsnt.htm (accessed May 2008).

Karplus, Heinrich. "Medical Ethics in Paolo Zacchia's 'Quaestiones medico-legales.'" In *International Symposium on Society, Medicine and Law, Jerusalem, 1972*, ed. Heinrich Karplus, 125–34. Amsterdam, 1973.

Kaufman, Suzanne K. *Consuming Visions: Mass Culture and the Lourdes Shrine*. Ithaca, NY: Cornell University Press, 2005.

Kiple, Kenneth F., ed. *The Cambridge World History of Human Disease*. Cambridge: Cambridge University Press, 1993.

Klaniczay, Gabor. "Miracoli di punizione e maleficia." In *Miracoli dai segni alla storia*, ed. Sofia Boesch Gajano and Marilena Modica, 109–35. Rome: Viella, 1999.

Koenig, Harold G., et al. "Religion, Spirituality and Medicine: A Rebuttal to the Skeptics." *International Journal of Psychiatry and Medicine* 29 (1999): 123–31.

Kselman, Thomas Albert. "Miracles and Prophecies; Popular Religion and the Church in Nineteenth-Century France." PhD thesis, University of Michigan, 1978.

Kunstmann, Pierre. *Treize miracles de Notre Dame tirés du manuscrit BN fr. 2094*. Ottawa: Editions de l'Université d'Ottawa, 1981.

Ladurie, Emmanuel le Roy. *Montaillou: The Promised Land of Error*. Trans. Barbara Bray. New York: Vintage, 1979.

Lappin, Anthony. "Miracles in the Making of Twentieth-Century Spanishness." In *Signs, Wonders, and Miracles: Representations of Divine Power in the Life of the Church*, ed. Kate Cooper and Jeremy Gregory, 464–75. Woodbridge, Suffolk: Boydell Press, 2005.

Larmer, Robert A., ed. *Questions of Miracle*. Montreal: McGill-Queen's University Press, 1996.

———. *Water into Wine: An Investigation of the Concept of Miracle*. Montreal: McGill-Queen's University Press, 1988.

Laugier, Laurence, ed. and trans. *Paul Zacchias. Questions médico-légales: des fautes médicales sanctionnées par la loi*. Aix-en-Provence: Presses Universtaires d'Aix-Marseille, 2006.

Lehrman, Arthur. "The Miracle of St. Cosmas and St. Damian." *Plastic and Reconstructive Surgery* 94 (1994): 218–21.

Leone, Francesco. *Ristretto delle vite de cinque santi: Lorenzo Giustiniani, Giovanni di Capistrano, Giovanni di S. Facondo, Giovanni d'Iddio, e Pasquale Baylon*. Rome: Giov. Batt. Molo, 1690. BAV Barb. T.IV.52.

Lilly, Steven M. "A 'STEP' in the Right Direction." *American Heart Journal* 152, no. 4 (2006): e31.

Linders, Tullia, and Gullög Nordquist, eds. *Gifts to the Gods: Proceedings of the Uppsala Symposium, 1985, Studies in Ancient Mediterranean and Near Eastern Civilization*. Uppsala: Boreas, 1987.

Llot de Ribera, Miguel. *De laudabili vita et de actis hactenus . . . Raymundi Penia Forti*. Rome: Dominici Gilotti, 1595. BAV Barb.U.III.89

Lloyd, Geoffrey E. R. *Magic, Reason, and Experience. Studies in the Origins and Development of Greek Science.* Cambridge: Cambridge University Press, 1979.

Macdonald, Michael. "Religion, Social Change and Psychological Healing in England, 1600–1800." In *The Church and Healing. Studies in Church History,* vol. 19, ed. W. J. Sheils, 101–26. Oxford: Basil Blackwell for the Ecclesiastical History Society, 1982.

Maeder, Hanspeter. "Die Frau im 17. Jahrhundert im Spiegel der 'Quaestiones Medico-Legales' des Paolo Zacchia (1584–1659)." MD thesis, Medizinischen Fakultät der Universtadt Bern, 1981.

Mahier, E. *Les questions médico-légales de Paul Zacchias médecin romain. Etudes bibliographiques.* Paris: Bailliere, 1872.

Marini, Gaetano. *Degli archiatri pontifici.* 2 vols. Rome: Stamperia Pagliarini, 1784.

Mangiapan, Théodore. "Le contrôle médical des guérisons à Lourdes." In *Histoire des miracles. Actes de la sixième rencontre d'histoire religieuse, 8–9 octobre 1982,* 143–64. Angers: Presses de l'Université d'Angers, 1983.

Mariani, Giordana Canova. *Storia dell'Arte Medievale. II. Duecento a Venezia,* Università degli Studi di Padova, 2002. http://www.moda.lettere.unipd.it/sfondi/sanmarco.pdf (accessed May 2008).

Mathaler, Bernard L., ed. *New Catholic Encyclopedia.* 15 vols. Washington, DC: Catholic University of America, 2003.

Matthews, Dale A. "Prayer and Spirituality." *Rheumatic Diseases Clinics of North America* 26 (Feb. 2000): 177–87.

———. "Religious Commitment and Health Status; a Review of the Research and Implications for Family Medicine." *Archives of Family Medicine* 7 (Mar–Apr. 1998): 118–24.

Matthews, Dale A., and D. B. Larson. "Faith and Medicine; Reconciling the Twin Traditions of Healing." *Mind/Body Medicine* 2 (1997): 3–6.

Maulitz, Russell C. "In the Clinic: Framing Disease at the Paris Hospital." *Annals of Science* 47, no. 2 (1990): 127–37.

McCreanor, Sheila J. *Sainthood in Australia: Mary MacKillop and the Print Media.* North Sydney, N.S.W.: Sisters of Saint Joseph of the Sacred Heart, 2001.

McVaugh, Michael R. "Bedside Manners in the Middle Ages." *Bulletin of the History of Medicine* 71 (1997): 201–23.

———. *Medicine before the Plague: Practitioners and Their Patients in the Crown of Aragon, 1285–1345.* Cambridge: Cambridge University Press, 1993.

Menesto, Enrico, ed. *Il processo di canonizzazione di Chiara da Montefalco.* Firenze: La Nuova Italia, 1984.

Micheli, Giuseppe. *L'Isola Tiberina e i Fatebenefratelli. La storia dell'insula inter duos pontes.* Milan: Editrice Cens, 1995.

Moss, Sandra. "Floating Kidneys." In *Clio in the Clinic. History in Medical Practice,* ed. Jacalyn Duffin, 92–104. New York and Toronto: Oxford University Press and University of Toronto Press, 2005.

Mullin, Robert Bruce. *Miracles and the Modern Religious Imagination.* New Haven, CT: Yale University Press, 1996.

————. "Science, Miracles, and the Prayer Gauge Debate." In *When Science and Christianity Meet,* ed. David C. Lindberg and Ronald L. Numbers, 203–24. Chicago: University of Chicago Press, 2003.

Neyrey, Jerome H. "Miracles, in Other Words: Social Science Perspectives on Healings." In *Miracles in Jewish and Christian Antiquity: Imagining Truth,* ed. John Cavadini, 19–55. Notre Dame, IN: University of Notre Dame Press, 1999.

Occhioni, Nicola. *Il processo per la canonizzazione di S. Nicola da Tolentino.* Rome: Ecole Française de Rome and Padri Agostiniani di Tolentino, 1984.

O'Connell, Marvin R. "The Roman Catholic Tradition since 1545." In *Caring and Curing: Health and Medicine in the Western Religious Traditions,* ed. Ronald L. Numbers and Darrel W. Amundsen, 108–45. New York: Macmillan, 1986.

Orsi, Robert A. "'He Keeps Me Going': Women's Devotion to Saint Jude Thaddeus and the Dialectics of Gender in American Catholicism, 1929–1965." In *Belief in History: Innovative Approaches to European and American Religion,* ed. Thomas Kselman, 137–69. Notre Dame, IN.: University of Notre Dame Press, 1991.

Palazzini, Pietro Card. "La perfettibilità della prassi processsulae di Benedetto XIV nel giudizio di Pio XII." In *Miscellanea in occasione del IV Centenario della Congregazione per le cause dei santi (1588–1988),* ed. CCS, 61–87. Città del Vaticano: Guerra, 1988.

Park, Katharine. "The Criminal and the Saintly Body: Autopsy and Dissection in Renaissance Italy." *Renaissance Quarterly* 47, no. 1 (1994): 1–33.

————. *Secrets of Women: Gender, Generation, and the Origins of Human Dissection.* Cambridge, MA: Zone Books and MIT Press, 2006.

Pastor, Ludwig von. *Storia dei Papi.* 20 vols. Rome: Desclée, 1908–1934.

Peitzman, Steven. "From Bright's Disease to End-Stage Renal Disease." In *Framing Disease: Studies in the Cultural History of Disease,* ed. Charles Rosenberg and Janet Golden, 3–19. New Brunswick, NJ: Rutgers University Press, 1992.

Pellegrini, Carlo. *Acta et processus sanctitatis vitae et miraculorum venerabilis patris Hieronymi Aemiliani, Fonte per la storia dei Somaschi (9).* Rome: Curia Generalizia dei Padri Somaschi, 1980. BAV Storia.IV.24815(9)

Peña, Francisco de. *Relatione sommaria della vita, santità, miracoli e atti della canonizzazione di S. Caroli Card. Borromeo.* Coloniae Agrippinae: Ioan. Kinckium, 1625. BAV T.IV.119

Peschel, Richard E., and Enid Rhodes Peschel. "Medical Miracles from a Physician-Scientist's Viewpoint." *Perspectives in Biology and Medicine* 31, no. 3 (1988): 391–404.

Pickstone, J. V. "Establishment and Dissent in Nineteenth-Century Medicine: An Exploration of Some Correspondence and Connections between Religious and Medical Belief Systems." In *The Church and Healing,* ed. W. J. Sheils, 165–89. Oxford: Basil Blackwell and the Ecclesiastical History Society, 1982.

Pierini, Giovanni, ed. *Venefici dalle "Quaestiones medico-legales" di Paolo Zacchia.* Milan: Mimesis, 2001.

Pomata, Gianna. "Malpighi and the Holy Body: Medical Experts and Miraculous Evidence in Seventeenth-Century Italy." *Renaissance Studies* 21 (2007): 568–86.

Popper, Karl. *Conjectures and Refutations: The Growth of Scientific Knowledge.* London: Routledge and Kegan Paul, 1963.

Porter, Roy. "The Patient's View: Doing Medical History from Below." *Theory and Society* 14 (1985): 175–98.

Porterfield, Amanda. *Healing in the History of Christianity.* New York: Oxford University Press, 2005.

Ramirez, Melchior. *Relatione sommaria della vita, santità, miracoli e atti della canonizatione di S. Isidoro Agricola.* Rome: Zannetti, 1622. BAV Barb.T.V.22

Ramsey, Ian T. "Miracles: An Exercise in Logical Mapwork [1952]." In *The Miracles and the Resurrection: Some Recent Studies,* Theological Collections 3, ed. Ian T. Ramsey, G. H. Booyer, F. N. Davey, M. C. Perry, Henry J. Cadbury, 1–30. London: S.P.C.K., 1964.

Ramsey, Matthew. *Professional and Popular Medicine in France, 1770–1830: The Social World of Medical Practice.* Cambridge: Cambridge University Press, 1988.

Ratzinger, Joseph Card., and Tarcisio Bertone. *Istruzione circa le preghiere per ottenere da Dio la guarigione.* Città del Vaticano: Libreria editrice del Vaticano, 2000.

Ratzinger, Joseph Card., Tarcisio Bertone, and Congregazione per la dottrina della fede. *Nota dottrinale circa alcune questioni riguardanti l'impegno e il comportamento dei cattolici nella vita politica.* Città del Vaticano: Libreria Editrice del Vaticano, 2002.

Resch, Andreas. *Miracoli dei Beati, 1983–1990.* Città del Vaticano: Libreria Editrice Vaticano, 2002.

———. *Miracoli dei Beati, 1991–1995.* Città del Vaticano: Libreria Editrice Vaticano, 2002.

———. *Miracoli dei Santi, 1983–1995.* Città del Vaticano: Libreria Editrice Vaticano, 2002.

Risse, Guenter B. *Mending Bodies, Saving Souls: A History of Hospitals.* New York: Oxford University Press, 1999.

Robbins, Russell Hope. *The Encyclopedia of Witchcraft and Demonology.* 3rd ed. London: Spring Books, 1959.

Rocca, Fr. Angelo. *De canonizatione sanctorum commentarium,* ed. Jose Luis Gutierez. Rome: Guillelmum Facciotum; Pubblicazioni Agostiniane, 2004 [reprint of 1601].

Russotto, P. Gabriele. "La constituzione dei Fatebenefratelli del 1596." *Vita Ospedaliera* 19, no. 6–12 (1964): 3–80.

Sabourin, Leopold. *The Divine Miracles Discussed and Defended.* Rome: Catholic Book Agency, 1977.

Sacra Congregatio pro Causis Sanctorum (SCCS). *Barcinonen seu Quiten. Beatificationis et canonizationis de ven. servi Dei Fratris Michaëlis (in saec. Francisco Febres Codero). Positio super miraculo.* Rome: Guerra et Belli, 1977. BAV R. G. Riti.II.723

———. *Compendium . . . Oliver Plunket.* Rome: Guerra e Belli, 1975. Archive of CCS B10/10

———. *Compendium . . . Raphaëlae Mariae a S. Corde Iesu.* Rome: Guerra e Belli, 1976. BAV R. G. Riti.III.25(16)

———. *Quiten seu Barcinonen. Canonizationis beati Fratris Michaëlis in saec Francisci Febres Codero. Positio super miraculo.* Rome: Guerra, 1983. BAV R. G. Riti.II.723A

———. *Regolamento per il Collegio dei medici periti istituito presso la Sacra congregatione per le cause dei santi*. Città del Vaticano: Tipografia Poliglotta Vaticana, 1976. BAV R. G. Medic.III.823(4)

Sacra Rituum Congregatio (SRC also Congregatio Sacrorum Rituum). *Andegaven. Beat. et can. . . . Mariae Euphrasiae Pelletier. Fama*. Rome: Guerra et Mirri, 1901. BAV R. G. Riti.II.381(3)

———. *Antiochena maronitarum. Beat. et can. . . . Sarbelli Makhlouf a Beqà Kafra. Novissima positio super miraculis*. Rome: Guerra e Belli, 1965. BAV R. G. Riti.III.15

———. *Aquen. Beat. et can. . . . Mariae Domenicae Mazzarello*. Rome: Guerra e Belli. *Novissima positio super miraculis*, 1938; *Positio super miraculis*, 1950. BAV R. G. Riti. II.537(1, 3)

———. *Asten seu Taurinen. Beat. et can. . . . Domenici Savio*. Rome: Guerra e Belli. *Positio super miraculis*, 1946; *Nova positio super miraculis*, 1949. BAV R. G. Riti. II.115(8, 9)

———. *B. Andreae Avellini. Positio super dubio*. Rome: Rev. Camera Apostolica, 1695. BAV Barb.LL.III.55

———. *Beat. et can. . . . Joannae Antidae Thouret*. Rome: Guerra e Mirri. *Nova positio super miraculis*, 1933; *Novissima positio super miraculis*, 1933. BAV R. G. Riti.II.195 (8, 9)

———. *Beatificationis seu declarationis martyrii . . . Joannis de Britto*. Rome: Joseph Brancodor. *Positio super dubio*. 1851, Rome: Pontificia Università Gregorianae. *Novissima positio super miraculis*, 1941. BAV R. G. Riti.II.251(6,7)

———. *Bononien. Canonizationis Beatae Catharinae a Bononia. Positio super dubio*. Rome: Rev. Camera Apostolica, 1681. BAV Chigi.II.80

———. *Brevissimum compendium . . . beatorum Caietani Thienaei, Francisci Borgiae, Philippi Benitii, Ludovici Bertrandi, Rosae de S. Maria [Lima]*. Rome: Rev. Camera Apostolica, 1671. BAV Chigi.V.2344(9)

———. *Calaritana. Beat. et can. . . . Ignatii a Laconi. Positio super miraculis*. Rome: Guerra et Belli, 1937. BAV R. G. Riti.III.285(3)

———. *Commentarium actorum omnium canonizationis Iosephat Kuncewicz, Petri de Arbues, XIX Martyrum Gorcomiensium, Pauli a Cruce, Leonardo a Portu Mauritio, Mariae Francescae a Vulneribus, Germana Cousin*. Rome: Officinatores Mensae Apostolicae, 1868. BAV R. G. Storia.II.1423

———. *Compendium . . . Aloysii Gonzagae Societate Jesu*. Rome: Rev. Camera Apostolica, 1726. BAV Miscell.F.149(25)

———. *Compendium . . . Alphonsi Mariae de Ligorio*. Rome: Rev. Camera Apostolica, 1839. BAV Ferr.II.790(26)

———. *Compendium . . . Angelae Mericiae*. Rome: Rev. Camera Apostolica, 1807. BAV Ferr.III.525(3)

———. *Compendium . . . Antonii M. Gianelli*. Cortonae: Tipografico Commerciale, 1951. BAV R. G. Riti.II.66(16)

———. *Compendium . . . Antonii Mariae Pucci, O.S.M. confessoris*. Vatican: Typis Polyglottis, 1962. BAV RG.Vite.II.275(3)

———. *Compendium . . . et martyrii beati Fidelis a Sigmaringa*. Rome: Rev. Camera Apostolica, 1746. BAV Miscell.H.1(5)

Sacra Rituum Congregatio (SRC also Congregatio Sacrorum Rituum). *Compendi-um . . . Gemmae Galgani, virginis.* Vatican: Typis Polyglottis, 1939. BAV R. G. Miscell.II.167(31)

———. *Compendium . . . Germanae Cousin.* Rome: Rev. Camera Apostolica, 1867. BAV Ferr.II.790(7)

———. *Compendium . . . Hieronymi Aemiliani.* Rome: Rev. Camera Apostolica, 1767. BAV Chigi.III.800(4)

———. *Compendium . . . Hiacyntae Mariscottiae.* Rome: Rev. Camera Apostolica, 1807. BAV Ferr.III.525(5)

———. *Compendium . . . Io. Francisci Regis.* Rome: Rev. Camera Apostolica, 1737. BAV Miscell.F.149(26)

———. *Compendium . . . Ioannis de Deo.* Rome: Rev. Camera Apostolica, 1690. BAV Miscell.H.67(16)

———. *Compendium . . . Ioannis Iosephi a Cruce.* Rome: Rev. Camera Apostolica, 1839. BAV Ferr.II.790(27)

———. *Compendium . . . Iohannae de Valois.* Vatican: Typis Polyglottis, 1949. BAV R. G. Miscell.II.46(6)

———. *Compendium . . . Iohannae Franciscae Fremiot de Chantal.* Rome: Rev. Camera Apostolica, 1767. BAV Chigi.III.800(6)

———. *Compendium . . . Iosephi a Leonissa.* Rome: Rev. Camera Apostolica, 1746. BAV Miscell.H.1(8)

———. *Compendium . . . Iosephi Calasanctii.* Rome: Rev. Camera Apostolica, 1767. BAV Chigi.III.800(2)

———. *Compendium . . . Iulianae Falconieri.* Rome: Rev. Camera Apostolica, 1738. BAV Miscell.H.1(13)

———. *Compendium . . . Mariae Franciscae a Vulneribus.* Rome: Rev. Camera Apostolica, 1867. BAV Ferr.II.790(15)

———. *Compendium . . . Mariae Theresiae Goretti virginis.* Vatican: Typis Polyglottis, 1950. Archive of CCS G47/12

———. *Compendium . . . Michaelis de Sanctis.* Rome: Rev. Camera Apostolica, 1862. BAV Ferr.II.790(17)

———. *Compendium . . . Pii V.* Rome: Rev. Camera Apostolica, 1712. BAV Miscell. H.67(21)

———. *Compendium . . . Roberti S.R.E. Card. Bellarmino.* Vatican: Typis Polyglottis Vaticanis, 1930. Archive of CCS B21/16

———. *Compendium . . . Seraphini ab Asculo seu de Monte Granario.* Rome: Rev. Camera Apostolica, 1767. BAV Chigi.III.800(5)

———. *Harlemen. Canonizationis seu declarationis martyrii servorum Dei novemdecim Martyrum Gorcomiensium. Positio super dubio et de quibus miraculis constet in casu etc.* Rome: Rev. Camera Apostolica, 1674. BAV Chigi.II.66

———. *Lausanen. Beatificationis . . . Petri Canisii. Positio super miraculis.* Rome: Brandacoro, 1860. BAV R. G. Riti.II.614(4)

———. *Leopolien. Canonizationis . . . B. Ioannis de Dukla. Positio super dubio.* Rome: Rev. Camera Apostolica, 1732. BAV Barb.LL.IV.79

———. *Majoricen. Beat. et can. . . . Alphonsi Rodriguez.* Rome: Rev. Camera Apostolica. *Positio super dubio, 1822; Nova positio super miraculis, 1823; Novissima positio super miraculis, 1824.* BAV R. G. Riti.II.74(1,2,3)

———. *Massilen. Beat. et can . . . Aemiliae de Vialar. Positio super miraculis.* Rome: Guerra e Belli, 1950. BAV R. G. Riti.II.691(5)

———. *Matriten. Beat. et can. Vincentiae Mariae Lopez Vicuña.* Rome: Guerra e Belli. *Positio super miraculis, 1949; Nova positio super miraculis.* 1949. BAV R. G. Riti.II.514(5,6)

———. *Nivernen seu Tarbien et Lourden. Can. . . . Beatae Mariae Bernardae Soubirous.* Rome: Guerra e Mirri. *Positio super miraculis, 1932; Nova positio super miraculis, 1933; Novissima positio super miraculis, 1933.* BAV R. G. Riti.II.182(5,6,7)

———. *Parisien. Canonizationis . . . beatae Catharinae Labouré.* Rome: Guerra e Belli. *Positio super miraculis, 1944;. Nova positio super miraculis, 1945.* BAV R. G. Riti.II.78(7,9)

———. *Passavien. Beat. et can. . . . Conradi a Parzham.* Rome: Guerra e Belli. *Positio super miraculis, 1930; Positio super miraculis, 1933.* BAV R. G. Riti.II.197(6,7)

———. *Polona seu Luceorien. Beat. et can. ven. s. d. Andreae Bobola.* Rome: Rev. Camera Apostolica. *Animadversiones . . . Responsio,* 1830, Rome: Pontificia Università Gregoriana; *Positio super miraculis, 1936.* BAV R. G. Riti.II.31(3,10)

———. *Positio super dubio an constet di miraculis, tum in vita, tum post obitum ab ipsomet b. Ioanne patratis* [de Capistrano]. Rome: Rev. Camera Apostolica, 1664. BAV Chigi.II.1074(7)

———. *Lusitana seu Conimbricen . . . Theresiae et Sanciae. Positio super miraculis* Rome: Rev. Camera Apostolica, 1709. BAV Barb.LL.VII.33(13)

———. *Quebecen. Canonizationis beatorum martyrum Ioannnis de Brebeuf, Isaaci Jogues, et sociorum Societate Jesu. . . . novissima positio supra miraculis.* Rome: Guerra e Mirri, 1930. BAV R. G. Riti.II.395(2)

———. *Romana seu Neapolitana. Beat. et can. . . . Josephi Mariae Pignatelli. Positio.* Rome, 1933. BAV R. G. Riti.II.619(11)

———. *Romana seu Setina. Can. . . . beati Caroli a Setia. Positio super miraculis.* Rome: Guerra e Belli, 1956. BAV R. G. Riti.II/73(2)

———. *Savonen. Beat. et can. . . . Mariae Josephae Rossello. Positio super miraculis.* Rome: Guerra e Belli, 1946. BAV R. G. Riti.II.635(6)

———. *Spoletana. Canonizationis beatae Clarae a Cruce de Monte Falco . . . Positio super miraculis.* Rome, 1881. BAV R. G. Riti.II.84(1)

———. *Suffragia in canonizatione S. Andreae Corsini Carmelitani Episcopi Fesulani.* Rome: Rev. Camerae Apostolicae, 1629. BAV Chigi.V.2350(2)

———. *Tarvisina. Beat. et can. . . . Mariae Bertillae Boscardin. Positio super miraculis.* Rome: Guerra e Belli, 1951. BAV R. G. Riti.II.396(4)

———. *Taurinen. Beat. et can. . . . Ioannis Bosco. Positio super miraculis.* Rome: Typis Vaticanis, 1907. BAV R. G. Riti.II.254(2)

———. *Tridentina. Beatificationis . . . Ioannae Mariae a Cruce. Positio super dubio.* Rome: Rev. Camera Apostolica, 1737. BAV Barb.LL.VII.33(16)

———. *Tullen. Beat. . . . Petri Forerii.* Rome: Rev. Camera Apostolica, Memoriale, 1703; *Nova animadversiones, 1710; Factum concordatum . . . super tribus miraculis, 1729.* BAV Barb.LL.VII.15(14, 2, 1 [respectively])

Sacra Rituum Congregatio (SRC also Congregatio Sacrorum Rituum). *Tullen. Beat. et can.* . . . *Petri Forerii. Novae animadversiones.* Rome: Rev. Camera Apostolica, 1726. BAV Barb.LL.III.41

———. *Vicen seu Barcinonen. Can. et beat.* . . . *Ioachimae de Vedruna, viduae de Mas.* Rome: Guerra e Belli, *Positio super miraculis,* 1936; *Positio super miraculis,* 1955. BAV R. G. Riti.II.237 (3,6)

———. *Viennen. Beat. et can.* . . . *Dominici à Iesu Maria. Positio super dubio.* Rome: Rev. Camera Apostolica, 1677. BAV Chigi.II.48

Sallman, Jean-Michel. *Naples et ses saints à l'âge baroque: 1540–1750.* Paris: Presses Universitaires de France, 1994.

———. "Sainteté et société." In *Santità, culti, agiografia. Temi e prospettive,* ed. Sofia Boesch Gajano, 327–40. Rome: Viella, 1997.

Schlauch, Margaret. *Medieval Narrative.* New York: Prentice Hall, 1934.

Schlich, Thomas. "How Gods and Saints Became Transplant Surgeons: The Scientific Article as a Model for the Writing of History." *History of Science* xxxiii (1995): 311–31.

Schultz, Nancy L. *A Capital Miracle: Biography of a Cure.* New Haven: Yale University Press, forthcoming.

Schutte, Anne Jacobson. *Aspiring Saints: Pretense of Holiness, Inquisition, and Gender in the Republic of Venice, 1618–1750.* Baltimore, MD: Johns Hopkins University Press, 2001.

Sharpe, Jim. "History from Below." In *New Perspectives on Historical Writing,* ed. Peter Burke, 24–41. Cambridge: Polity Press, 1991.

Sigal, Pierre André. *L'homme et le miracle dans la France médiévale.* Paris: Editions du Cerf, 1985.

Siraisi, Nancy G. *The Clock and the Mirror: Girolamo Cardano and Renaissance Medicine.* Princeton, NJ: Princeton University Press, 1997.

———. *Medicine and the Italian Universities, 1250–1600.* Leiden: Brill, 2001.

Skinner, Patricia. *Health and Medicine in Early Medieval Southern Italy.* Leiden: Brill, 1996.

Sloan, R. P., E. Bagiella, and T. Powell. "Religion, Spirituality, and Medicine." *Lancet* 353 (Feb. 20, 1999): 664–67.

Smoller, Laura Ackerman. "A Case of Demonic Possession in Fifteenth-Century Brittany: Perrin Hervé and the Nascent Cult of Vincent Ferrer." In *Voices from the Bench: the Narratives of Lesser Folk in Medieval Trials,* ed. Michael Goodich, 149–76. Houndmills, Basingstoke, Hampshire: Palgrave Macmillan, 2006.

Sodano, Giulio. "Miracolo e canonizzazione. Processi napoletani tra XVI e XVIII secolo." In *Miracoli dai segni alla storia,* ed. Sofia Boesch Gajano and Marilena Modica, 171–96. Rome: Viella, 1999.

Stone, Lawrence. *The Family, Sex and Marriage in England, 1500–1800.* Abridged ed. New York: Harper Colophon Books, 1979.

Surius, Laurentius. *Vita del gran patriarca S. Bruno Carthusiano.* Rome: Zannetti, 1621. BAV Barb.T.IV.84

Szabo, Jason. "Seeing Is Believing? The Form and Substance of French Medical Debates over Lourdes." *Bulletin of the History of Medicine* 76 (2002): 199–230.

Taves, Ann. *The Household of Faith; Roman Catholic Devotions in Mid-Nineteenth Century America*. Notre Dame, Ind.: University of Notre Dame Press, 1986.

Temkin, Oswei. *Hippocrates in a World of Pagans and Christians*. Baltimore, MD: Johns Hopkins University Press, 1991.

Thomas, Louis-Vincent. *Le cadavre de la biologie à l'anthropologie*. Brussels: Editions Complexe, 1980.

Torres, Andrea. *Predica per la canonizzazione di S. Andrea Corsini*. Rome: Rev. Camera Apostolica, 1629. BAV R. G. Miscell.D57(6)

Trambusti, Giuseppe. *Della vita del beato Gio. Battista Rossi*. Rome: Bernardino Morini, 1861. BAV Ferr.II.790(1)

Turchini, Angelo. *La fabbrica di un santo: Il processo di canonizzazione di Carlo Borromeo e la Controriforma*. Casale Monferrato: Marietti, 1984.

Urban VIII. *Decreta servanda in canonizatione e beatificatione sanctorum accedunt instructiones e declarationes*. Rome: Rev. Camera Apostolica, 1642. BAV R. G. Miscell.D.57(7)

Valauri, Giacomo Antonio. *Vita di S. Giovanni da San Facondo*. Rome: Giacomo Komarek Boemo, 1690. BAV Chigi.IV.216

Valenzuela, Gabriele Maria de. *Historia vitae, martyrii et prodigiorum b. Ioannis Nepomuceni*. Rome: Io. Zempel e Io. de Mey, 1729. BAV Barb.U.V.121

Valladier, André. *Speculum sapientae matronalis ex vita sanctae Franciscae Romanae*. Paris: Ioannem Richer, 1609. BAV Palatina.III.21

Vallon, Charles, and Georges Genil-Perrin. *La psychiatrie médico-légale dans l'oeuvre de Zacchias (1584–1659)*. Paris: Octave Doin et fils, 1912.

Van Dam, Raymond. *Saints and Their Miracles in Late Antique Gaul*. Princeton, N.J.: Princeton University Press, 1993.

Van der Hart, O., R. Lierens, and J. Goodwin. "Jeanne Fery: A Sixteenth-Century Case of Dissociative Identity Disorder." *Journal of Psychohistory* 24, no. 1 (1996): 18–35.

Vauchez, André. *La sainteté en occident aux derniers siècles du Moyen Age d'après les procès de canonisation et les documents hagiographiques*. Rome: Ecole française de Rome, 1981.

———. "Les procès de canonisation médiévaux comme sources de l'histoire de la religion populaire." In *La religion populaire. Colloque international du Centre National de la Recherche Scientifique, no. 576, Paris 17–19 octobre 1977*, ed. Guy Dubosq, Bernard Plongeron and Daniel Robert, 109–14. Paris: Editions du Centre National de la Recherche Scientifique, 1979.

Veraja, Fabijan. *Le cause di canonizzazione dei Santi: Commento alla legislazione e guida pratica*. Vatican: Libreria Editrice Vaticana, 1992.

Voragine, Jacques. *La légende dorée*. Paris: Honoré Champion, 1997.

Ward, Benedicta. *Miracles and the Medieval Mind: Theory, Record, and Event, 1000–1215*. Philadelphia: University of Pennsylvania Press, 1982.

———. "Monks and Miracle." In *Miracles in Jewish and Christian Antiquity: Imagining Truth*, ed. John Cavadini. Notre Dame, IN: University of Notre Dame Press, 1999.

Ward-Perkins, J. B. "Memoria, Martyr's Tomb and Martyr's Church." *Journal of Theological Studies* N.S. XVII, Pt. I (1966): 20–37.

Warner, John Harley. *The Therapeutic Perspective: Medical Practice, Knowledge, and Identity in America, 1820–1885*. Cambridge, MA: Harvard University Press, 1986.

Weninger, Fr. F. X. "An Interesting Letter from Father Weninger, S.J.: Miraculous Cures through the Intercession of Blessed Peter Claver." *Ave Maria* 22, no. 13 (March 1886): 250–51.

Wilson, Adrian F. *The Making of Man-Midwifery: Childbirth in England, 1660–1770*. London: UCL Press, 1995.

———. "On the History of Disease Concepts: The Case of Pleurisy." *History of Science* 38 (2000): 271–319.

Wilson, Stephen, ed. *Saints and Their Cults: Studies in Religious Sociology, Folklore, and History*. Cambridge: Cambridge University Press, 1983.

Woodward, Kenneth L. *Making Saints: How the Catholic Church Determines Who Becomes a Saint, Who Doesn't, and Why*. New York: Simon and Schuster, 1990.

———. *The Book of Miracles: The Meaning of the Miracle Stories in Christianity, Judaism, Buddhism, Hinduism, Islam*. New York: Simon and Schuster, 2000.

Wyshogrod, Edith. *Saints and Postmodernism: Revisioning Moral Philosophy*. Chicago: University of Chicago Press, 1990.

Yarrow, Simon. *Saints and Their Communities: Miracle Stories in Twelfth-Century England*. Oxford: Clarendon Press, 2006.

Young, Kathleen Z. "The Imperishable Virginity of Saint Maria Goretti." *Gender and Society* 3, no. 4 (1989): 474–82.

Zacchia, Paolo. *Quaestiones medico-legales*. Avenione: Joannes Piot, 1657.

———. *Quaestionum medico-legalium in tres tomos divisae*, ed. J. D. Horst and Lanfranco Zacchia. Noribergae: Joannis Georgii Lochneri, 1725.

———. *Die Beseelung des menschlichen Fötus. Buch IX Kapitel I der Quaestiones medico-legales*, ed. and trans. Beatrix Spitzer. Köln: Böhlau Verlag, 2002.

Ziegler, Joseph. "Practitioners and Saints: Medical Men in Canonization Processes in the Thirteenth to Fifteenth Centuries." *Social History of Medicine* 12, no. 2 (1999): 191–225.

Zimmerman, Kees W., ed. *One Leg in the Grave: The Miracle of the Transplantation of the Black Leg*. Maarsen: Elsevier/Bunge, 1998.

Index

DATE DUE

Demco, Inc. 38-293